TATIANA TROUVÉ

216939290

TATIANA TROUVÉ

Arts

Verlag der Buchhandlung Walther König, Köln

ISBN 978-3-86560-352-4

Managing Editor: Maria Muhle
Copyediting: Ben Fergusson, Matthew Gaskins
Translation: Will Bishop
Design: Jérôme Saint-Loubert Bié, Paris
Production: Printmanagement Plitt, Oberhausen

Published by
Verlag der Buchhandlung Walther König, Köln
Ehrenstr. 4, 50672 Köln
Tel: +49 (0) 221 20 59 653
Fax: +49 (0) 221 20 59 660
verlag@buchhandlung-walther-koenig.de

Co-published by Centre National d'Art Contemporain de la Villa Arson, Nice, MAC/VAL, Musée d'Art Contemporain du Val-de-Marne, Vitry-sur-Seine, Frac des Pays de la Loire, Carquefou

With the support of Galerie Johann König, Berlin, Galerie Emmanuel Perrotin, Miami & Paris, Galerie Almine Rech, Brussels & Paris

Die Deutsche Bibliothek
– CIP-Einheitsaufnahme
Ein Titelsatz für diese Publikation ist bei Der Deutschen Bibliothek erhältlich

Printed in Germany

DISTRIBUTION

Europe
Buchhandlung Walther König, Köln
Ehrenstr. 4
D-50672 Köln
Tel: +49 (0) 221 20 59 653
Fax: +49 (0) 221 20 59 660
verlag@buchhandlung-walther-koenig.de

Switzerland
Buch 2000
c/o AVA Verlagsauslieferungen AG
Centralweg 16
CH-8910 Affoltern a.A.
Tel: +41 (0) 1 762 42 00
Fax: +41 (0) 1 762 42 10
a.koll@ava.ch

UK & Eire
Cornerhouse Publications
70 Oxford Street
GB-Manchester M1 5NH
Tel: +44 (0) 161 200 15 03
Fax: +44 (0) 161 200 15 04
publications@cornerhouse.org

Outside Europe
D.A.P./Distributed Art Publishers, Inc.
155 6th Avenue, 2nd Floor
New York, NY 10013
Tel: +1 (212) 627 1999
Fax: +1 (212) 627 9484
eleshowitz@dapinc.com

THE LONGEST ECHO

Tatiana Trouvé

For a long time, I was hesitant to finish anything I would undertake. Thus, for a long time, I thought I was a scattered kind of person. Yet scattered things don't hold up very well over time. In the end, accumulated elements, systems of classification, projects, intentions, and titles are all articulated and find a common meaning: for me, this was the *Bureau of Implicit Activities*. To get there, you have to wait, but also to think of time not as a process of evolution, with something that begins and ends, nor even as a cycle, but rather as a linear projection and a stratification of events: a Monday is a Monday, a Tuesday is a Monday, a Wednesday is a Monday.[1] Time has to be thought of in terms of its imperceptible movements, either because they are too fast for us to gain a clear image of them, or because they are too slow for us to discern their movement. If the time in which I am interested produces neither a clear image nor a perceptible movement, it also leaves few traces and does not appear in any historical register[2]. It does, nonetheless, have the capacity to unite what was destined to be separate and to separate what was destined to be united. In this sense, it brings about movements like those of an echo.

1/ Cf. *Bureau of Implicit Activities, Annex* to the *Modules of Waiting* (2004)

2/ Cf. *Bureau of Implicit Activities, Administration* (1997–2003)

Therefore, I have started to sculpt echoes, as it were. I'm rather fond of the idea that things appear from the moment they are deformed, in the play between what is identical and different, between repetition, alteration, and renewal—like the movement my voice makes in its journey in front of the mountain's belly, which allows me to measure the architecture of the mountain. I hear my voice at the same time as I produce it, but what is the distance I am measuring? What is the distance separating me from my voice or the distance separating me from the mountain? It is probably both, since I am simultaneously separated from my voice and from the mountain. This separation now constitutes its own unique matter—the echo—which is thus the form of divided architecture.

Although I have sometimes used a sound apparatus in my work,[3] this remains rare and has never served as a way to give concrete form to the acoustic phenomena of echoes. Indeed, in a visual or sculptural sense, the concept of divided architecture has found a more fitting home in my sculptures and installations.

3/ Cf. *Polder* with microphones, radios, and amplifiers (2002) and *Bureau of Implicit Activities, Annex to the Modules of Waiting* (2003)

For example, these echoes have sometimes taken the form of little elevators presented with their doors ajar and their ceiling lit up, as if they had just opened or were going to close.[4] In reality, it is important to keep in mind that these doors close very slowly—so slowly, in fact, that from one exhibition to another, we do not see the change. The show would have to last for a decade to measure the progression of their closing. Here, a division into three types of time takes place in one piece of architecture: the time it takes to visit the exhibition, the duration of the exhibition itself, and the movement of the elevator, which has been suspended. And to these three kinds of time, we could even add another: the time of our memory. It is the layering of these different times in one place that gives the work its unity.

4/ *Expansion of a Closure* (2007)

In an even more direct way, I have brought these layers of time into play in the same place by burying an exhibition under sand, or at least submitting the duration of an exhibition to an uninterrupted and regular process of burial. Black sand was running uninterruptedly through the walls, day and night, filling the room of an exhibition by emptying another one that remained invisible and whose dimensions, when considered in this context, might seem unlimited. Where is this running sand at my feet coming from? Will its flow ever be interrupted? And if so, when? When the exhibition closes? Does it flow all night long while I'm asleep? When did all this start? When should I have noticed? Should I be expecting an event? Will that event happen after I have left? Has it already happened? Will it ever happen?

If reality only assumes form in our memories, and if the present is only the past passing, then works of art, too, are constituted from the moment they leave our field of vision. The time we will have taken to contemplate them is preparation for the time we will need to return to them, to grasp them, and finally, to interpret and deform them—and, through these different moments, to formulate the questions they ask us.

The work I do on space in my installations is determined by creating physical laws different from those that cross through and constitute our reality. I imagine magnetic sectors or singular atmospheric densities, speeds that could, in turn, sculpt forms, sometimes contradicting the laws of gravity by sucking matter and objects up to the ceiling, deforming or compressing them, but also by fixing them in movements of falling or equilibrium.[5]

5/ I was able to do this with sockets, freezers, deformed cubes, or stopped objects falling down.

When I am not building installations, I draw. Most often I draw spaces where the borders between what is shown of a piece of architecture and what actually constitutes it remain indeterminate. That has given way to a series I have named *Intranquility.* In these drawings, interiors and exteriors, reflections and mirrors, overexposures or erasures are juxtaposed and dwell together within the same space. With these drawings, I was not attempting to make the representation of a real space tangible, but to give body to what produces a place in our minds. I've done this by allowing what viewers project onto any given place to settle, by creating intervals or voids that are capable of prodding mental projections.

Very recently, I returned to these drawings, in somewhat the same way you go back to a site years later. Other drawings came from this, in black pencil on black paper, where silhouettes are effaced and disappear into a space that absorbs their contours, where the notions of interior and exterior are more indistinct than ever and appear in tentative accord with the distance and place that are being observed—reflections of pencil and pencil lead allow contours, objects, and eventually a place to be glimpsed, furtively.

These slippages of time into space, their manifestations on visual planes, their sculptural forms, their points of correspondence with direct experience, with consciousness, with the memory of events, determine, I think, the contours of a sculptural territory that I have explored for some time now.

Following pages:
Model of the Bureau of Implicit Activities, 1997
Wood, Formica, imitation leather, plastic, sand, metal, tape, mirror, Plexiglas, paper,
140 x 120 x 50 cm [55 x 47¼ x 19¾ in.]

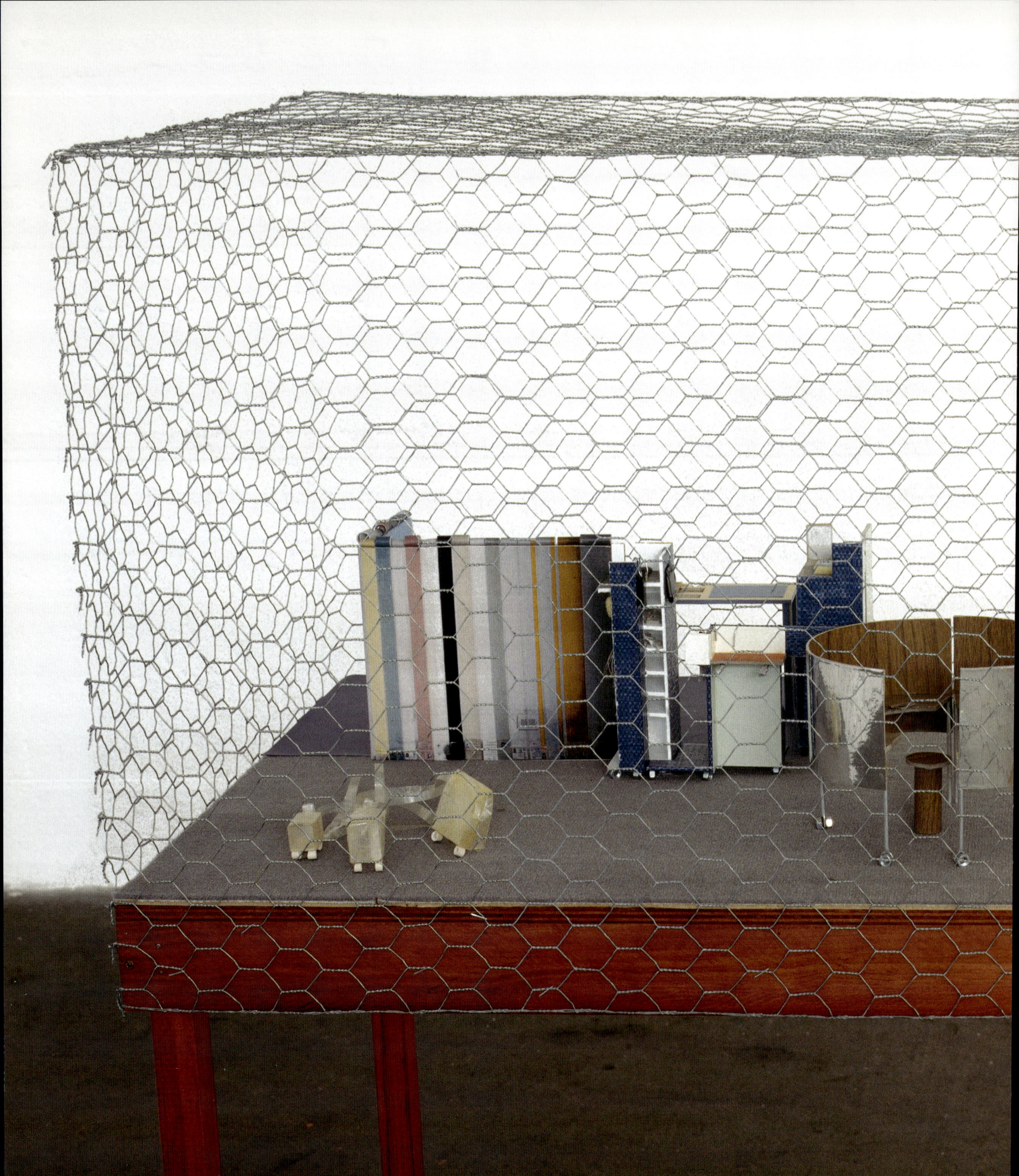

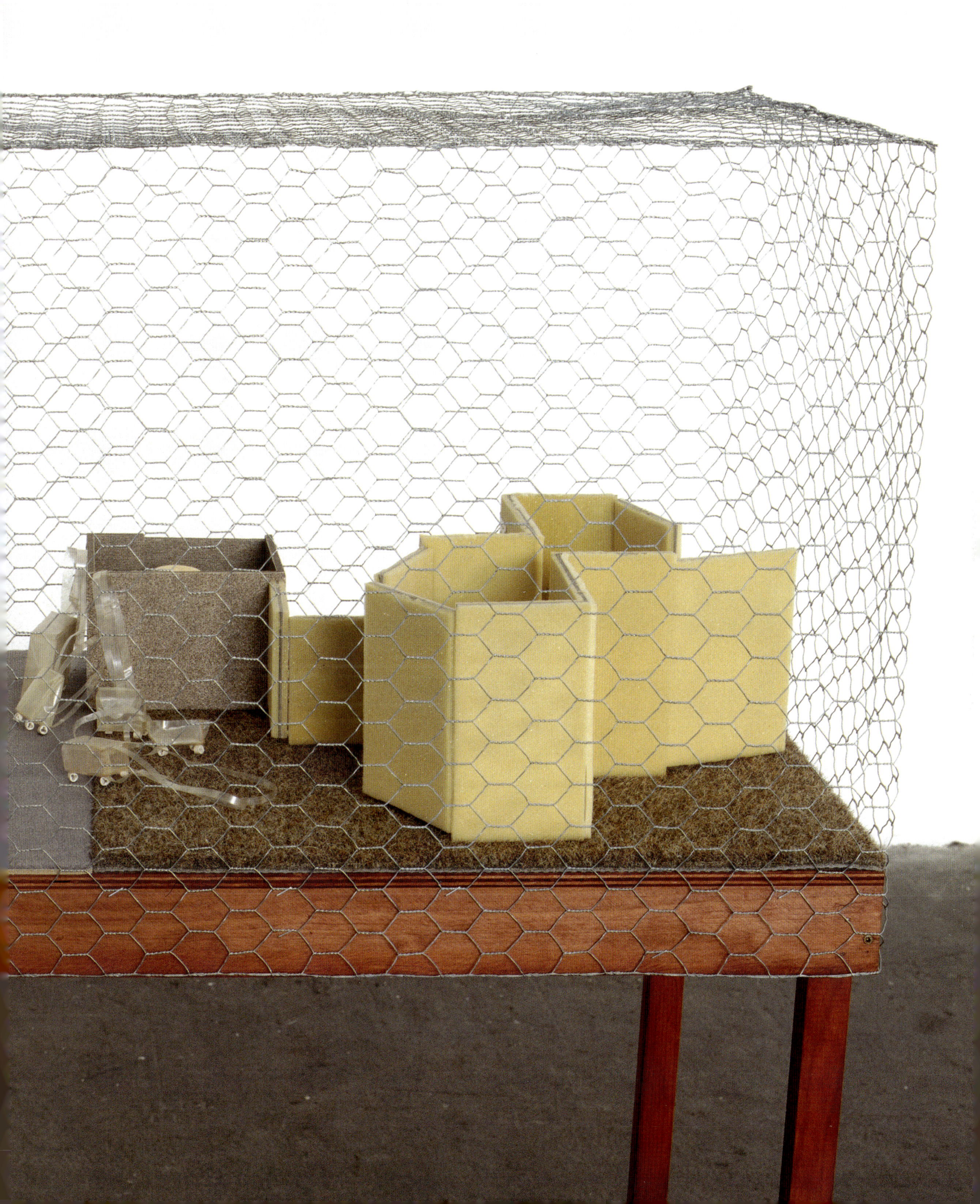

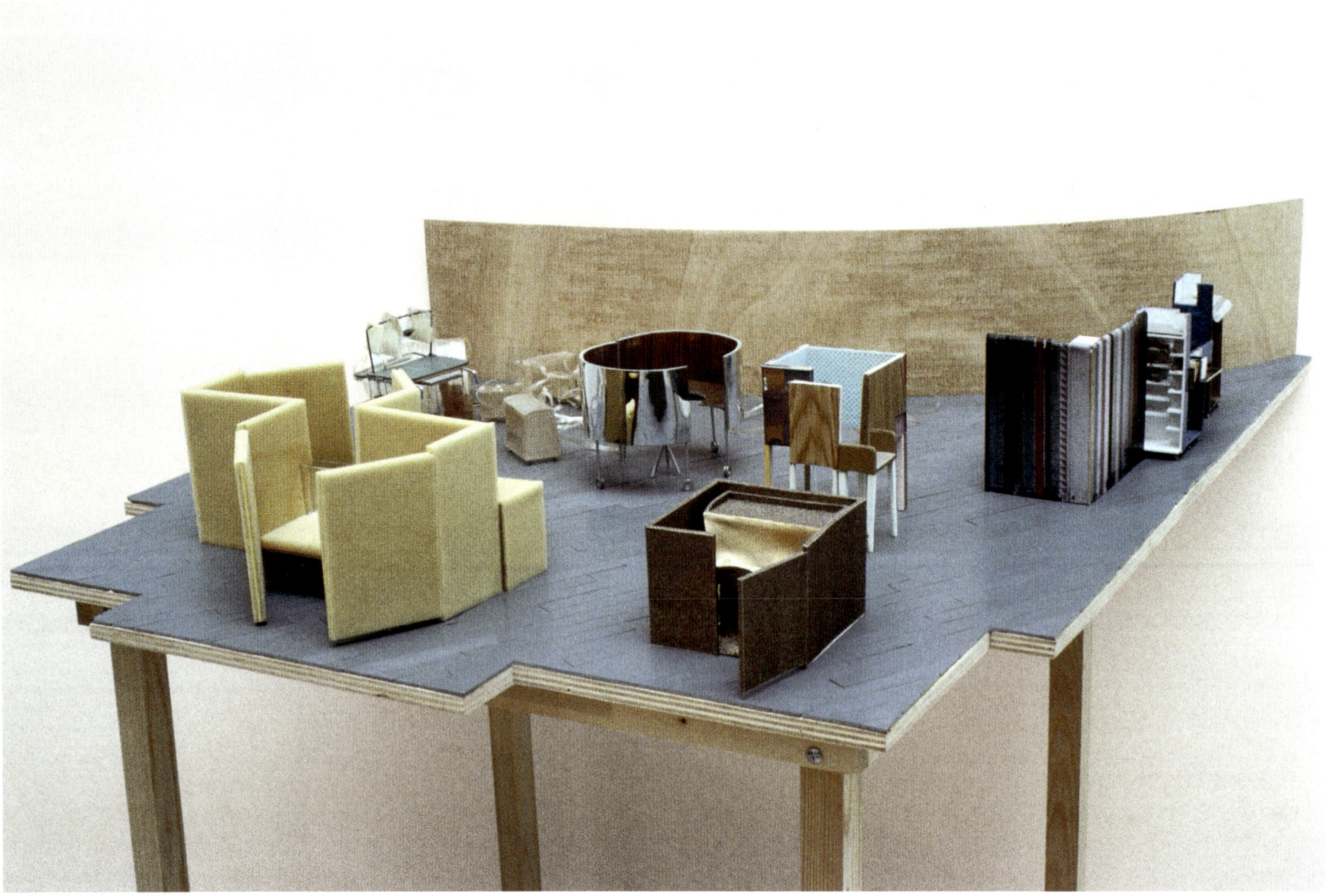

Model of the Bureau of Implicit Activities, 1999
Wood, Formica, imitation leather, plastic, sand, metal, tape, mirror, Plexiglas, paper, 137 x 102 x 101 cm [54 x 40¼ x 39¾ in.]

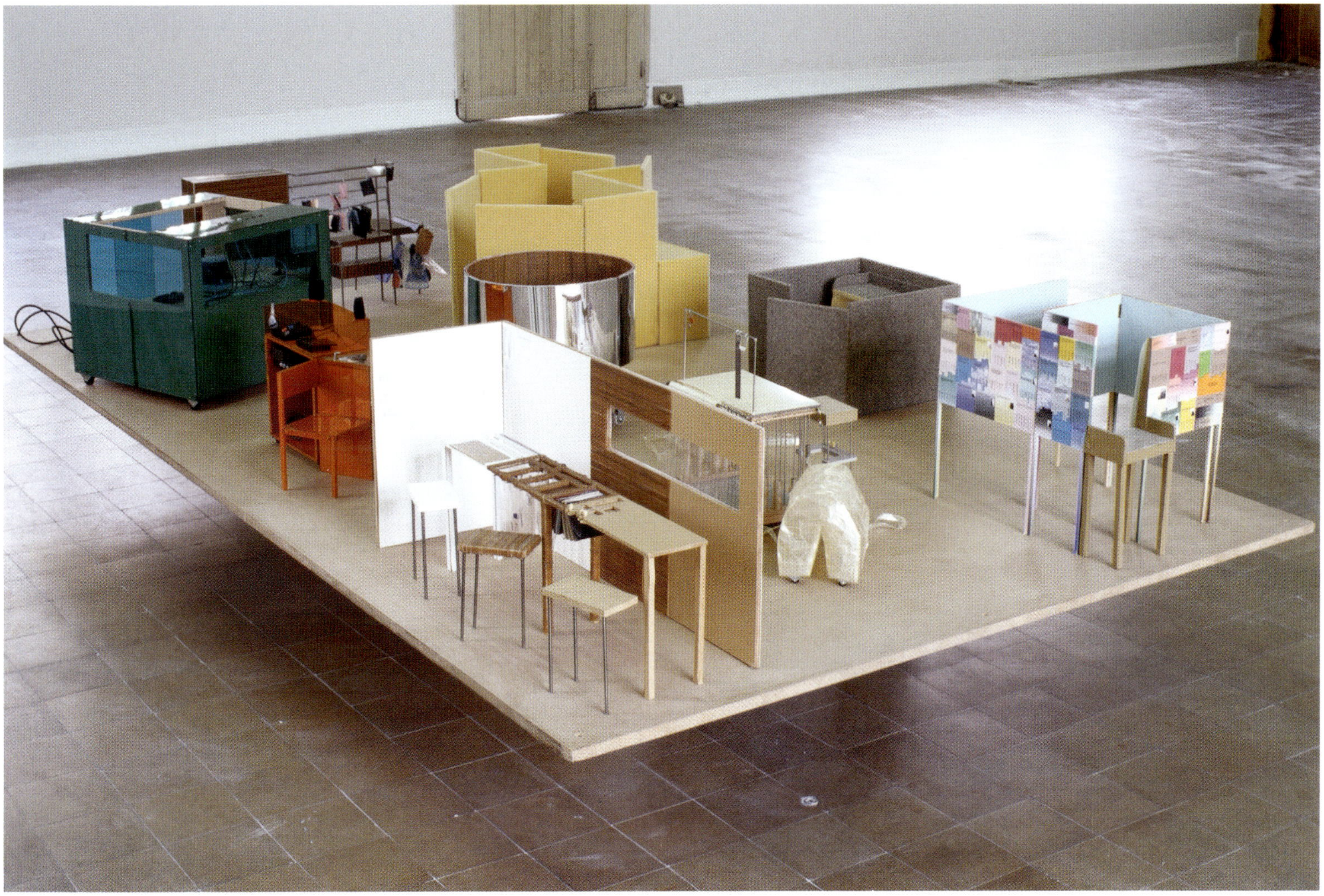

Model of the Bureau of Implicit Activities, 2001
Wood, Formica, imitation leather, plastic, sand, metal, tape, mirror, Plexiglas, paper, 40 x 200 x 300 cm [15¾ x 78¾ x 118 in.]

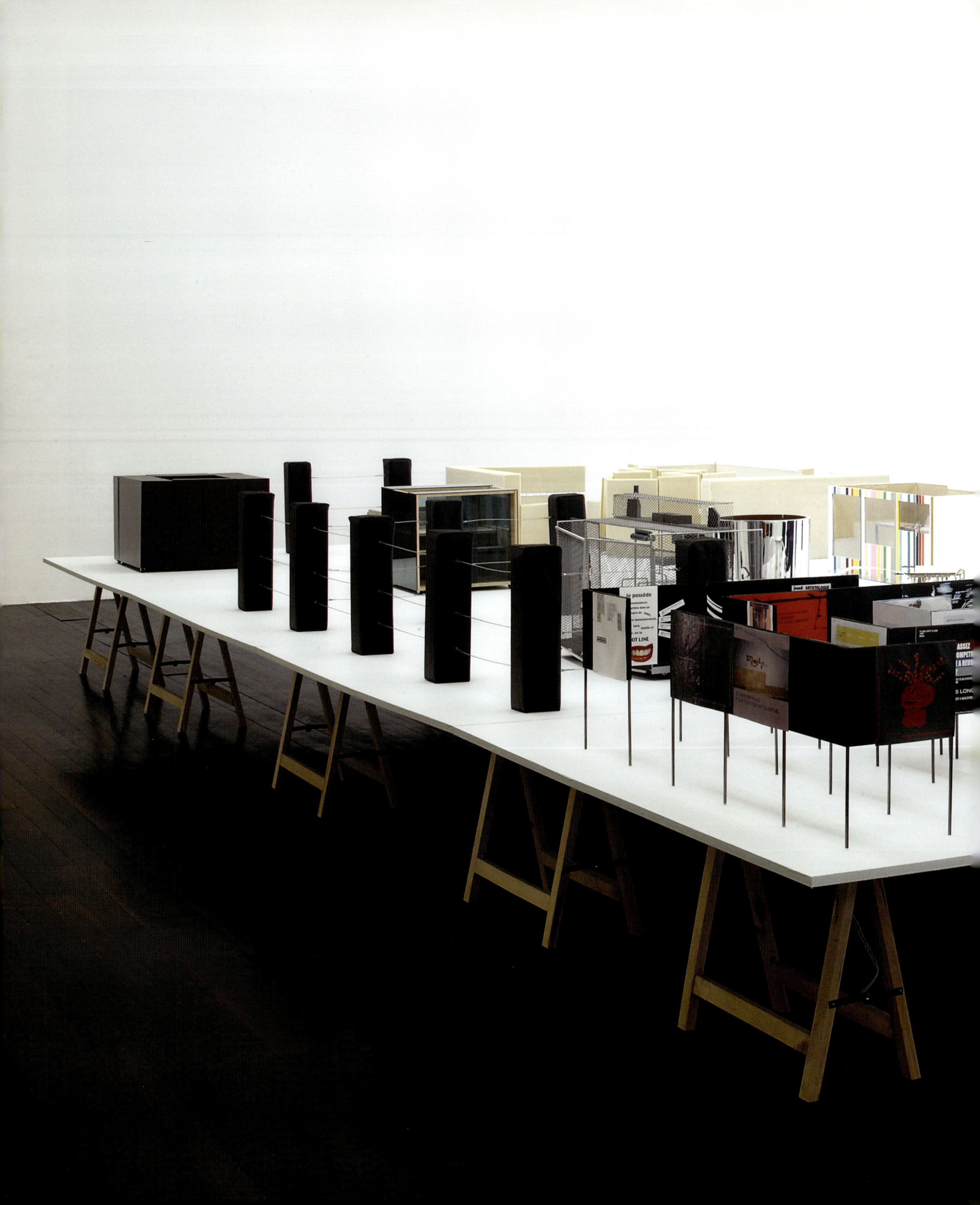
Je possède
ARTISTOLOGIE

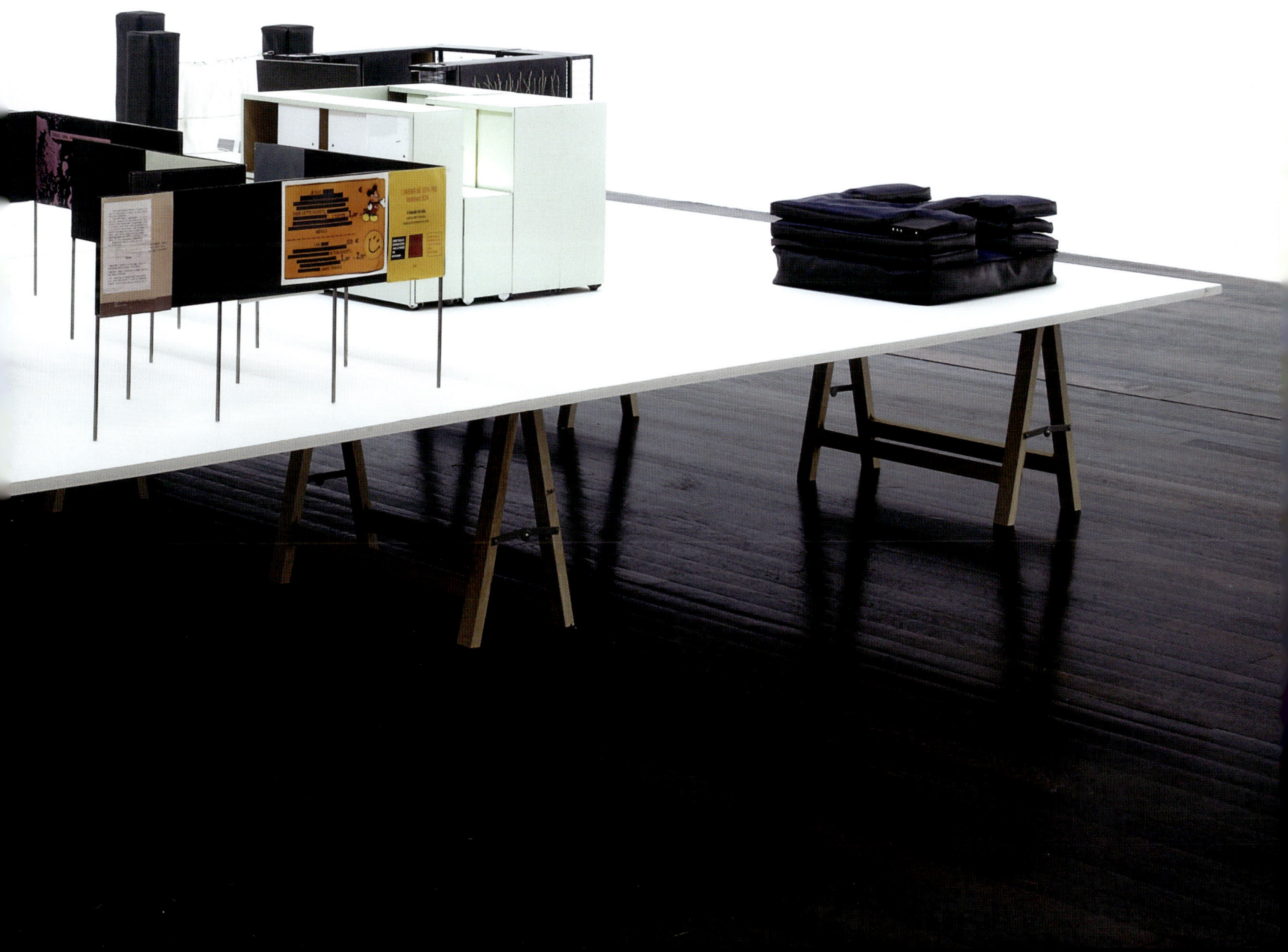

Previous pages:
Model of the Bureau of Implicit Activities, 2007
Wood, Formica, imitation leather, plastic, sand, metal, tape, mirror, Plexiglas, paper,
90 x 740 x 370 cm [35½ x 291 x 145¾ in.]

SOMEWHERE A PLACE

Robert Storr

By now we know memories are made. They do not just happen. There is no process of absorption and metabolic transformation that fills our minds with the reserves of sense data that order our thoughts and disorder our dreams. No natural mental equivalent of photosynthesis exists whereby light is transformed into storable energy for future reference or use. The verbs and locutions we use when we speak about memory tell the tale of active construction within the brain's many mansions.

To memorize is a deliberate act, usually performed against the resistance of primal drives that seeks only to exert their power over palpable things or to spend themselves in states of elated, purposeless self-assertion. Which is why school children called upon to recite poetry in class have such a difficult time of it. Nevertheless in a country like France, where this is still done beyond the age of nursery rhymes, a stuttering teenage student who engages in the sadomasochistic ritual of publicly failing to remember—or at least failing to properly perform his or her humiliating subjugation to the teacher's authority through a forced subjugation to someone else's text rendered in halting, inarticulate bursts—after returning to the fold of fellow students, may well be found in a bar outside school speaking the same lines with lexical precision and passion.

"To commit to memory" is a stronger expression of the same phenomenon, since all commitments summon the will's overridingly deliberate character as a counterforce to human nature's persistent whimsicality. At this point, spontaneous desire is disciplined by intentions presaging greater but deferred gratification. The difference between these two aspects of the will and their coincident or at least sequential operations explains why the student I referred to earlier seems to have been remembering and forgetting at the same time, or at least within the interval between facing a demand from outside his or her psyche and responding to a craving emanating from within it, oscillating between relative obliviousness or approximate recollection and vivid, all-consuming recall.

But, aesthetically speaking, we are still in the domain of preexisting realities or artifacts—words we hear on a staircase, through walls or on stage, on television or the radio; words we struggle to keep fresh in our ear in order that they may flow easily to our lips when we wish to hear them again or tell someone else about them; things seen on the street, on the page or on screens that we attempt to photograph with our mind's eye. "I am a camera," Christopher Isherwood's doppelganger declared in *The Berlin Stories* (1946). However, we know full well that our eye filters out 99 percent of everything in our field of vision, with the aim of fashioning a Gestalt from the remaining one percent, a nugget subsequently regarded as having somehow crystallized all that was inherently "memorable". Making allowance for the social, cultural and psychological preferences of the person whose ear, eye and grey matter are making these "recordings", this suggests that we are all born with a retrospective Identikit, crammed with something akin to the readymades and assisted readymades that compose Marcel Duchamp's portable *Boîte-en-valise,* as if everyman and everywoman awoke to themselves and the world with such a portable archive-museum at hand, just waiting to be filled.

I choose a Duchampian analogy for consciousness in order to correct both the objective pretense of Isherwood's realism and conversely the Surrealist assumption that revelation feeds on remembrance like a man or woman in a restaurant dipping a spoon into cerebral soup in search of especially succulent subconscious morsels. More to the point

Bureau of Implicit Activities, Archive Module ("drawings"), 2003
Metal, Formica, Plexiglas, neon light, slide projector, overhead projector, copies of drawings, 163 x 220 x 220 cm [64¼ x 86½ x 86½ in.]

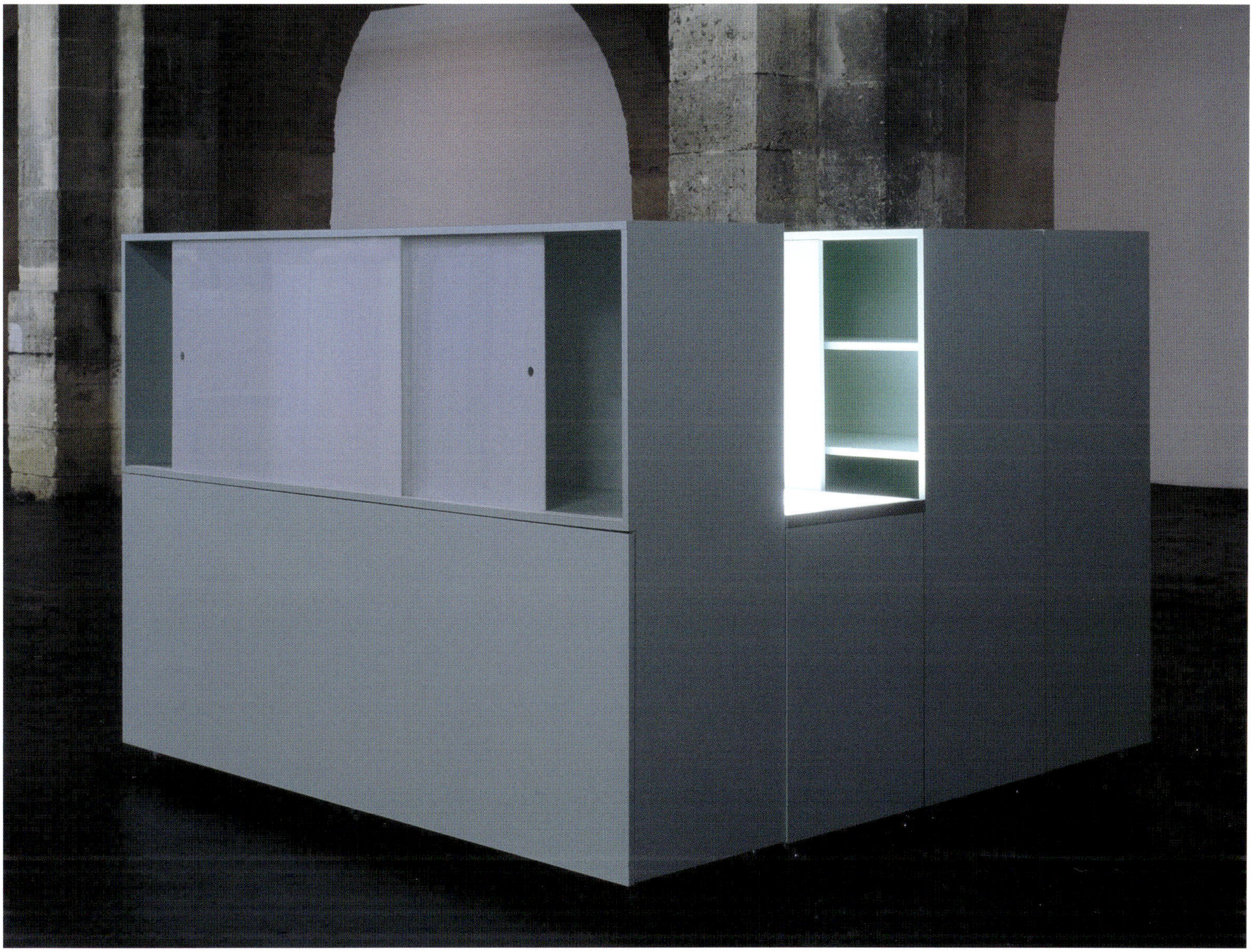

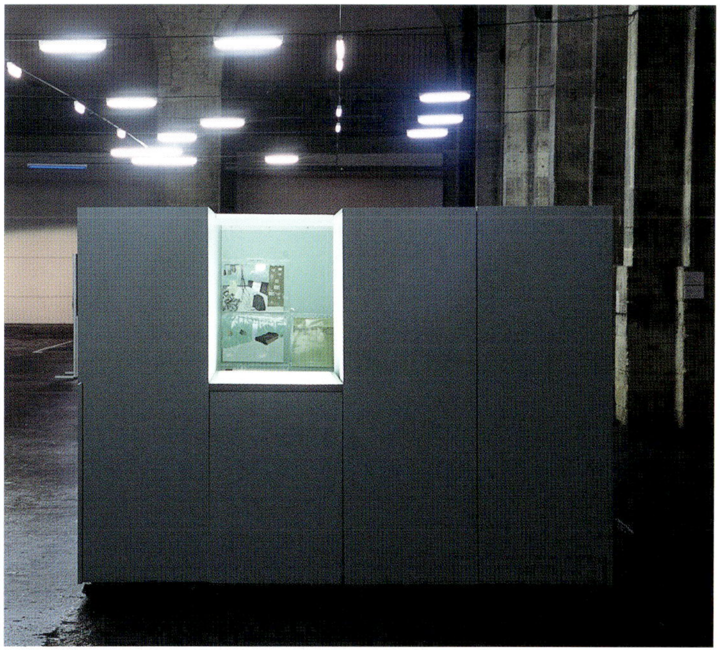

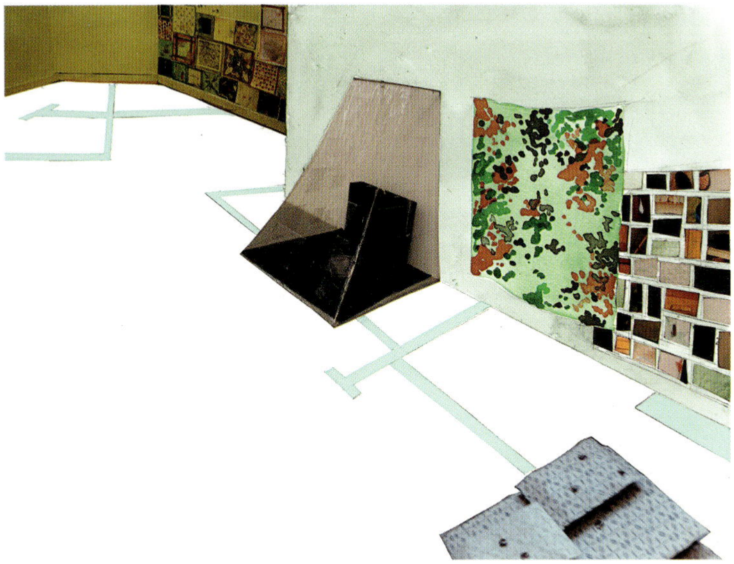

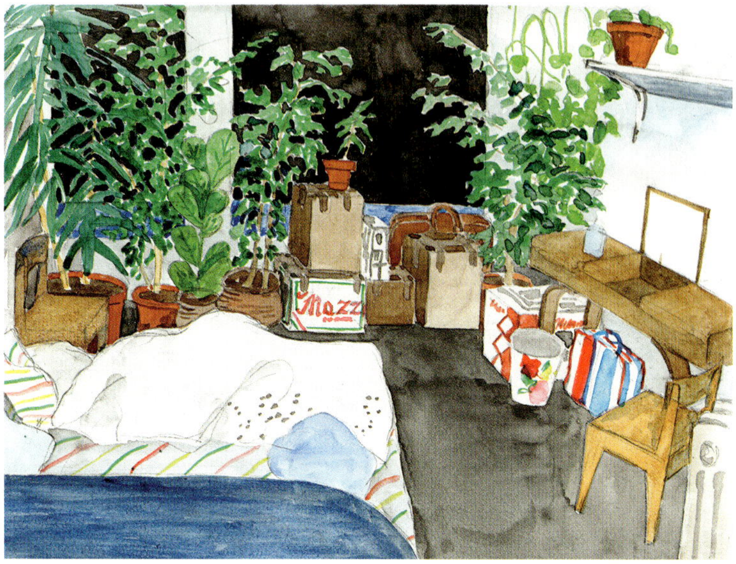

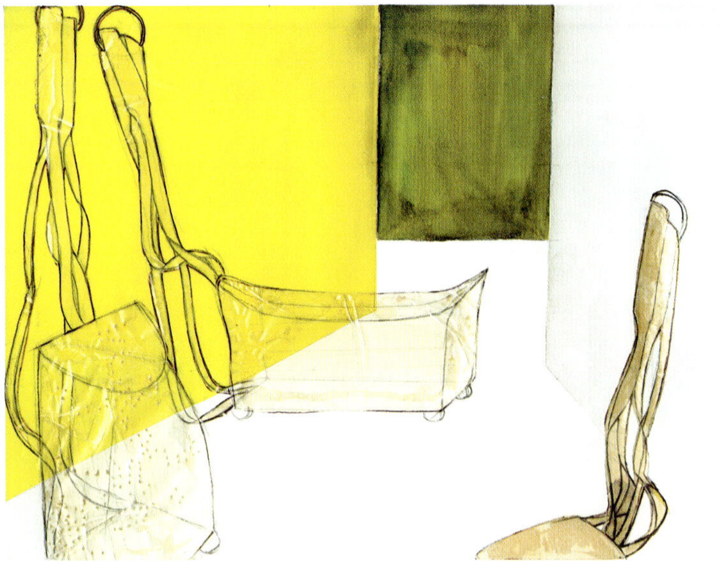

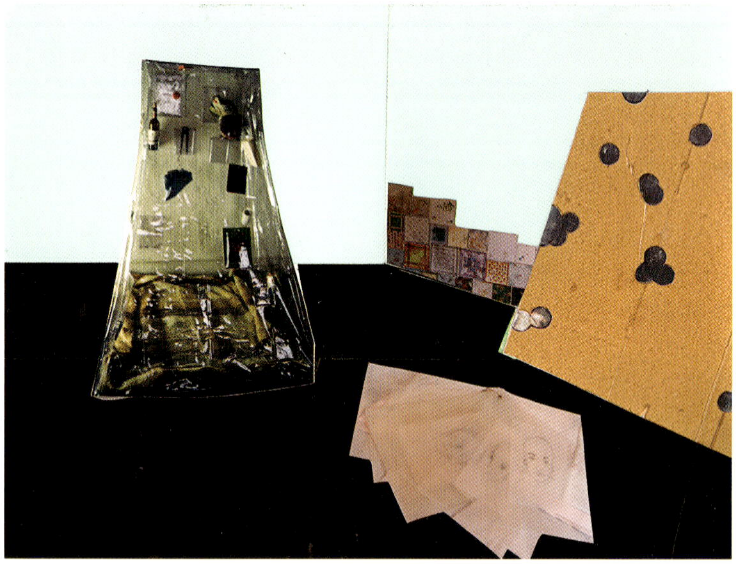

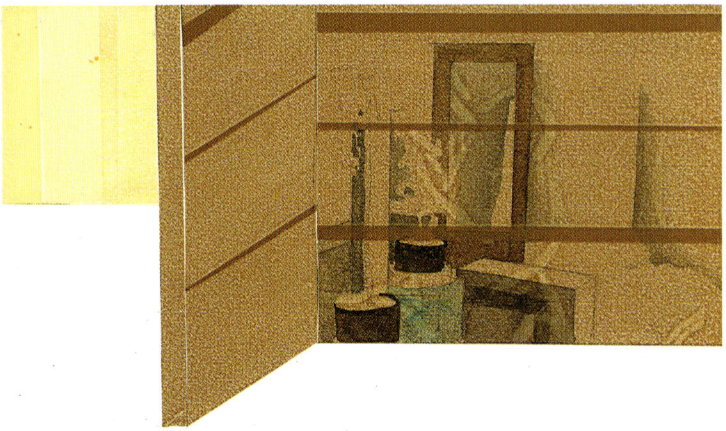

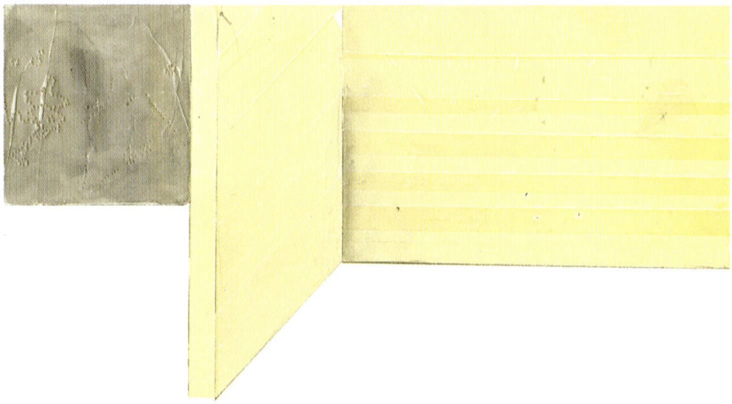

Quelques murs pour Odette

Sample drawings from the *Archives Module ("drawings"),* 2003

is Duchamp's invention of *cervellités,* or thought-objects, that prime the pump of memory even as they test the limits of logic. This concept is the predicate for a much wider range of practices in which truth to experience or mnemonic accuracy matters less—if it matters at all—than the jarring recognition of things and situations that are in fact wholly unfamiliar or radically estranged. Nevertheless, these thought-objects prompt emotions and activate the mechanisms of recovery in ways that mimic actual remembering, a quality of alertness to immediate sensation and of searching introspection that might, for want of better words, be called the "memory effect".

This is the zone Tatiana Trouvé inhabits. It is where she works and welcomes all comers, and these, roughly speaking, are the basic problematics of her multi-media, multi-dimensional and frequently multi-chambered enterprise. As in all situational art, Trouvé's installations make the person who explores them as much a protagonist of that situation as the artist who invents them and occupies them while they are being articulated—even though many spaces within her installations are, by design, shut off from physical access, while many of the others only permit partial visual access, so that the artist alone really experiences the whole environment. (About the drawings more later, but for now one may say that they too are "occupied" prior to being made available to the viewer.) And so the process of discovery, of following clues, of navigating a labyrinth from which the Minotaur has been evacuated, falls to individual members of the public. And on that score it is worth stressing that a woman—not a later-day Daedalus—is the architect of these mazes; that ordinary women and men—rather than a heroic modern Theseus—are the ones who penetrate these mysteries; and that Picasso is nowhere in sight.

Indeed, there is almost a forensic aspect to the process, as if the spectator were gathering evidence of things that had happened before his or her arrival. Moreover, with straps, chains, locks and various fasteners being prominent features of the setting along with bars and cages, there is a pronounced though never exaggerated element of the ominous in the installations as well, as if the furniture of bureaucratic, scientific or industrial reality had been roused from a state of passive hostility towards the human need for warmth and comfort to one of actively sinister waiting. Waiting, that is, for someone—anyone—to enter and eventually surrender to the regime of confinement and restraint implicit in such details and in the structure of the site overall. But Trouvé's formal discretion prevents these attributes and the atmosphere they engender from becoming one-dimensionally spooky or threatening. Instead of imposing themselves on the viewer with the inevitability of a fright-film narrative, they uncannily suggest scenarios, which are ultimately impossible to pin down or even anticipate more than a few steps ahead of where one is standing at any given point. What hides behind the locked cabinet door under which light shines? Where do these electrical wires originate or end up? What is being stored in the packages on the floor, what music emanated from those speakers, what work went on here amidst these loose scraps of material? Did everyone who was here leave in a hurry? Did they drift away? Did they simply not show up as they have always done before? Other than oneself and perhaps a scattering of other spectators, where is everybody?

The forms of the questions and even some of their specifics will seem like *déjà vu* to those who follow installation art in general, and especially to those who have carefully studied what Ilya Kabakov has called "Total Installation". That genre within the genre of situational art so dramatically immerses

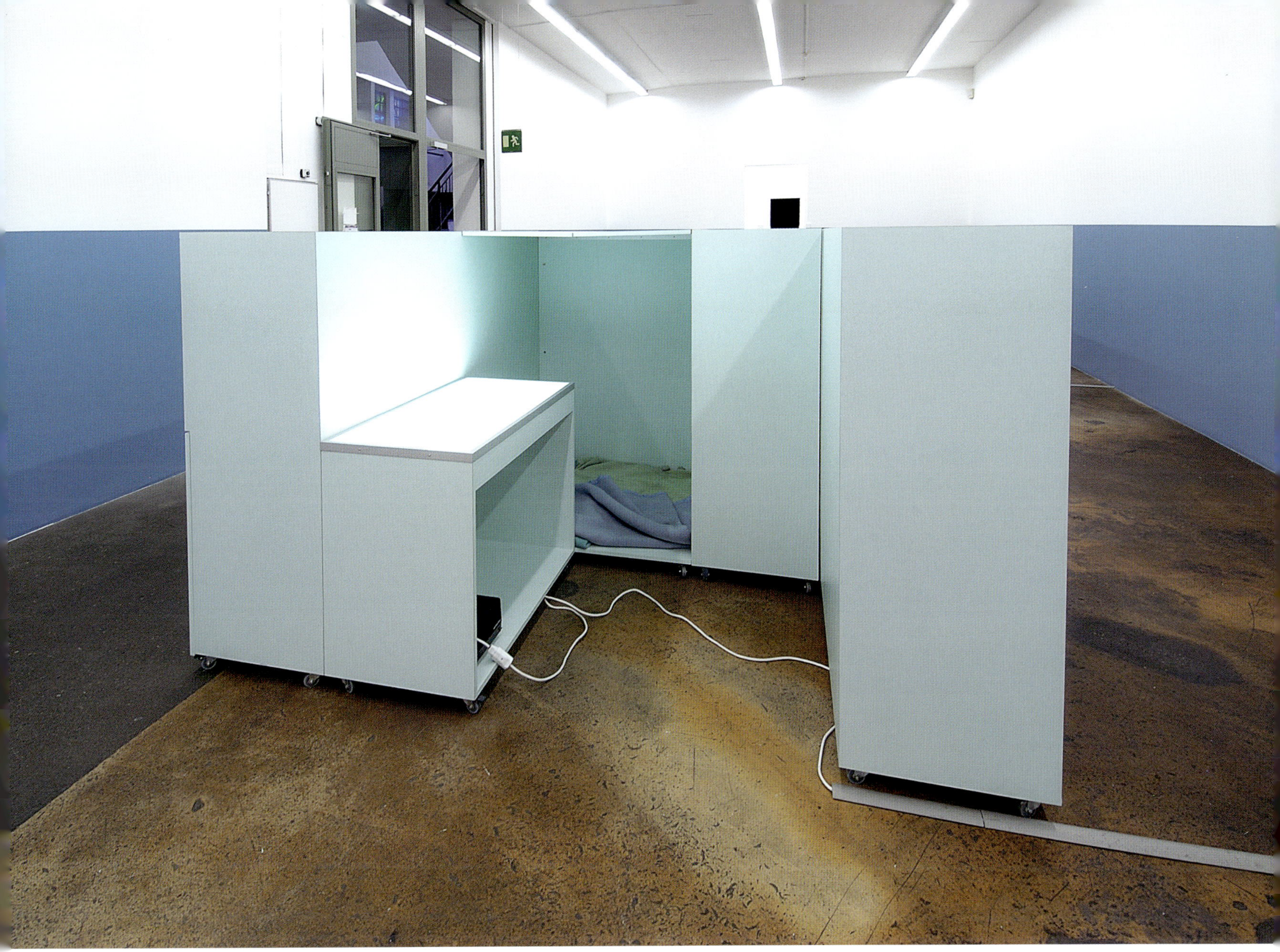

Bureau of Implicit Activities, Archives Module („drawings"), 2003
Metal, Formica, Plexiglas, neon light, slide projector, overhead projector, copies of drawings, 163 x 220 x 220 cm [64¼ x 86½ x 86½ in.]

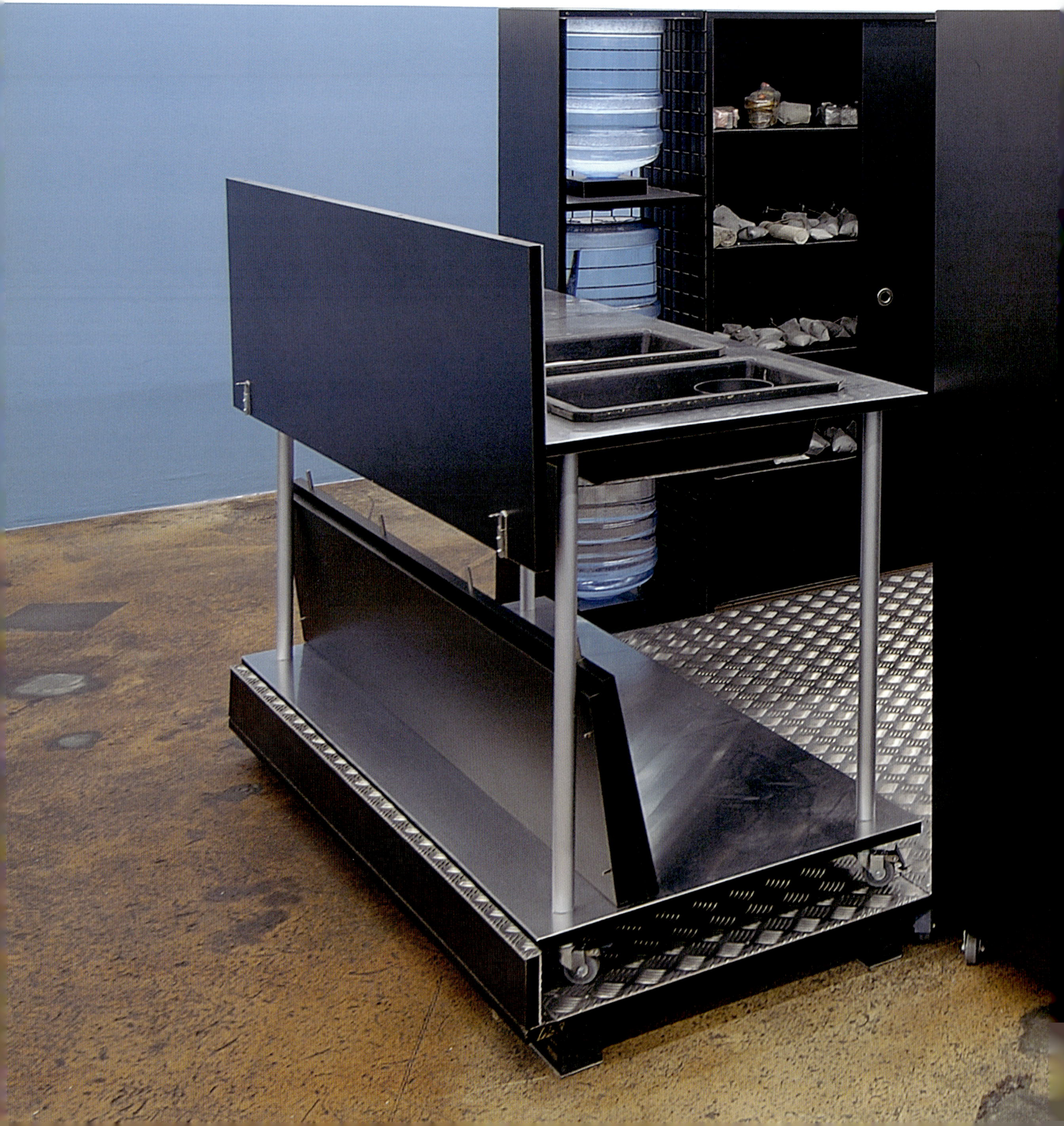

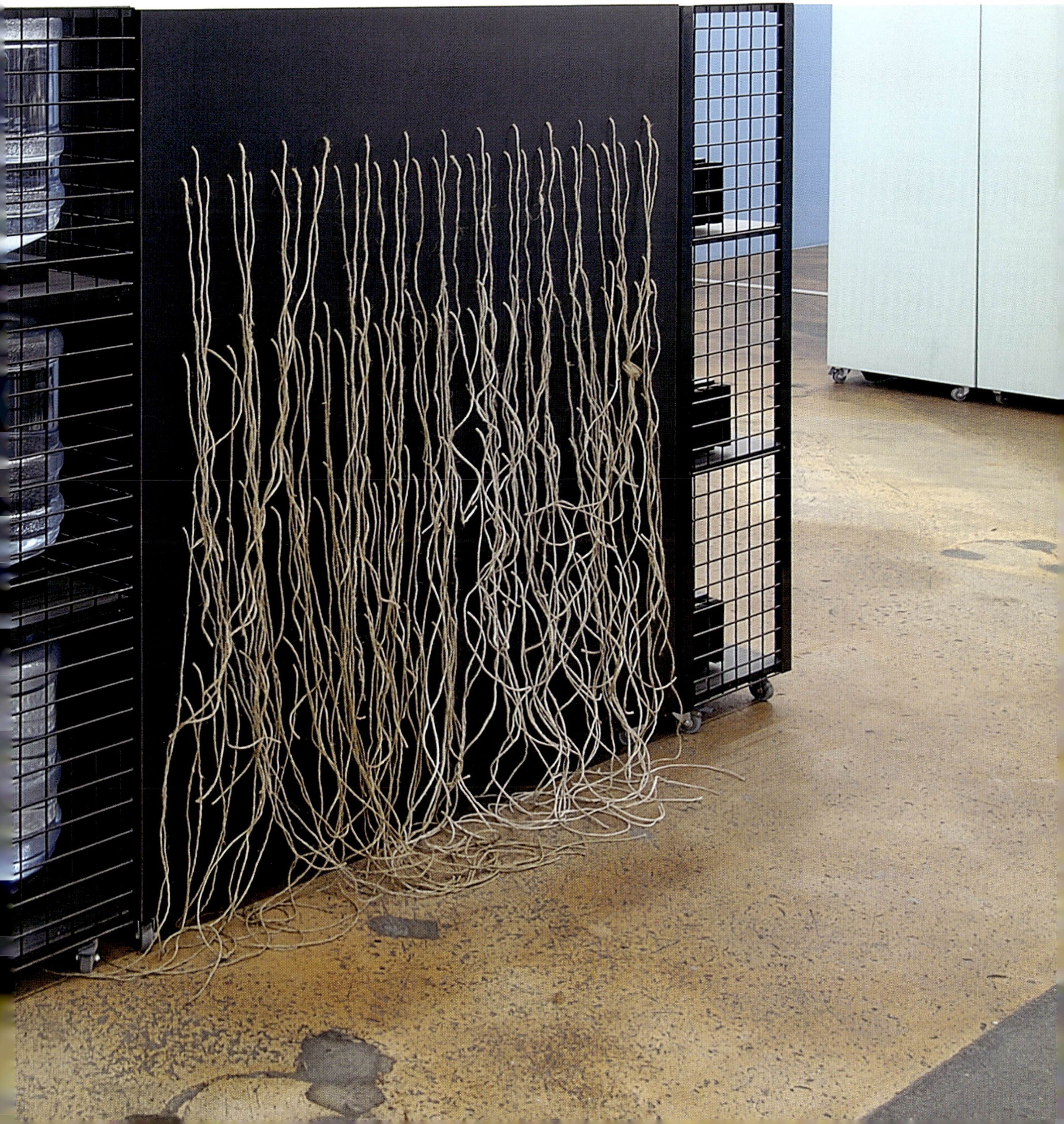

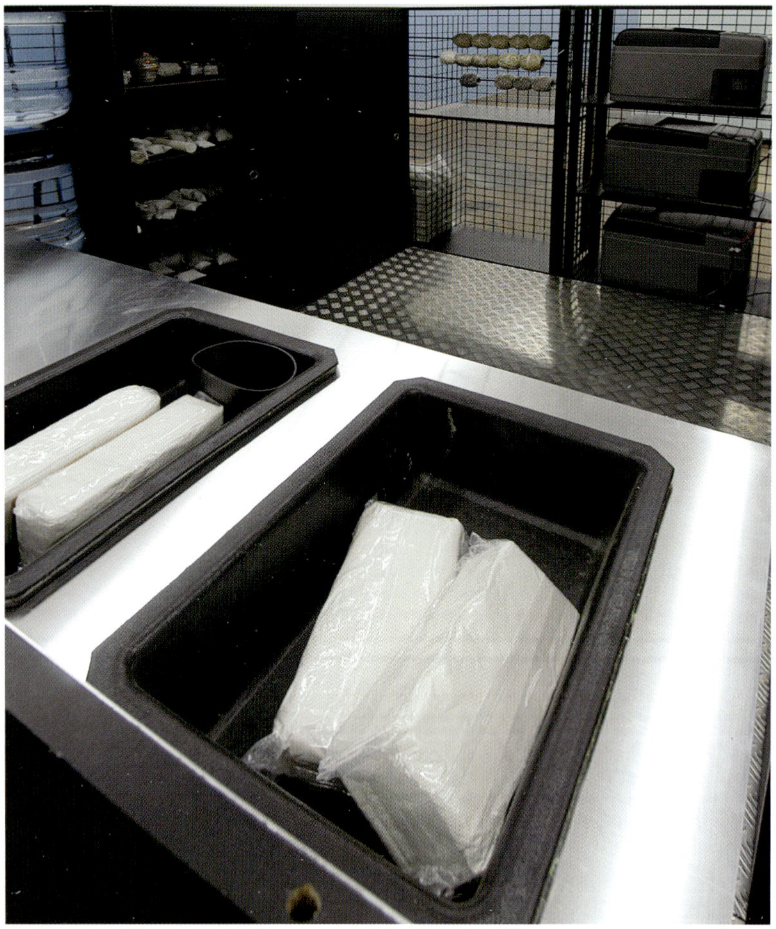

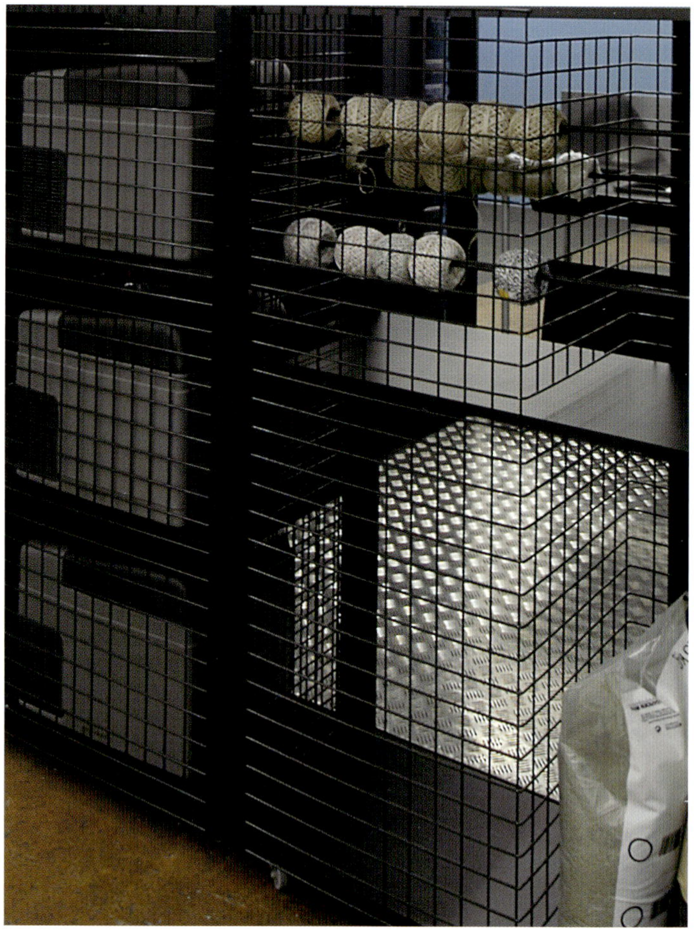

Previous pages and above:
Bureau of Implicit Activities, Archives Module (“Secrets” and “Lies”), 2003
Wood, Formica, cement, freezers, water, rope, metal,
163 x 220 x 220 cm [64¼ x 86½ x 86½ in.]

the spectator in the illusion of having been transported to another place entirely than the one left behind at the installation's doorstep—without for all that ever wholly losing sight of the fact that one is caught up in a periodically self-betraying illusion for which unexpected glimpses at the theatricality of the set-up or back into the world one has just left are jarringly essential dimensions of an overall alienation from the real and a partial assimilation to its simulacrum—that he or she adapts to the new surroundings as if taking up temporary residence in a sublet or looking for a safe haven to curl up in when stranded in a strange yet vaguely familiar city.

To that extent, memory is embedded in the very habits of adaptation as much as in the particulars that the spectator might recall from their own existence. But what of those particulars? In Kabakov's case they are a combination of two strands of Soviet life, the sketchy outlines of a never-realized Utopia and the squalidness of that Utopia constructed on the cheap, with both aspects being manifestly anachronistic. Trouvé's spaces prompt dual associations as well. To my mind the first is the chill futurism of Jean-Luc Godard's Dystopian *Alphaville;* the second is the sublime banality of the *bureau paysage,* the commercial laboratory and the light manufacturing and warehouse districts previously mentioned but grounded in the actuality of such places as they currently exist in Paris, not least the interstitial urban area where Trouvé has her studio.

Kabakov commemorates a tomorrow that never happened and an everyday for every man and woman that seemed to go on forever. In sharp and equally disorienting contrast, Trouvé encapsulates today remembered tonight or earlier in the evening, remembered in the long dark night of the soul that is 3:00 am, which is to say "the day after" before it dawns and when one doubts that it will dawn—the metaphor, of course, is F. Scott Fitzgerald's, stripped of his jittery Jazz Age effervescence by cold-sweat exhaustion of the spirit. And in the spatial and temporal nether regions where Trouvé stages her viewer-animated non-events it is virtually impossible to imagine that a day has so few as 24 hours, or a year so few as 365 days. Thus, at the artist's prompting assistance, memory plays tricks on us. Not by telescoping the remote historical or emotional past or the desired or feared future into time present, but by dilating that present and suspending it in a twilight realm where near immediacy and partial recognition compel that viewer to fill in the gaps with his or her own recollections and projections. In other words, Trouvé catches us coming and going, looking over our shoulders and around corners, with the "memory effect" being the trigger she pulls—or rather the wire of the booby trap our movement trips—releasing muffled explosions of feeling, longing, disquiet, anxiety over loosing one's way coupled with a still deeper desire to just "get lost".

The latter half of this psycho-situational ying-yang is a basic trope of "contemporaneity"—Chet Baker named one version of that dialectic by turning it into the invitation "let's get lost" and then vocally drenched that plea in erotic lassitude. It is a counter image of the quotidian dutifulness and orderliness, an emblem of the craving for escape, either from the maze or deeper into it. Cinematic correlations include the *terrains vagues* of Italy's postwar Neorealism and of a good deal of current science fiction worldwide, though in the former the city's edge is a demilitarized zone between the class wars of a beleaguered peasantry and urban workers and the unemployed, while in more recent films a step off the sidewalk or onto a road leading out of town may be an irrevocable detour into wilderness and tribal regression. Trouvé's *terrain*

Bureau of Implicit Activities, Archives Module ("Secrets" and "Lies"), 2003
Wood, Formica, cement, freezers, water, rope, metal,
163 x 220 x 220 cm [64¼ x 86½ x 86½ in.]

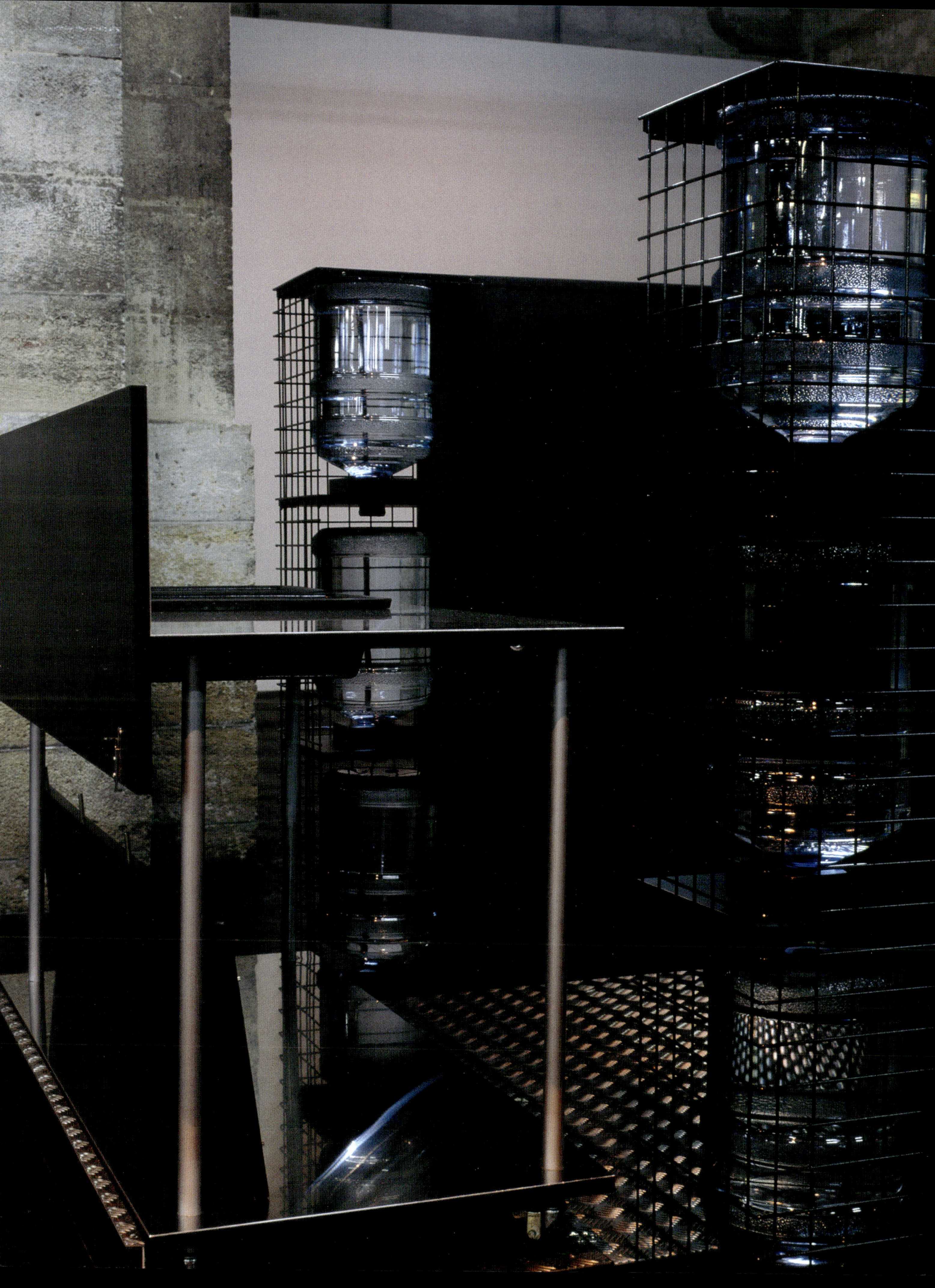

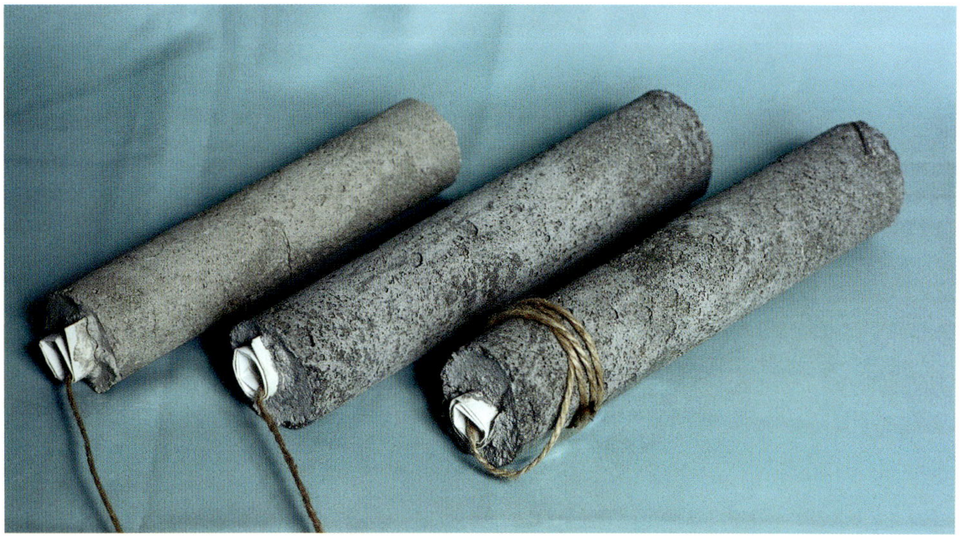
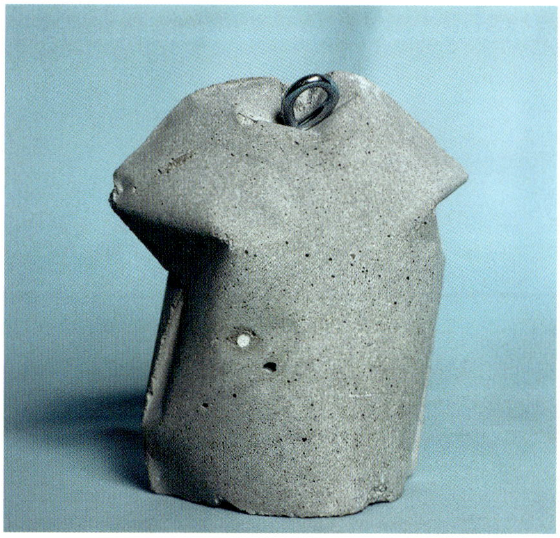
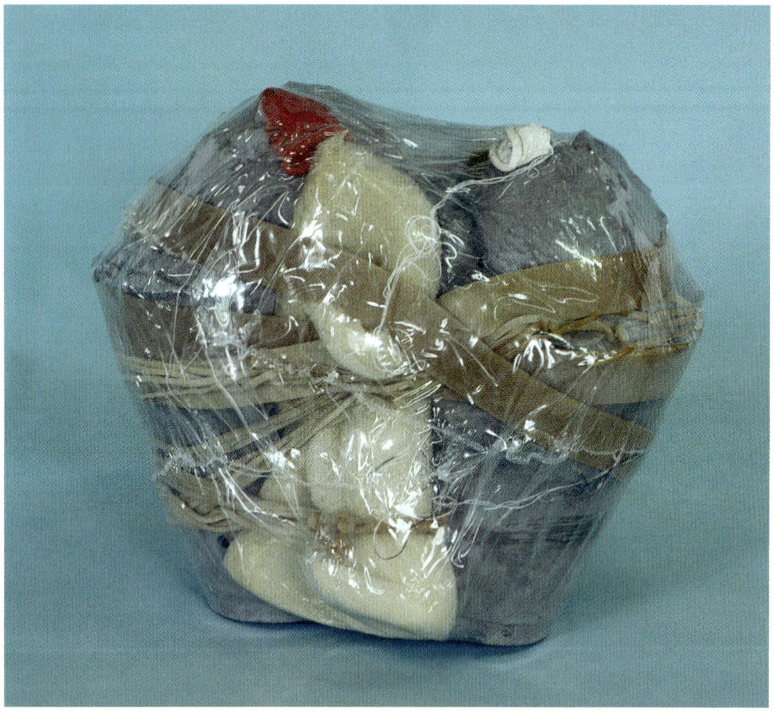
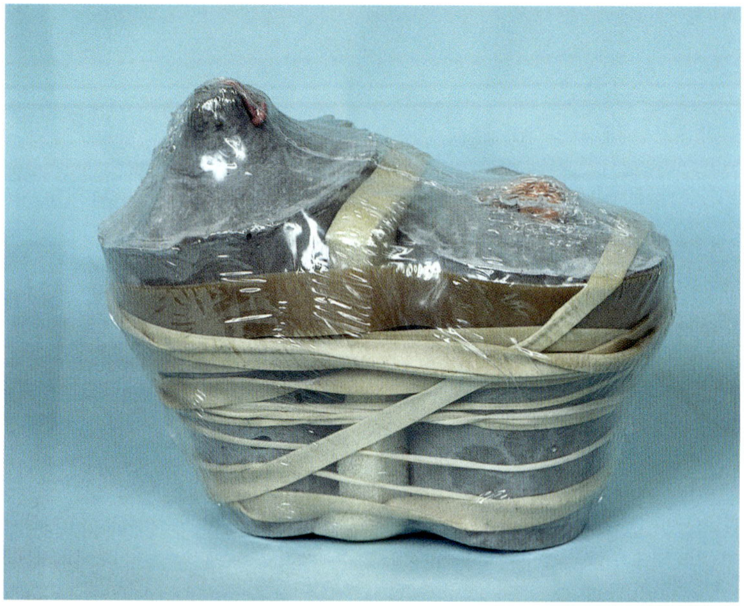
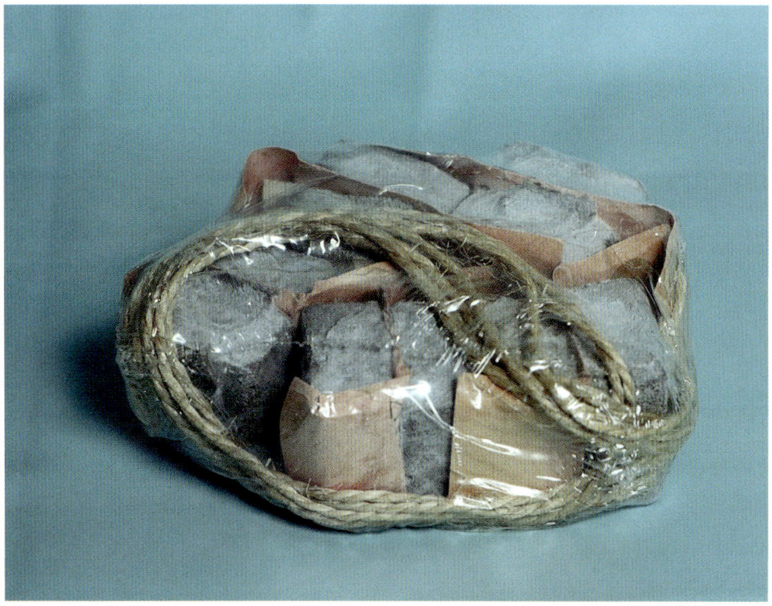
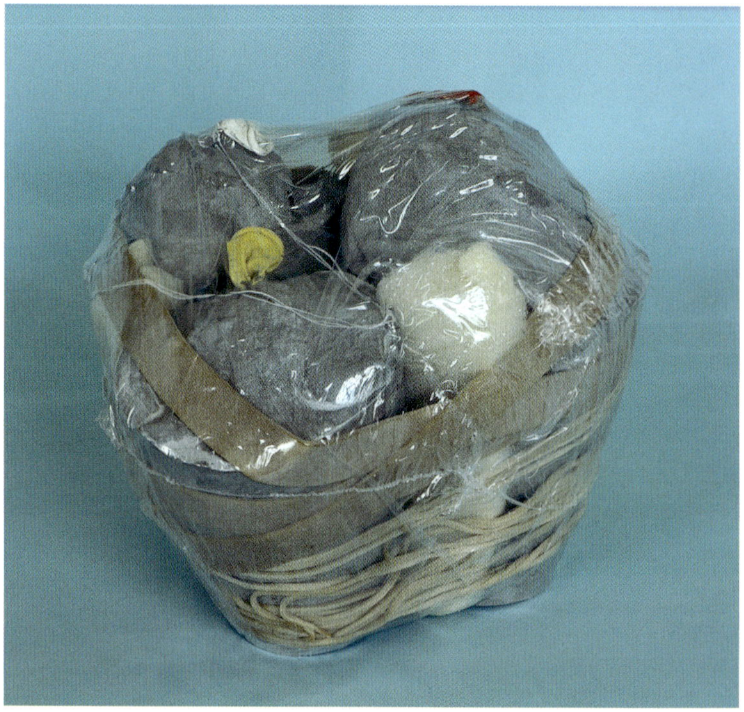

"Secrets" and "Lies", 1997–2003
(Bureau of Implicit Activities, Archives Module [2003])
Cement, rope

vagues are interior rather than exterior. With their freestanding sculptural elements—knotted conduit, blackened metal forms, rocks and more—dispersed across a generally neutral but enveloping background, Trouvé's compositons are at times reminiscent of Yves Tanguy's surreal vistas folded into enclosed, squared-off structures rather than out into convoluted landscapes. As with Tanguy, the eye navigates from one strange landmark to the next, simultaneously gaining and losing one's bearings at each point of reference. But as with previous comparisons, invoking Tanguy's name and work is not intended to signal influence or aesthetic sympathy to any precise degree, but only to assist with filling in heretofore unclaimed locations on the map of the collective imagination's *Terrae incognitae.* And in such places the difference between inside and outside, closed and open, is relative, as those who have descended into caverns or walked the length of office building corridors, factory cellars and storage depots can attest. Such places beg for a new chapter in Gaston Bachelard's *Poetics of Space* (1957), a chapter that, absent Bachelard's posthumous inscription, Trouvé's installations go a long way to adumbrating.

By and large the spaces found in Trouvé's drawings are of a different order, and the recent proliferation of such graphic works write a fresh chapter in the story of her imaginative endeavour. With the most significant group to date being titled *Intranquillity,* what is instantly striking is that they are domestic scenes, fragmentary images of modernist houses on the verge of coming unstuck or, in some cases, past that point already. In them the furniture is less generic and more stylish than in most of Trouvé's previous installations, although some have been transformed into installation after having been sketched as works on paper. Indeed, they appear to be composites made up of bits and pieces gleaned from architecture and interior design magazines and catalogues, although—with the exception of bands of color and strips of copper tape—they are not collages but pencil renderings of things found in such sources. And given that perspective is suggested by patterned backgrounds, isolated architectural units, a row or windows, cabinetry—and the angle from which we see a standing lamp, a table or bed frame on the floor—but otherwise left to the imagination, the flatness of these composites pressurizes everything contained in them like butterflies and moths pinned to a mount, or specimens trapped between glass slides. (In this they also evoke the early open-and-shut Pop montage paintings of Richard Hamilton.)

Again a forensic aspect emerges and a "scene of the crime" curiosity creeps in. But we are not in film noir mode. In fact, but for the rich graphite that describes select details, strong contrasts of light and dark are suppressed in favour of modular hues and tones, and a mysterious hybrid of crisp delineation and ambient blandness conspires to intrigue us. The disquiet with which these paper installations are imbued—and whether or not they are realized in three dimensions they somehow manage to implicate and annex the viewer in two dimensions—is that of quietude pushed to an unnerving extreme, of the same suspended animation of Trouvé's environments unrelieved by the animate presence of the spectator—though we are nonetheless provoked to insinuate ourselves into these dislocated yet hyperstatic rooms. The only piece of the puzzle that moves visually are the copper filaments that run through some of them, catching light that flickers as if in a dull mirror, when that viewer changes position in front of the image.

For if it is true as Western tradition has it that all that representational art holds up a mirror to reality, then in the final analysis what kind of reality has Trouvé chosen to reflect back

"Secrets" and "Lies", 1997–2003
(Bureau of Implicit Activities, Archives Module [2003])
Cement, rope

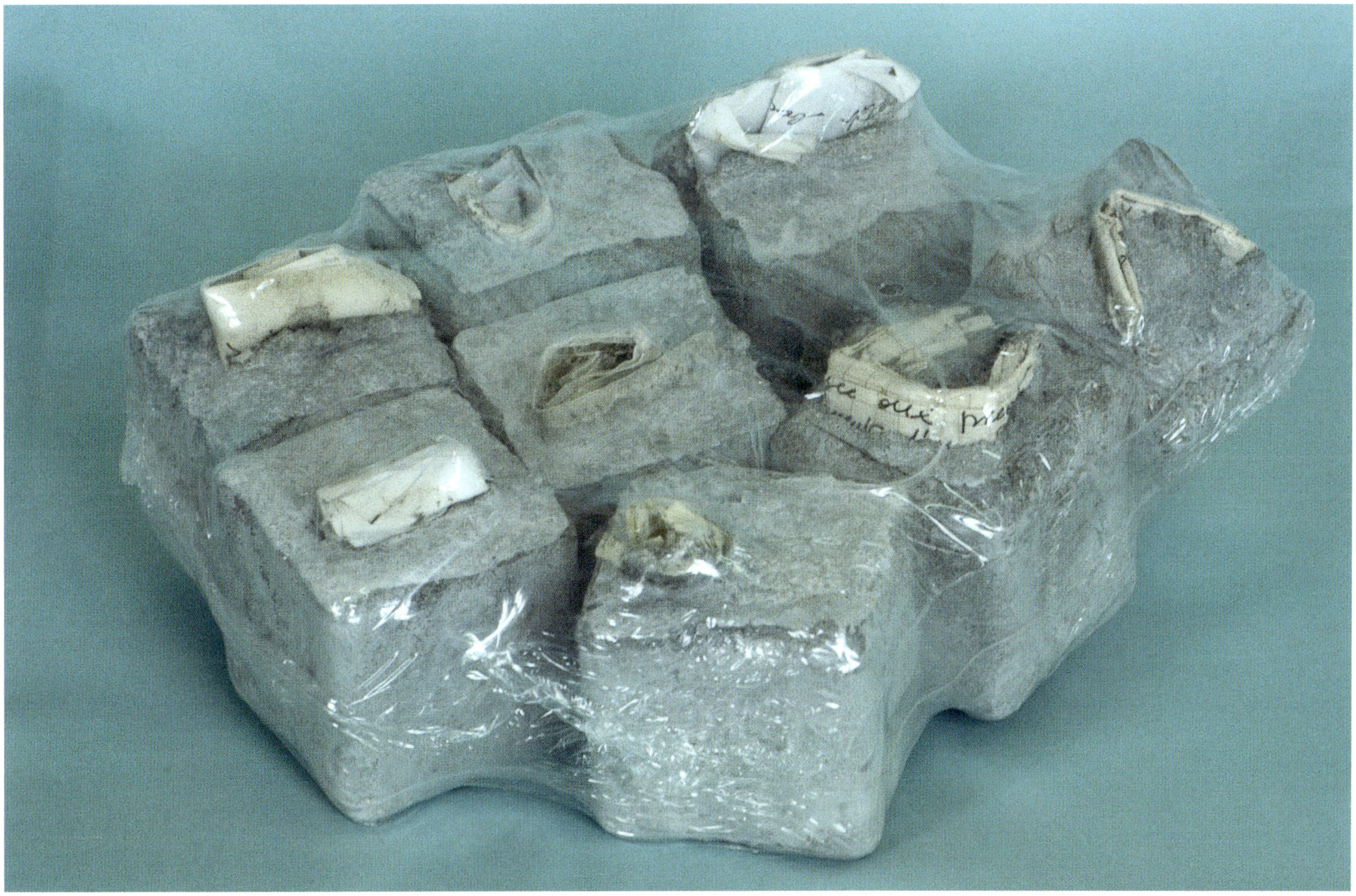

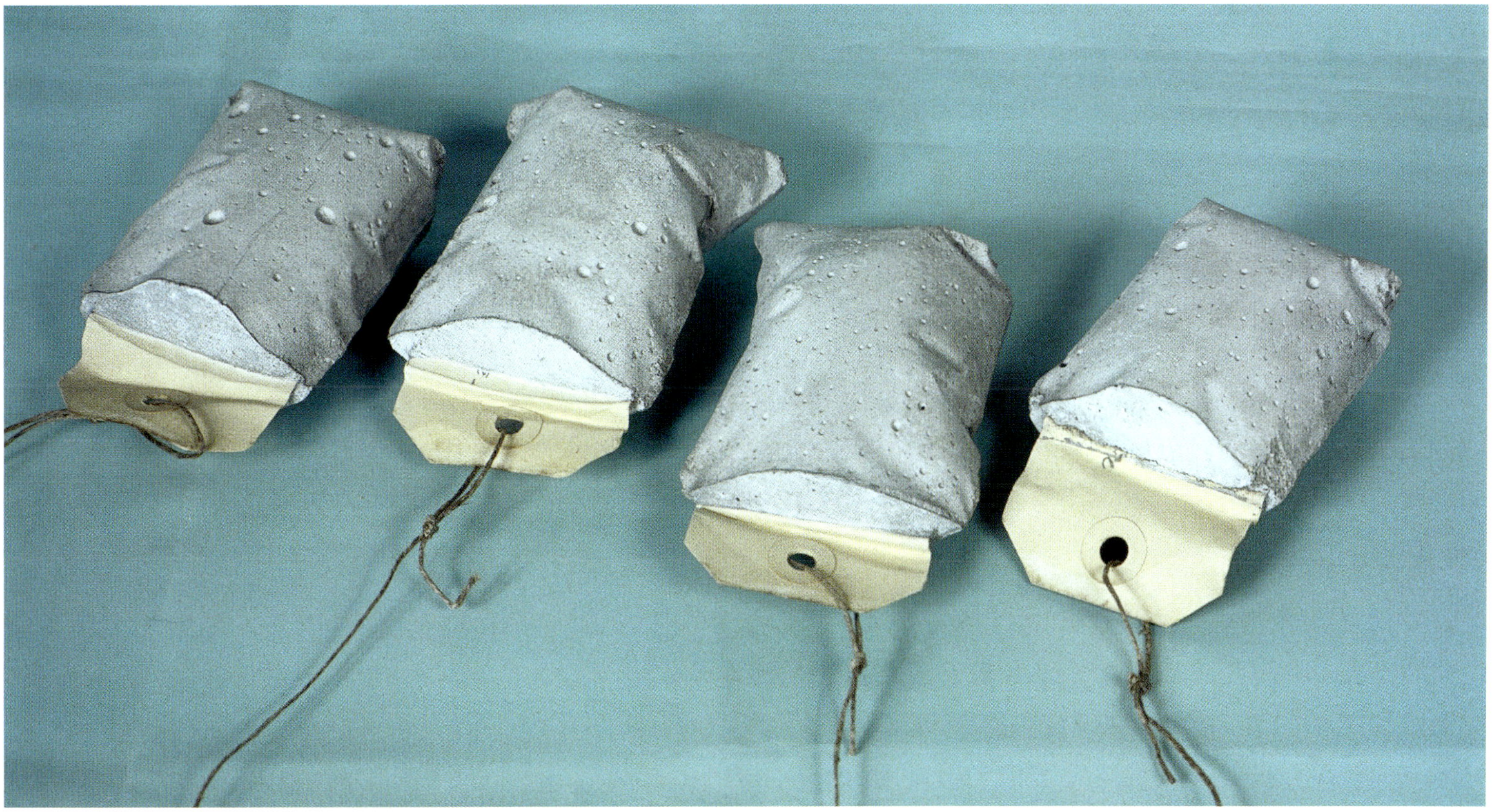

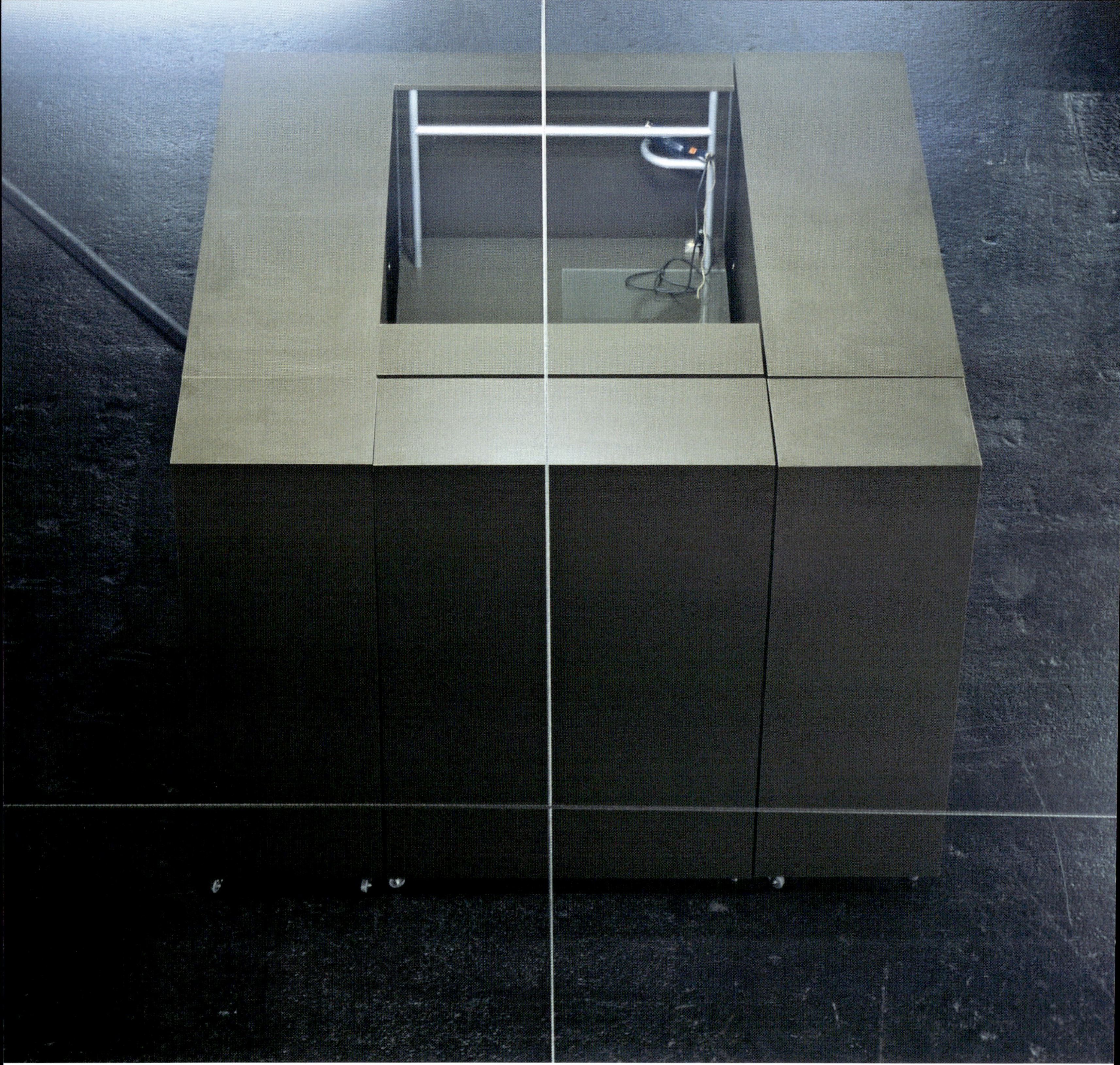

Bureau of Implicit Activities, Archives Module ("Correspondence"), 2003
Wood, Formica, Plexiglas, heat gun, letters (1999–2006),
163 x 220 x 220 cm [64¼ x 86½ x 86½ in.]

into the viewer's eye and consciousness, and what characterizes the several types of mirrors she uses? The easy way out of answering this essentially poetic question would be to align her with current trends and discourses. As to the former, her penchant for slightly dated but generally streamlined or at least austere styles partakes of a wider revival of interest in the postwar modernist décor, while her theoretical affiliations seem to remain at arms length due to a quite reasonable leeriness of becoming a technician of ideological systems as distinct from an artisan of untested possibilities. Thus in an interview with Richard Shusterman she demurs when offered the choice Ludwig Wittgenstein advocated of belonging to no school of thought and being a citizen of no community of ideas, by asserting that for her the crucial thing was to belong to no one community in particular, and to submit to no law in order to gain citizenship of whichever communities one might otherwise willingly associate with.[1] And so in an art context much given to programmatic production and strenuous position-taking and polemic, Trouvé stands out as both clear-headedly intuitive and pragmatic.

1/ Tatiana Trouvé in "Body without a Face," conversation with Richard Shusterman. See page 143 in this volume.

Notwithstanding such seemingly down-to-earth attitudes, the allegiances Trouvé does declare are with fiction writers who trafficked in fantasy of various sorts, chief among them Italo Calvino, Jorge Luis Borges, Georges Perec and Dino Buzzati, all of whom in their own way have explored the poetic license accorded to those who dream waking dreams and all of whom have fine-tooled the art of physical, conceptual, perceptual, emotional and spiritual displacement to exquisite aesthetic tolerances. On leaving one of Trouvé's installations or turning one's gaze away from one of her drawing, the reasons for that affinity are obvious. For we quickly find that that temporary experience of displacement—equally exquisite, equally disconcerting and imaginatively liberating despite its iconography of confinement—is indispensable preparation for at long last awakening to the unnatural, unfamiliar surroundings we are accustomed to thinking of as the ordinary. The necessity and history of doing this is as old as the first images that recast our world in the image of another much like it but fundamentally estranged from it. The challenge is to do this afresh, to charge the uncanny with untapped energy, to give its conductive polarities—the memory effect and the alienation effect—new facets in contact with the new dimensions of modernity. If I have alluded to only a few such precedents it is to spare the reader—and the artist—the burden of clearing away the vast accumulation of alternative realities in order to reach Trouvé's own. Indeed, one has only to cross its threshold to know where one is and isn't—and to become so alert to both that every sensory organ, of which the mind is the most alert of all, shivers.

"Unsent Correspondence", 1999–2006
(Bureau of Implicit Activities, Archives Module [2003])

Following pages:
Bureau of Implicit Activities, Archives Module ("Correspondence"), 2003
Wood, Formica, Plexiglas, heat gun, letters (1999–2006), 163 x 220 x 220 cm [64¼ x 86½ x 86½ in.]

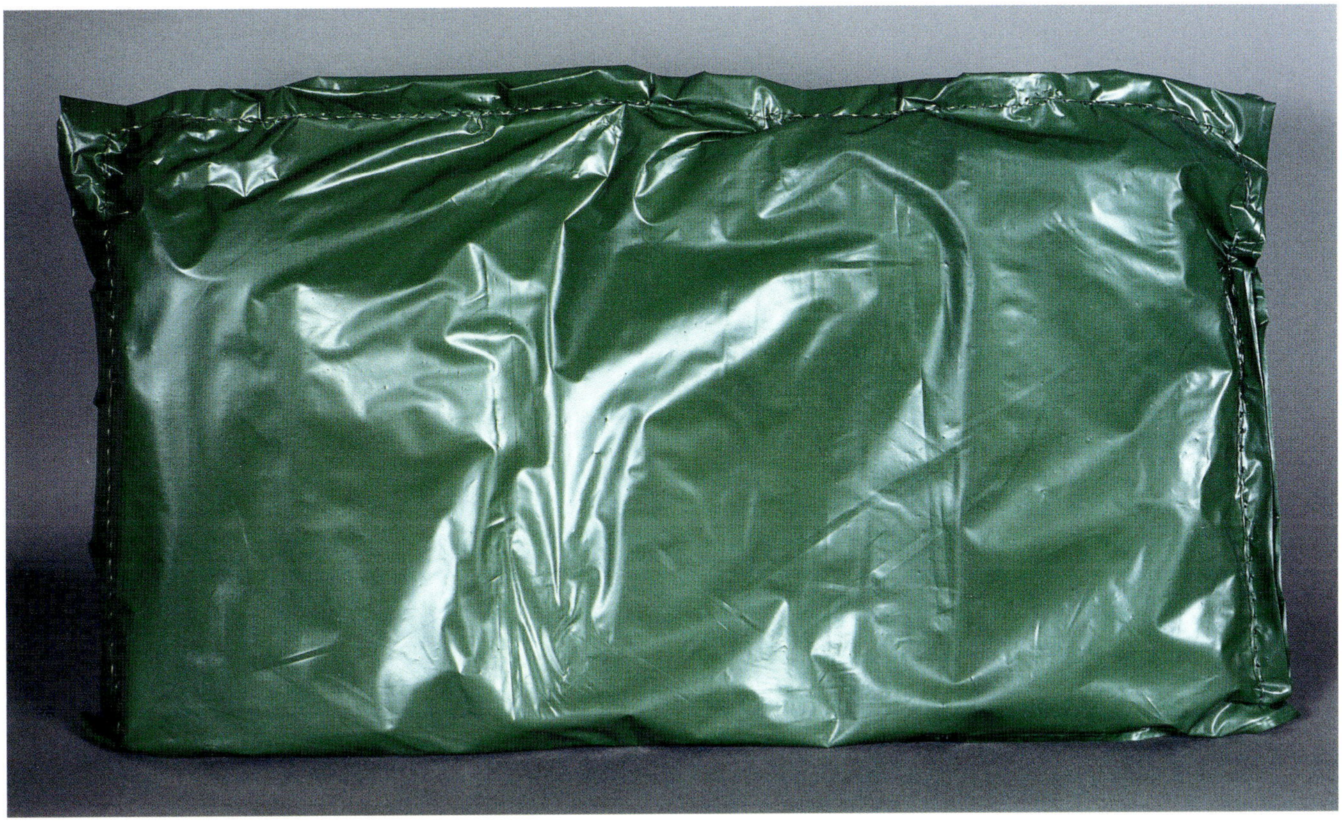

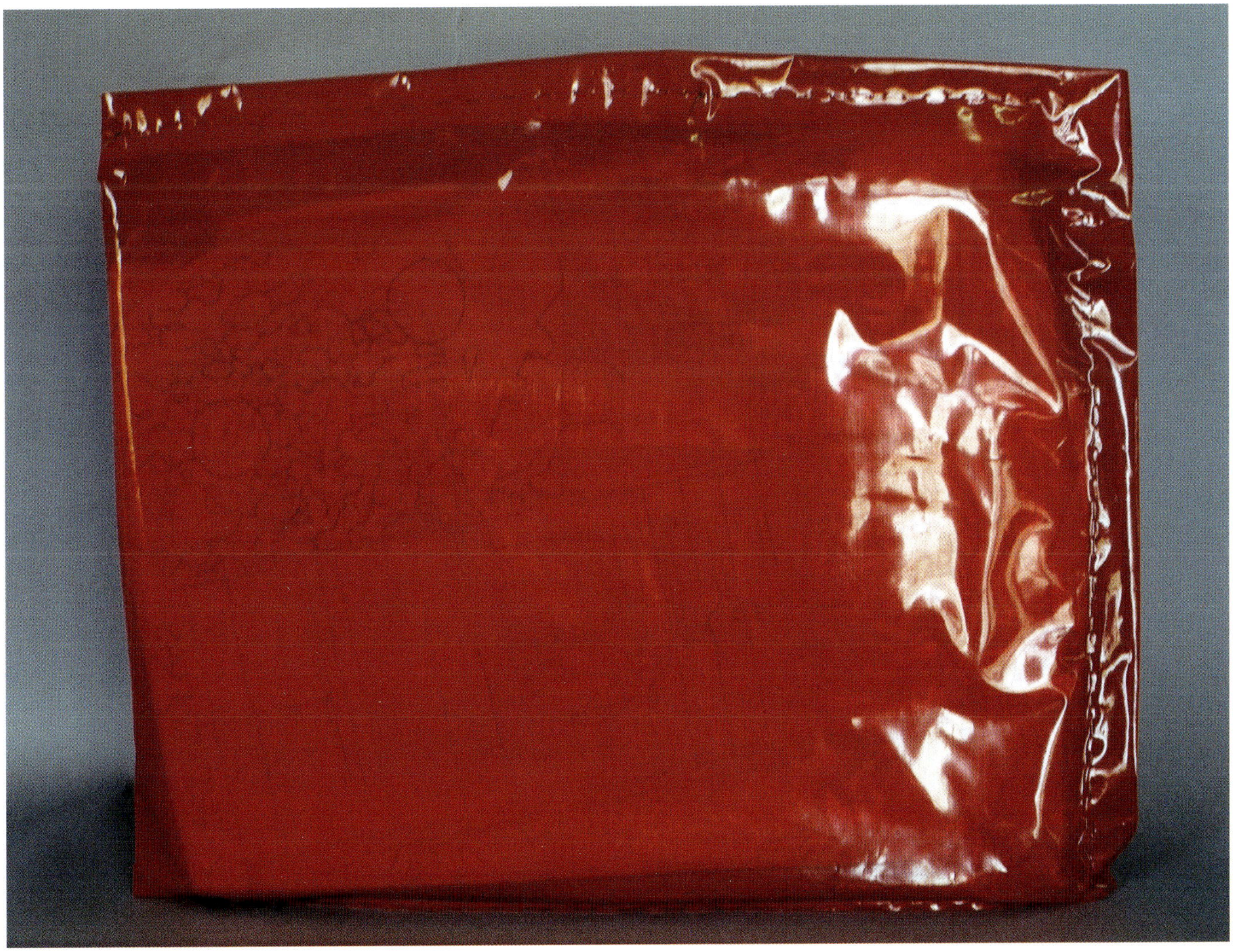

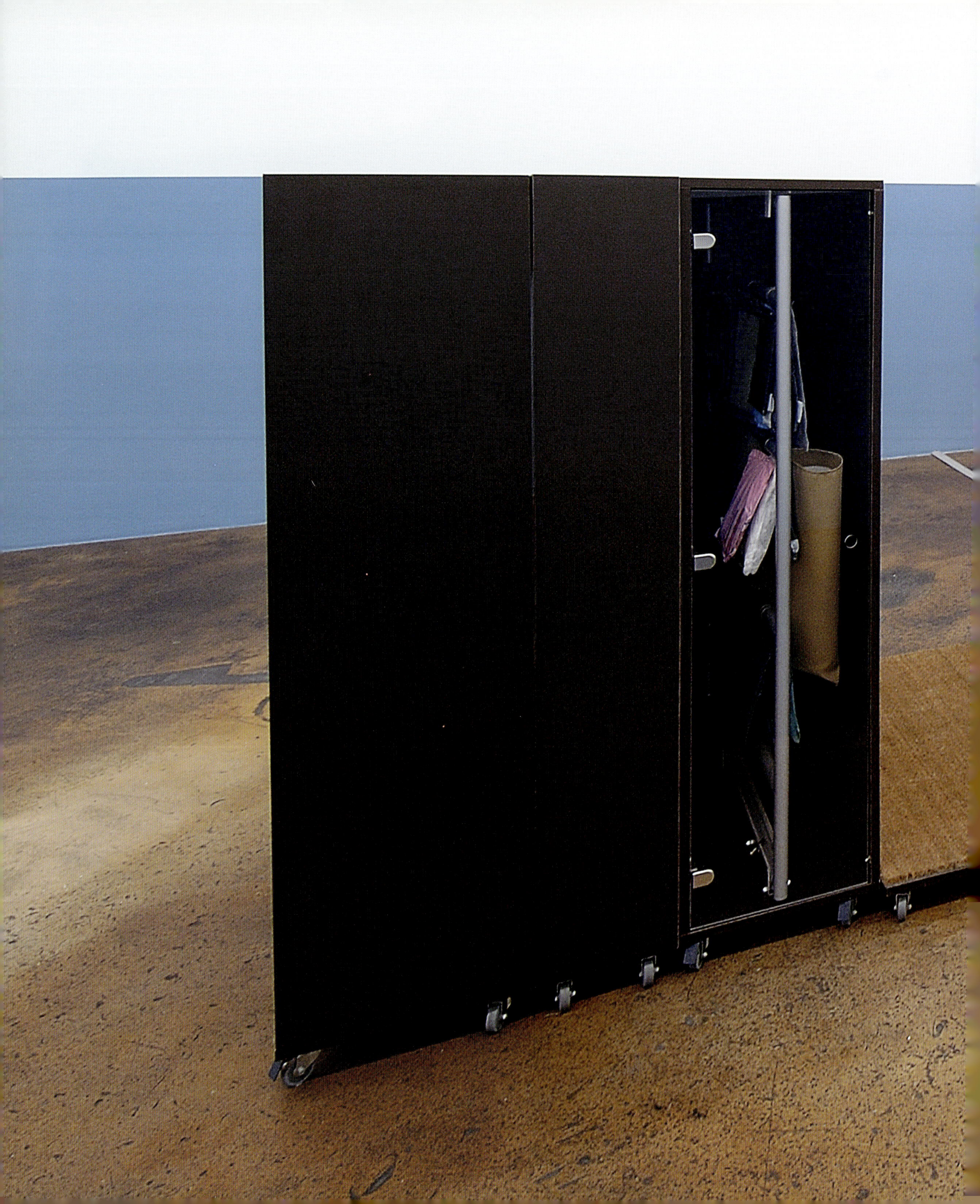

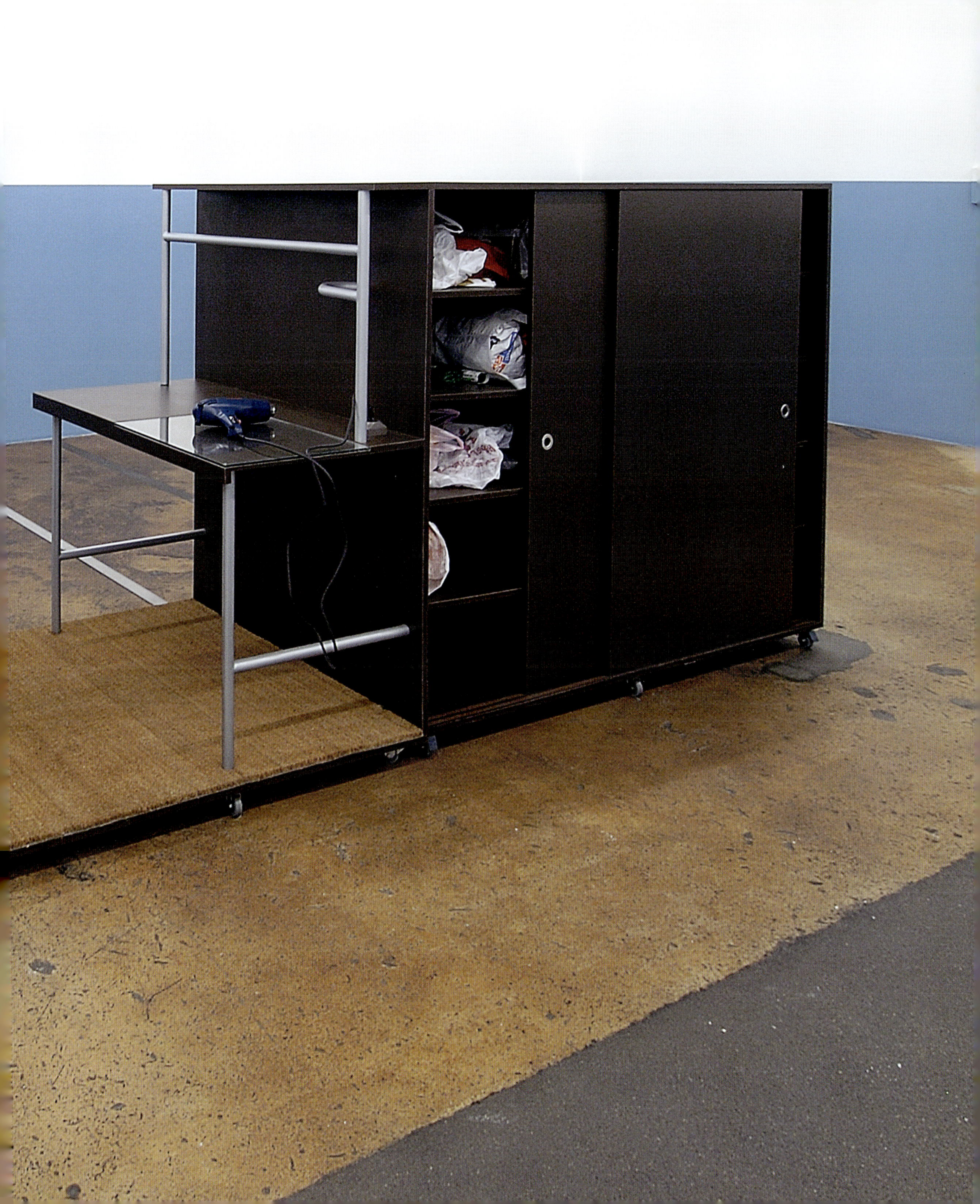

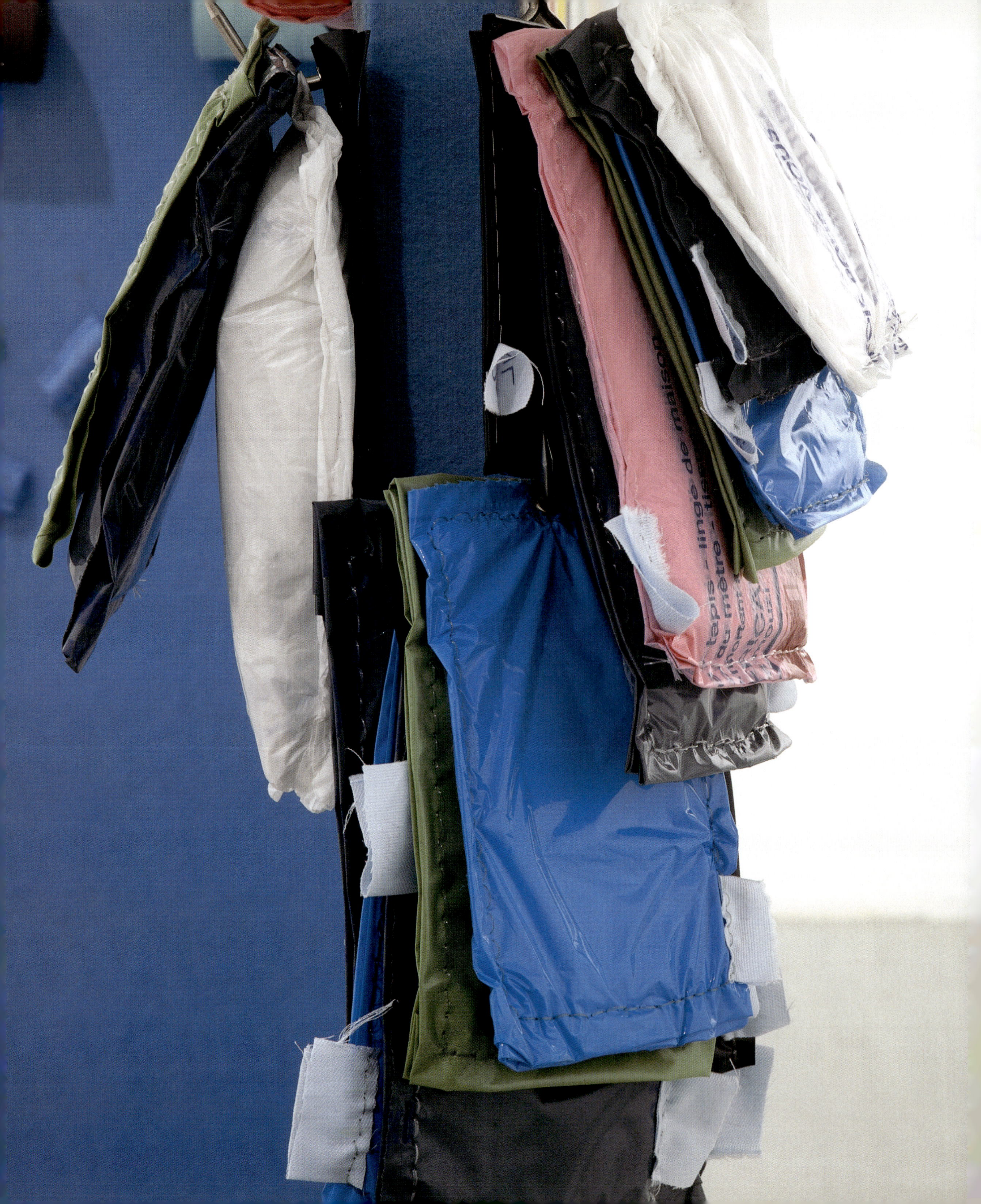
tapis - linge de maison

"Unsent Correspondence", 1999–2006
(Bureau of Implicit Activities, Archives Module [2003])

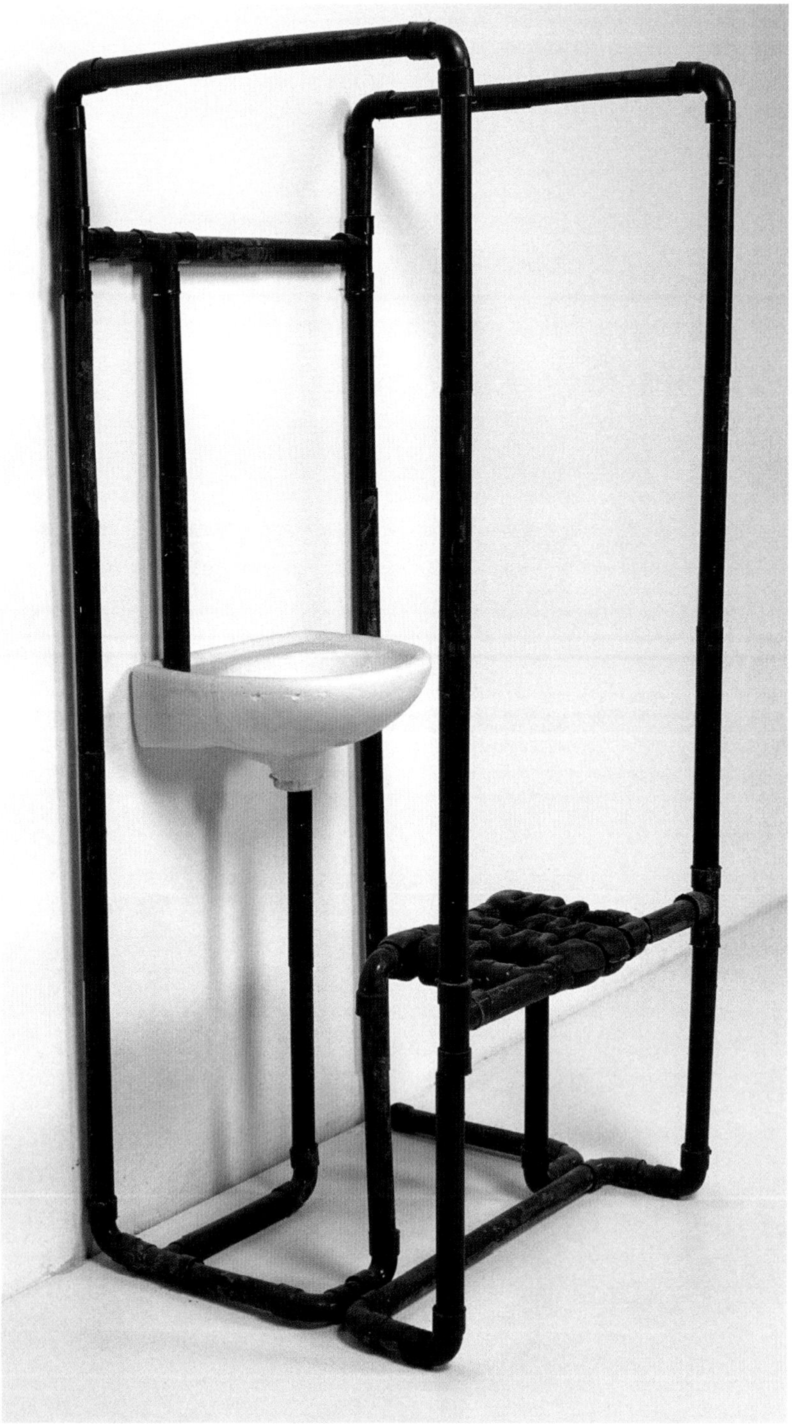

Bureau of Implicit Activities, Bulimia Booth, 2004
Black chocolate and white chocolate, 150 x 65 x 65 cm [59 x 25½ x 25½ in.]

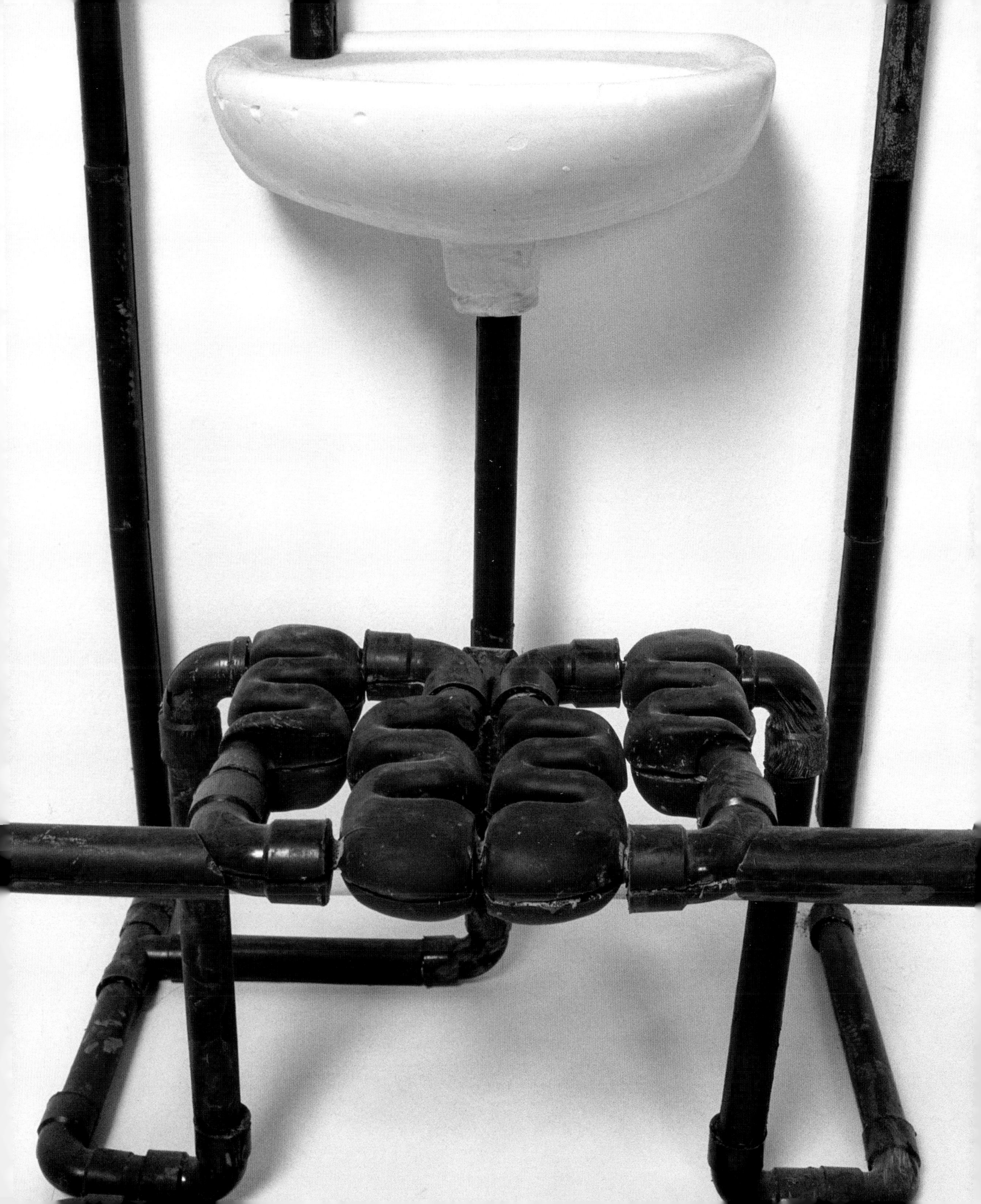

TATIANA TROUVÉ'S BACHELOR MACHINES

Catherine Millet

While scrolling on my computer screen through all the images I was given to prepare this text, my index finger suddenly raises off the mouse: my gaze remains fixed on the photo of a work from 2007 that I have never seen in reality—if, that is, you are ever truly in reality when viewing an exhibition by Tatiana Trouvé. Several large sheets, three black and one white, with haphazard outlines, are hanging limply over a long bar. One or more "windows," all relatively square in shape, have been cut into the sheets, allowing us to see the underlying sheet at the point of their intersection. My attention is drawn to this work, because the sheets remind me of the layer of "Milky Way flesh" that can be found in the uppermost panel of Marcel Duchamp's *The Large Glass*—that uncertain form in which one finds the three square "draft pistons." Upon closer inspection, however, I realize this is not entirely correct. Another work by Trouvé that is executed according to the same principle also includes colored sheets, one gray and one white, with a black sheet cut in such a way that only a few shreds of it are left at its center. After a few inquiries, I realize that these are, in fact, sheets of leather hanging over a wooden bar. Trouvé was obviously not thinking of *The Large Glass* when she began working with these skins, but she is very receptive to the comparison when I ask her about it.

This encourages me to follow my own intuition, all the more so since the thought of *The Large Glass* prompts me to take another look at Michel Carrouges's book on *The Bachelor Machines.* In its very first pages, I already find the following comment: "When we read, our imagination is set in motion through an automatic impulse that furnishes us with an unpremeditated interpretation of the text that excites it. Why do we allow these images to be born and die without paying direct attention to them? This is dreamlike behavior of a very particular kind, whose analysis would no doubt bring many revelations."[1] But would it not be possible for the author's comment to apply just as well to the consideration of a landscape or a work of art? This is how Carrouges justifies a project inspired by the spontaneous juxtaposition of Kafka's *In the Penal Colony* with Duchamp's *The Bride Stripped Bare by Her Bachelors, Even.* I, in turn, decide to pursue the analogy between Duchamp and Trouvé, carried away by something so obvious that I felt it could not be avoided: taken as a whole, Trouvé's work belongs to the prestigious genealogy of bachelor machines.

The most pertinent interpretation of *The Bride,* or *The Large Glass* as it is usually called, comes from Jean Clair. Clair emphasized Duchamp's interest in geometrical speculation, especially with respect to the fourth dimension. The premise of the fourth dimension is that, just as shadows and images are projections of three-dimensional models into two dimensions, our three-dimensional reality is the projection of a four-dimensional universe. According to Clair, Duchamp attempted to transcribe this universe into figures he carefully placed in perspective on a transparent medium—a medium, in other words, that is subject to more than one point of view. Trouvé is also interested in the passage from one space into another. Several times over the course of my visit to her studio, she insists on the fact that her sculpture ("I'm actually a sculptor," she says) comes from drawing—and returns to it, one should add.

More or less in the manner of drawings for interior design, her works on paper establish extremely pronounced perspectives (views of a bedroom? a living room? a studio? a gallery?) that are emphasized by the line of a plinth or a metallic structure, and look out on a distant natural world: a path through a park, or a fragment of a more wild landscape. Yet this perspective,

1/ Michel Carrouges, *Les Machines célibataires* (Paris: Nouvelles éditions du Chêne, 1976), p. 26. (First edition, Paris: éditions Arcanes, 1954.)

Bureau of Implicit Activities, Sand Cell, 1997
Wood, sand, suede, 100 x 140 x 131 cm [39½ x 55 x 51½ in.]

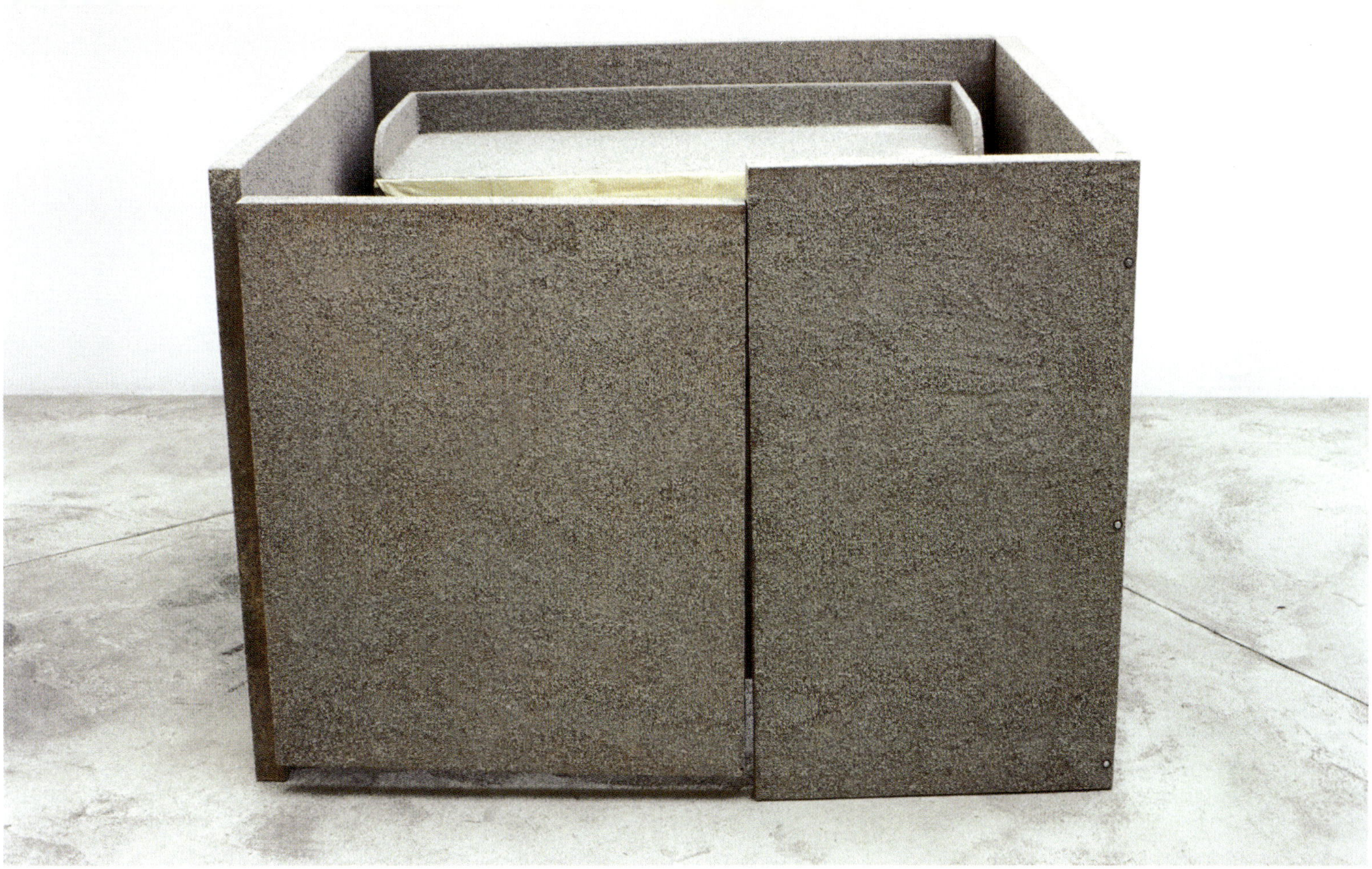

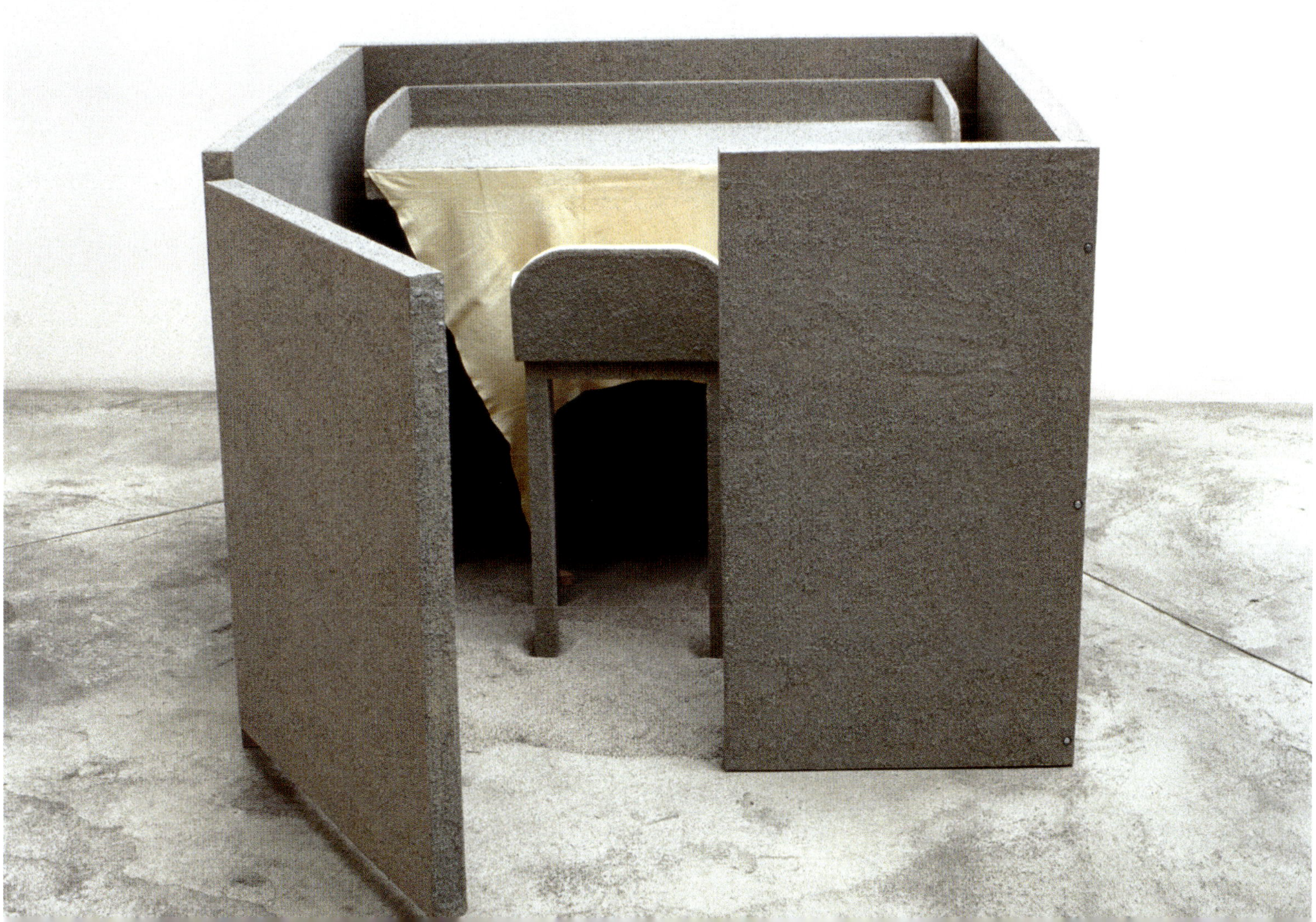

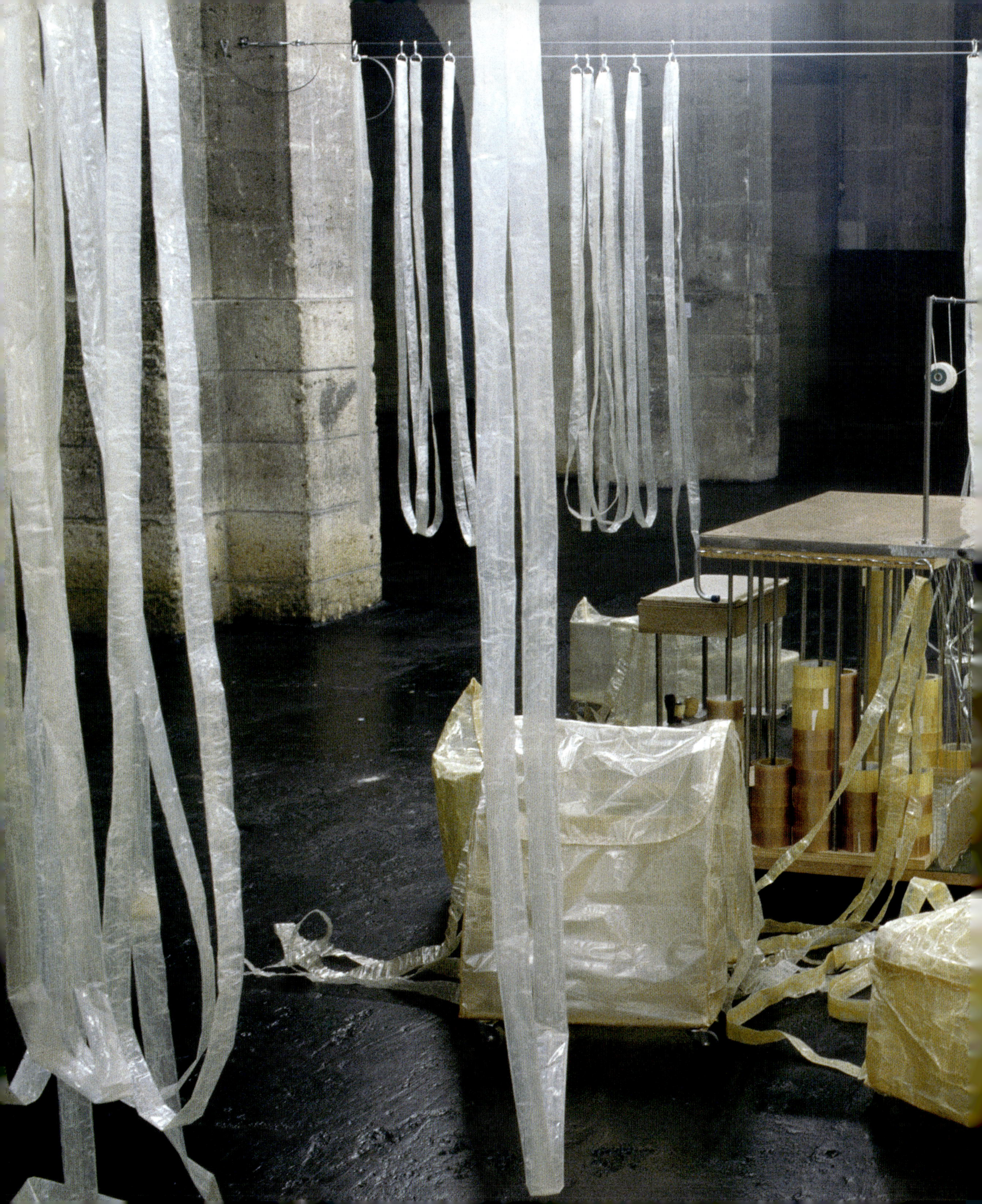

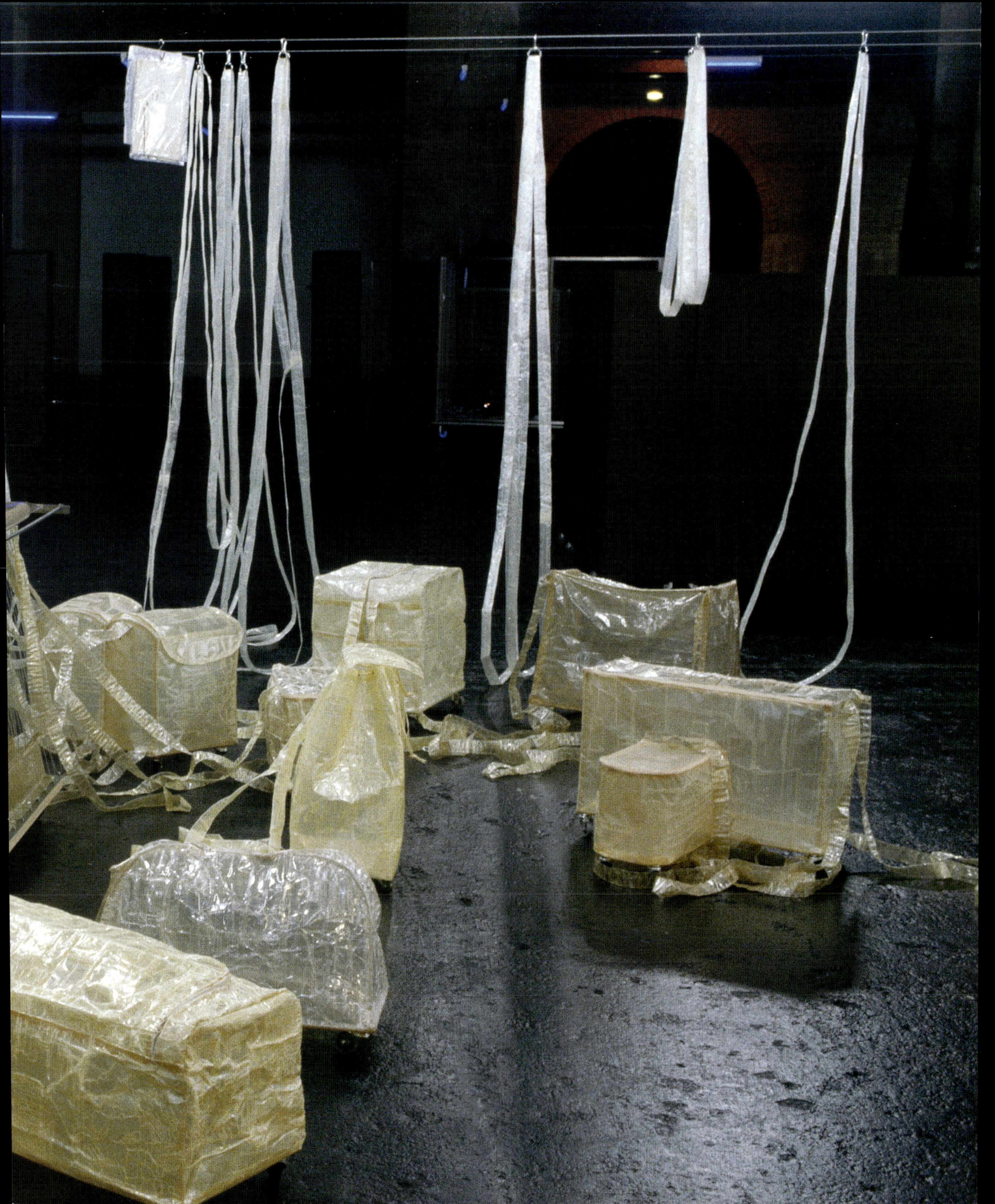

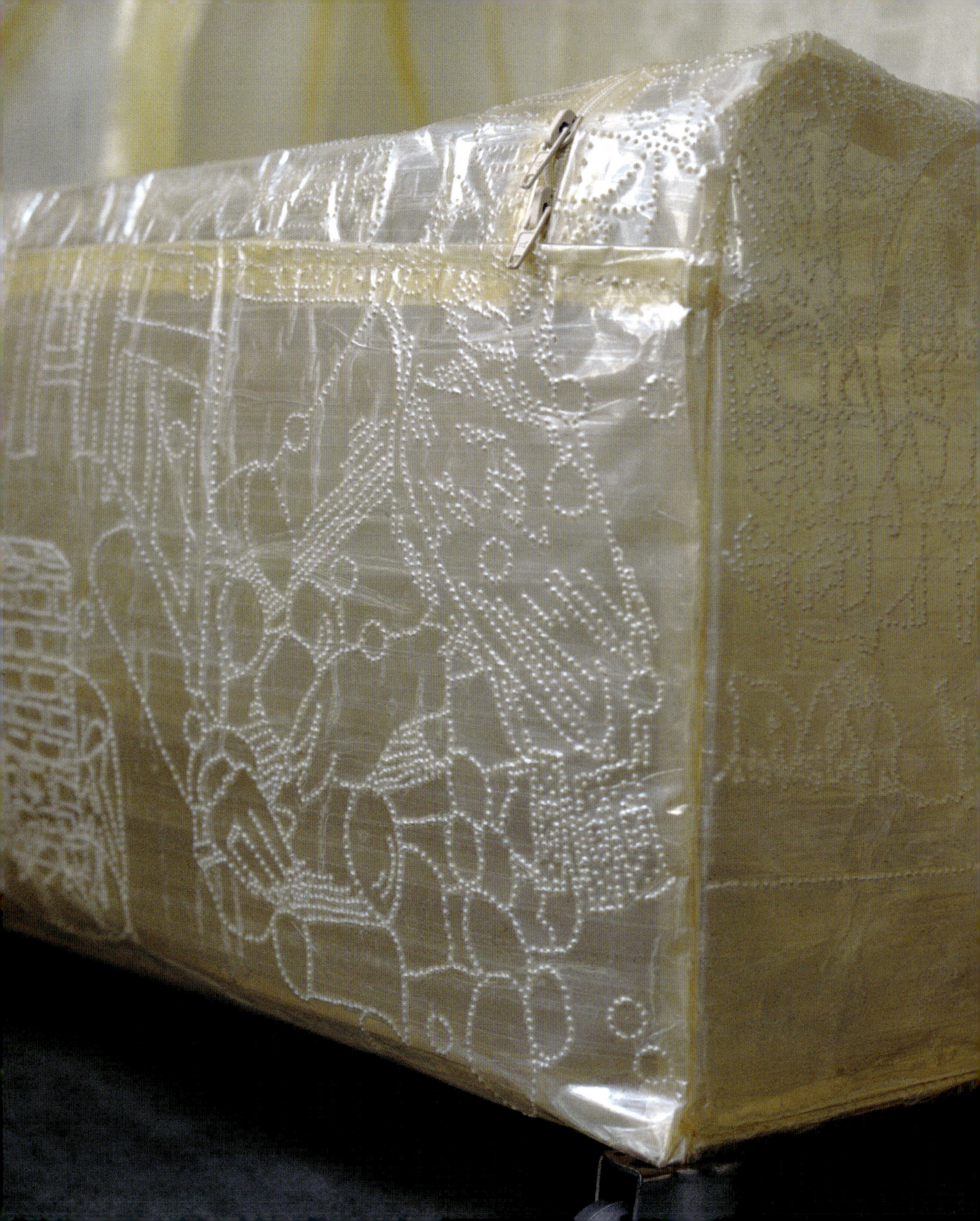

Previous pages:
Bureau of Implicit Activities, Ghost Matrix, 1999
Wood, metal, nylon, tape, PVC, imitation leather, tools, plastic,
147 x 108 x 80 cm [57¾ x 42½ x 31½ in.]

Left-hand page:
Ghosts, 1994–99
Tape, hole punches, stitches

which gives the viewer the illusion of entering a vast space and being able to walk around in it, corresponds to sculptures, which, even if they are situated in three-dimensions, occupy a space that the visitor is not entirely sure he shares. Faced with the sculptures, the visitor is almost as awkwardly positioned as if he were standing in front of a wall, or a screen, or some kind of obstacle. Sometimes the visitor is stuck in a physical sense: although he might like to get closer to a group of intriguing objects, or else to understand the accident that brought about the pile of black sand he sees, a glass window keeps him irremediably removed from it. Nothing is more frustrating than standing in front of that window, and the visitor will no doubt prefer to back up and enjoy the strange still-life he can nonetheless contemplate through the pane, as though he were in front of a painting. In fact, the sight of this apparatus through the glass partition's metal-set frame is not entirely unrelated to the "scene" represented in *The Large Glass,* for it is within this frame that objects (a piece of furniture, bedsprings, a rock) look familiar until a detail, or else a somewhat overly schematic configuration (the rock is in chains and the piece of furniture bizarrely placed), charges them with mystery, all the while giving us the feeling that there must be certain, yet distant, relationships between them.

In interviews, the artist has mentioned her childhood in Senegal and how much she has been influenced by the widespread belief there in Djinns: spirits and ghosts that live alongside humans but are invisible, in a parallel world. Trouvé explains, "I started imagining that perhaps we, not they, were the ghosts."[2] The perspective is reversed: if we can imagine that the three-dimensional world in which we live is perhaps nothing but the projection of another world in four dimensions, can we not also reason the other way around? Is it possible that this three-dimensional world is nothing more than the representation

2/ Tatiana Trouvé in conversation with Hans Ulrich Obrist, *Djinns* catalogue (Chatou: CNEAI éditions, 2005).

of a world in two dimensions (which it often actually is, whenever one goes from an architectural study on paper to an actual building)? And could we not then argue that, in this transfer, our imagination, so easily solicited by the drawing's two-dimensional space, can only thrive in three-dimensional space if it forgets the body that burdens it, going so far as to transform the body into a kind of ghost? Now that she is an adult, Trouvé no longer believes in Djinns, but she has made sure that she remains capable of assuring the coexistence of two parallel worlds while traveling, as an artist, from one to the other: "In the end, I think that artists, every time they do a piece, always do the same thing: they provide a double of that about which they are speaking."[3]

3/ Ibid.

Trouvé's drawings and sculptures also have several other contradictory effects. Her recent drawings on black paper divide space into different planes thanks to the varied use of certain media (pencil lead, collage with leaves of lead and tin); in spite of its opacity, the black surface catches our gaze and holds onto it even while the eye wanders from one plane to another. The body then also starts to move and vary its point of view, thus altering the way the light hits the planes, too, making them disappear and reappear. Other drawings, this time on a white background, similarly grab our attention because of the subtly suggested overlapping of planes. For example, in what looks like a bedroom, we can see a kind of armoire, which seems exaggeratedly long, perhaps because it is extended by its reflection in a mirror. The other objects reflected in this "mirror" are nonetheless seen either from an identical, and not inversed, angle (the ball and its shadow, the rope falling to the ground), or at an angle perpendicular to the orientation of the object in the foreground (the bed)! Add to this image a bar that has been placed in front of the armoire but somehow continues behind it, as though the armoire were transparent

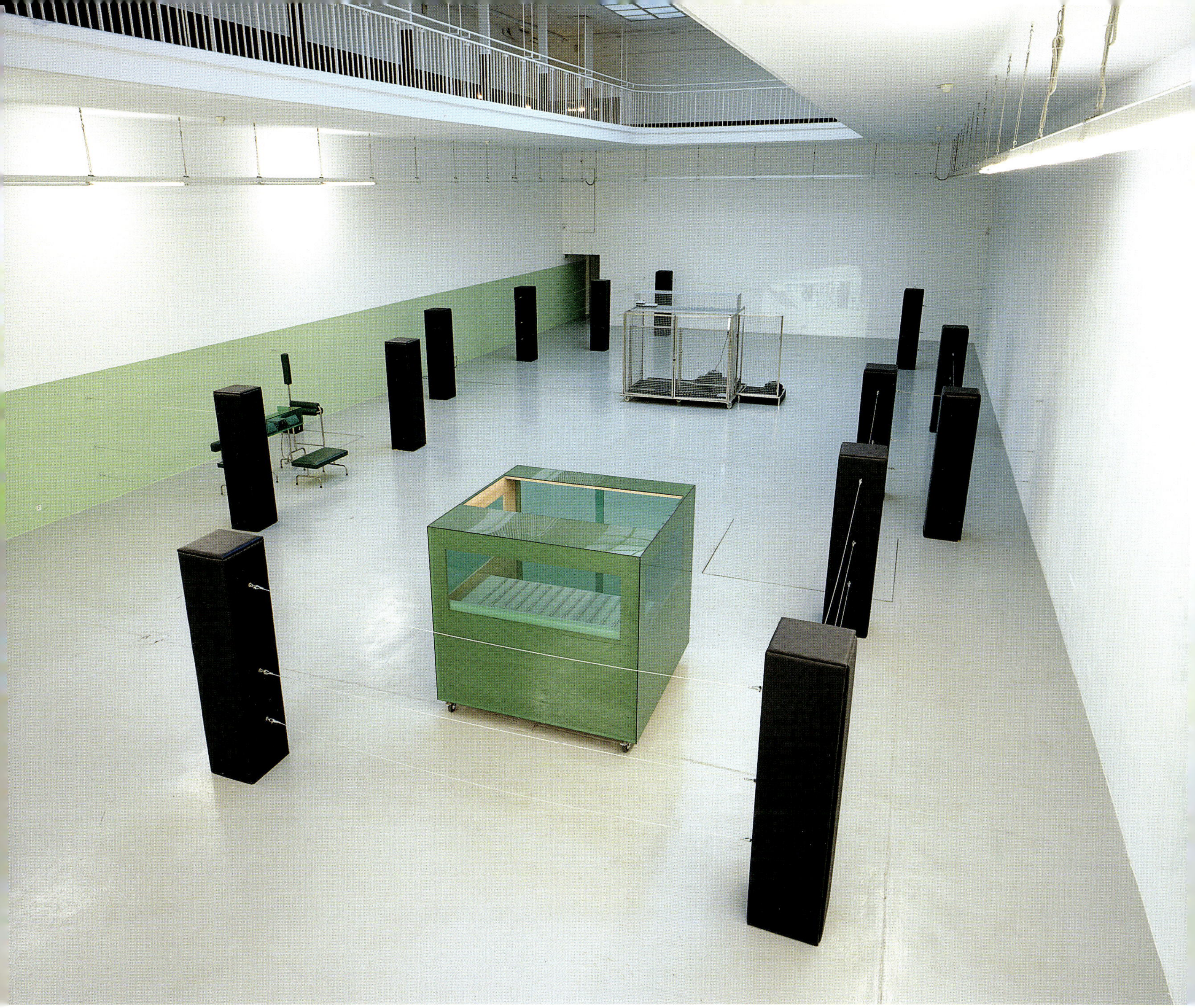

Bureau of Implicit Activities, Waiting Modules Annex, 2003
Wood, Plexiglas, paper, sound archives, 160 x 180 x 185 cm [63 x 70¾ x 72¾ in.]

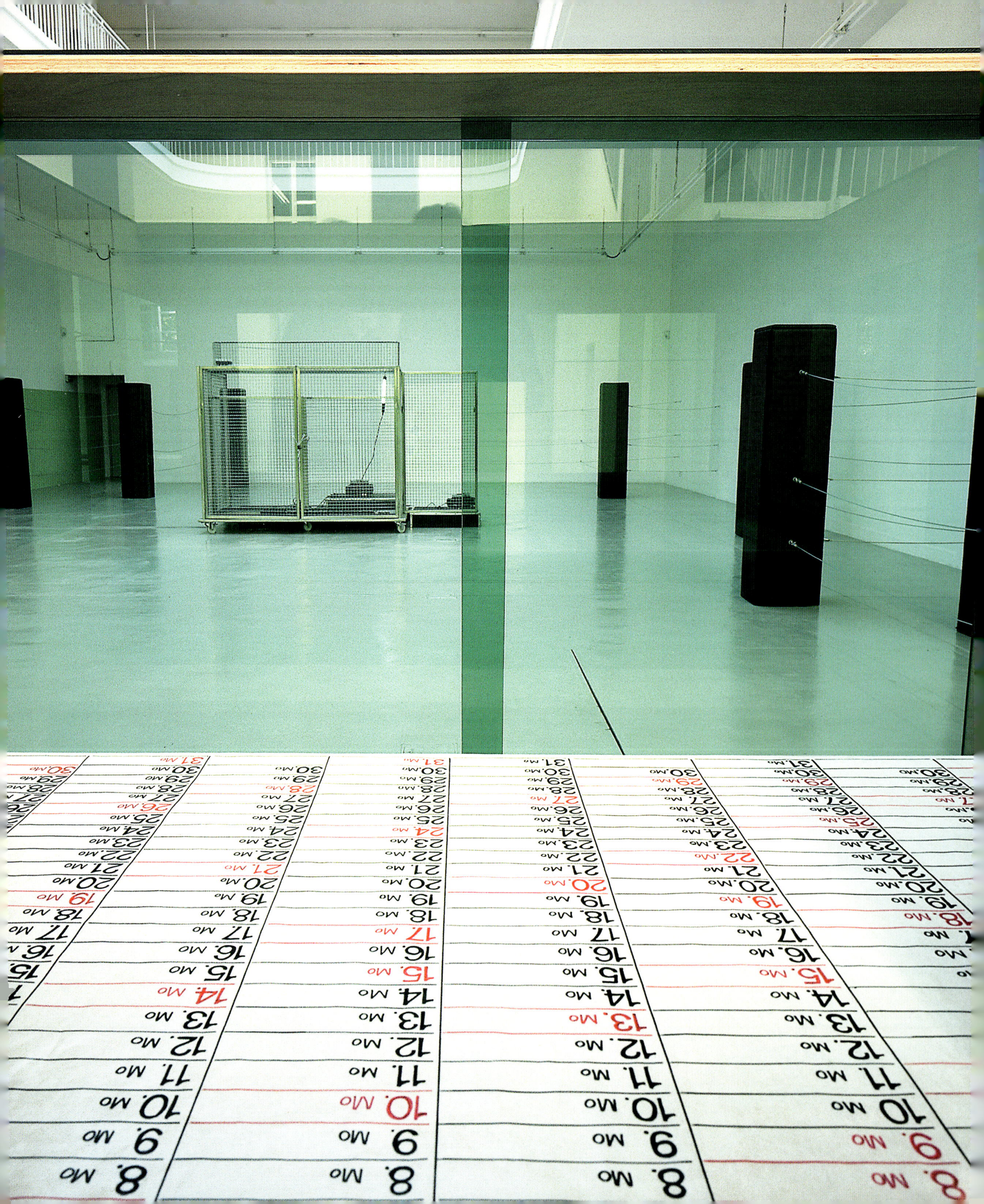

Bureau of Implicit Activities, Waiting Modules Annex (detail), 2003

and had been placed in front of another mirror. The space of these drawings, once we have entered it, is of infinite complexity, and yet our eyes adjust to it all the more readily since our imagination is provoked. On the other hand, if we were to find ourselves in a space constructed in this manner—if such a thing were even possible—we would be paralyzed, or at least stunned, thinking only of how we might escape! These drawings are populated by objects whose aesthetics are reminiscent of the 60s, which is perhaps why they recall other memories, such as the *Interiors* arranged by the very Duchampian artist Richard Hamilton in incompatible perspectives, with doorways opening onto other more or less coherent spaces where it would be entirely impossible to stand if one were to try to construct life-sized versions of them in real space.[4]

4/ And of course, before these, the famous collage *Just what is it that makes today's homes so different, so appealing.* "Appealing" is certainly the word.

As we know, Hamilton also created objects in three-dimensions, or environments. Some of these, like *Exhibit I* and *Exhibit II,* are abstract compositions with lines and monochrome planes arranged in space, showing the mark of the graphic designer Hamilton also was. Similarly, I note that Trouvé's sculptures are themselves increasingly graphic: metallic bars drawn in space; sheaths of leather are laced in a way that gives them the uncertain, frayed appearance of a painted or drawn line, while other sheaths, vertical or assembled, are set at the border of planes like hatch-marks in a drawing; or else a billiard stick whose base is probably filled with lead seems to stand obliquely, and miraculously, in space, like a line struck across the white space of a sheet of paper. There is nonetheless one major difference between Hamilton's environments and Trouvé's constructions: Hamilton's spaces are constructed in such as way that the visitor may enter and walk around within them. The visitor's pleasure comes from finding his way around and progressively understanding the spatial divisions (like the ones in the installation version of *Lobby*).[5] In Trouvé's sculptures, however, finding the "thread" (the metal bar, the chain, the cable) that links them together, far from allowing us to appropriate the logic of the group, only gets us increasingly lost. There is a way out of the paths Hamilton proposes, but there is no escape from the mental labyrinths of Trouvé's exhibitions. The race is lost before it starts, and the object of our visual desire is at an ever-receding distance. It is something our body will never be able to translate.

5/ Imagined in relation to the eponymous painting, this environment invites the visitor into a space that is *mise-en-abyme* by a painting that, placed inside the space itself, represents it and is reflected in a mirror. We should remember that Hamilton also executed didactic exhibitions.

Trouvé frequently places us in this terrible predicament. For example, she often creates an "inadequate" relationship of scale between the visitor and the objects presented in her exhibition. Objects too small for the visitor to be able to use, or to even imagine using, still look like seats, tables, or screens, or else machines or instruments for body-building. At the same time, they are too big to be considered easy-to-use toys. Doors are set into the walls of a museum gallery and left ajar, providing a glimpse of strongly lit spaces that make them all the more attractive. Yet these doors, on the same scale as the objects, don't allow us through towards the light, unless you happen to come from Lilliput.

Although Trouvé has recently brought her objects up to a scale much closer to that of the human body, she has also invented new and ingenious devices to ensure that the visitor finds himself drawn towards a hallway he cannot enter or, as I have described above, facing a glass barrier that blocks all passage. This causes the visitor to stare all the more intently at what Trouvé has prevented him from approaching physically. Has the mirror in that inaccessible space he sees in front of him been placed there to help in some way? Of course not! The mirror reflects objects that are not the ones he sees between the mirror and himself, and it is impossible to determine their location. He can stretch his neck or bend over and try to see through an opening situated at the bottom of the exterior barrier, but the forbidden scene remains a mystery. Duchamp comes to mind once again. As in Duchamp's *Given: 1 The Waterfall, 2. The Illuminating Gas,* Trouvé's recent sculptures excite our gaze but leave us at the door. One might say that they reduce us to supposition and speculation, but "reduce" is not exactly the right word, since the speculative imagination always leads us further than our bodies ever could.

At this stage of my reflection, my first intuition is confirmed: Tatiana Trouvé's sculptures are indeed bachelor machines. One sees this in their basically "industrial" aesthetics (even when they are made by the artist herself or artisans she commissions)—by which I mean their coldness and what one might think is their functionality. They are often juxtaposed and sometimes linked together as if they really were destined to produce something, but in a closed circuit, or at least without demanding any intervention on our part and, to the contrary, imposing their autonomy. Nonetheless, as further proof of my hypothesis, I would invite the reader to remember the artist's older works (let's turn on the time machine), the ones that brought her recognition in the late 1990s. It all started with what she called the *Bureau d'Activités Implicites* [Bureau of Implicit Activities], or *B.I.A.* Conceived of as a way to conserve the already abundant archives of her still young life, this "bureau" turned out to be well-adapted to the task of transforming unfinished processes and failures (rejection letters in reply to her requests for employment; titles of abandoned works) into creative projects. It provided the crucible where the negative could be transformed into the positive. As the artist herself notes, "Forgetting has a creative charge. If I recall a party with guests and I describe it as I remember it, and then I repeat the same exercise a day later, I'll remember the party and the description I gave of it. However, if I continue the experiment, my first memory will gradually begin to merge with the various subsequent representations I've made of it, making facts that really happened appear as a kind of genre painting. This protocol implies that newness is one of the possible horizons of forgetting."[6] The *Modules* where the archives can be consulted came from the *B.I.A.,* but they are also, in and of themselves, sculptural objects, small structures such as billboards, stands, and cages, closed in on themselves but which can generally be entered by the visitor. Then came the *Polders,* which, as their name indicates, are new territories torn from the void, from waiting, from inactivity, and which took on the reduced scale described above, capable of conserving the sediment of fantastic elaborations. Trouvé's bachelor machines are power switches for the imagination and, in their own way, join the tradition of pataphysics, the "science of imaginary solutions" that Alfred Jarry invented while elaborating, in his novels, fantastic bachelor machines and rather hair-raising mechanisms. Of course, we can also draw other connections. For example, does the very name of the Bureau of Implicit Activities not bring to mind the *Agentur für geistige Gastarbeit,* or "Agency for Spiritual Migrant Work," founded by Harald Szeeman, one of Alfred Jarry's main readers and, as it so happens, curator along with Jean Clair of the 1975 exhibition called *Bachelor Machines*? When asked about what she reads, Trouvé cites, among others, Georges Perec and especially Italo Calvino, both members of OuLiPo, the Workshop of Potential Literature [*Ouvroir de Littérature Potentielle*], which itself is closely tied to Jarry's *Collège de Pataphysique.*

6/ Tatiana Trouvé in "Body without a Face," conversation with Richard Shusterman. See pages 122–127 in this volume.

While chatting with the artist, I draw her attention to the fact that her objects, unlike traditional sculptures or what are called "installations," do not allow the visitor to believe

Bureau of Implicit Activities, Waiting Module no. 1, 2002
Plexiglas, imitation leather, metal, wood, stereo system, music, CD, 186 x 165 x 80 cm [73¼ x 65 x 31½ in.]

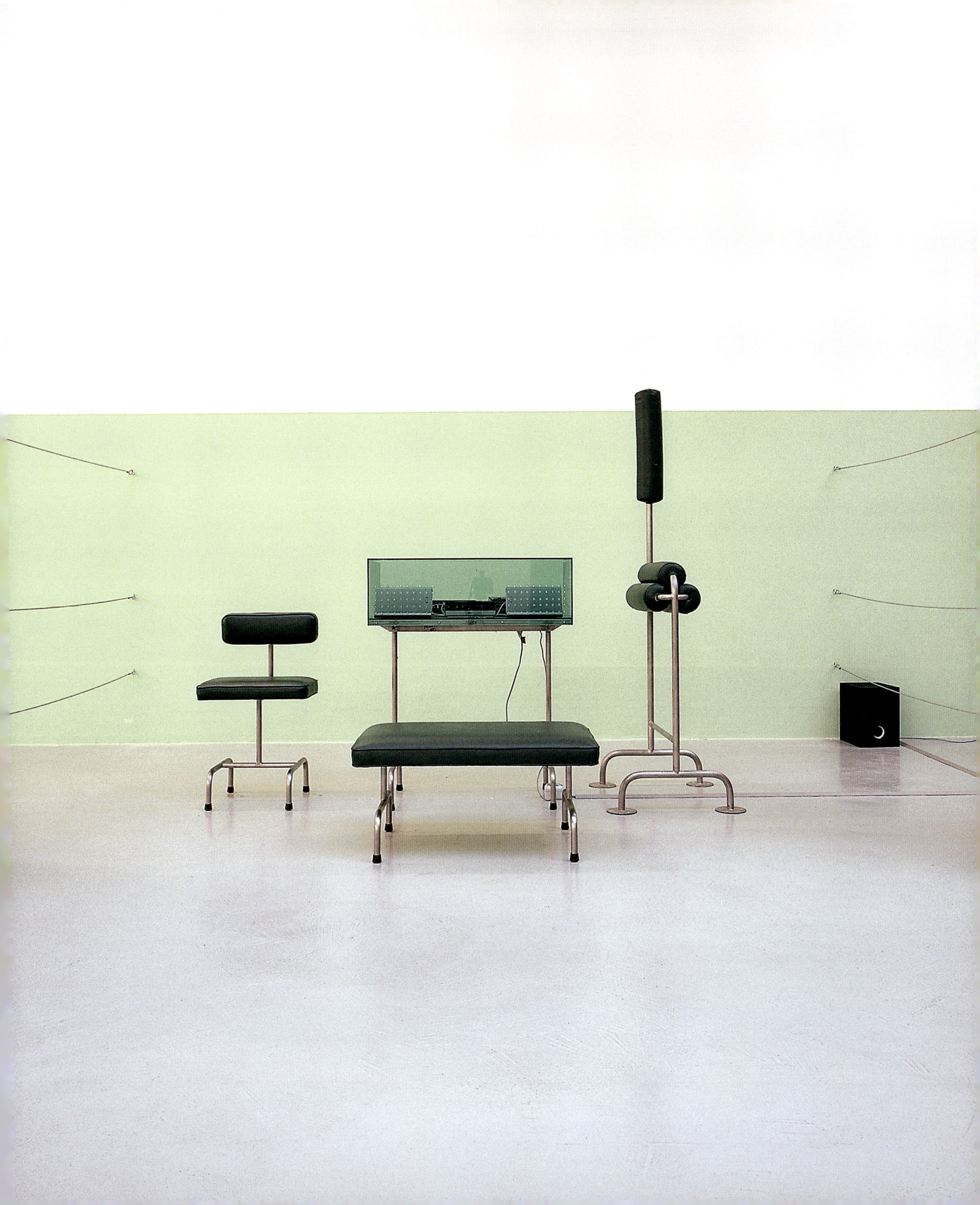

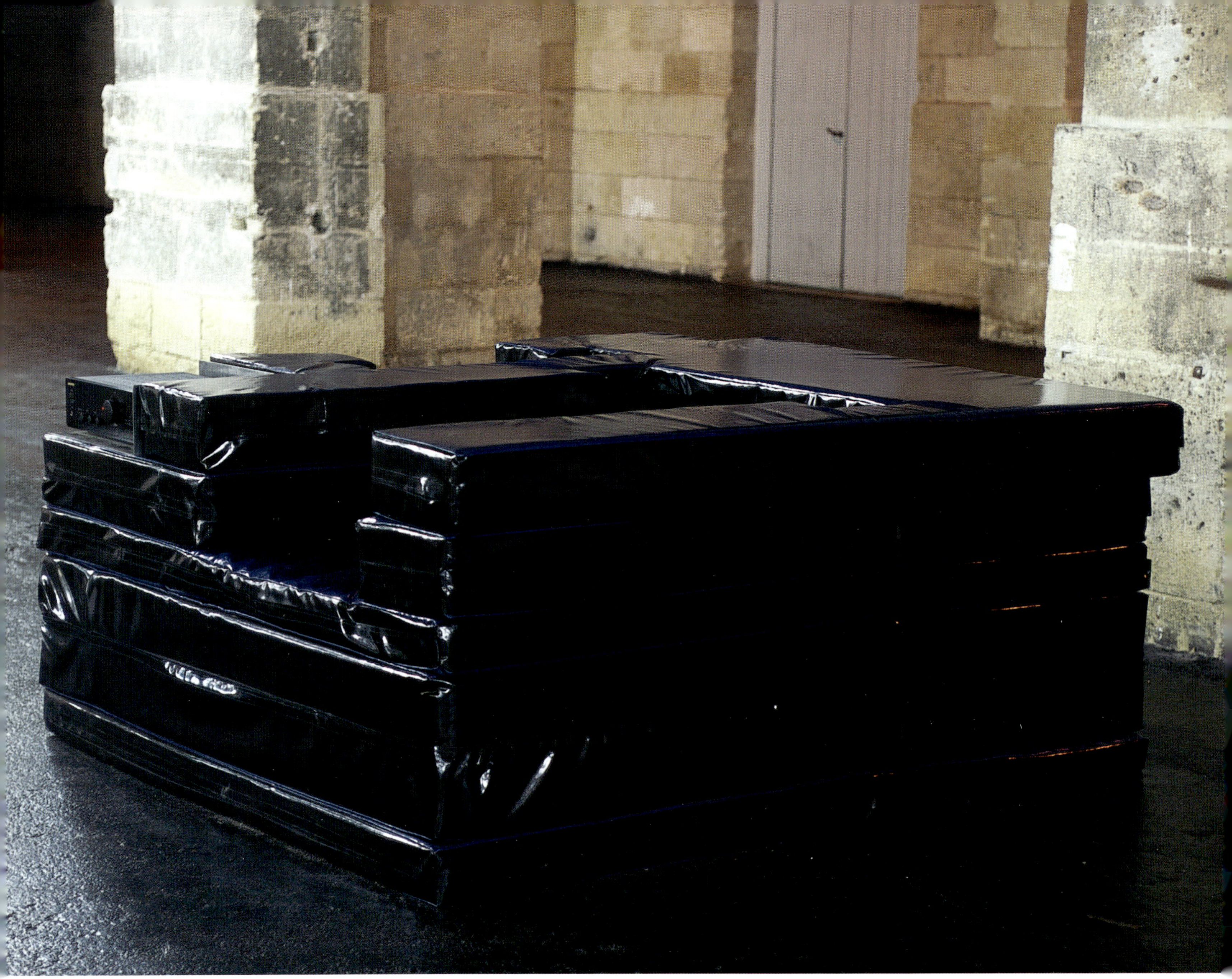

Bureau of Implicit Activities, Waiting Module no. 2, 2003
Foam, PVC, metal, stereo system, 65 x 186 x 165 cm [25½ x 73¼ x 65 in.]

a seamless understanding of them is even possible. We do not necessarily feel the desire to touch them; walking around them is also of little help; and entering one of these objects does not allow us to master its space. But Trouvé intervenes categorically: “In front of my sculptures, the body is simply of no use.” I readily agree. However, is this assertion not contradicted by those steel bars in the studio, wrapped as they are in a leather sheath and with lacing that allows their smooth surface to appear—just as gaiters give us a brief glimpse of a woman’s legs? Do these not appeal to our notions of sensuality? Have I not been able to identify horse saddles and bicycle seats in other projects? Oh, and as to the bicycle seat: is that not a characteristic element of bachelor machines? And what about all those metal and leather objects—those weights you might imagine being used to train a hypothetical athlete? Once they have been associated with the iron beds and those heavy chains, it is not difficult to conceive of them being used by someone adept in sadomasochism. Finally, we cannot neglect to mention those doors left ajar, and those corners into which we cannot walk. Is it not true that they are apt to awaken our voyeuristic impulses?

Such is the paradox of bachelor machines, which exclude our body or, more precisely, instrumentalize it to underscore the degree to which eroticism is a mental affair. Perhaps if that bed were of a more hospitable size its leather blanket would be pleasantly supple under the weight of our body. Perhaps we would rediscover our childhood reflexes if we could hang from those bars and jump into that saddle. Perhaps we would like to pick up those objects we see behind that door or that pane of glass, if only we could cross through them and understand, in the first place, *where* they really are. Perhaps. But it is impossible for us to know—a situation that affords our imagination all the more pleasure since it can continue to lose itself in the thousands of possibilities these appropriations would allow.

I like the idea that Trouvé, who refers to herself a sculptor, undoes the viewer's physical implication, steals the art of sculpture away from touch to offer it entirely to vision, and asks it to produce illusions—much as Duchamp did, in fact, by introducing the real and eminently prosaic object into art, which did not stop him from being a great illusion monger, passionate about the optical sciences. Trouvé's work would certainly trouble 18th-century authors who, if they were to come back to life, would have to revise their dichotomy between painting and sculpture. How would Diderot or Herder interpret a sculpture that, leaving behind its (approximate) claims to truth, invites us dream—the realm of painting? Contrary to what we might think, this division is not obsolete, but if it has been so resistant, it is through a reversal of judgment. Throughout the 20th century, we have had a tendency to be suspicious of art forms that were overly illusionist. We have privileged art that claimed to be anchored in reality. But it would be a mistake today to continue to believe that art has to share our space. We have indeed had fun, and we have expanded our field of knowledge in the company of artists who have invited us to share in their studio work, their parties, their dinners, their convictions, their lives. But by frequenting them too intimately, our pleasure has been spent. Today, the art amateur is a lover who knows his mistress's body all too well and turns around to look from afar at the unknown woman on the street whose curves he seeks under her dress. Vision is what awakens desire. Just guess where the bride is hidden in the traps Tatiana Trouvé has devised for our gaze.

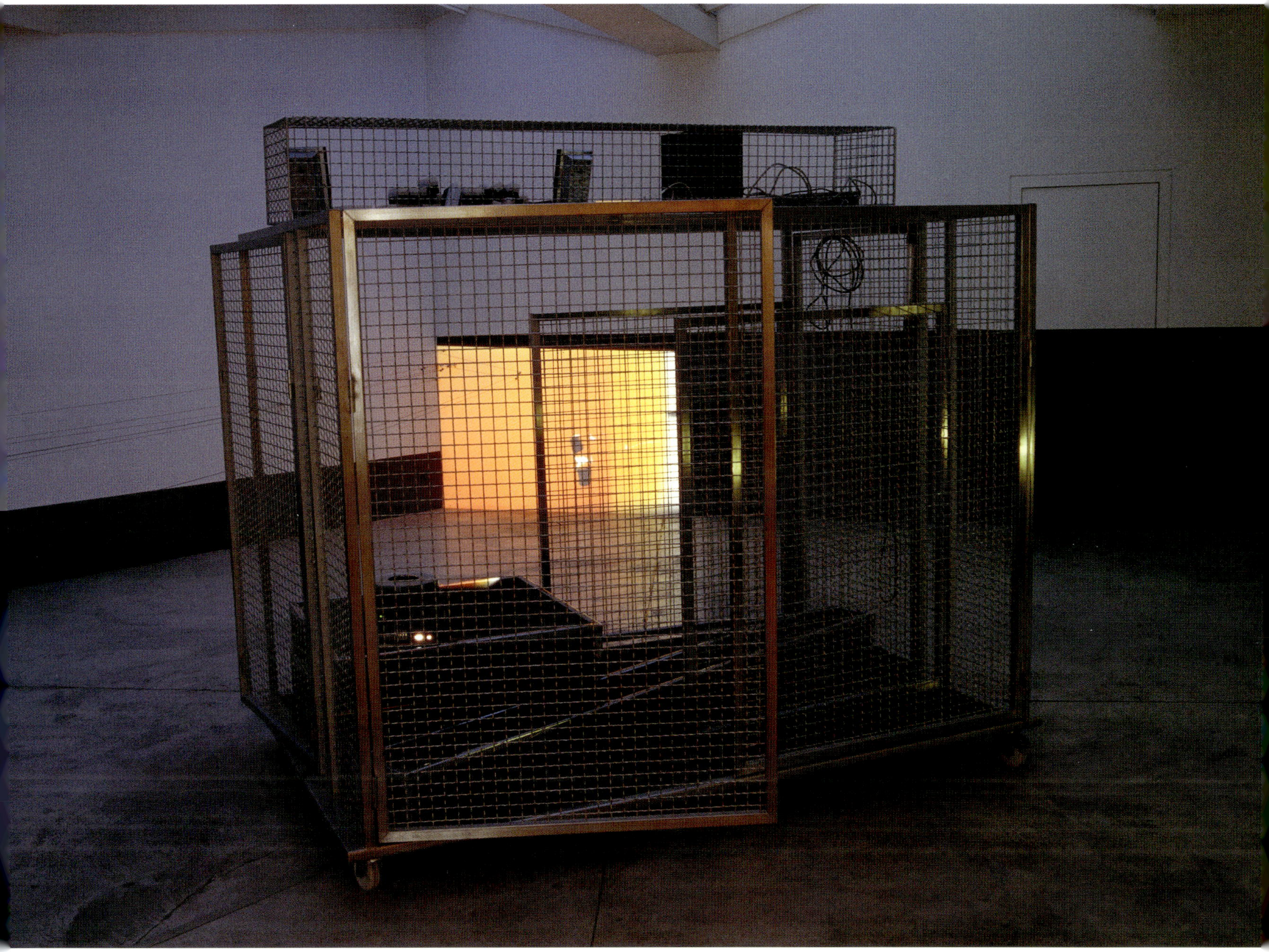

Above and following pages:
Bureau of Implicit Activities, Strike Module, 2002
Wood, metal, rubber, slides, slide projector, stereo system, imitation leather, walkman, 160 x 220 x 150 cm [63 x 86½ x 59 in.]

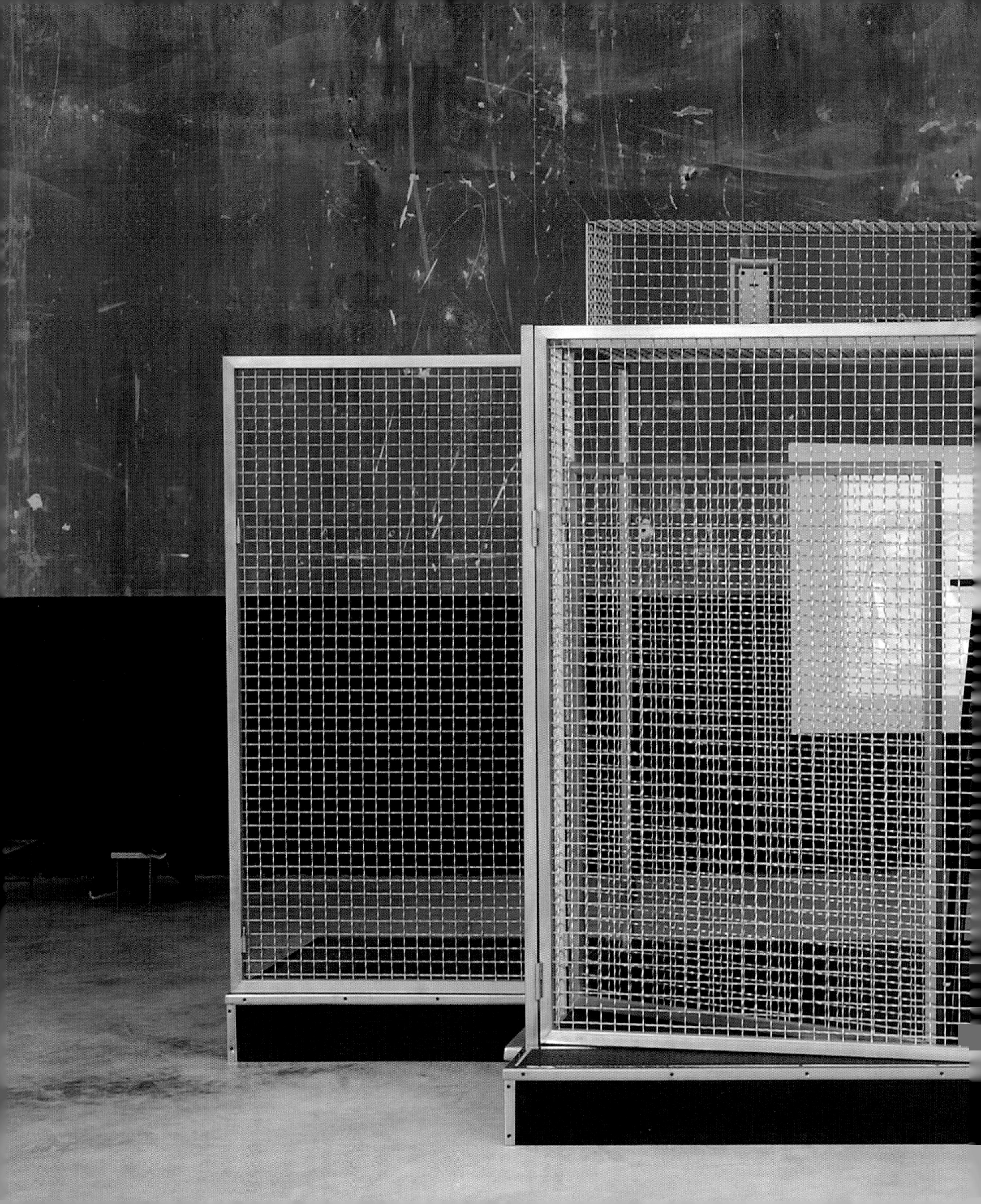

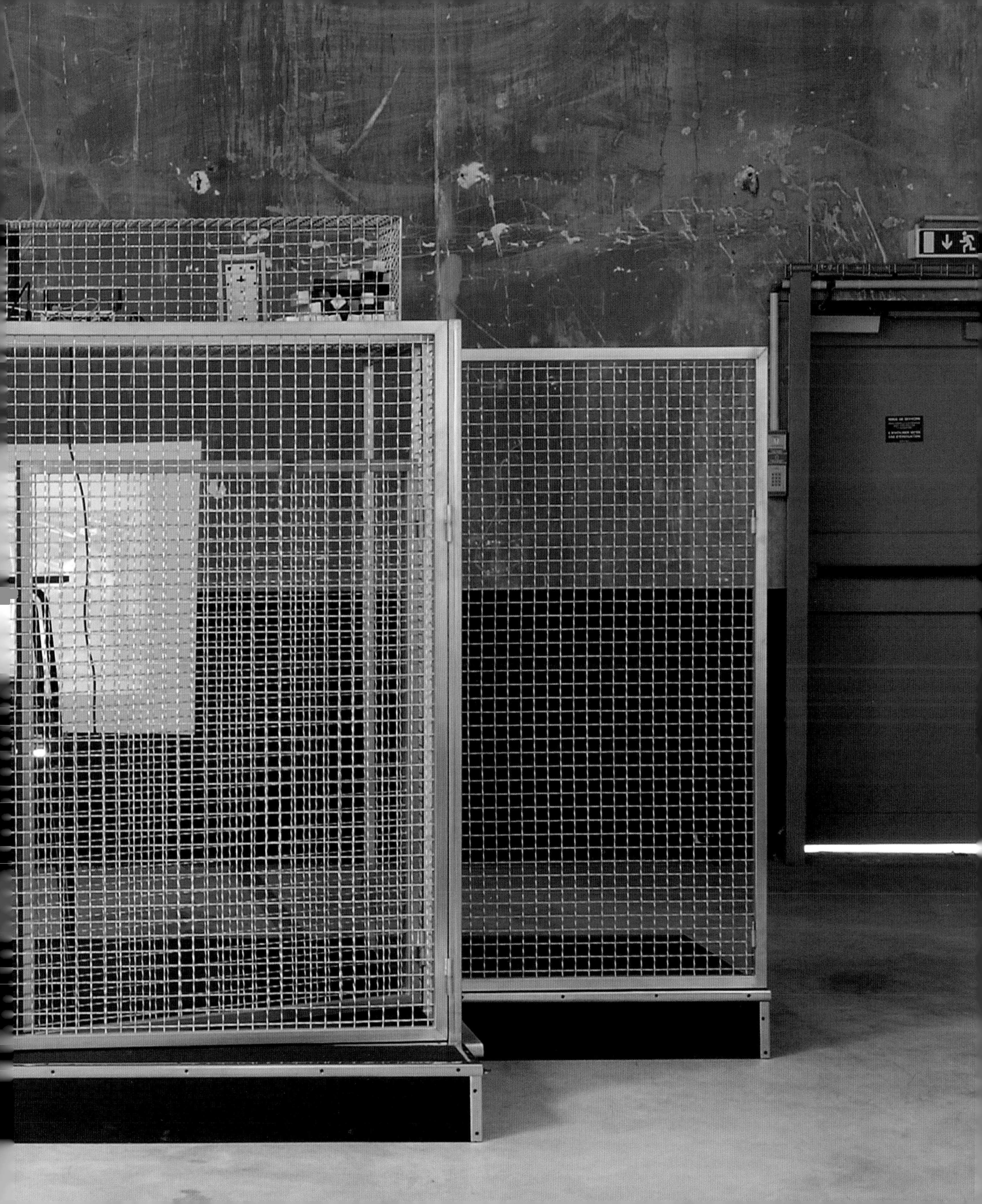

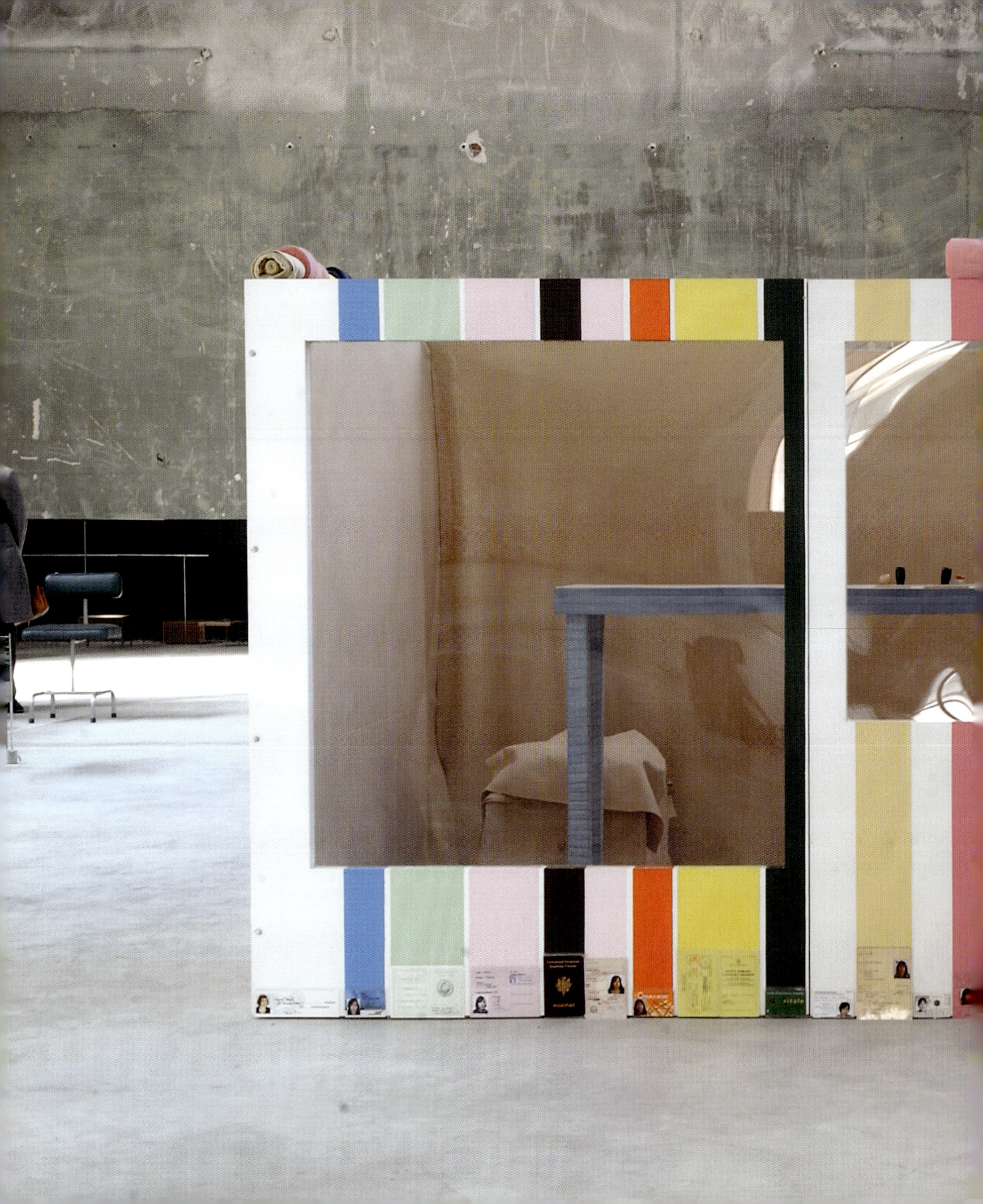

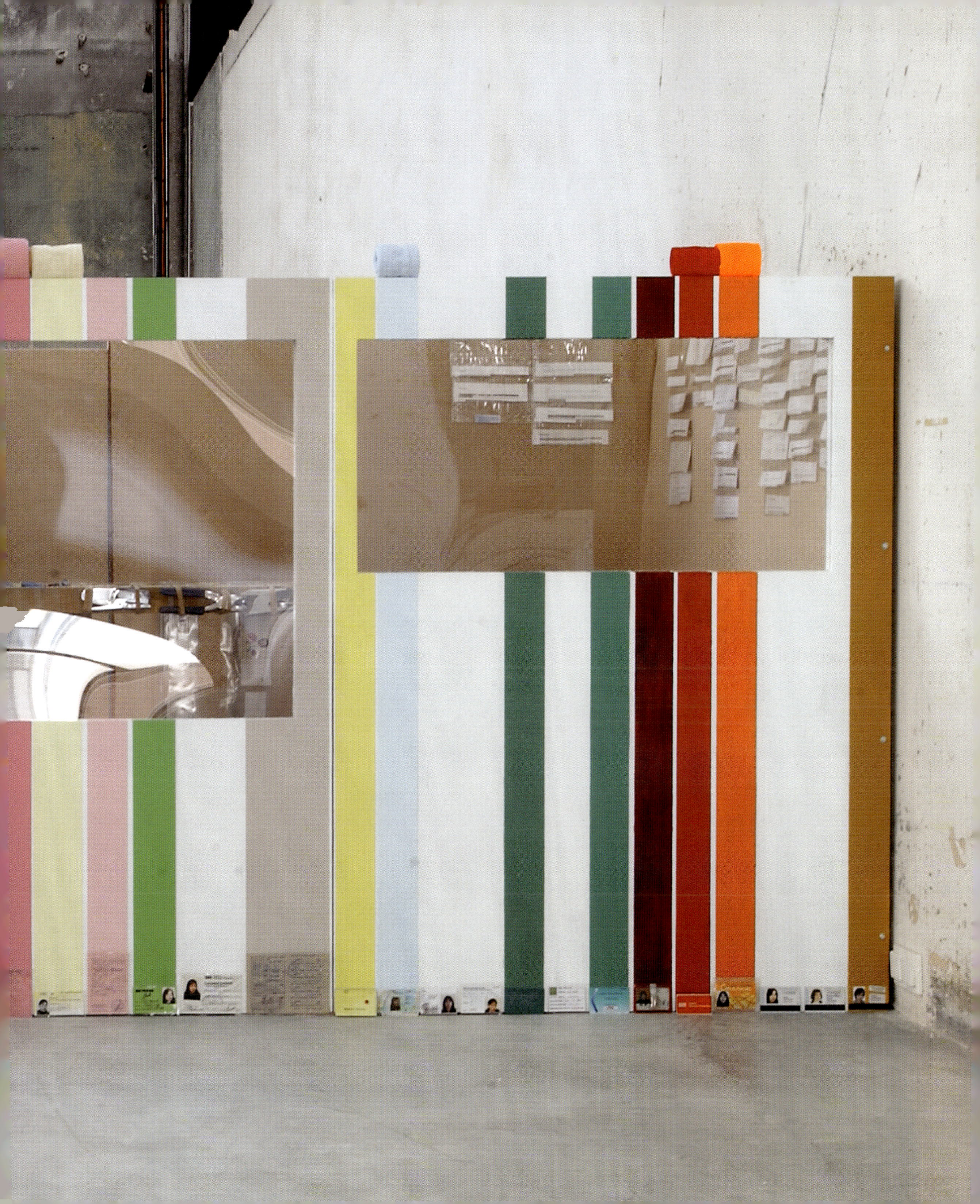

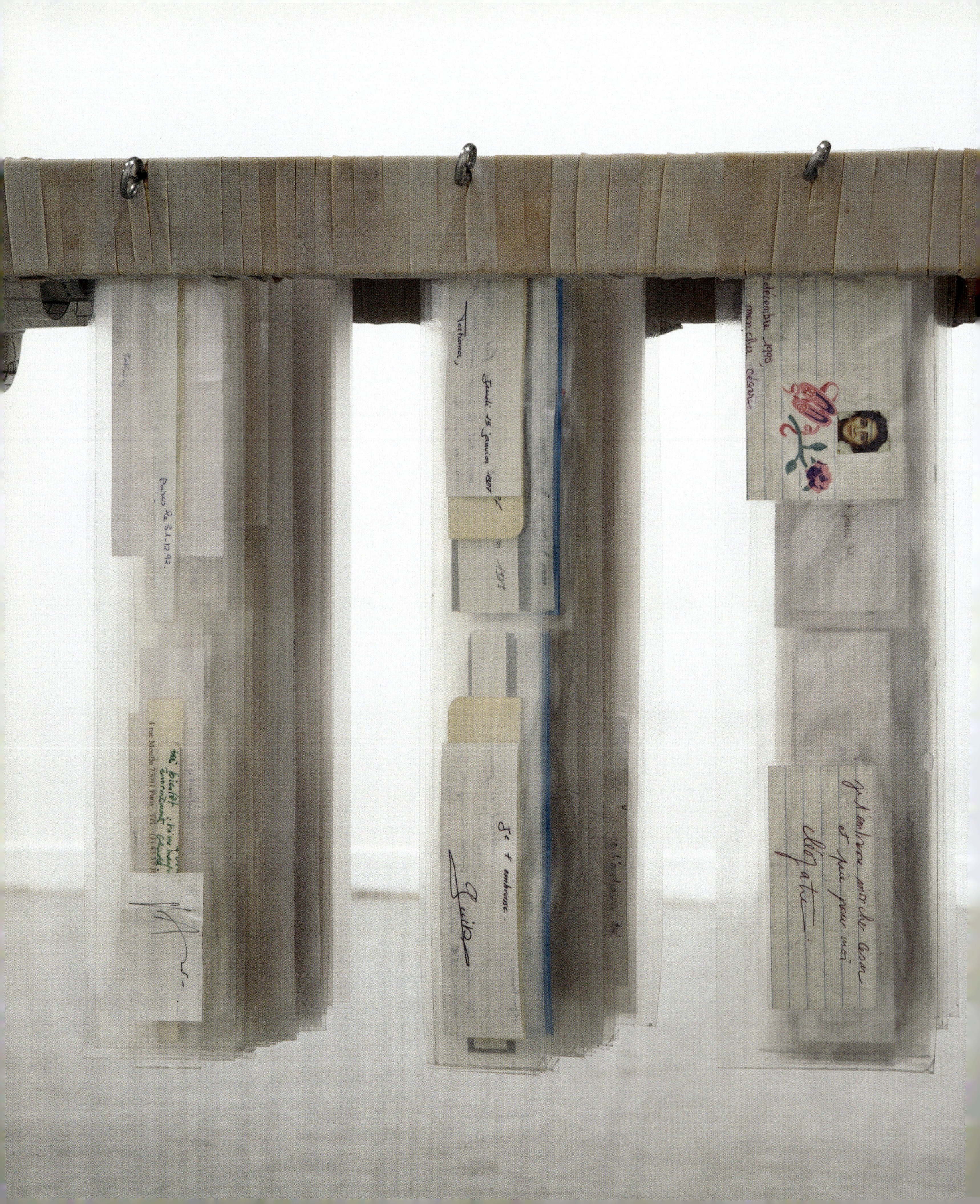

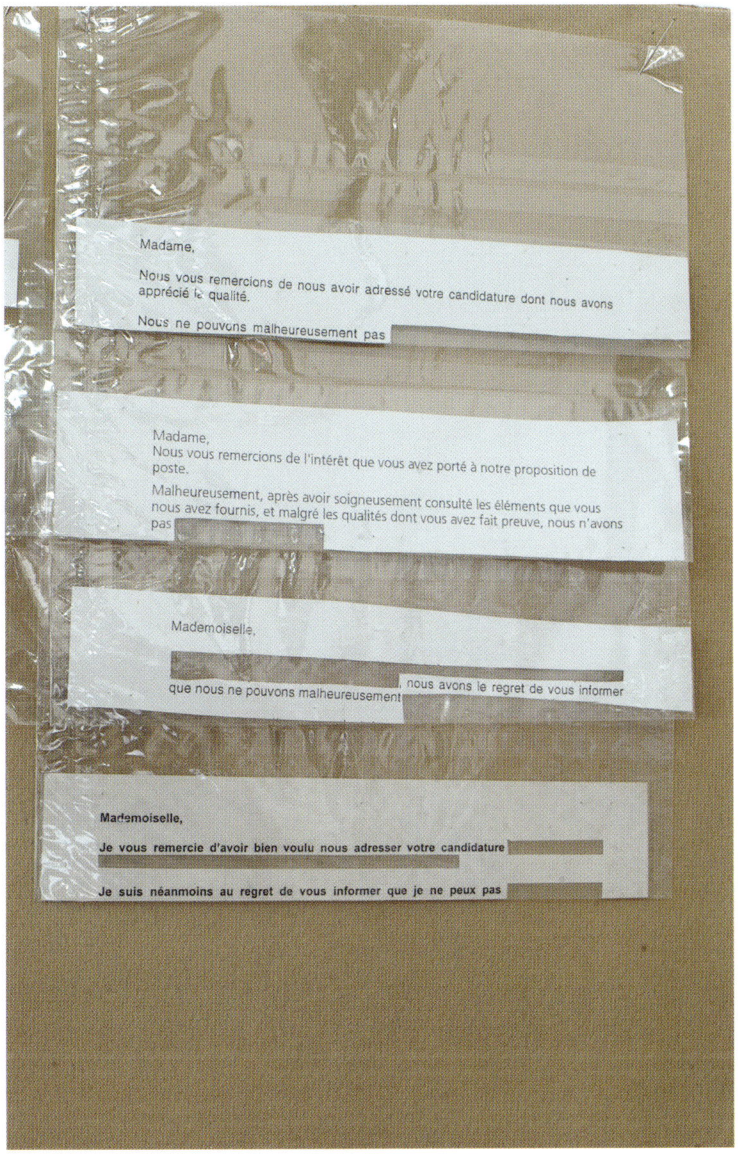

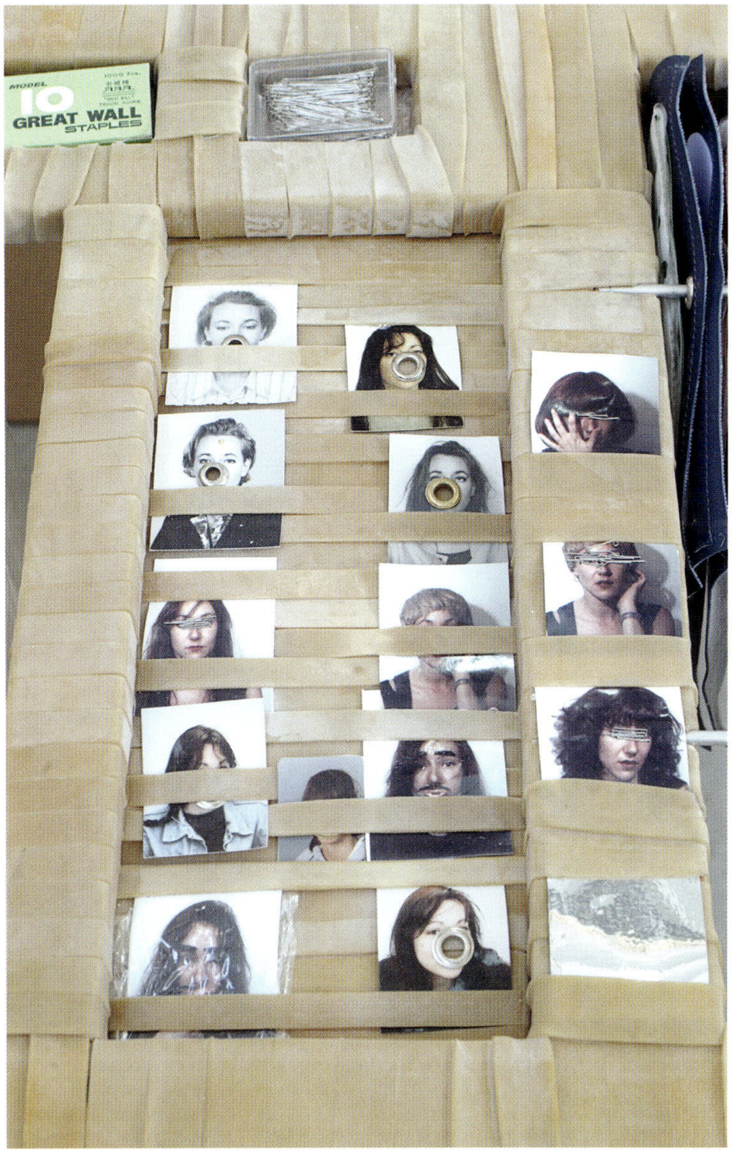

Previous pages:
Bureau of Implicit Activities, Administrative Module, 1997–2003
Wood, paint, identity cards, rubber bands, photographs, paper, plastic, metal, tools, felt, Plexiglas, 150 x 350 x 180 cm [59 x 138 x 70¾ in.]

Left-hand page and above:
Bureau of Implicit Activities, Administrative Module (detail), 1997–2003

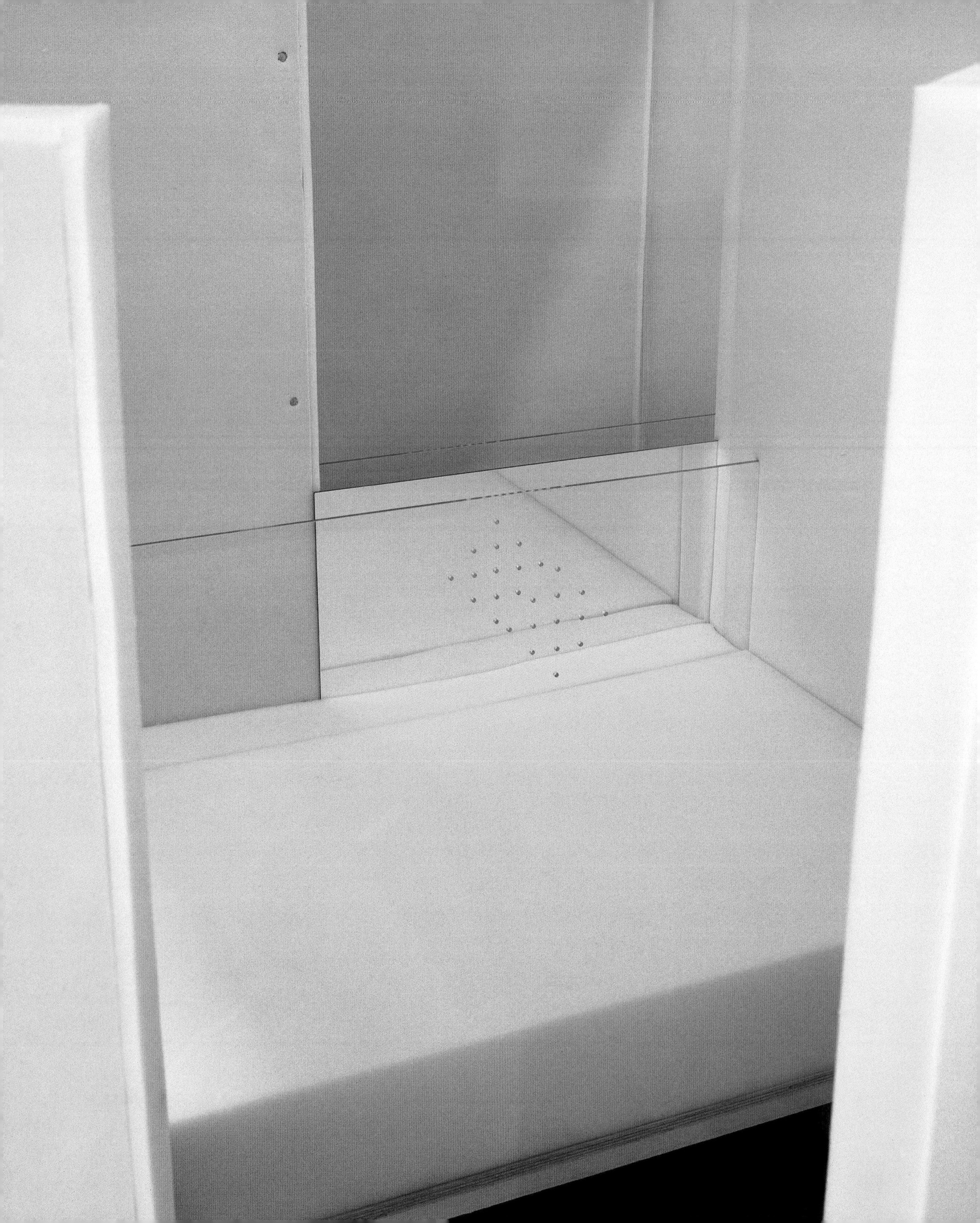

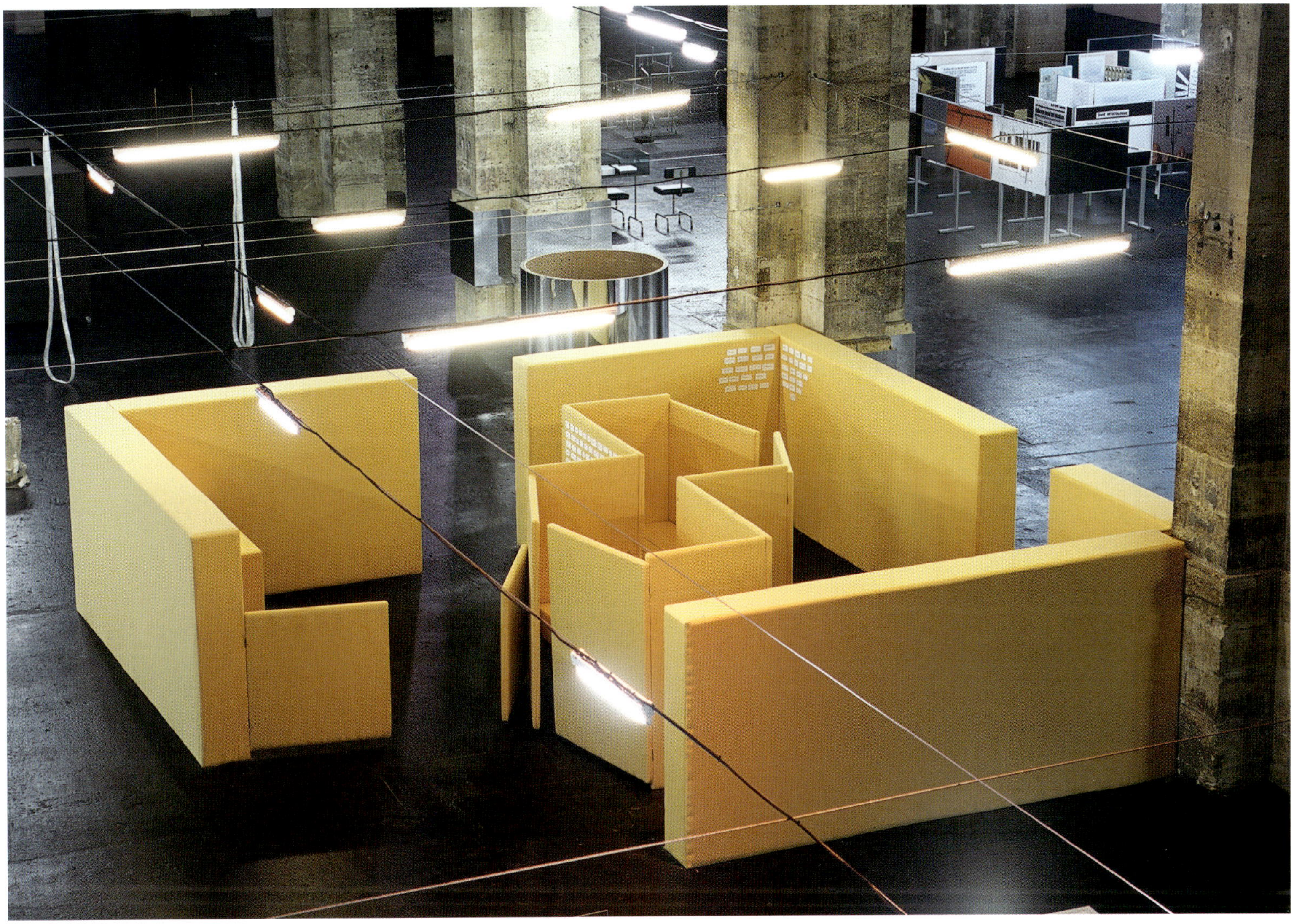

Bureau of Implicit Activities, Titles Module, 1999–2003
Wood, foam, fabric, mirror, Plexiglas, labels for titles, 150 x 650 x 650 cm
[59 x 256 x 256 in.]

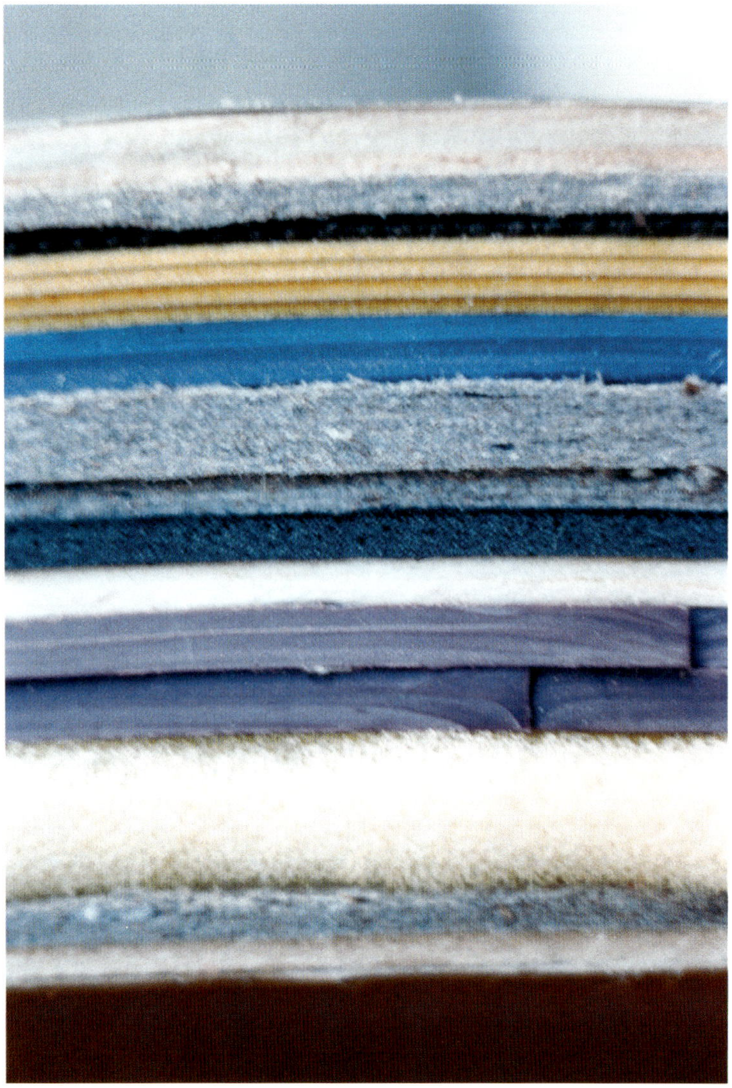

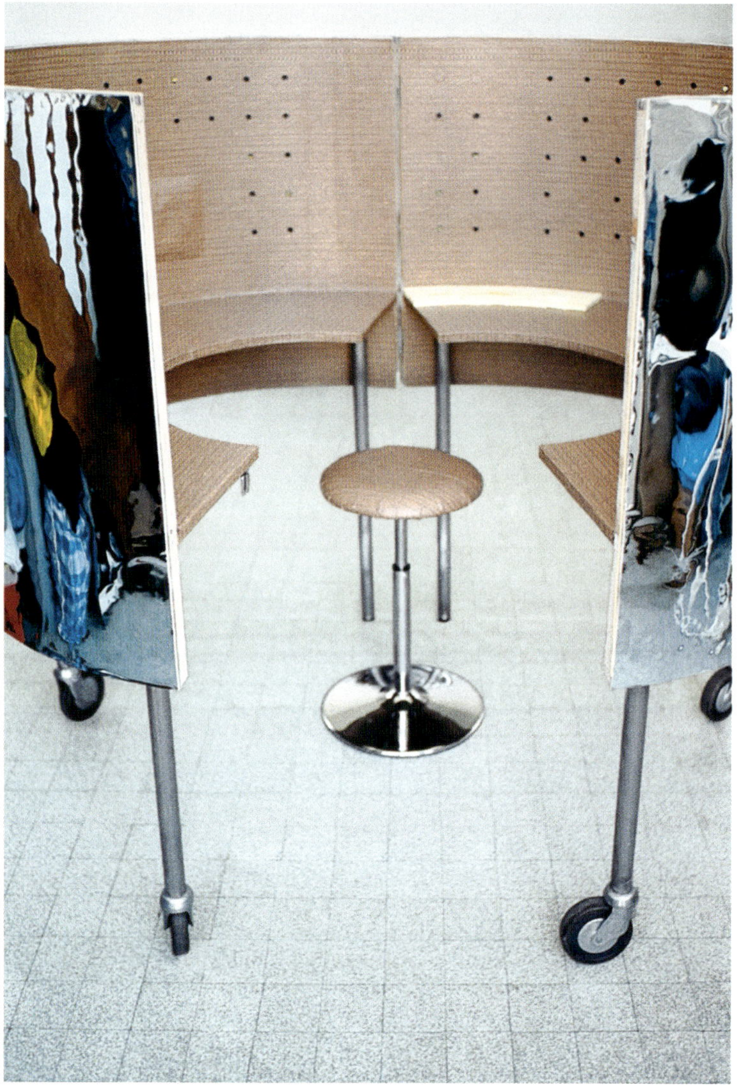

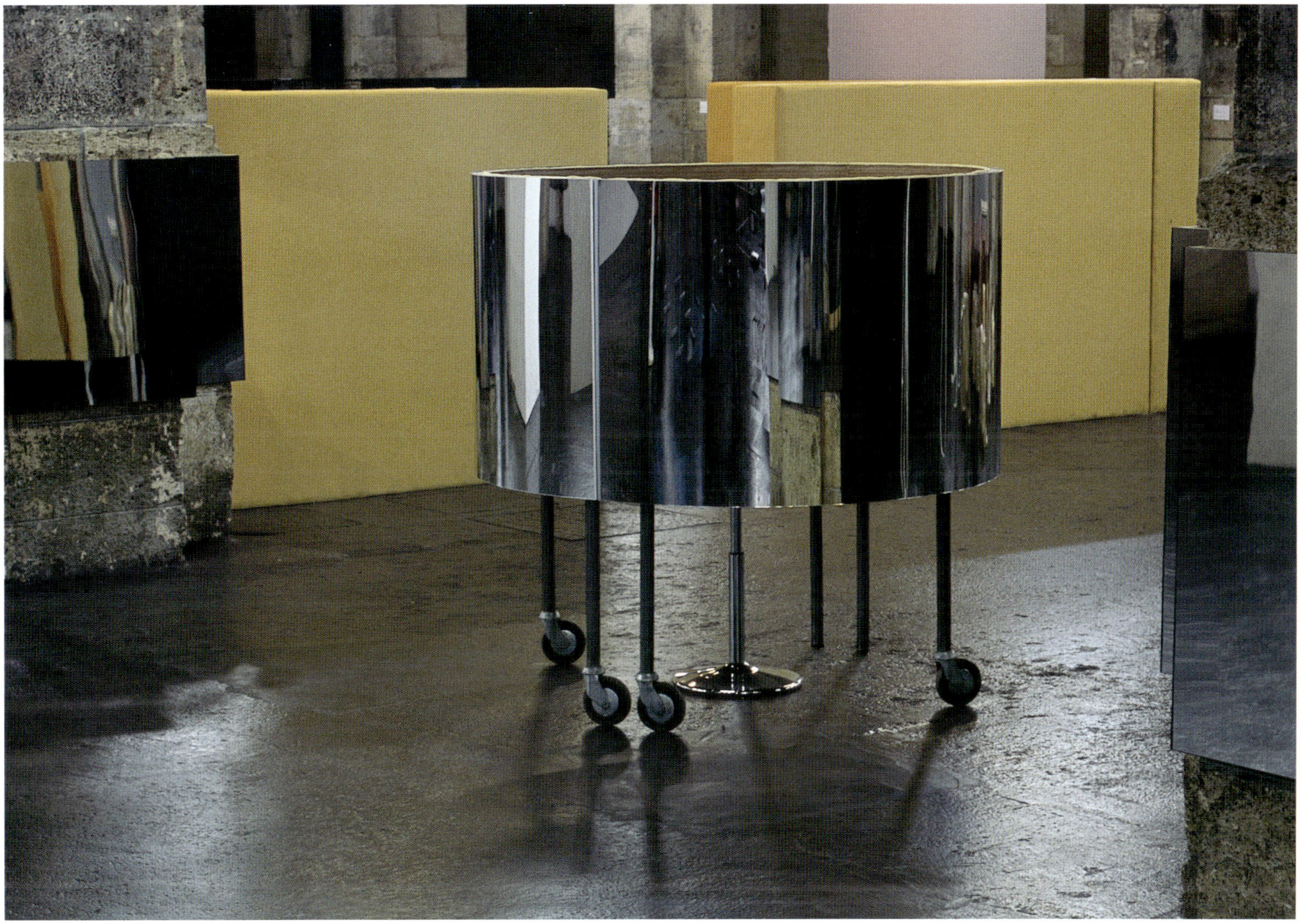

Bureau of Implicit Activities, Reminiscences Module,
1999–2003
Wood, plastic foam, metal, Plexiglas, mirror, silicone, Formica, rubber, cardboard, paper, 135 x 135 x 135 cm [53¼ x 53¼ x 53¼ in.]

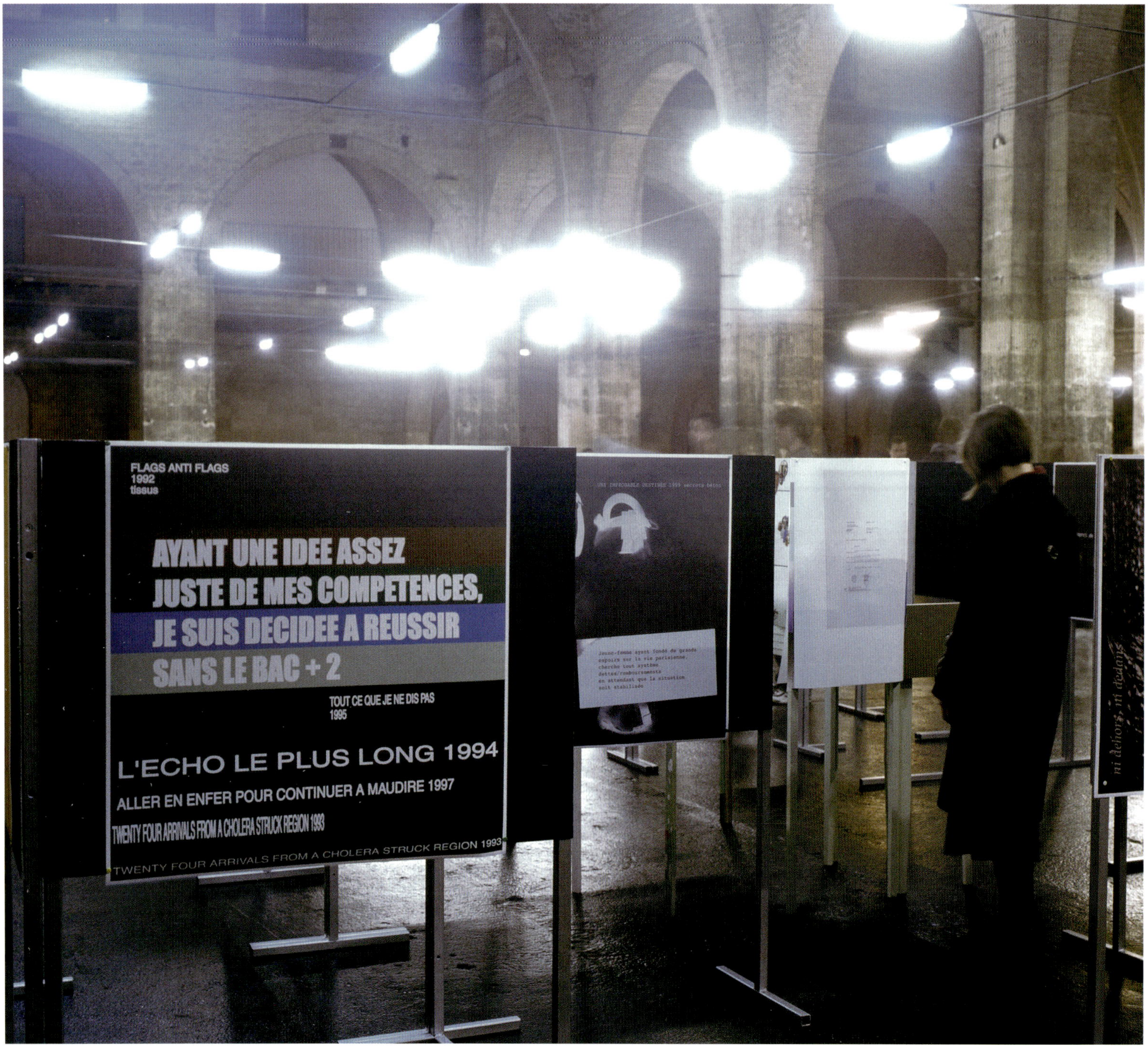
FLAGS ANTI FLAGS
1992
tissus
AYANT UNE IDEE ASSEZ
JUSTE DE MES COMPETENCES,
JE SUIS DECIDEE A REUSSIR
SANS LE BAC + 2
TOUT CE QUE JE NE DIS PAS
1995
L'ECHO LE PLUS LONG 1994
ALLER EN ENFER POUR CONTINUER A MAUDIRE 1997
TWENTY FOUR ARRIVALS FROM A CHOLERA STRUCK REGION 1993
TWENTY FOUR ARRIVALS FROM A CHOLERA STRUCK REGION 1993
ni dehors, ni dedans

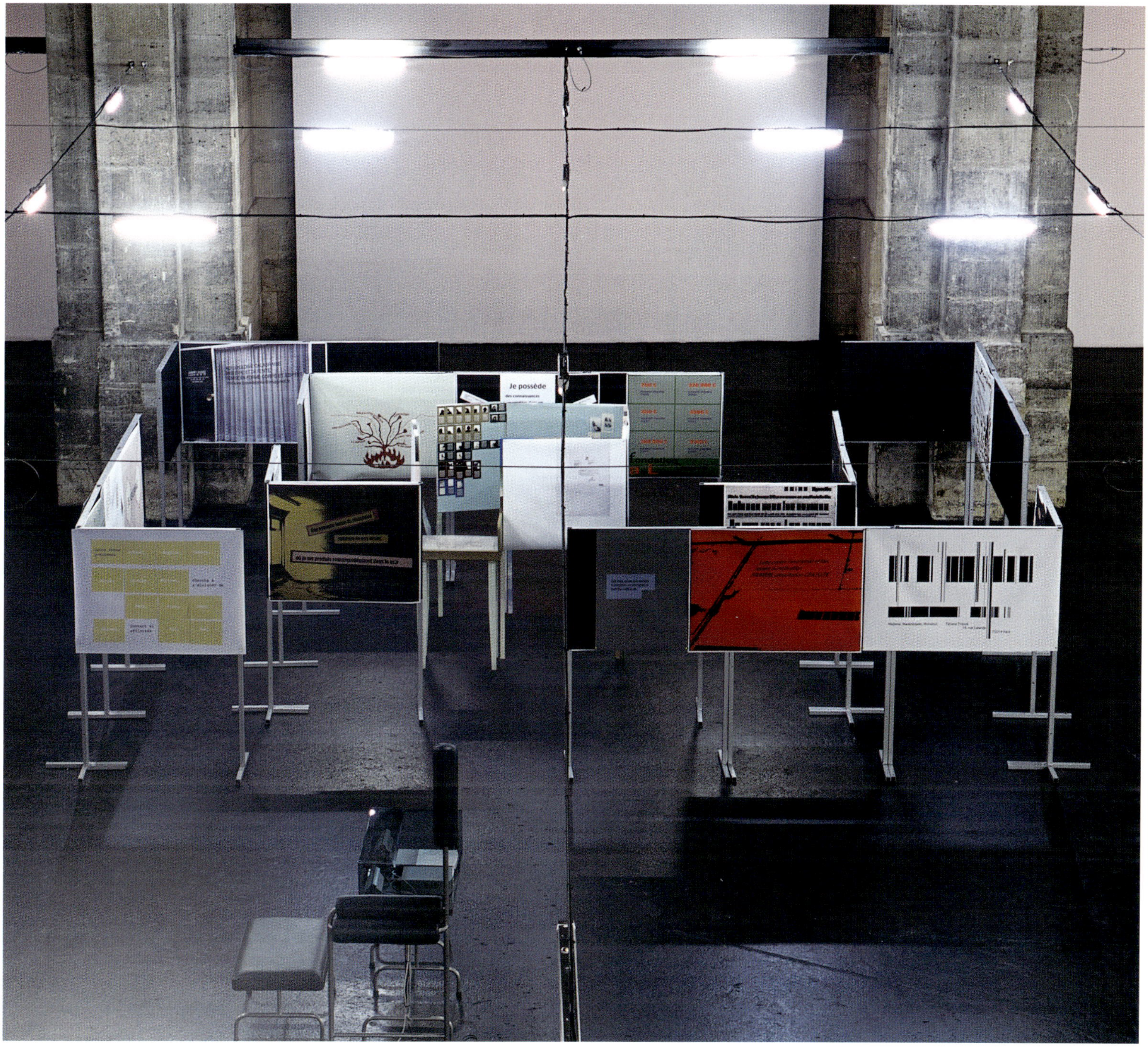

Bureau of Implicit Activities, Slips of the Tongue Module, 2000
Wood, ink-jet printing, paper, plastic, imitation leather, photographs, 150 x 600 x 400 cm
[59 x 236 x 157½ in.]

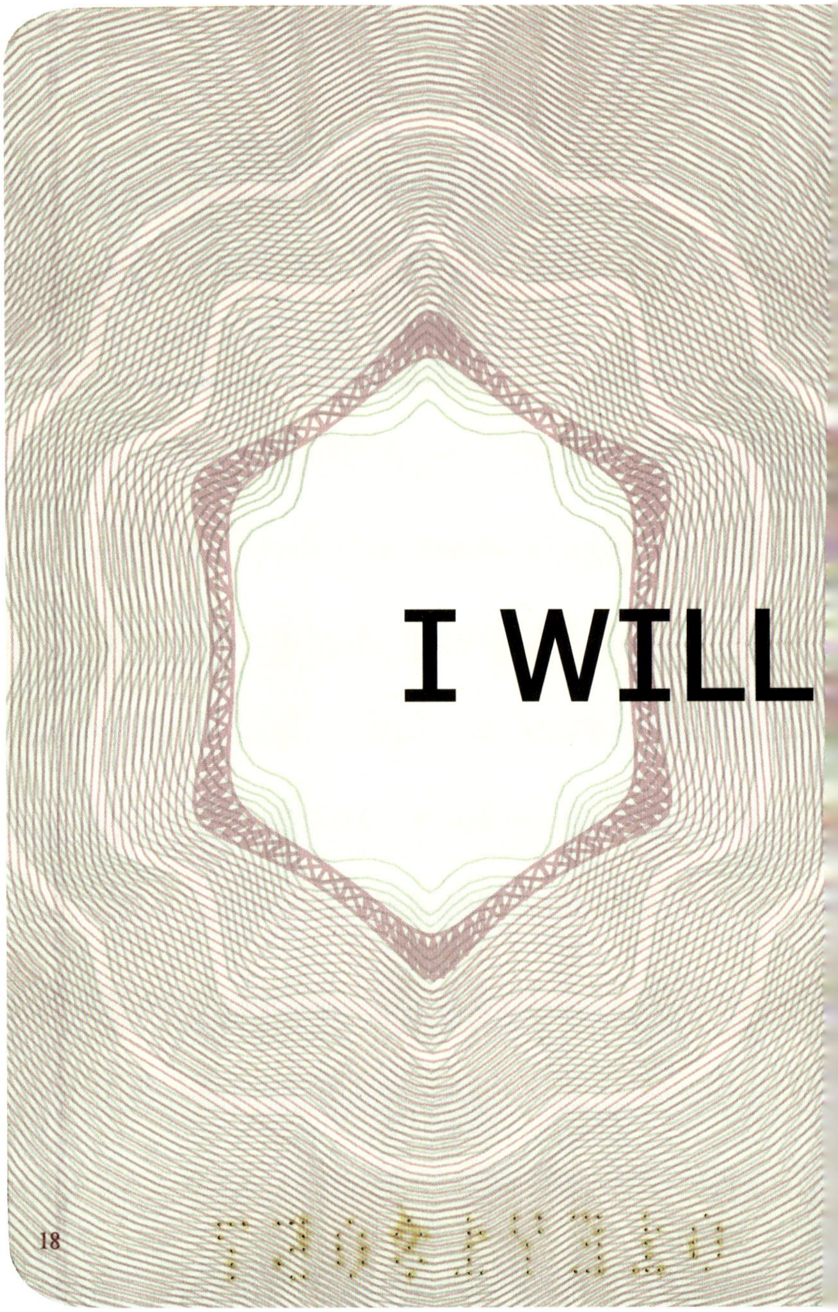
I WILL
18

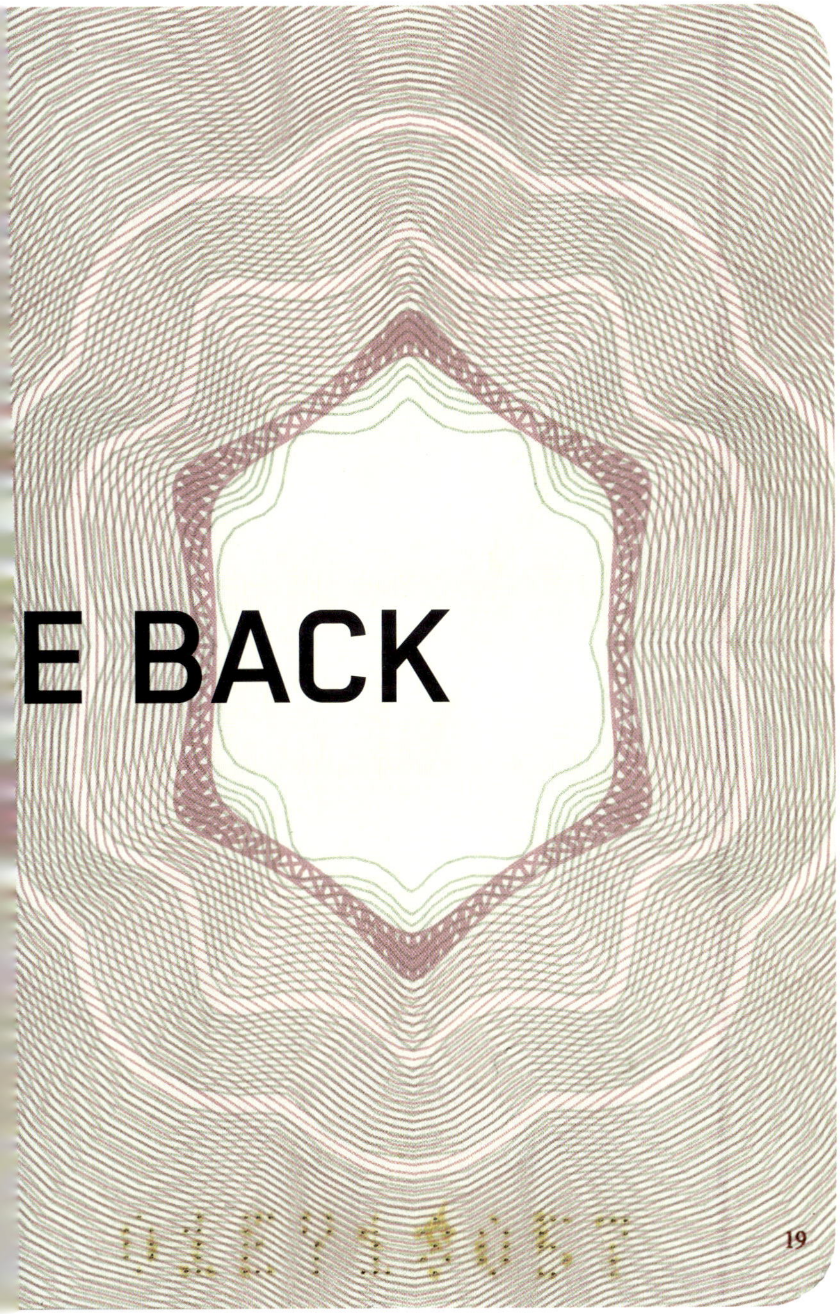

Print from the *Slips of the Tongue Module,* 2003

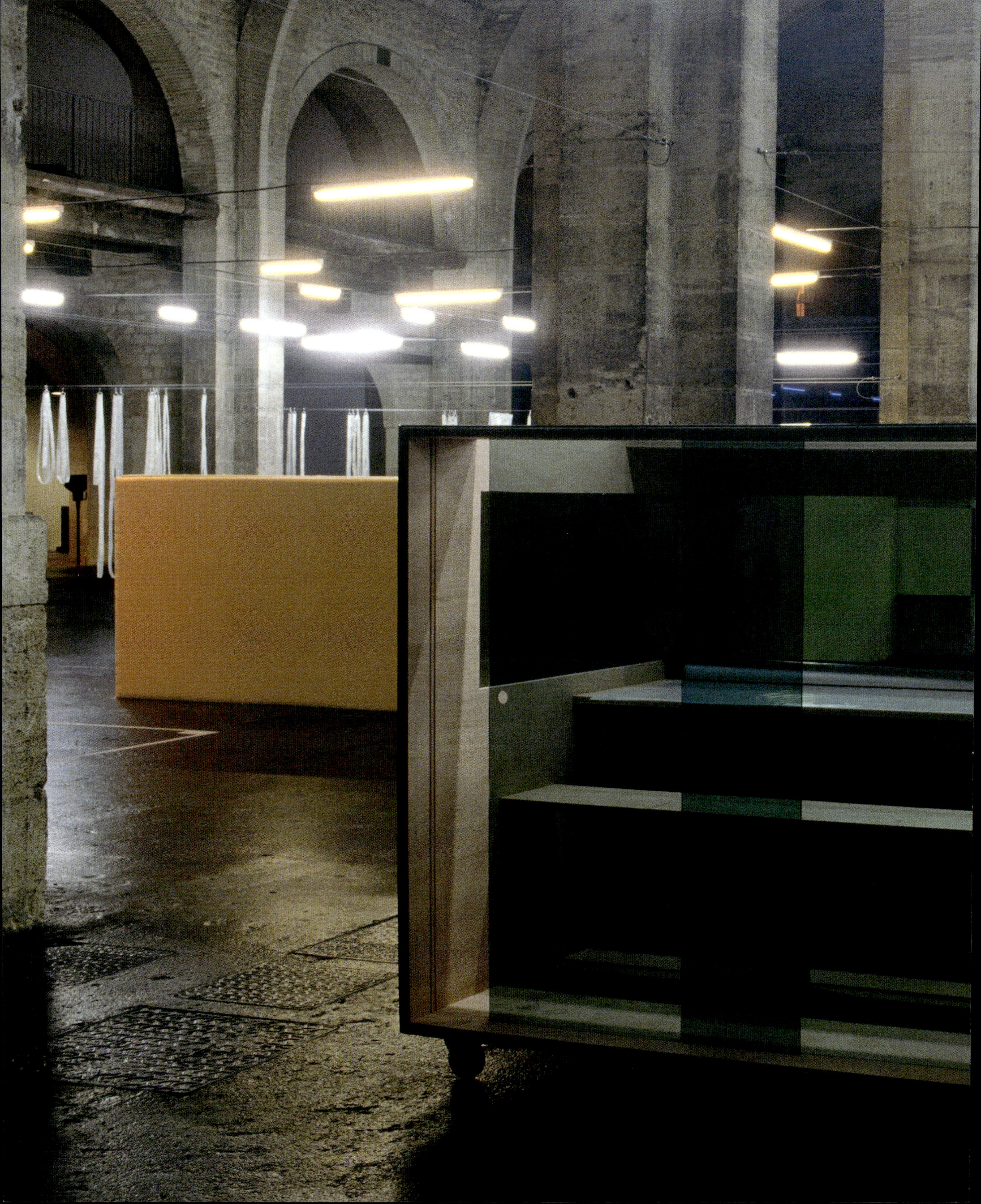

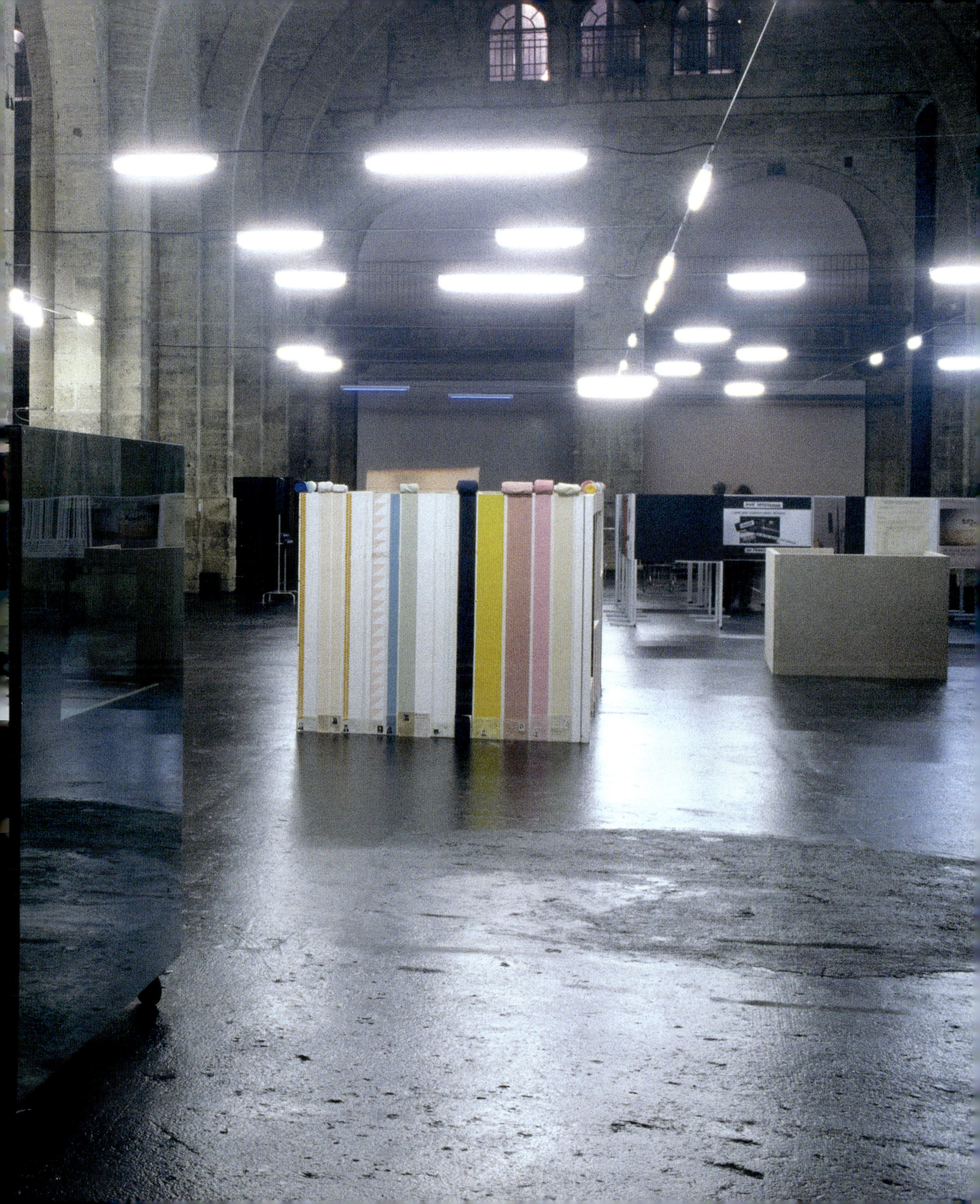

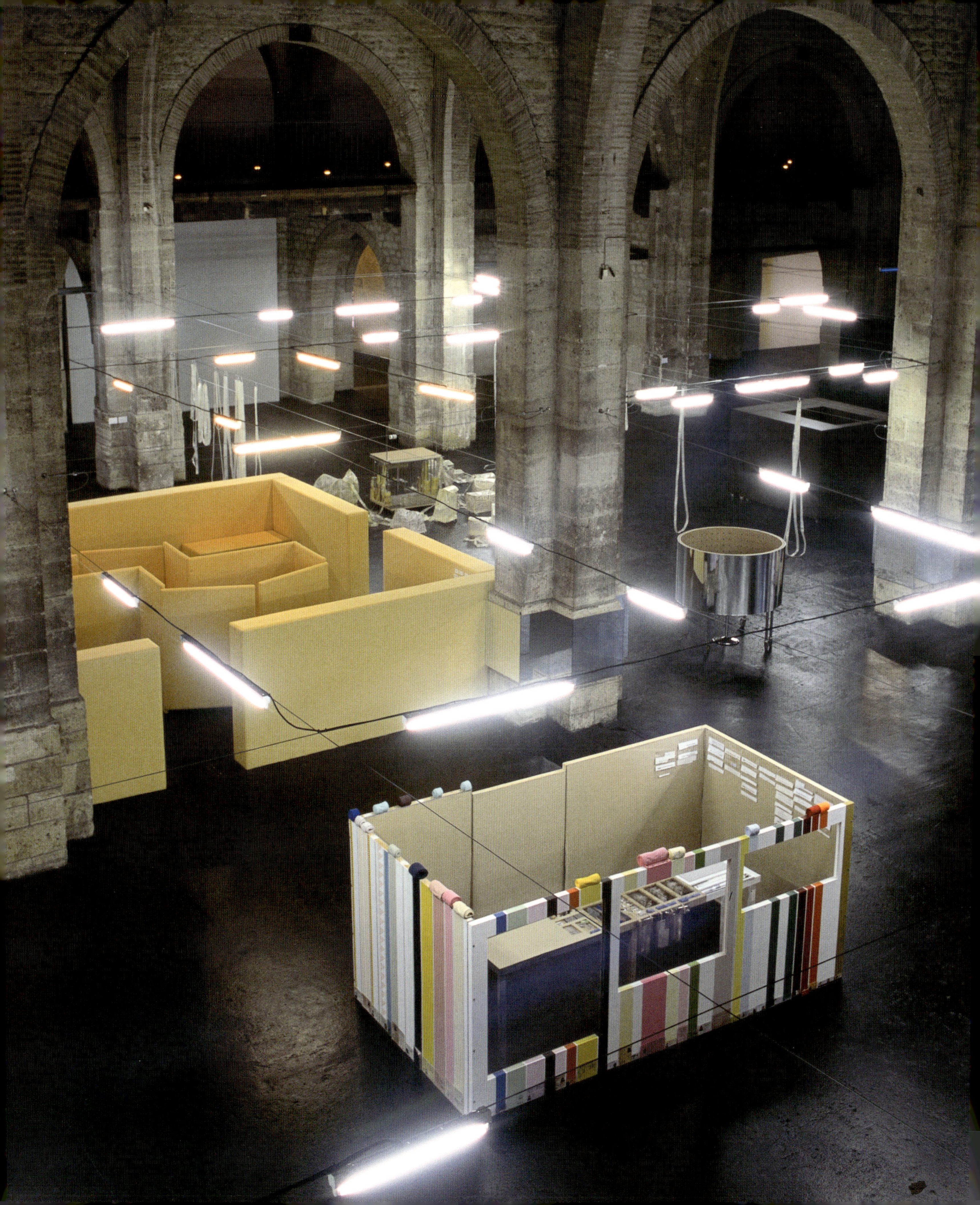

Previous and left-hand pages:
View of the exhibition *Aujourd'hui, hier, ou il y a longtemps* ("Today, yesterday, or long ago"), capcMusée d'art contemporain, Bordeaux, France, 2003

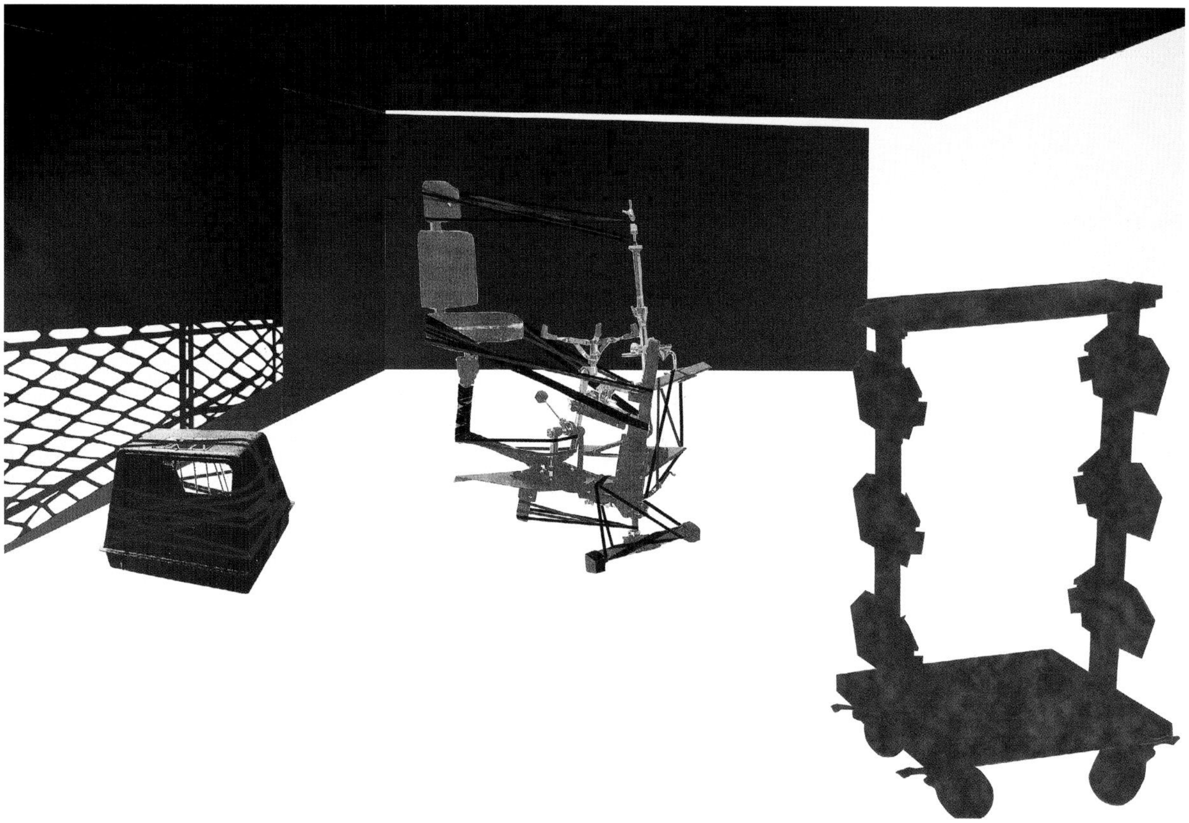

Untitled, 2005
Collage on paper, 75 x 110 cm [29½ x 43¼ in.]

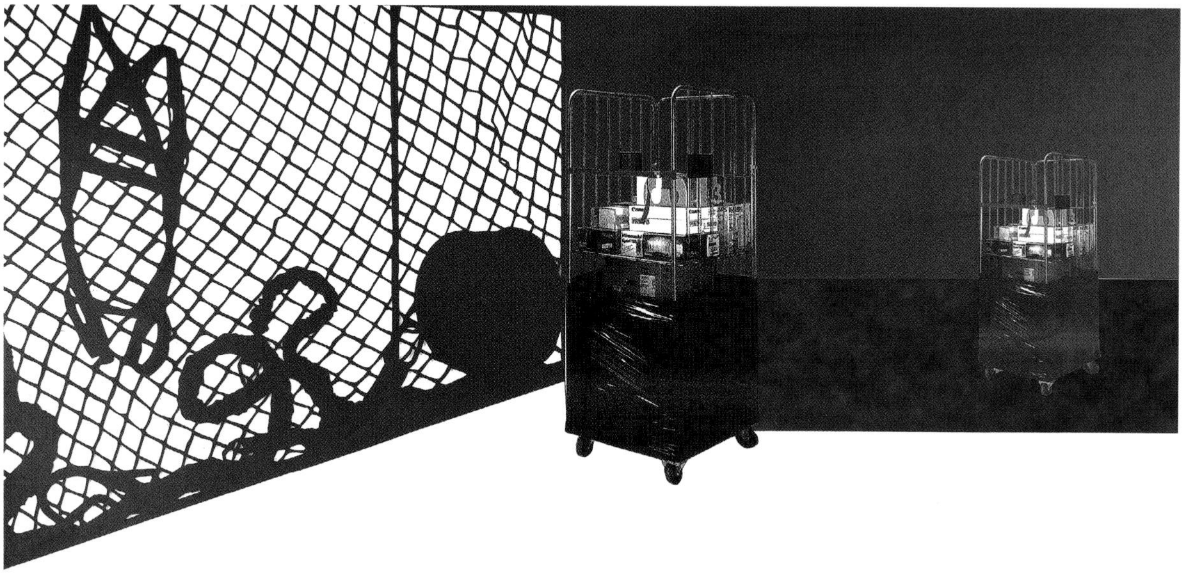

Untitled, 2005
Collage on paper, 75 x 110 cm [29½ x 43¼ in.]

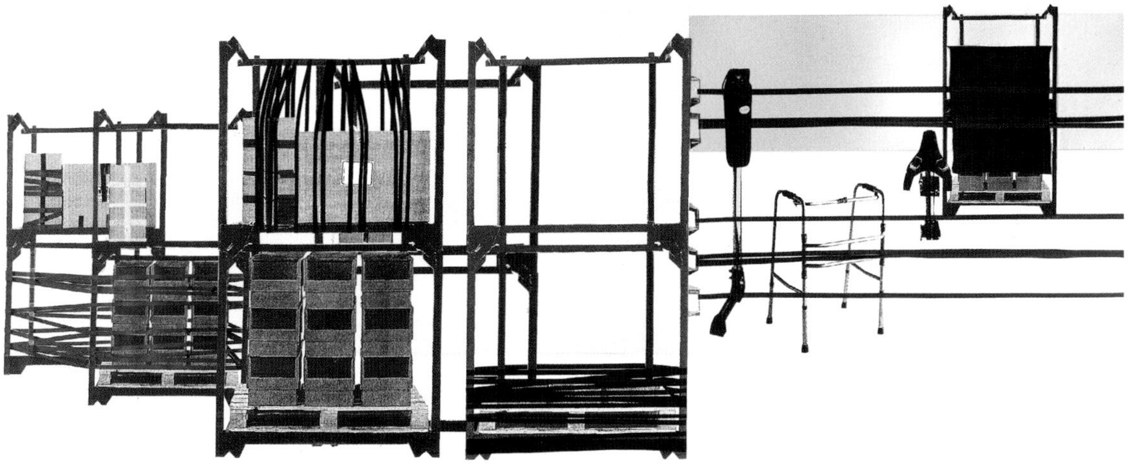

Untitled, 2005
Collage on paper, 75 x 110 cm [29½ x 43¼ in.]

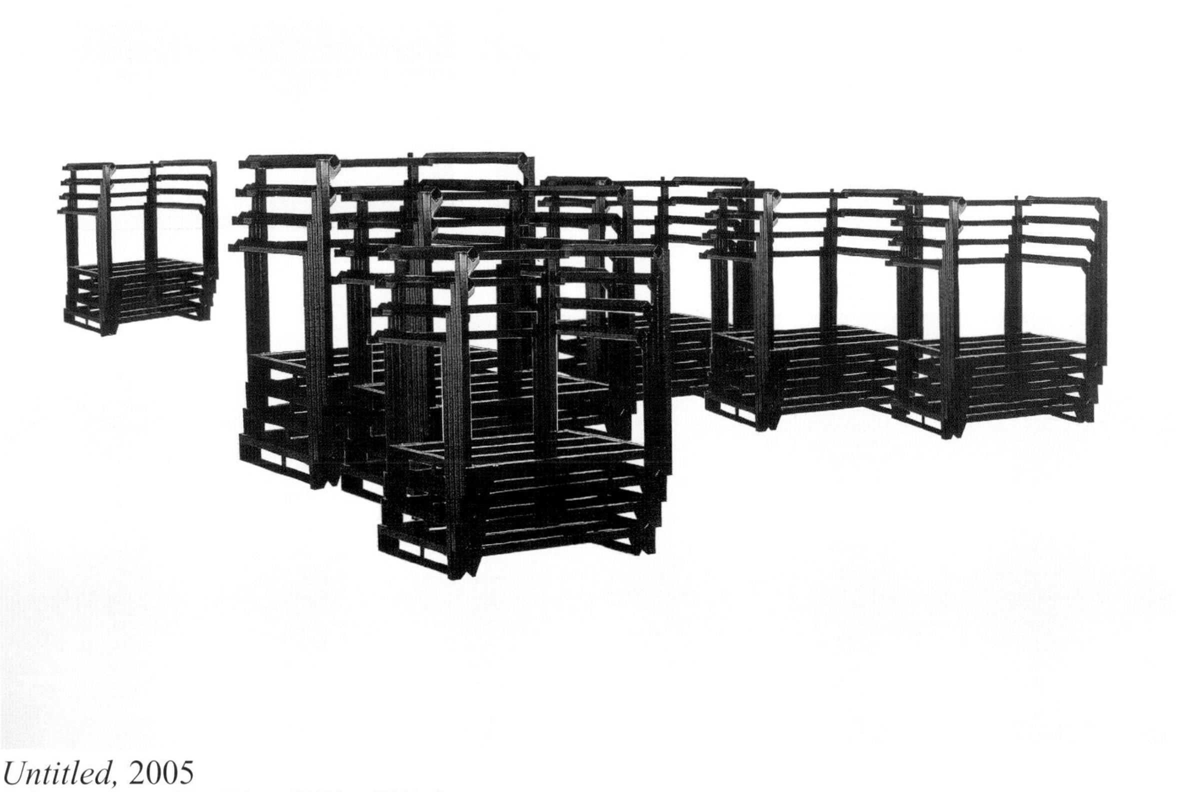

Untitled, 2005
Collage on paper, 75 x 110 cm [29½ x 43¼ in.]

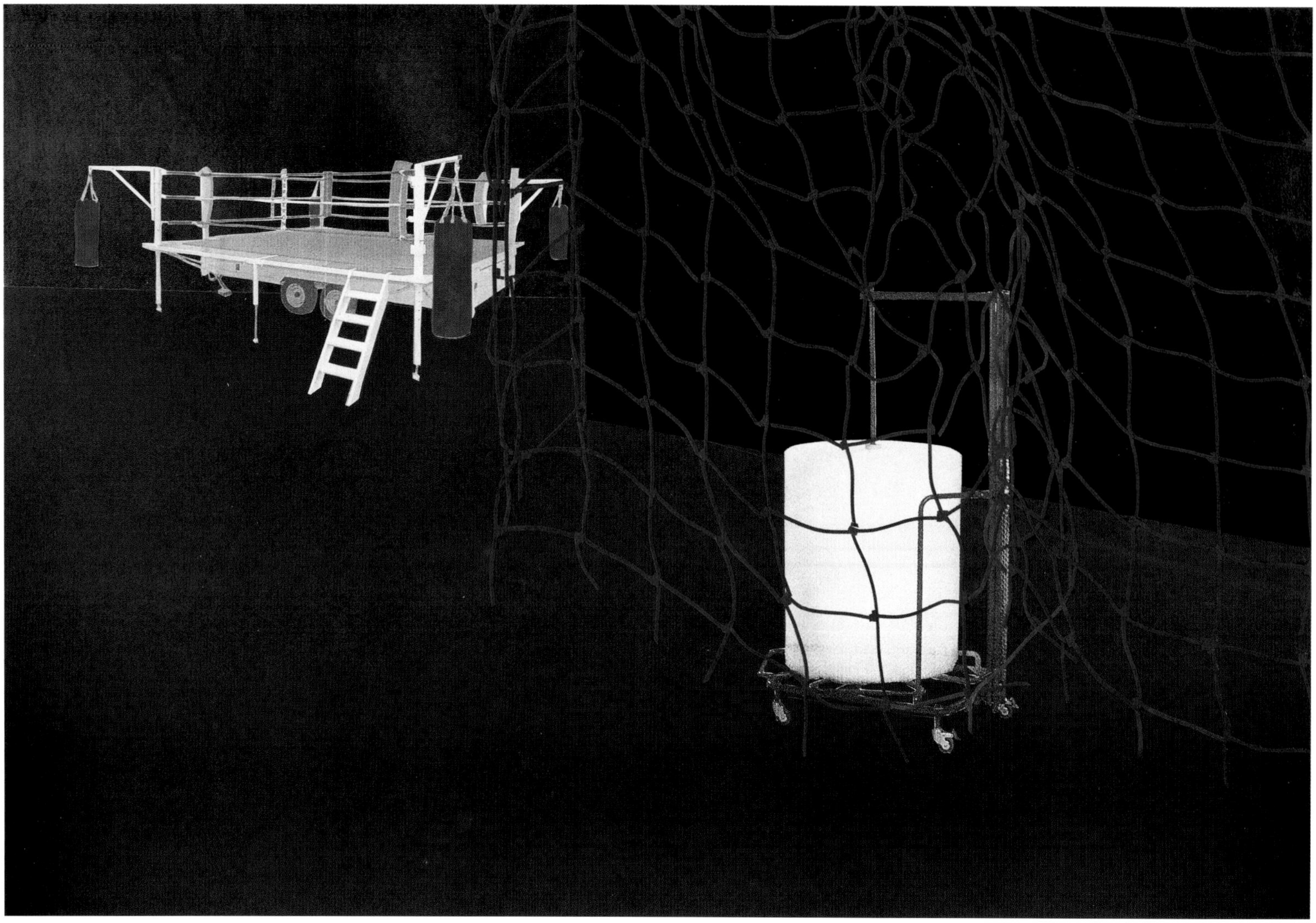

Untitled, 2005
Collage on paper, 75 x 110 cm [29½ x 43¼ in.]

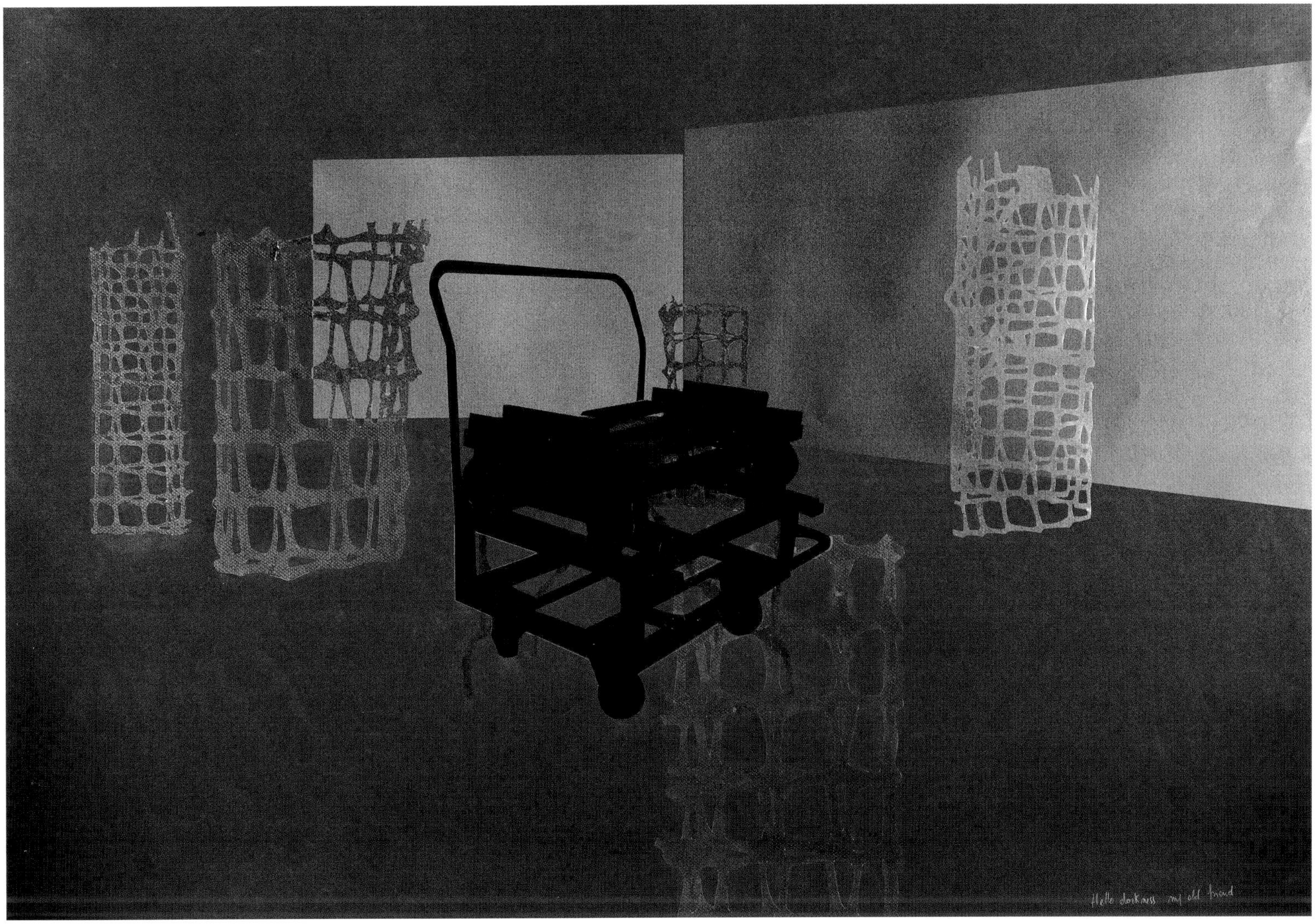

Untitled, 2005
Collage on paper, 75 x 110 cm [29½ x 43¼ in.]

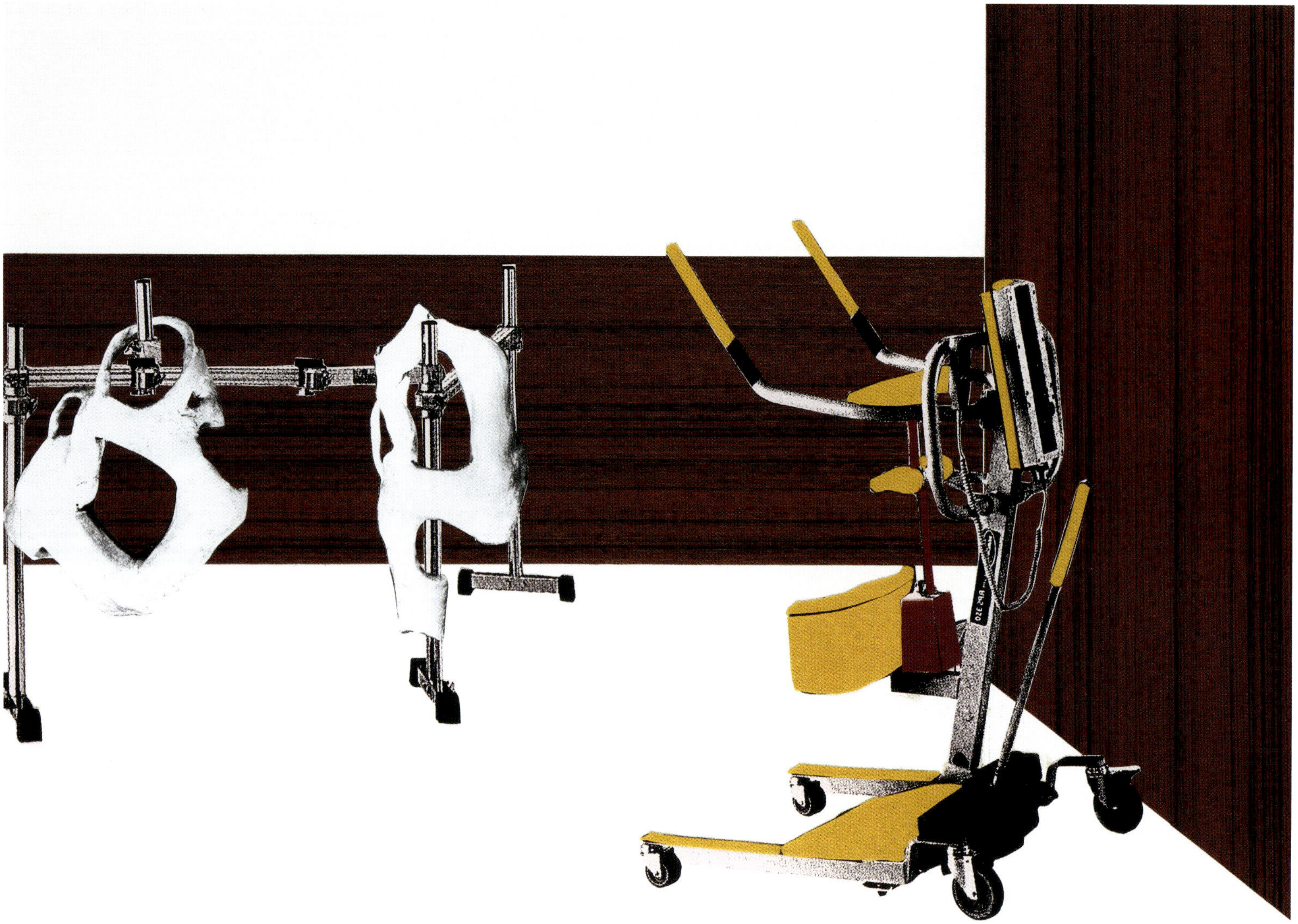

Untitled, 2003
Collage on paper, 49 x 65 cm [19¼ x 25½ in.]

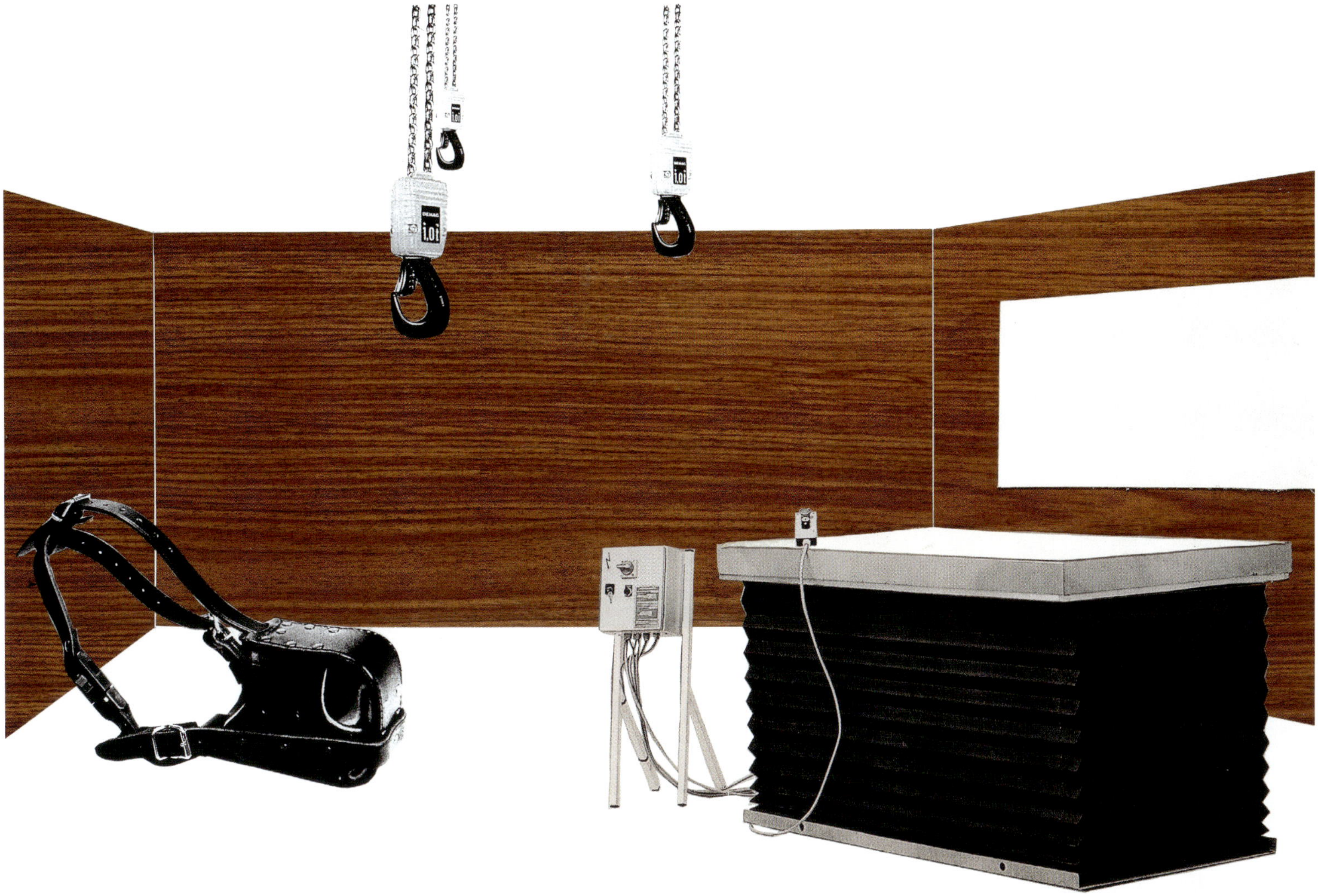

Above:
Untitled, 2004
Collage on paper, 49 x 65 cm [19¼ x 25½ in.]

Following pages:
Untitled, 2003
Collage on paper, 64.5 x 79.5 cm [25½ x 31¼ in.]

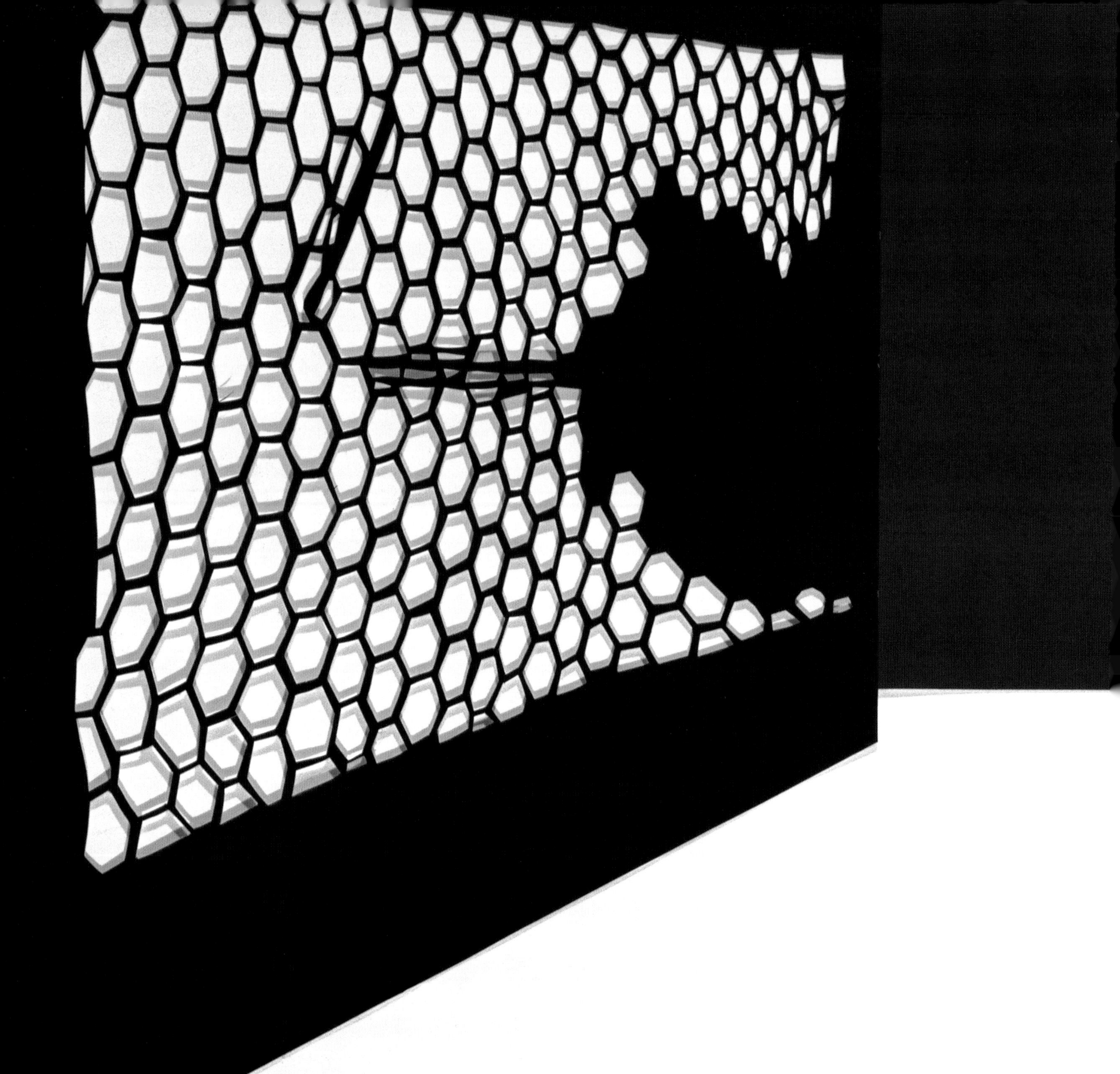

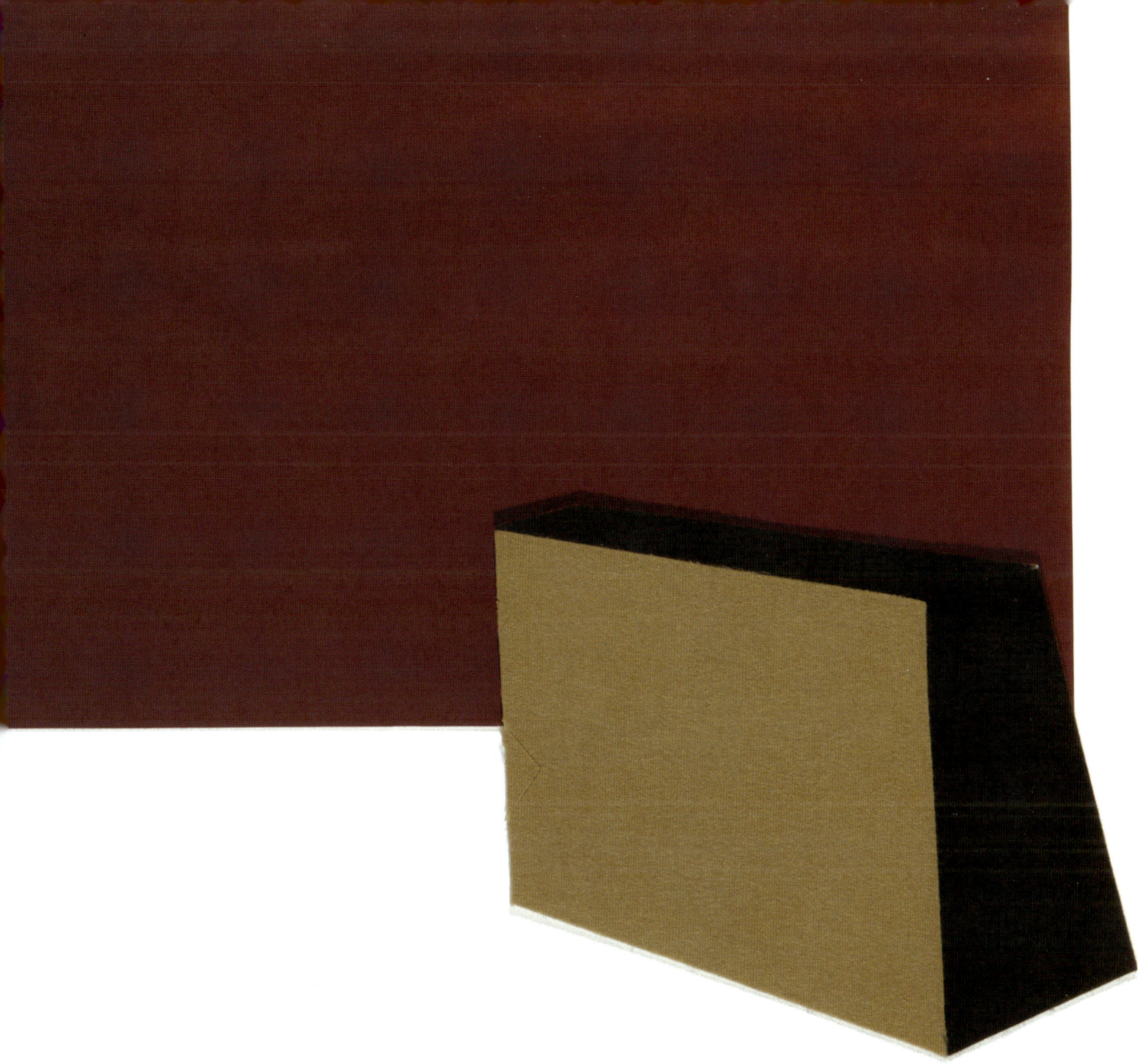

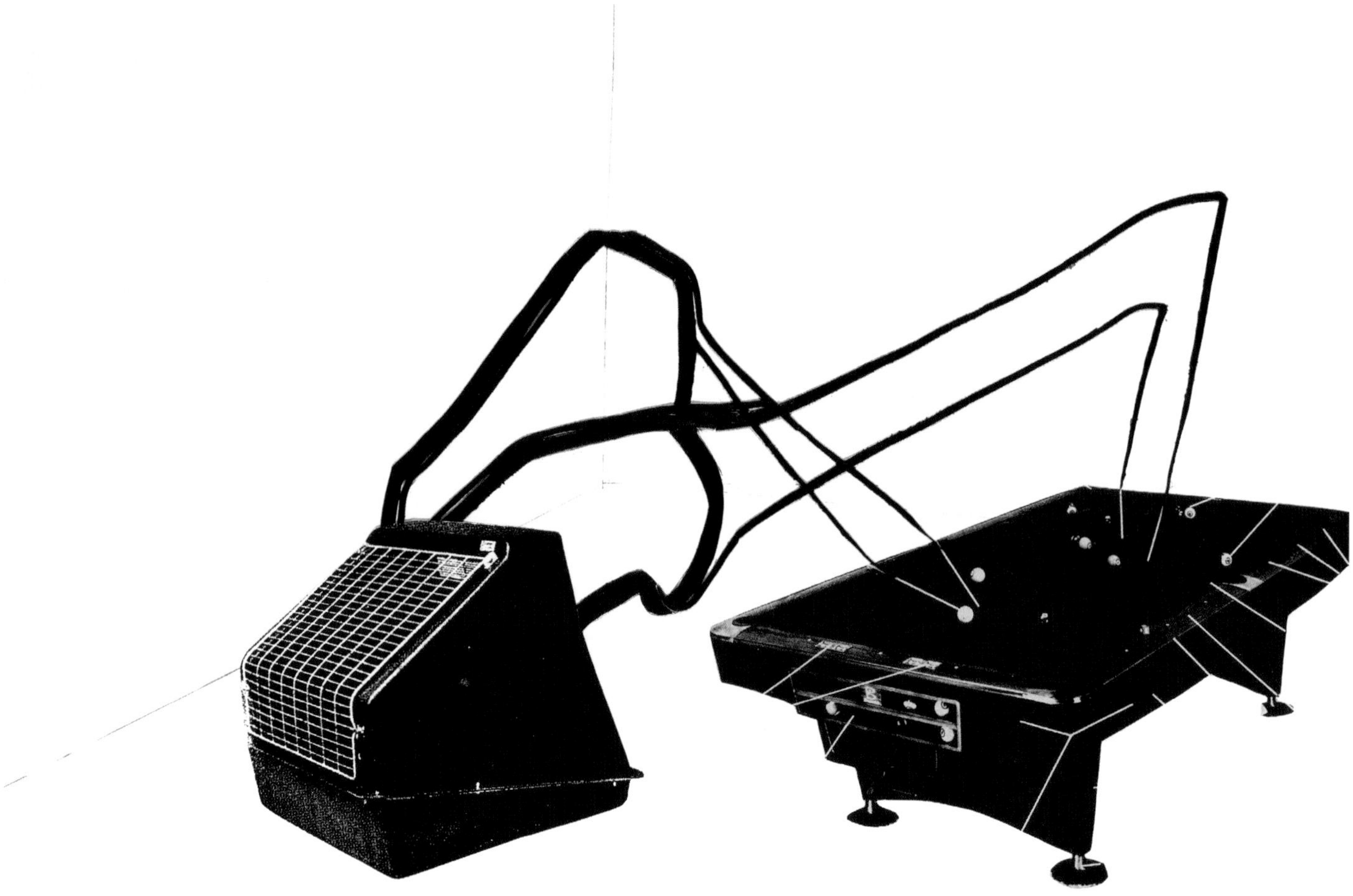

Untitled, 2003
Collage on paper, 51.5 x 66.5 cm [20¼ x 26¼ in.]

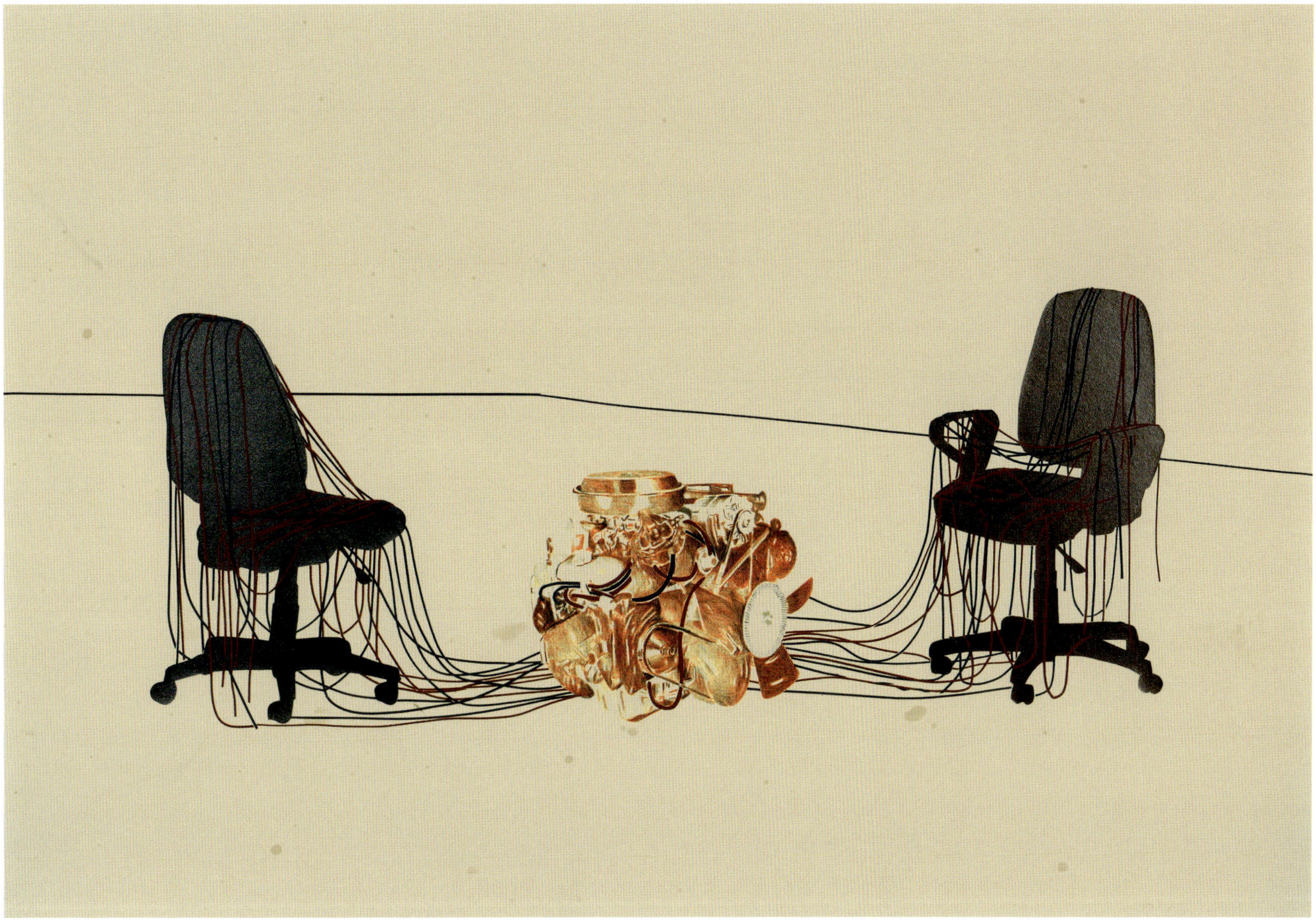

Untitled, 2005
Pencil on paper, collage, 76 x 113 cm [30 x 44½ in.]

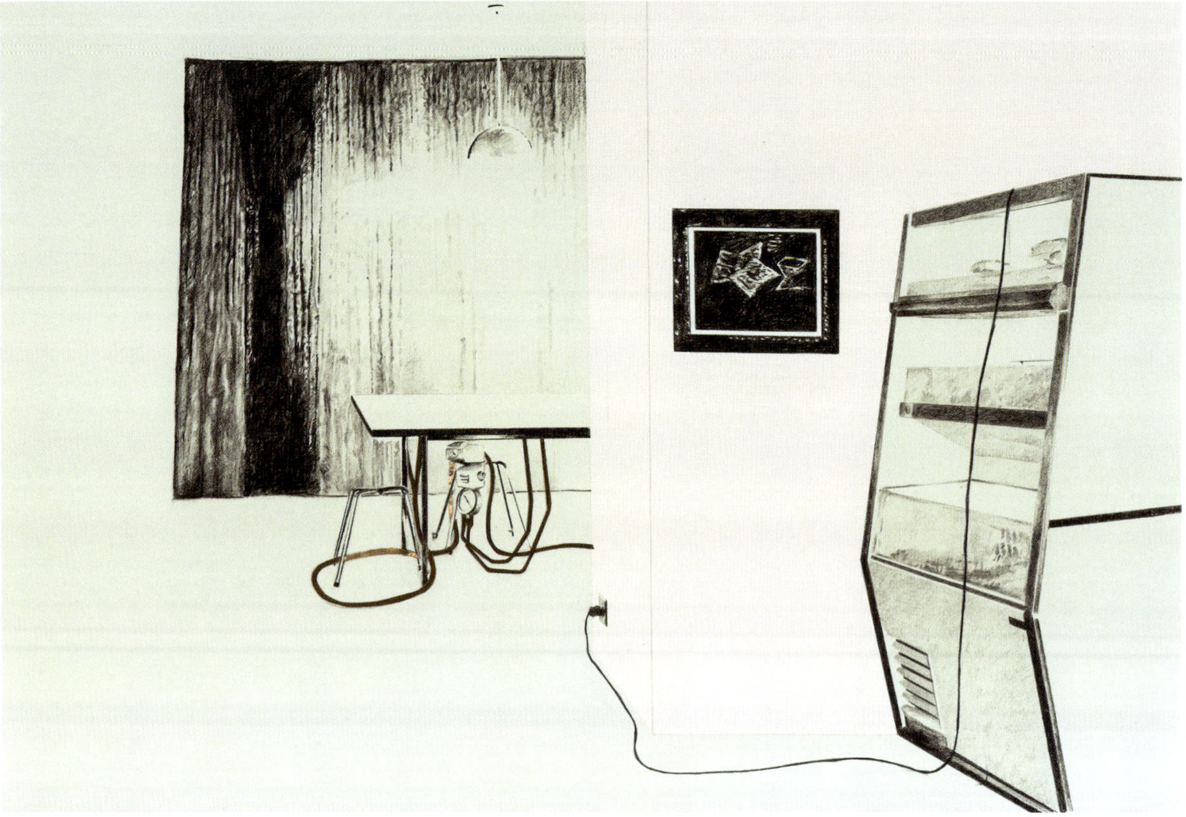

Untitled, from the series *Intranquillity,* 2006
Pencil on paper, plastic, copper, 76 x 113 cm [30 x 44½ in.]

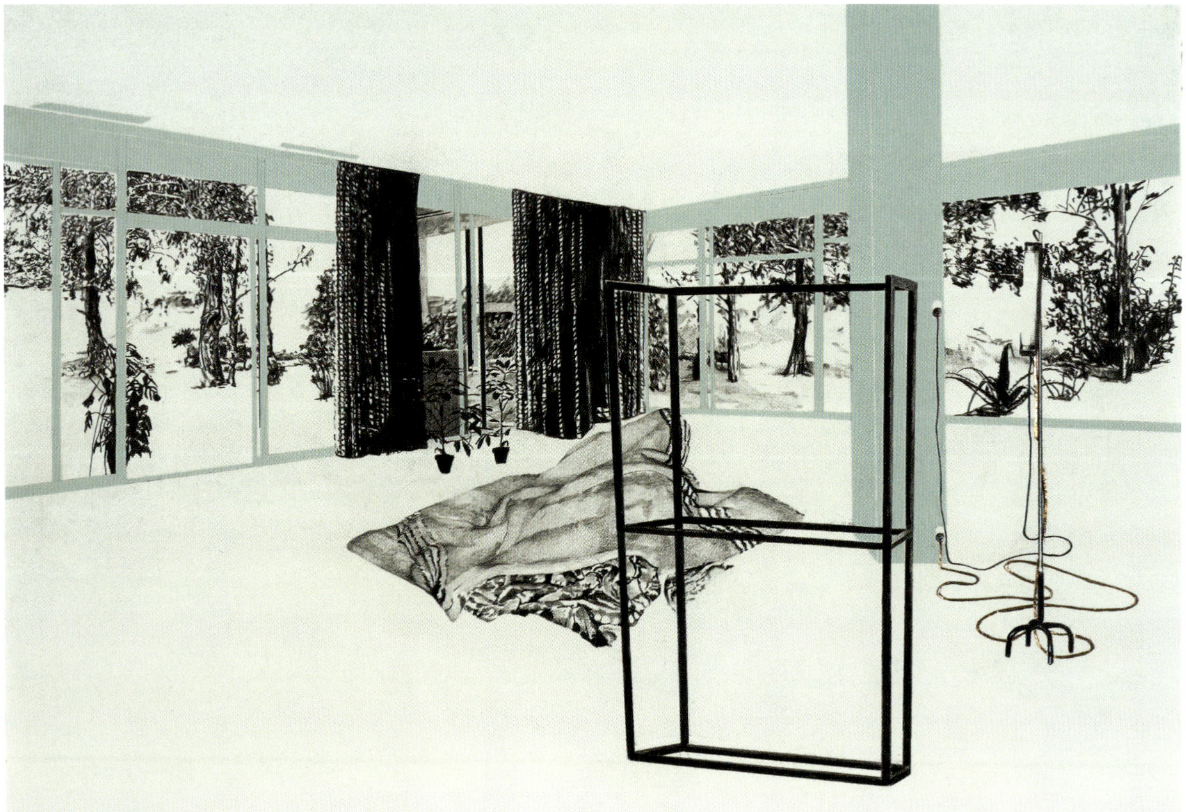

Untitled, from the series *Intranquillity,* 2006
Pencil on paper, plastic, copper, 76 x 113 cm [30 x 44½ in.]

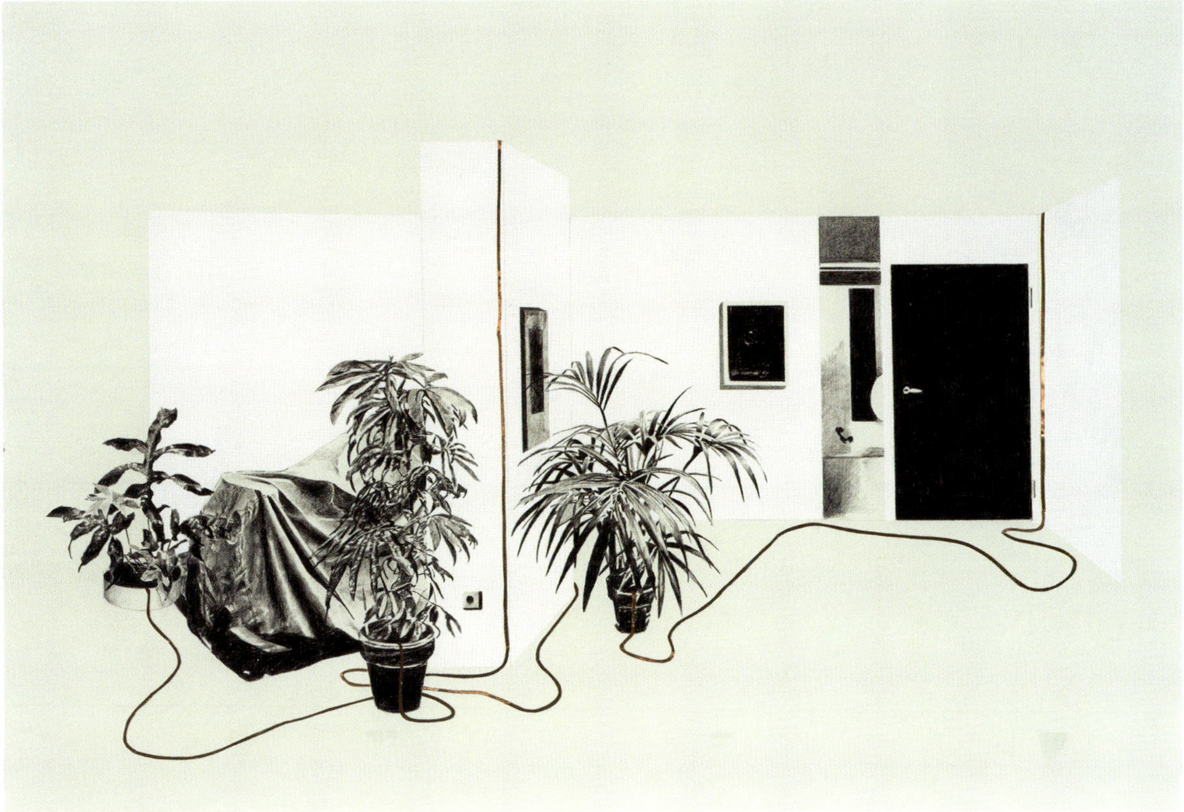

Untitled, from the series *Intranquillity,* 2006
Pencil on paper, plastic, copper, 76 x 113 cm [30 x 44½ in.]

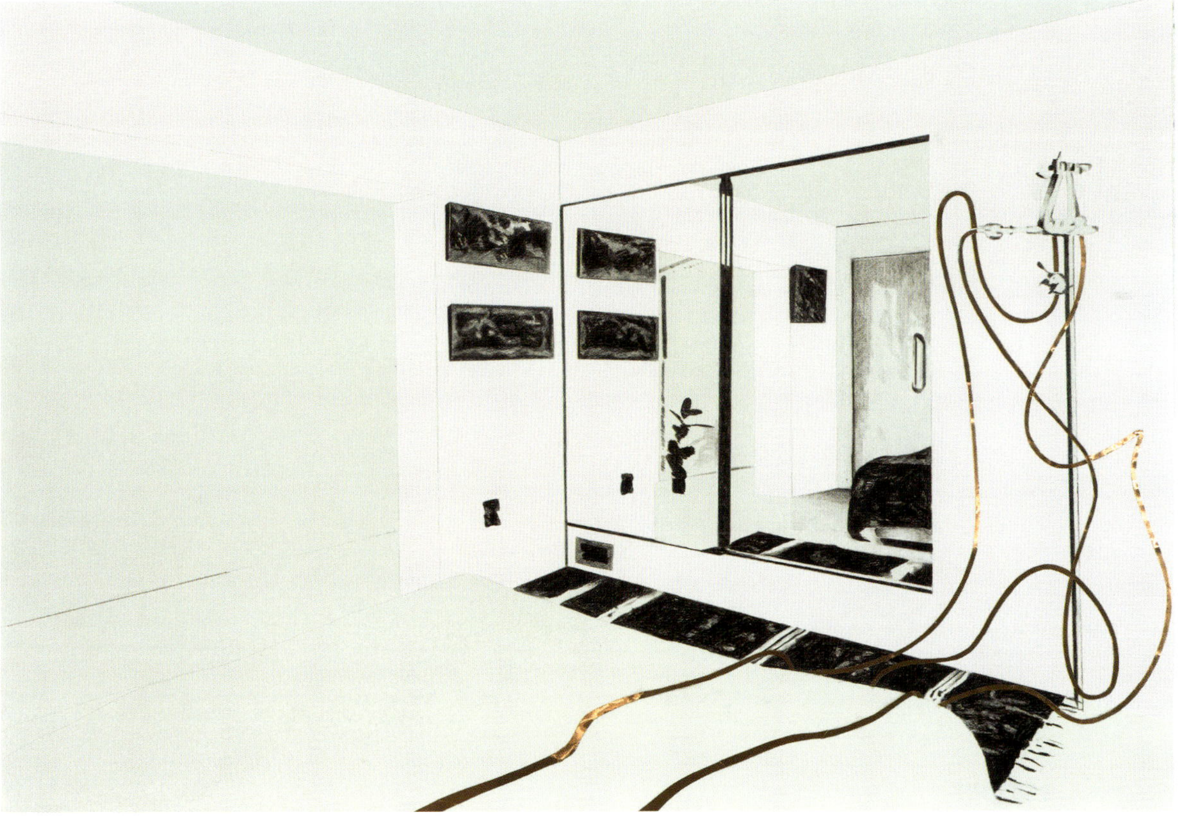

Untitled, from the series *Intranquillity,* 2006
Pencil on paper, plastic, copper, 76 x 113 cm [30 x 44½ in.]

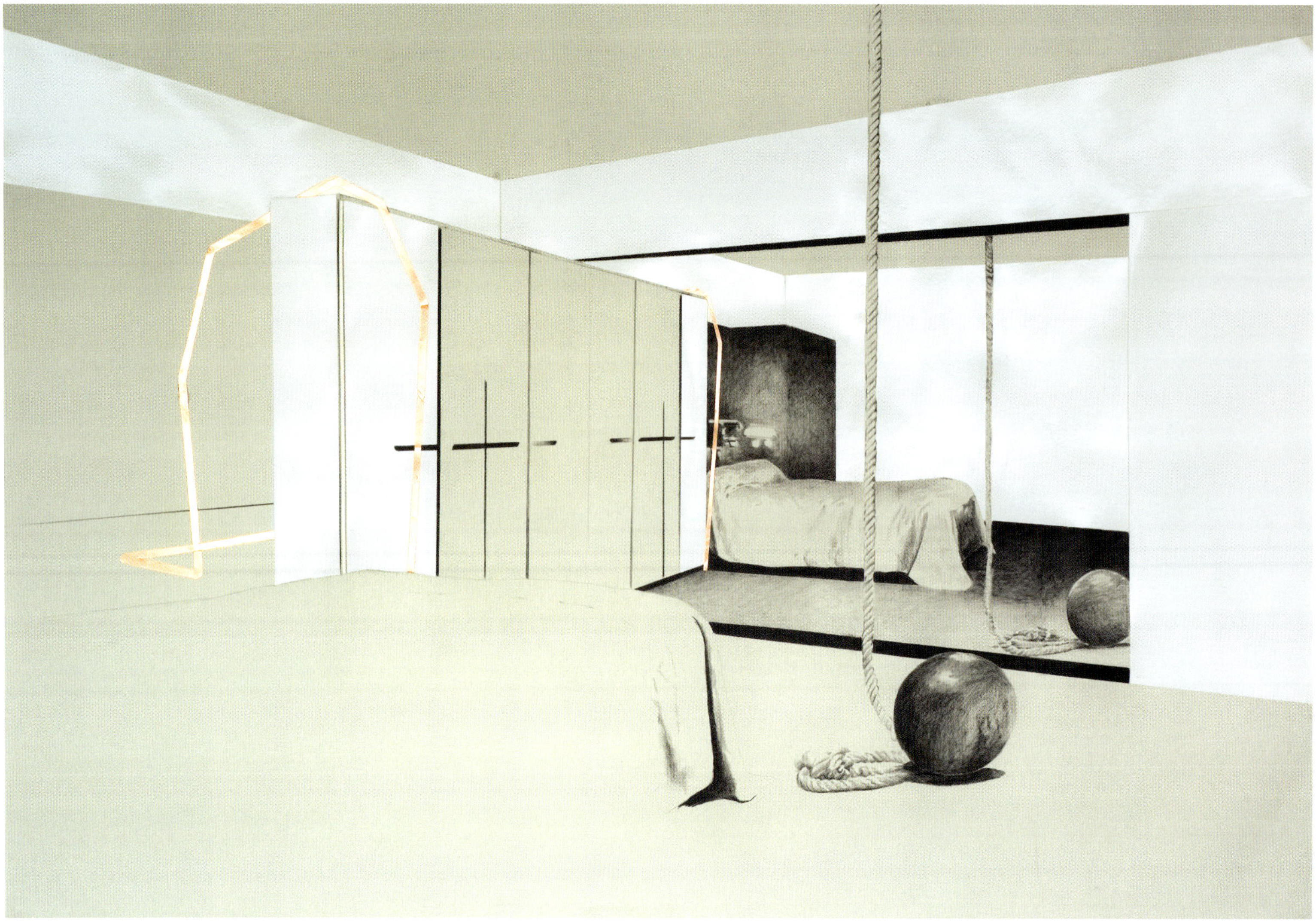

Untitled, from the series *Intranquillity,* 2007
Pencil on paper, plastic, copper, 76 x 113 cm [30 x 44½ in.]

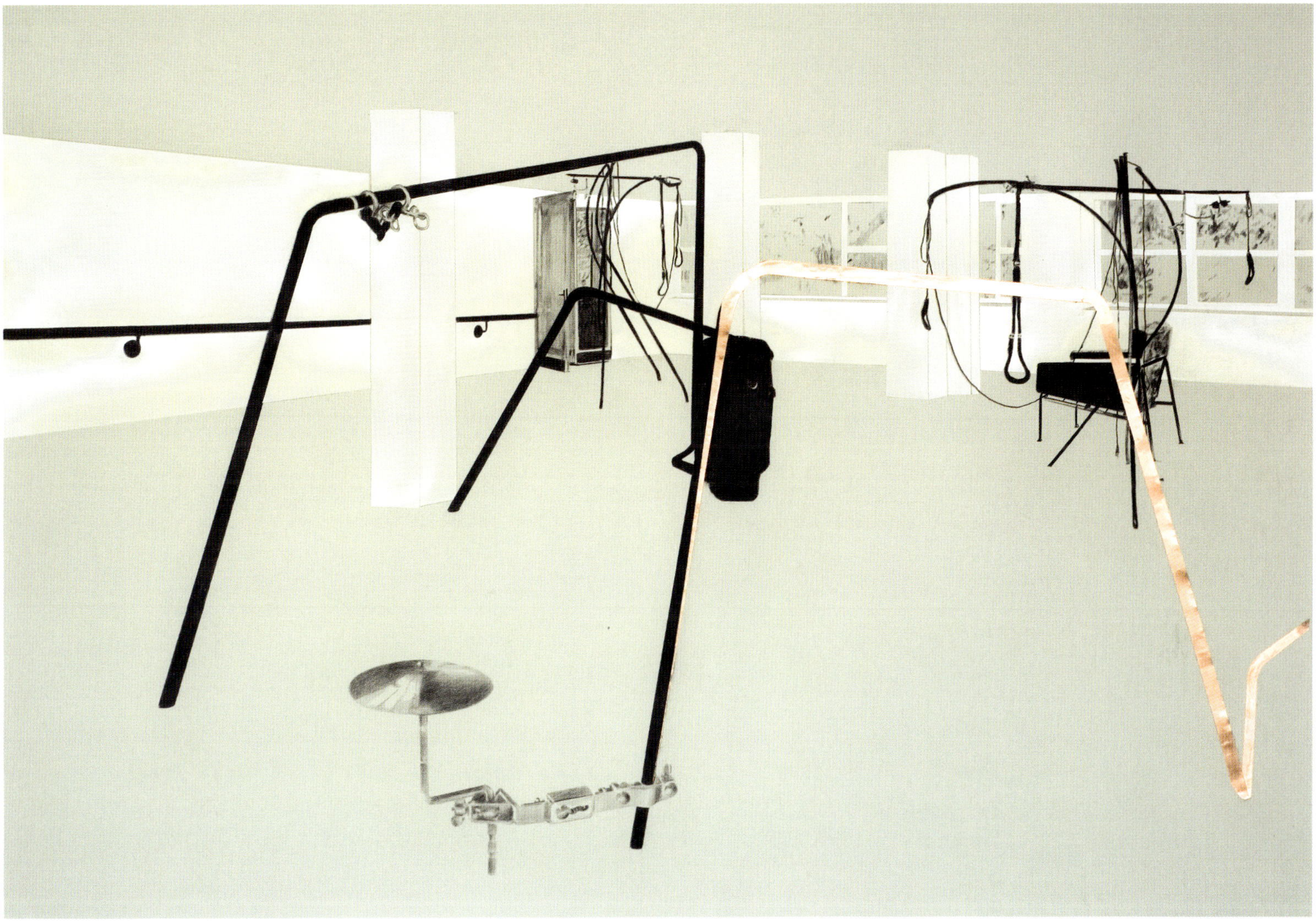

Above:
Untitled, from the series *Intranquillity,* 2007
Pencil on paper, plastic, copper, 76 x 113 cm [30 x 44½ in.]

Pages 102–103:
Untitled, from the series *Intranquillity,* 2007
Pencil on paper, plastic, copper, 76 x 113 cm [30 x 44½ in.]

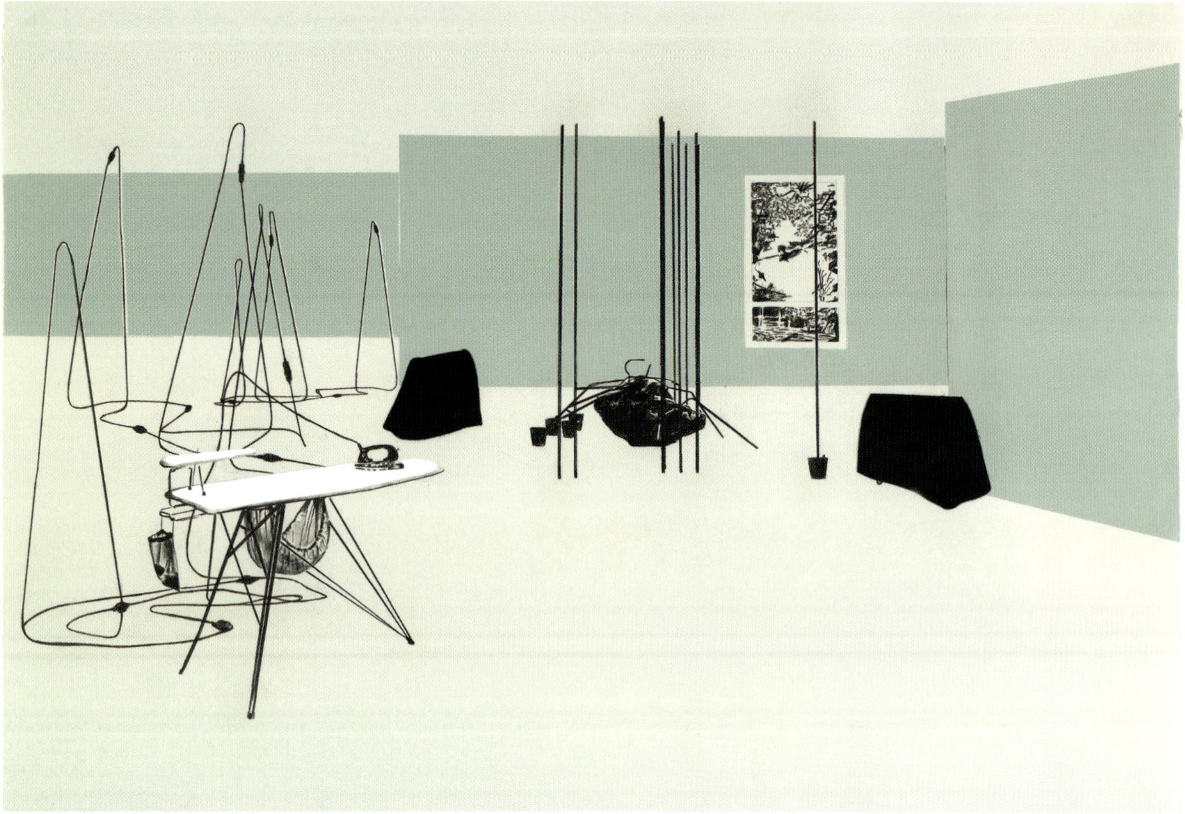

Untitled, from the series *Intranquillity,* 2007
Pencil on paper, plastic, copper, 76 x 113 cm [30 x 44½ in.]

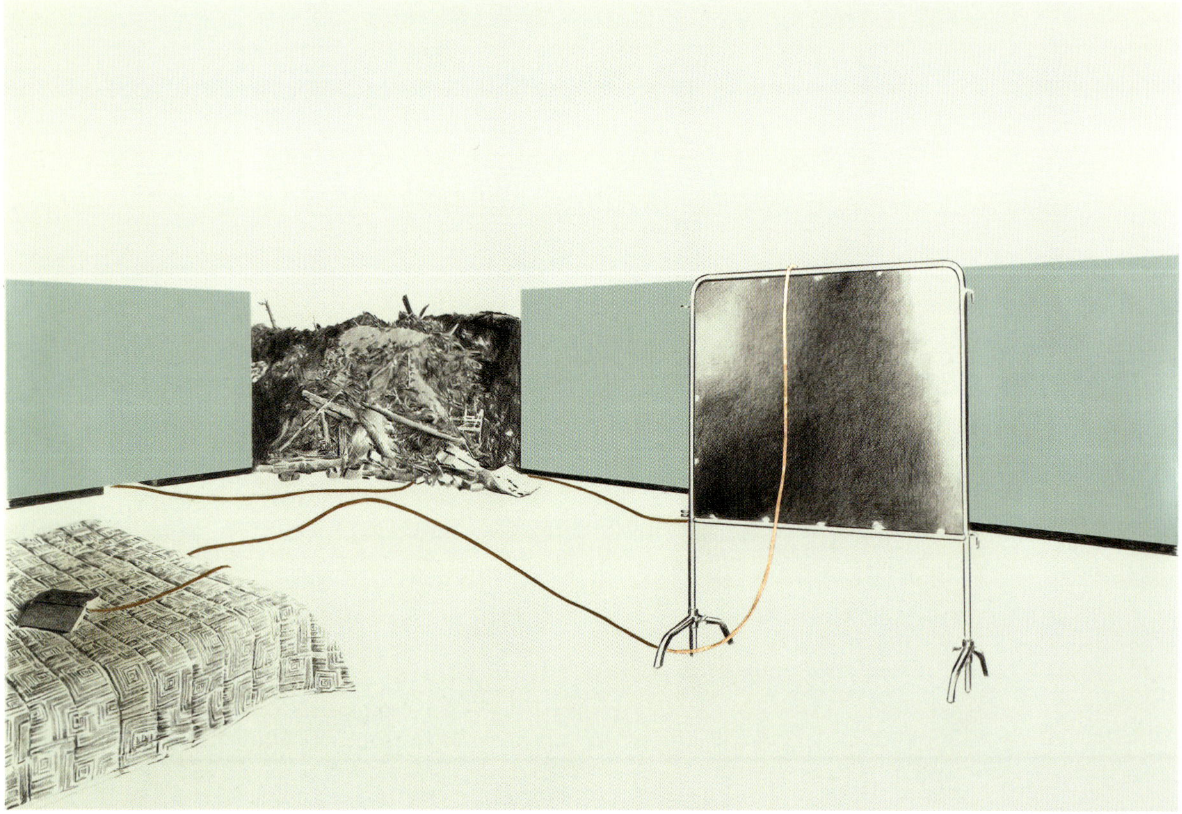

Untitled, from the series *Intranquillity,* 2007
Pencil on paper, plastic, copper, 76 x 113 cm [30 x 44½ in.]

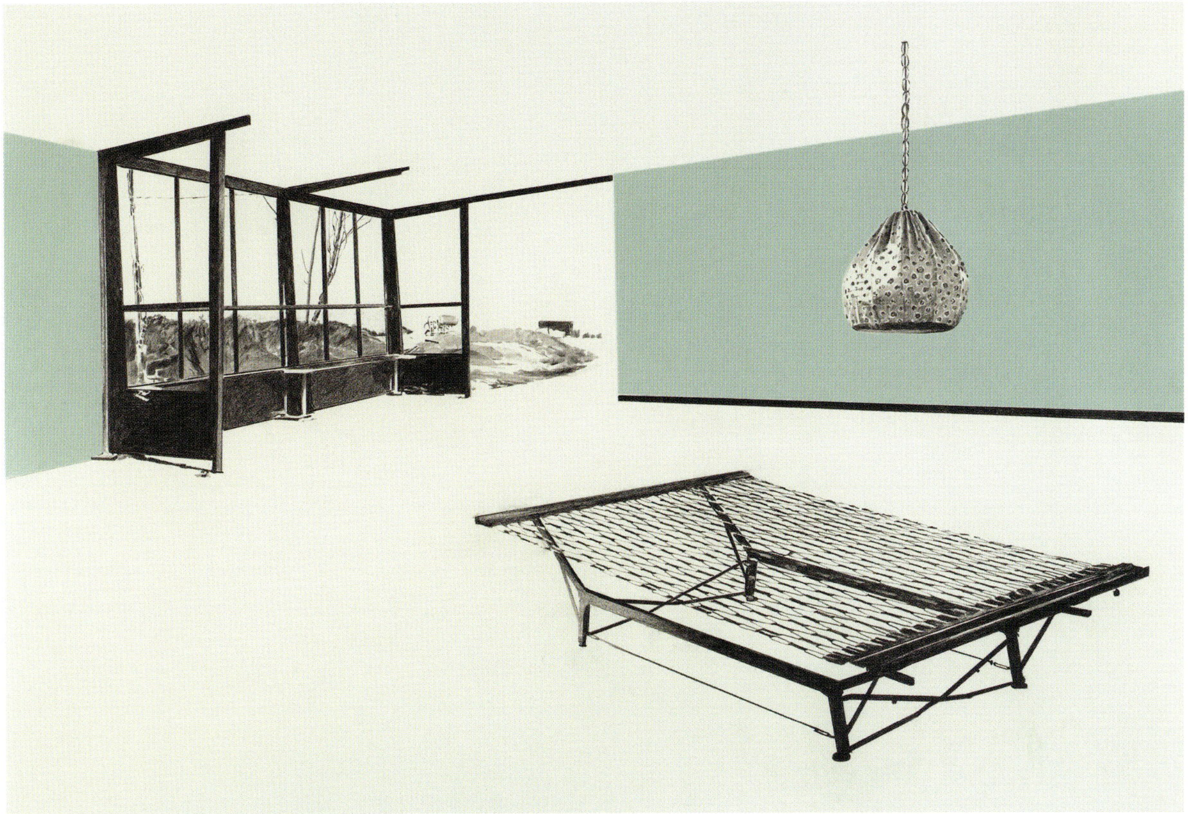

Untitled, from the series *Intranquillity,* 2007
Pencil on paper, plastic, 76 x 113 cm [30 x 44½ in.]

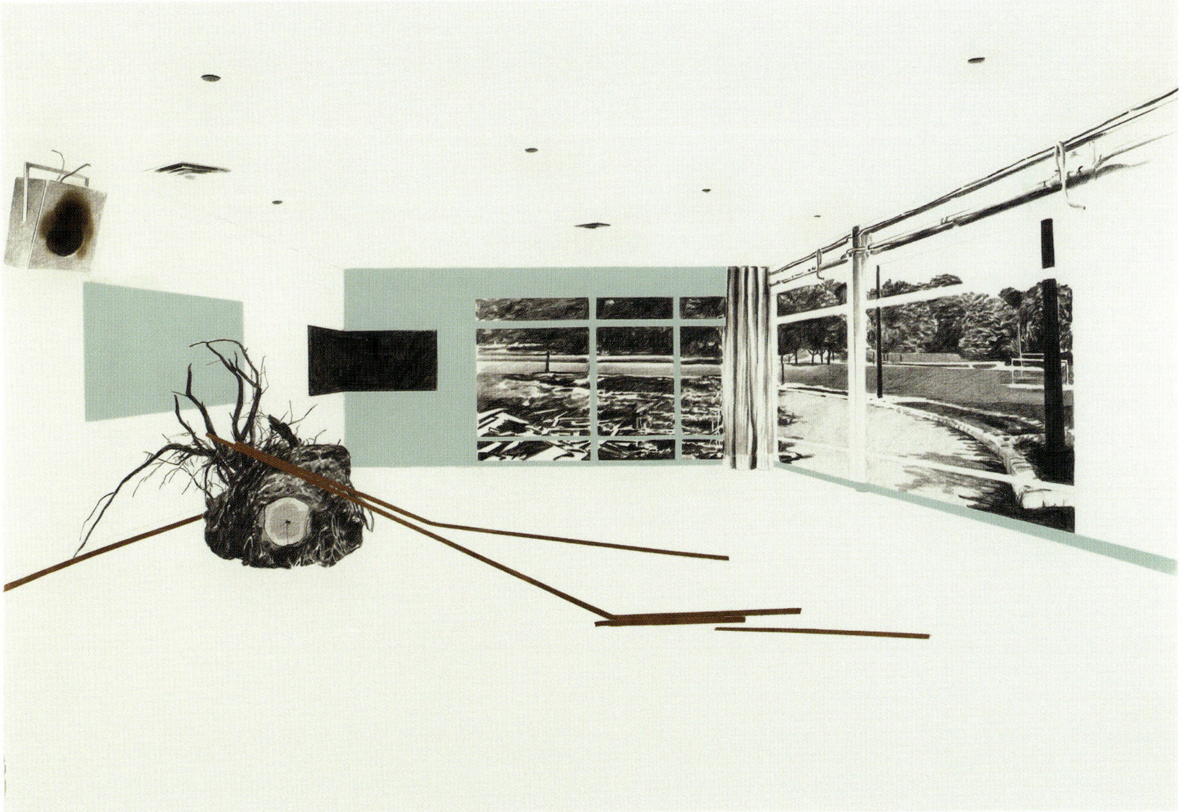

Untitled, from the series *Intranquillity,* 2007
Pencil on paper, plastic, copper, 76 x 113 cm [30 x 44½ in.]

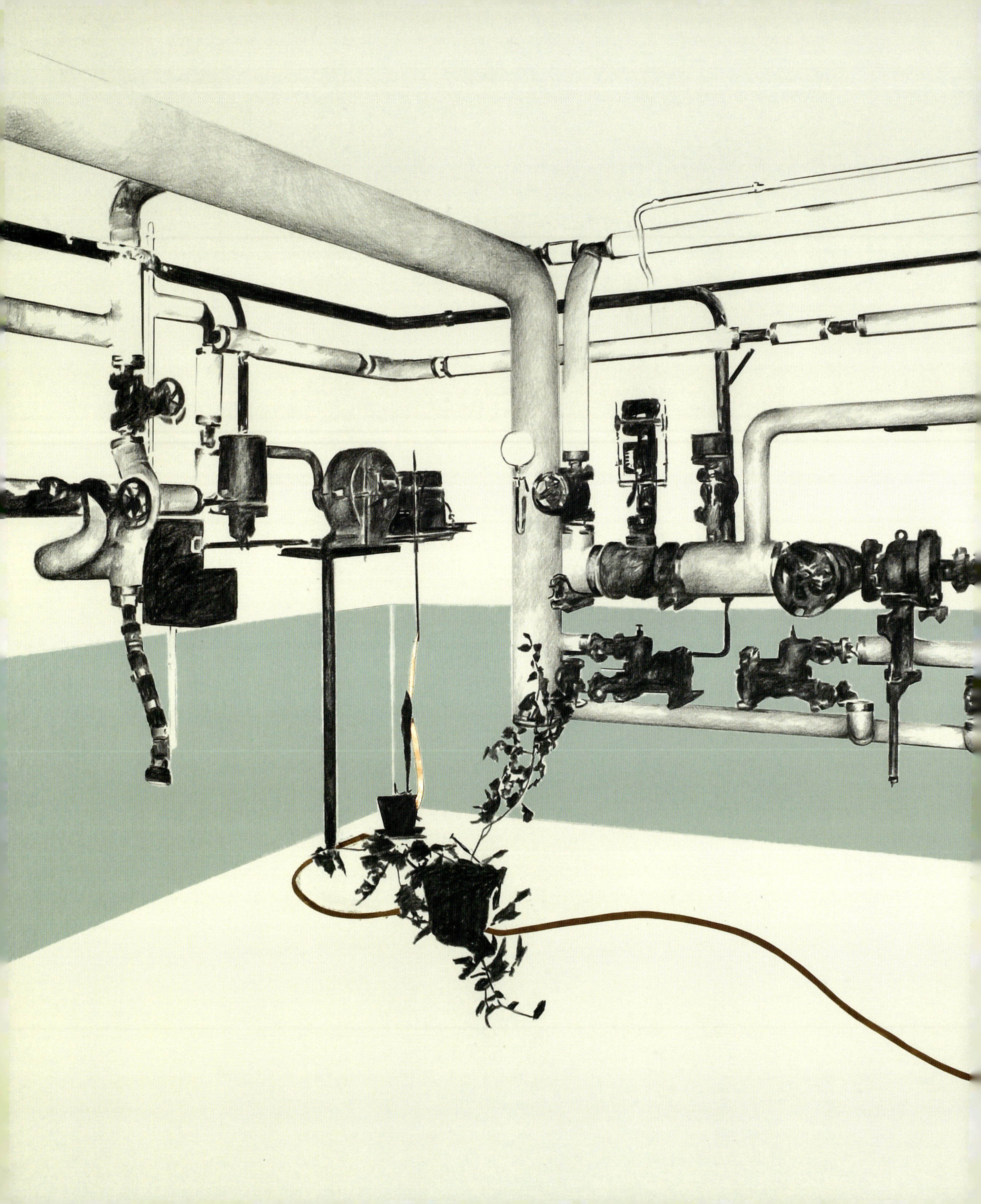

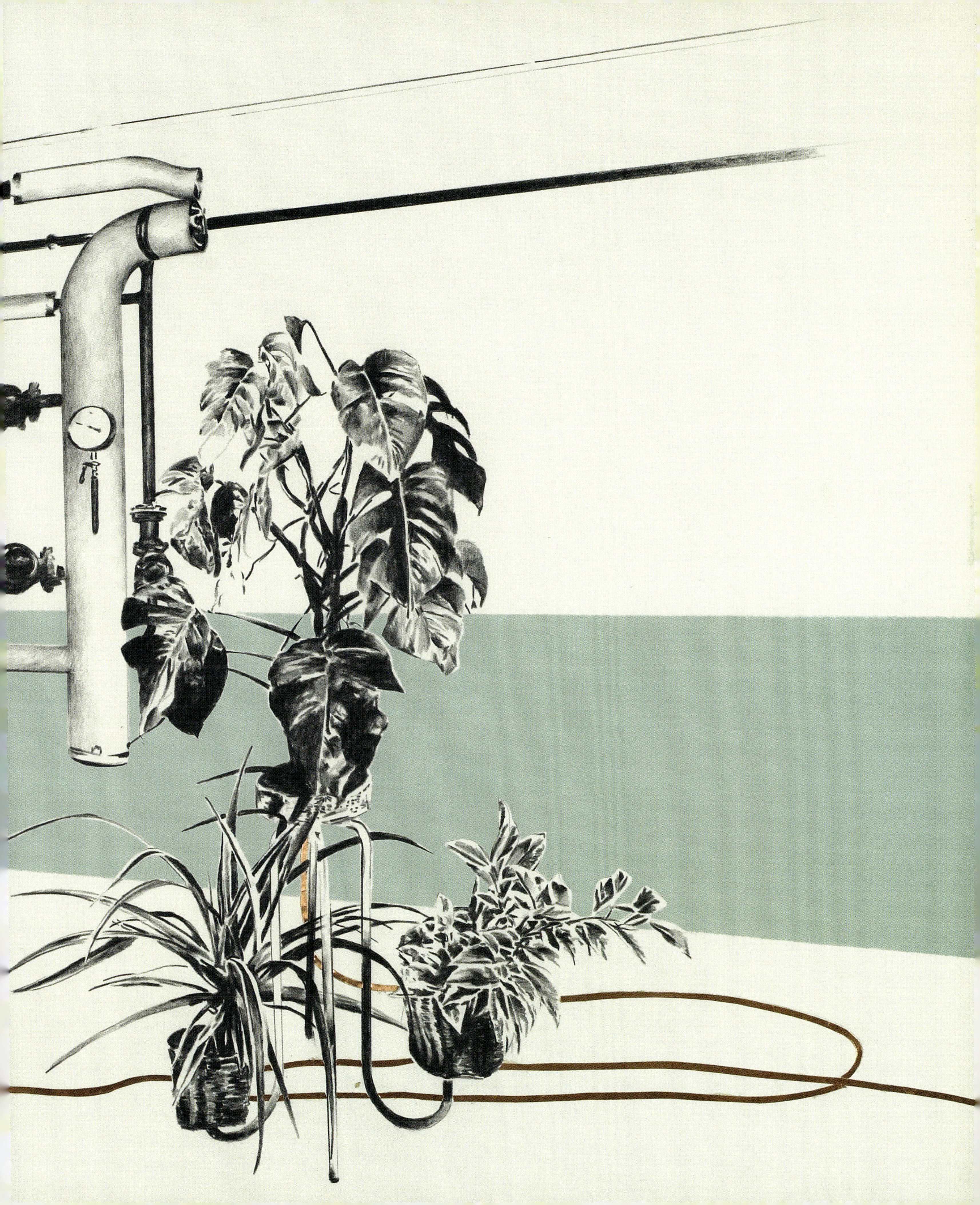

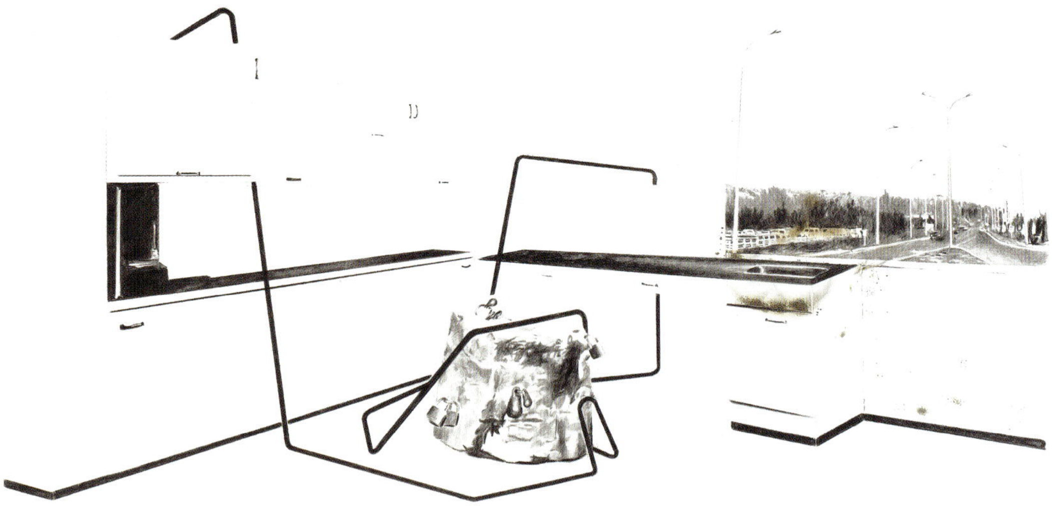

Untitled, from the series *Intranquillity,* 2007
Pencil on paper, plastic, 76 x 109 cm [30 x 43 in.]

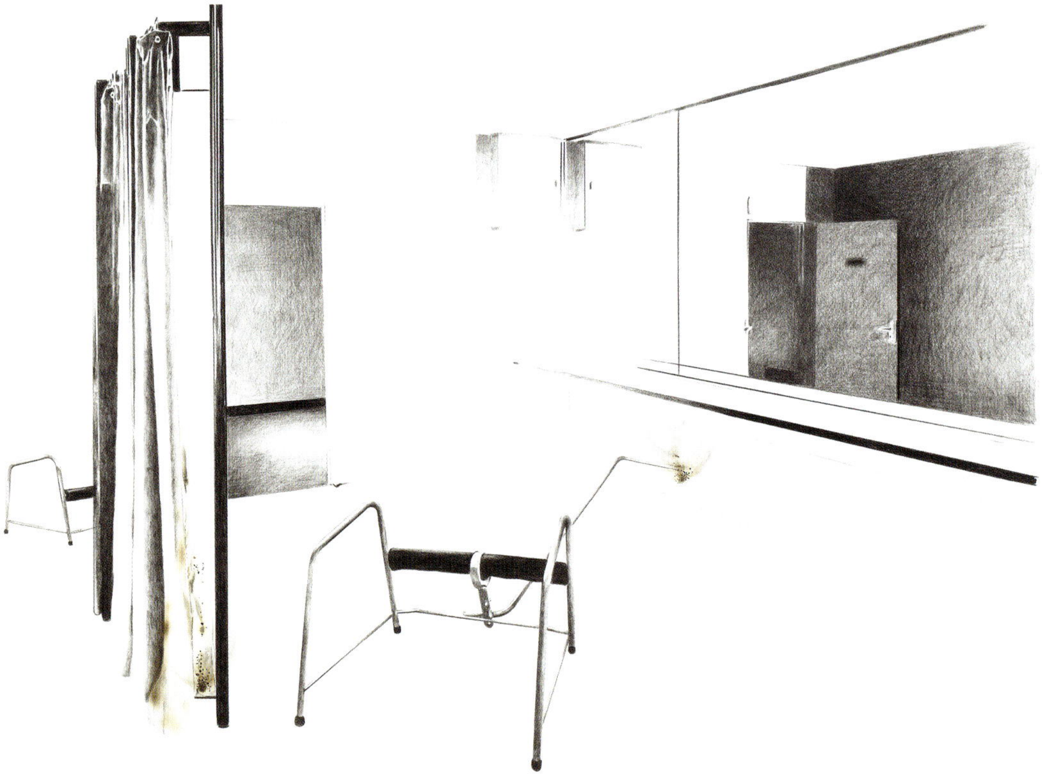

Untitled, from the series *Intranquillity,* 2007
Pencil on paper, plastic material, burns, 76 x 113 cm [30 x 44½ in.]

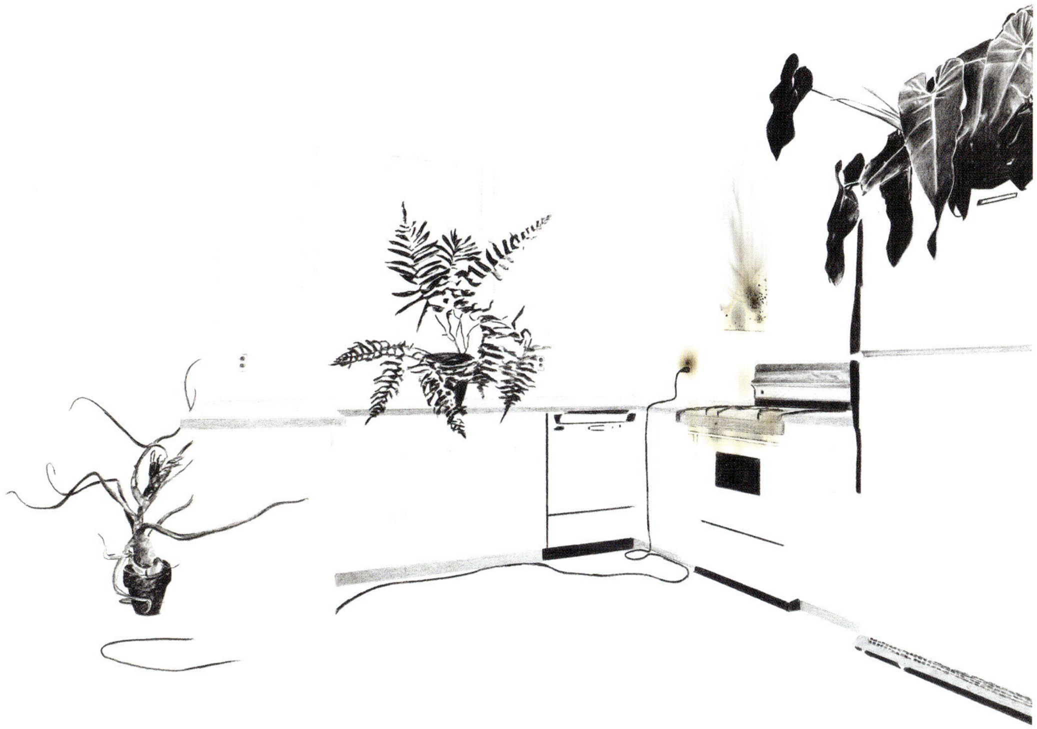

Untitled, from the series *Intranquillity,* 2006
Pencil on paper, plastic, burns, 57 x 76.5 cm [22½ x 30¼ in.]

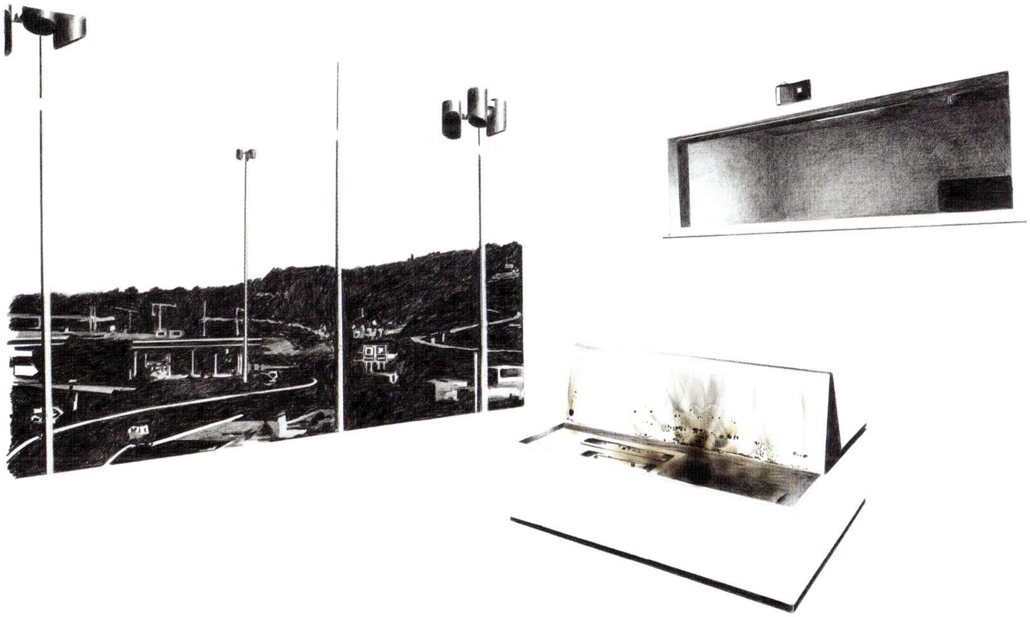

Untitled, from the series *Intranquillity,* 2007
Pencil on paper, plastic, burns, 76 x 113 cm [30 x 44½ in.]

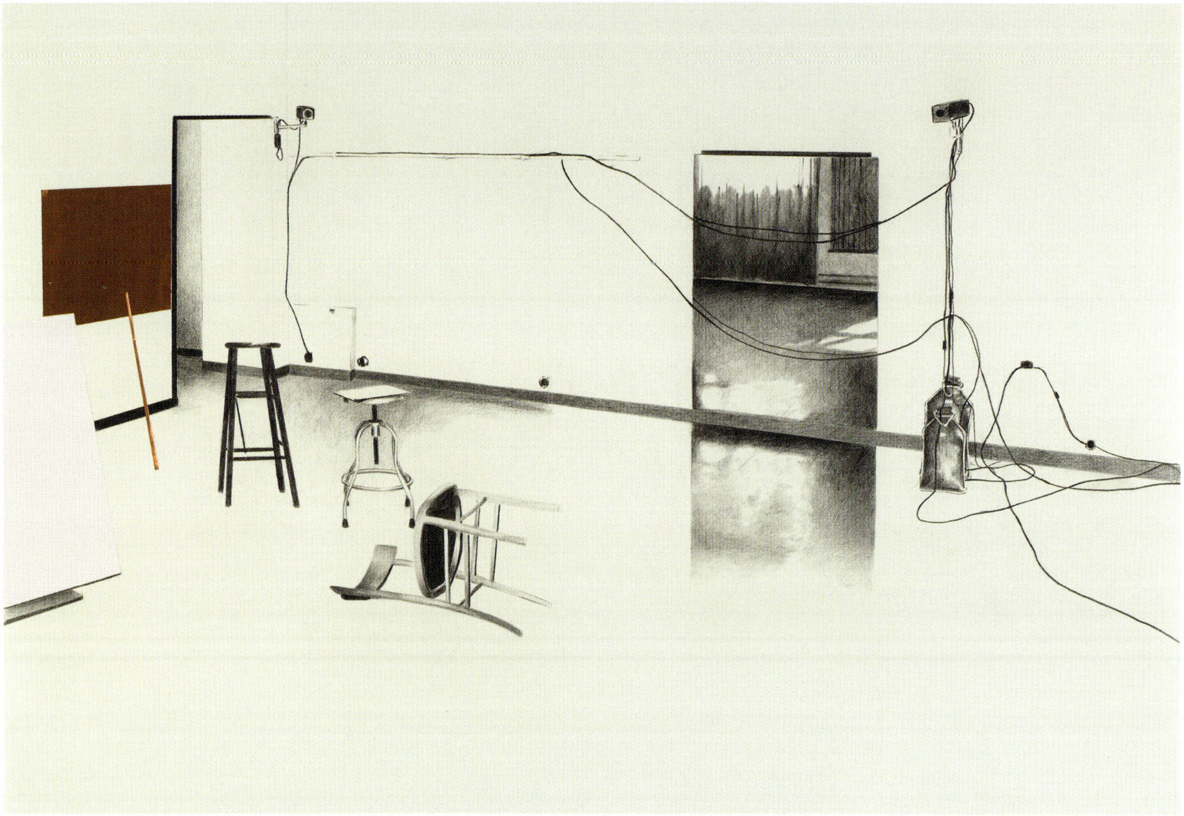

Untitled, from the series *Intranquillity,* 2007
Pencil on paper, plastic, copper, 76 x 113 cm [30 x 44½ in.]

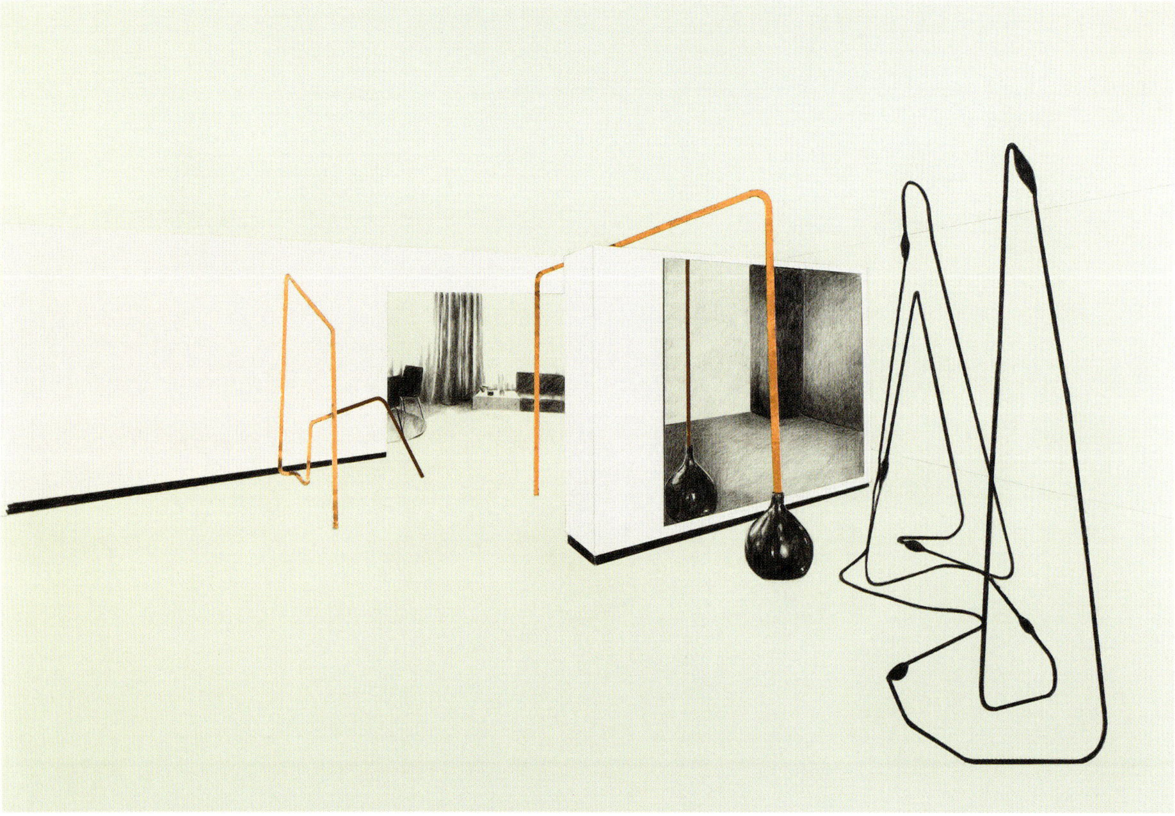

Untitled, from the series *Intranquillity,* 2007
Pencil on paper, plastic, copper, 76 x 113 cm [30 x 44½ in.]

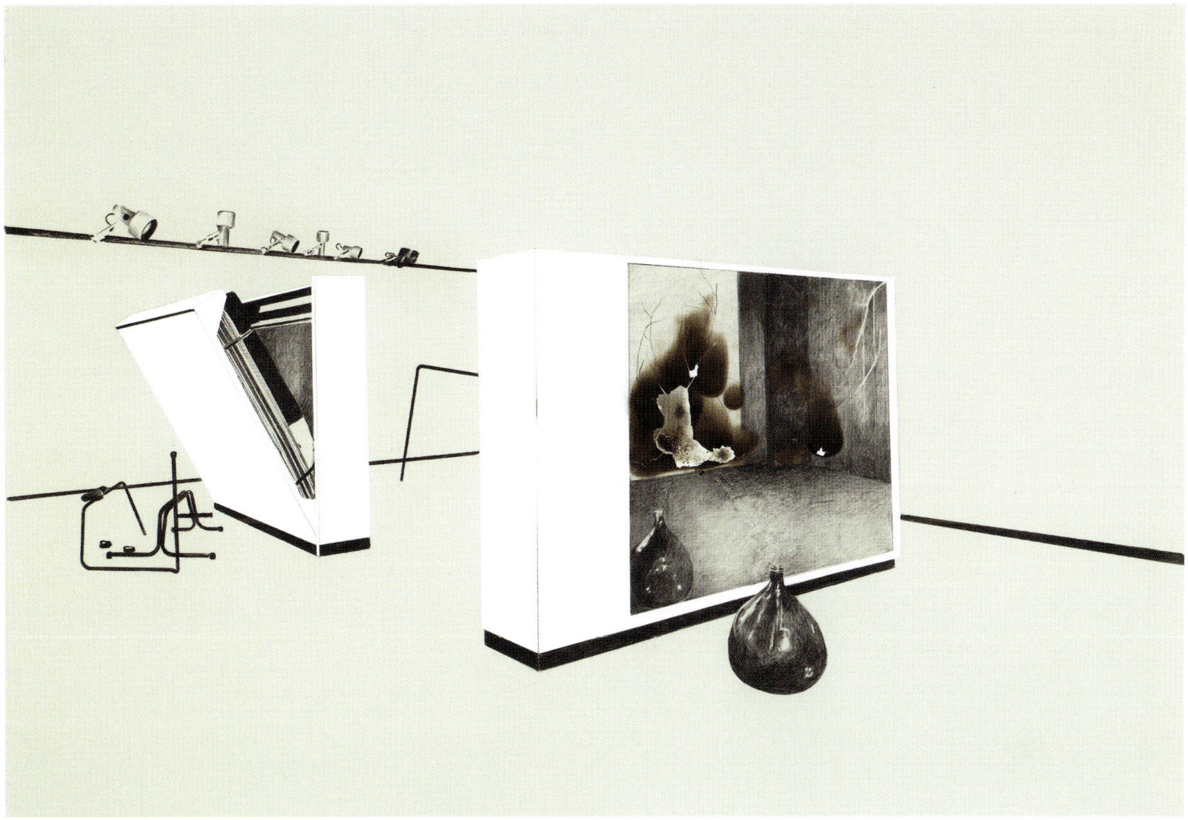

Untitled, from the series *Intranquillity,* 2007
Pencil on paper, plastic, burn, 76 x 113 cm [30 x 44½ in.]

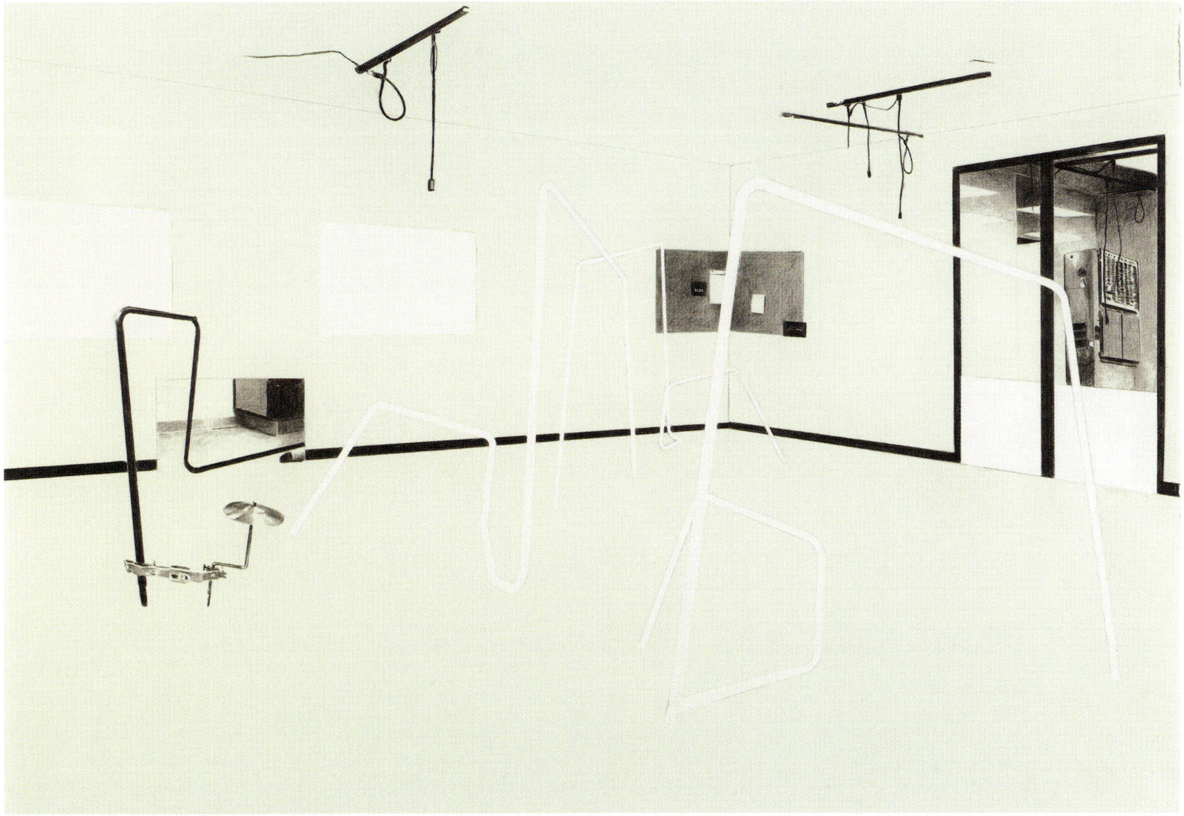

Untitled, from the series *Intranquillity,* 2007
Pencil on paper, plastic, 76 x 113 cm [30 x 44½ in.]

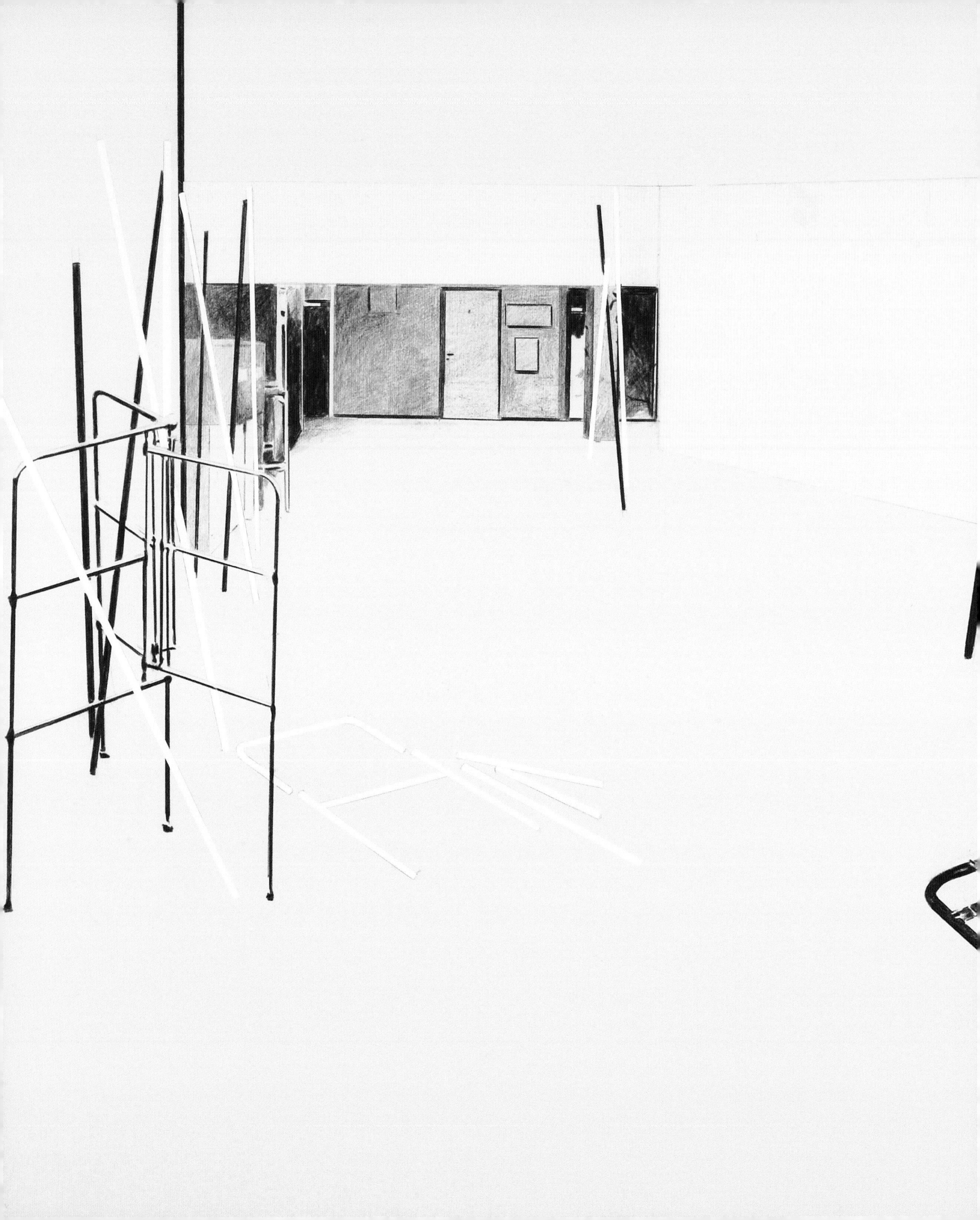

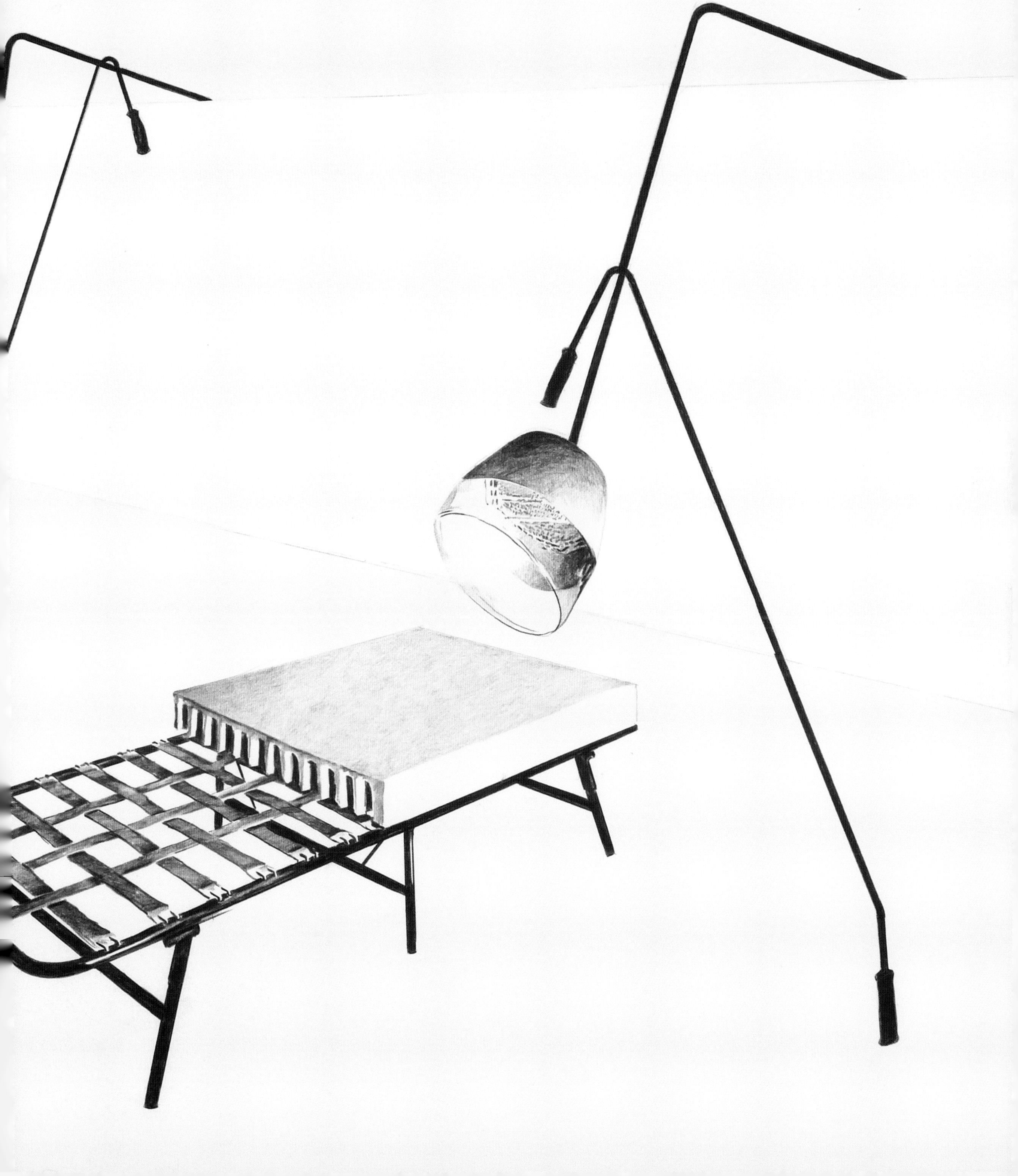

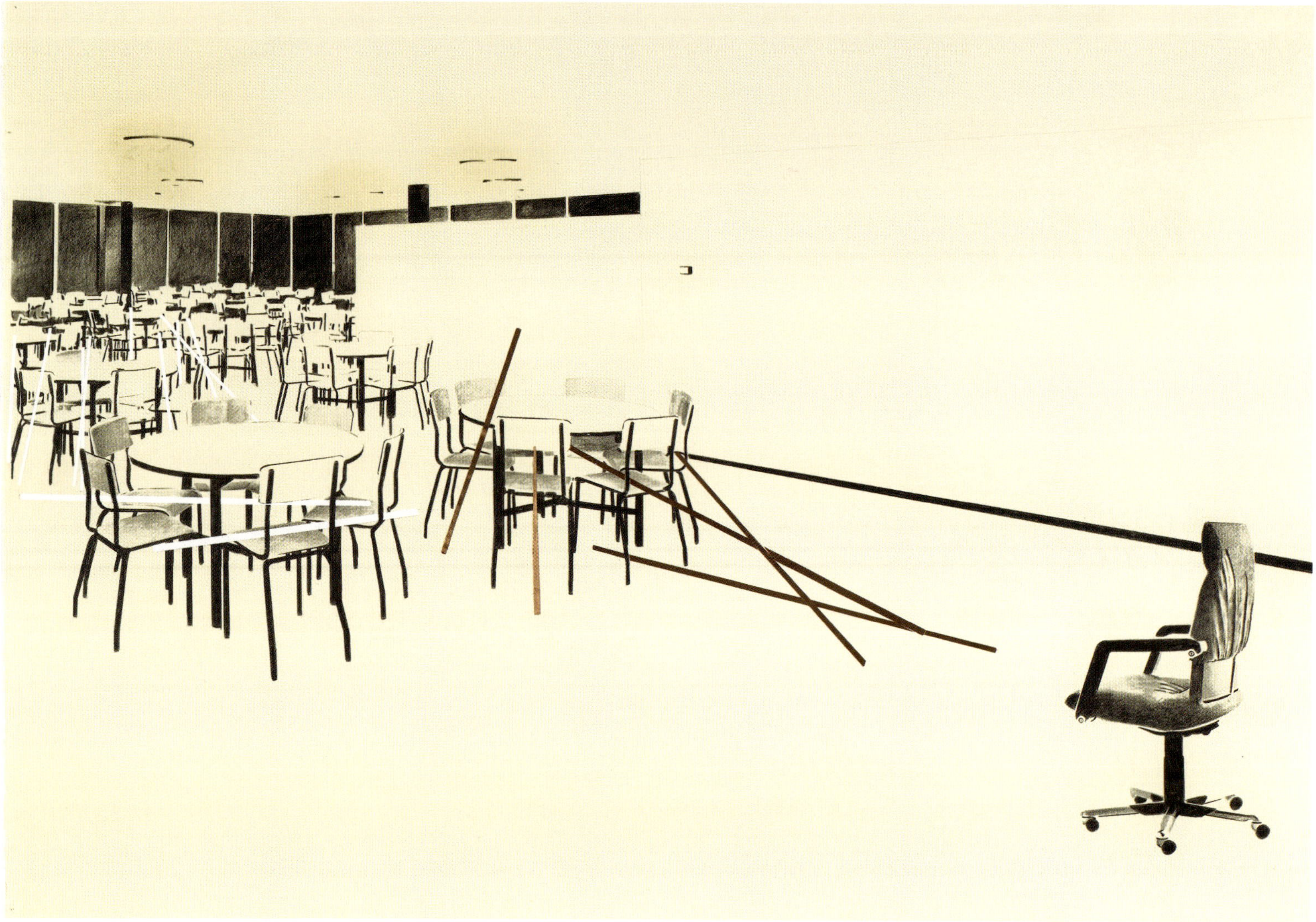

Previous pages:
Untitled, from the series *Intranquillity,* 2007
Pencil on paper, plastic, copper, 76 x 113 cm [30 x 44½ in.]

Above:
Untitled, from the series *Intranquillity,* 2007
Pencil on paper, plastic, copper, 76 x 113 cm [30 x 44½ in.]

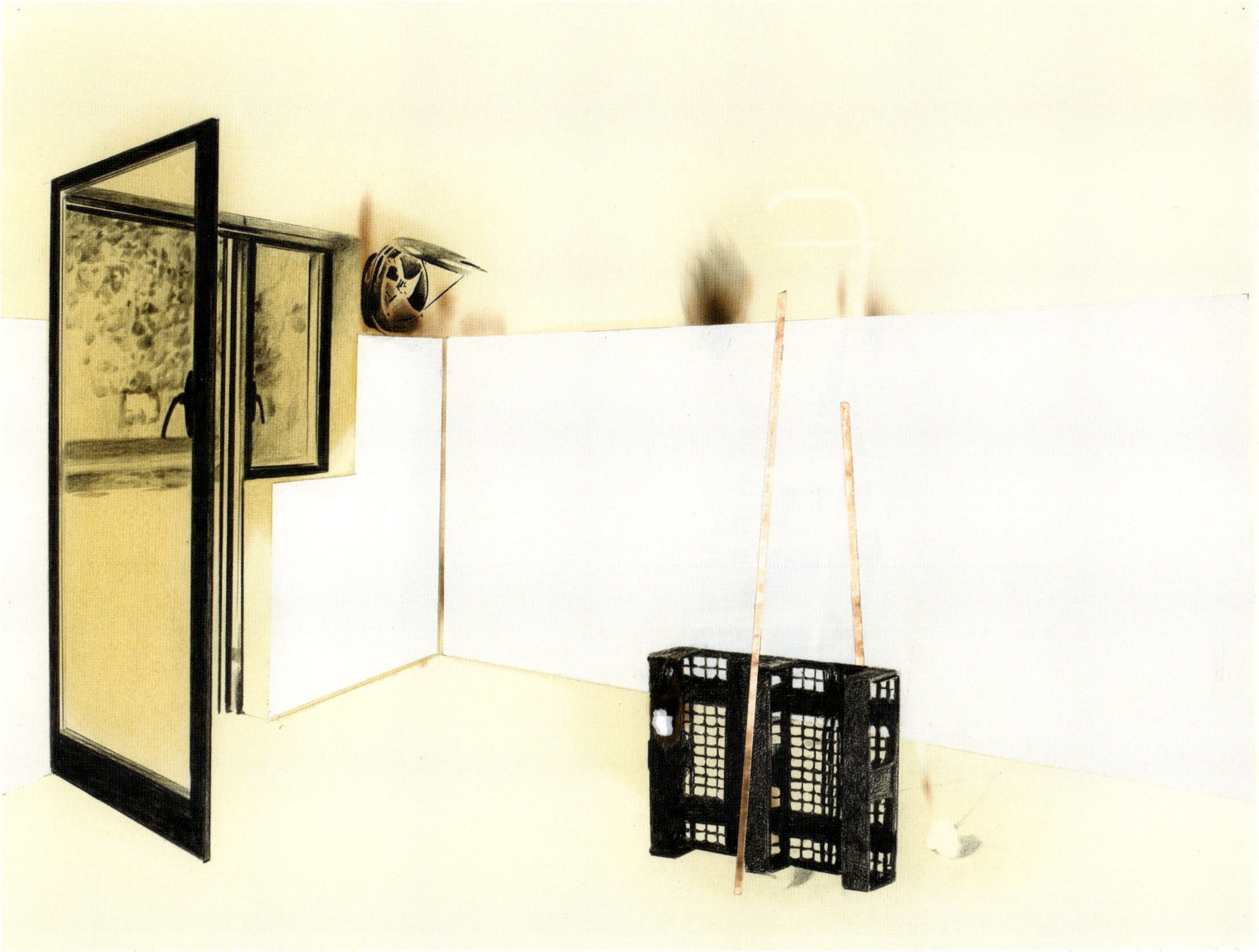

Untitled, from the series *Intranquillity,* 2007
Pencil on paper, plastic, copper, 57 x 76.5 cm [22½ x 30¼ in.]
Drawing part of the installation *Untitled,* 2007

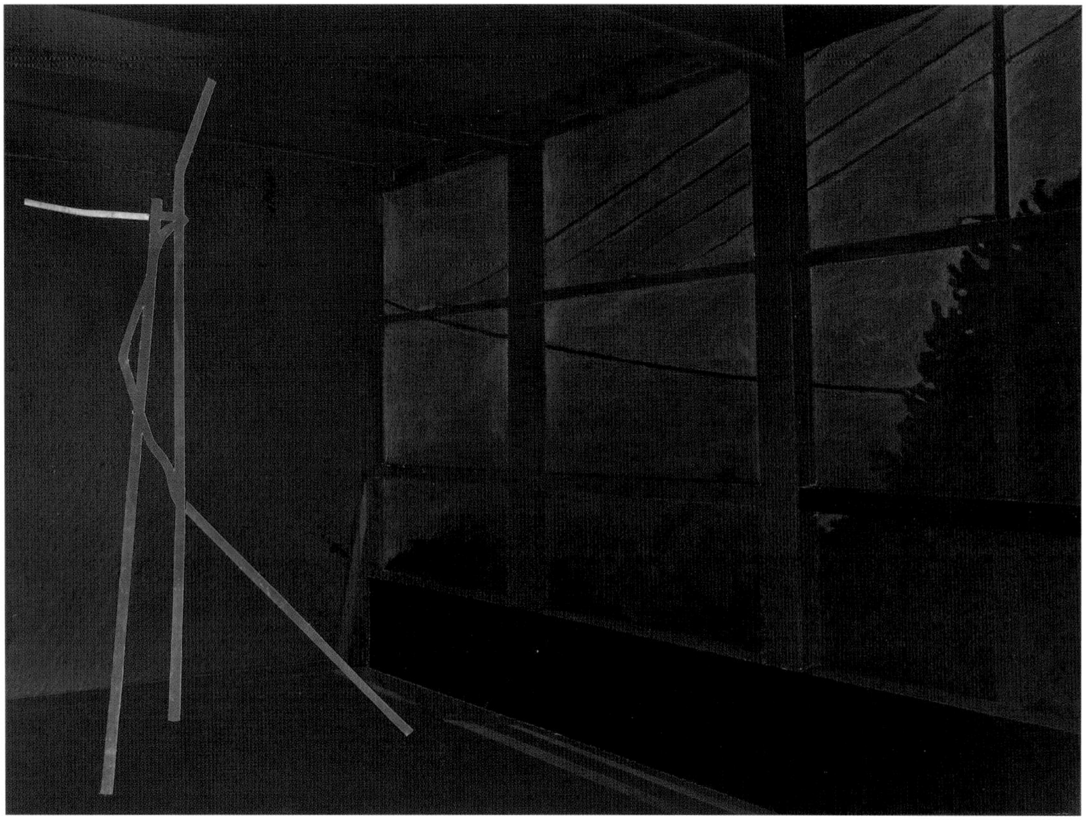

Untitled, from the series *Remanence,* 2008
Pencil on paper, pencil lead, lead, plastic, 57 x 76.5 cm [22½ x 30¼ in.]

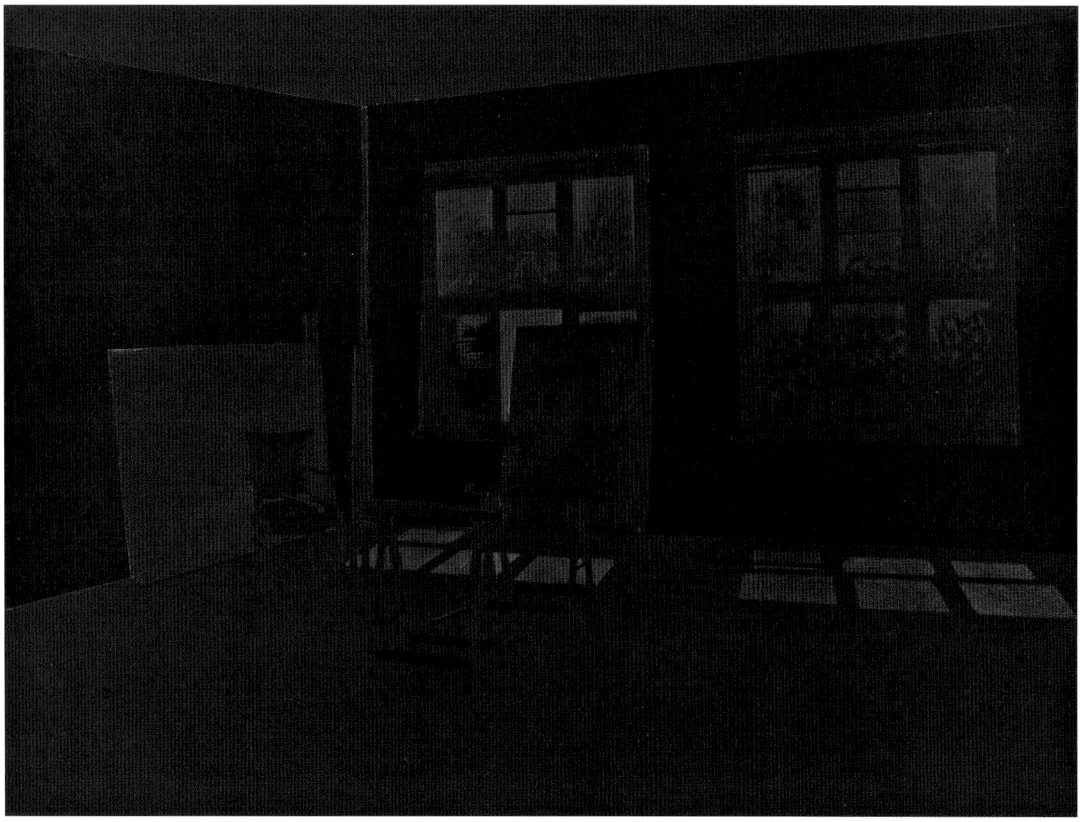

Untitled, from the series *Remanence,* 2008
Pencil on paper, pencil lead, plastic, 57 x 76.5 cm [22½ x 30¼ in.]

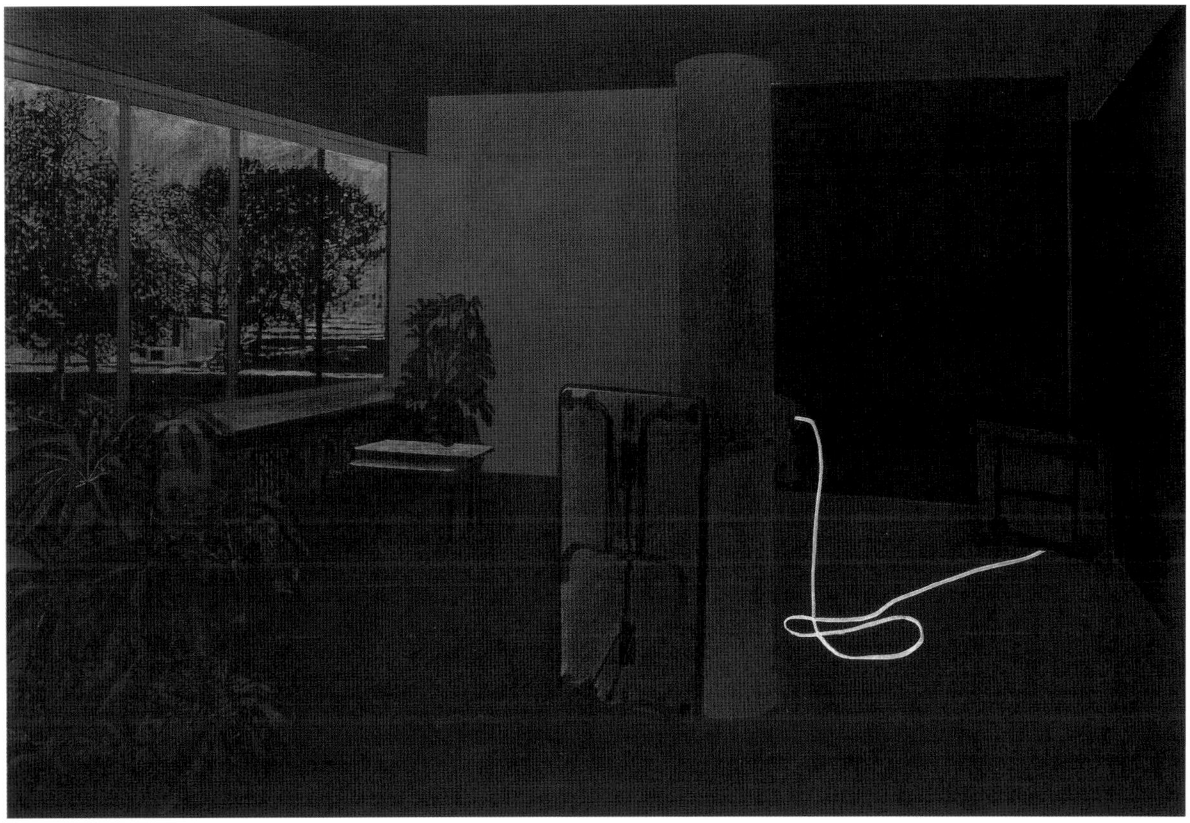

Untitled, from the series *Remanence,* 2008
Pencil on paper, pencil lead, tin, plastic, 76 x 113 cm [30 x 44½ in.]

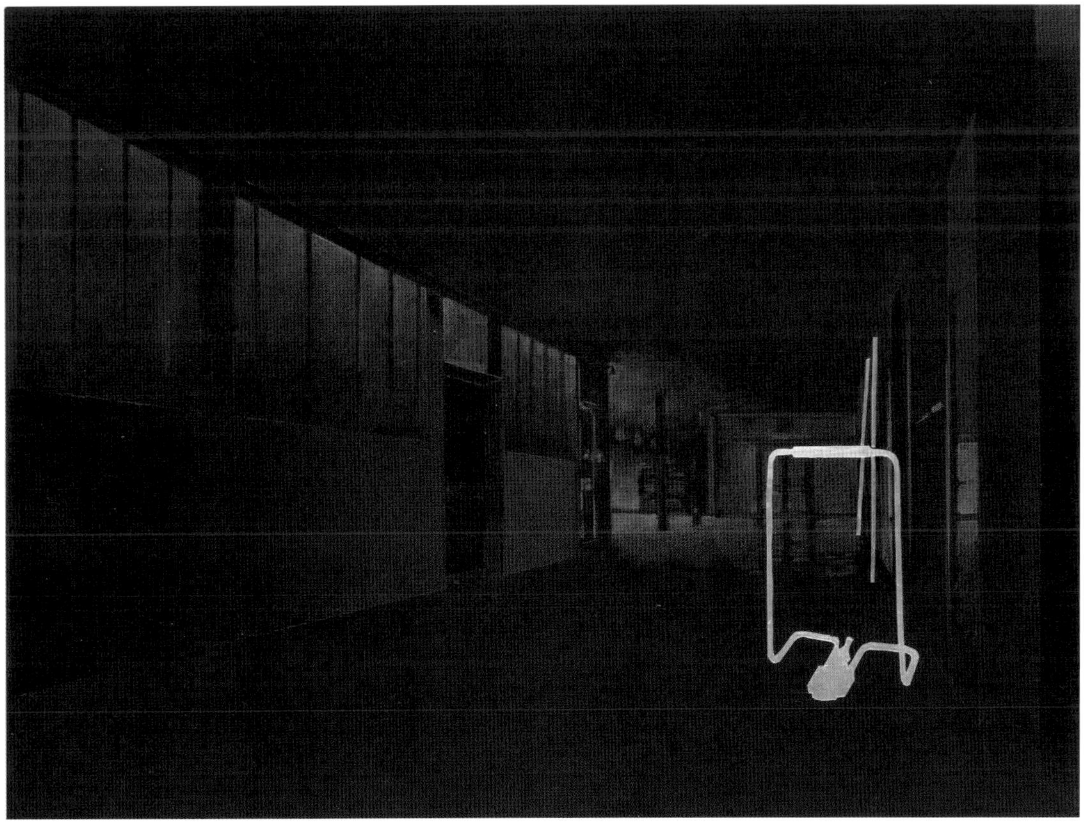

Untitled, from the series *Remanence,* 2008
Pencil on paper, pencil lead, tin, plastic, 57 x 76.5 cm [22½ x 30¼ in.]

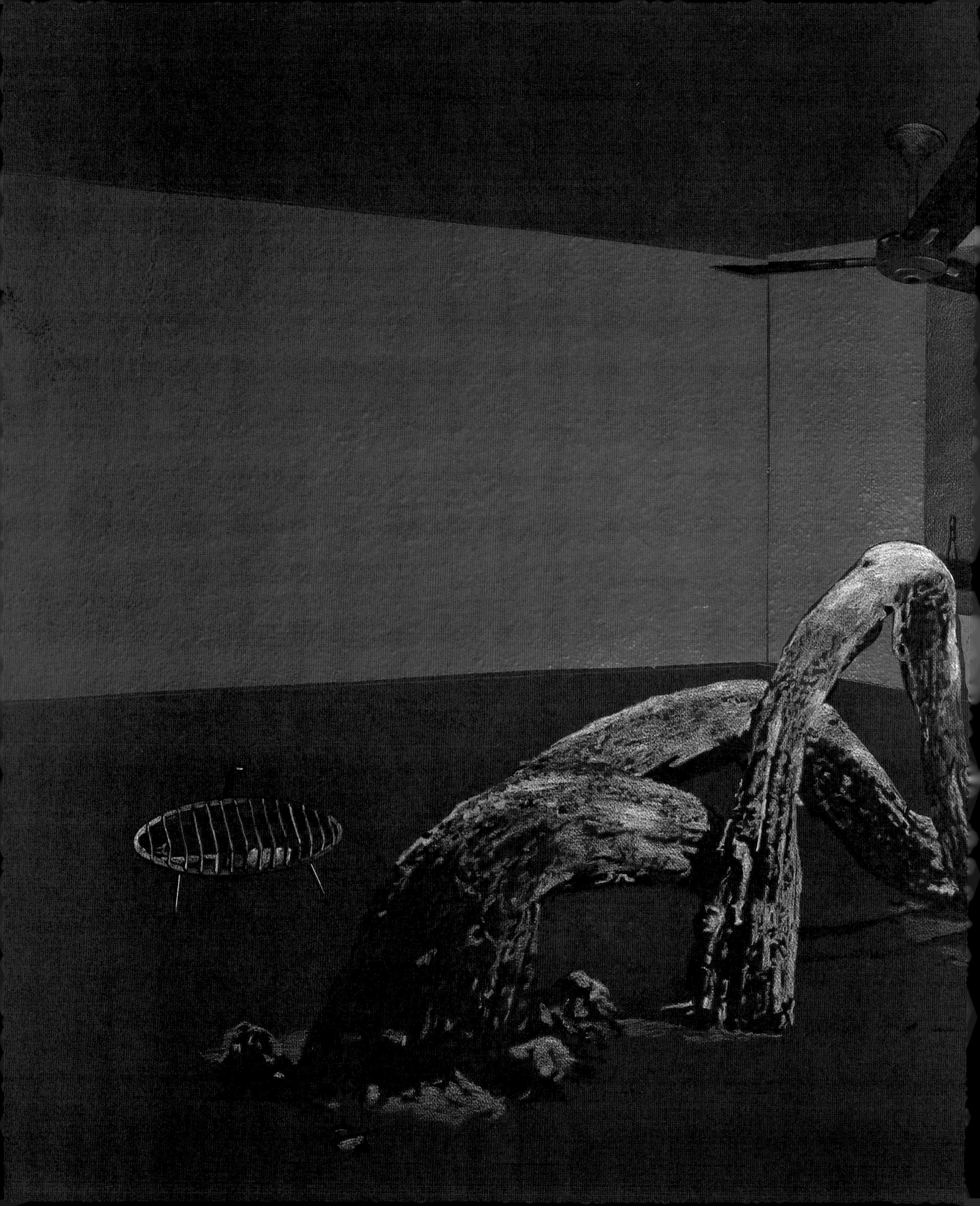

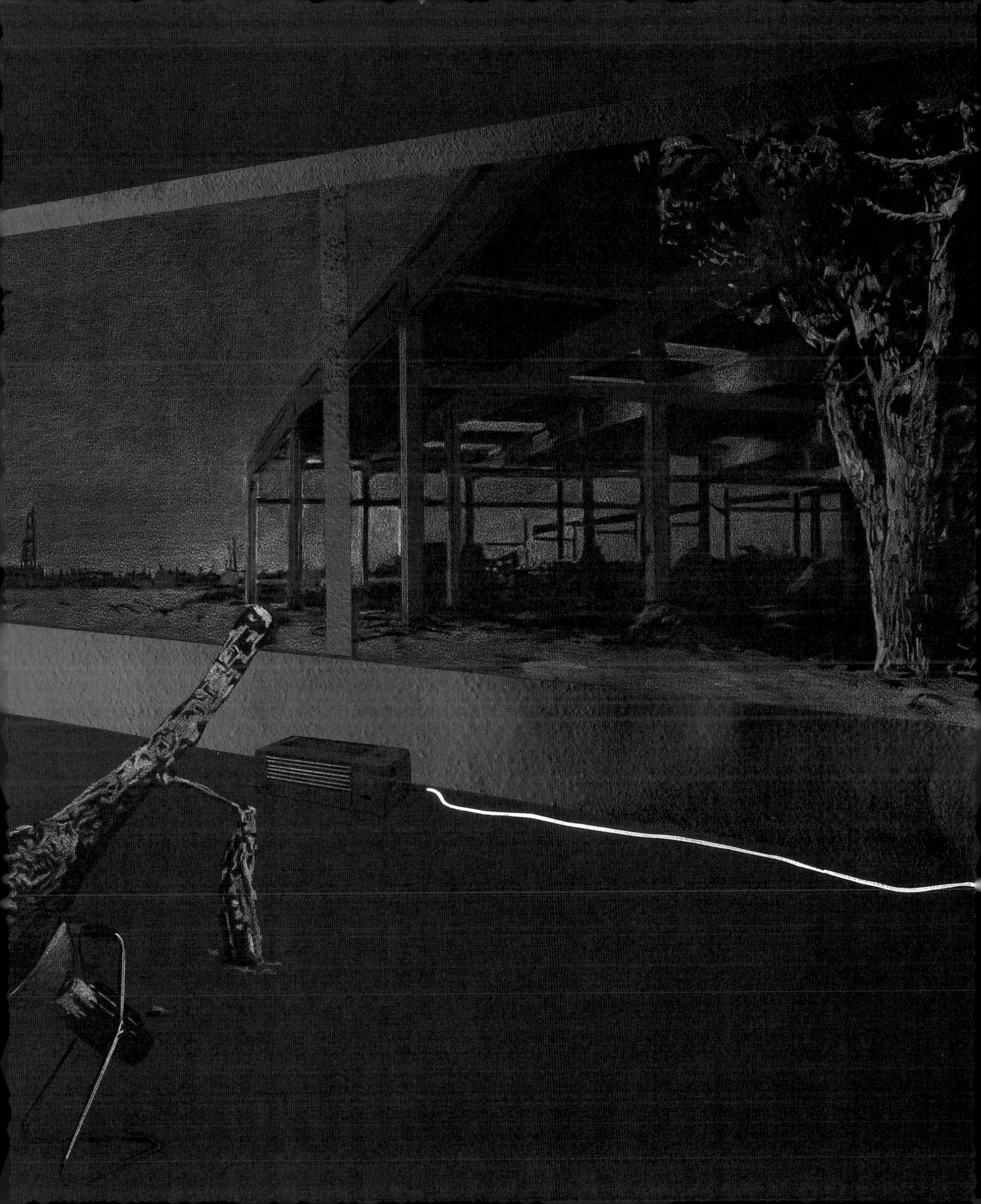

Previous pages:
Untitled, from the series *Remanence,* 2008
Pencil on paper, pencil lead, tin, plastic, 76 x 113 cm [30 x 44½ in.]

"BODY WITHOUT A FACE"

A conversation between Tatiana Trouvé
and Richard Shusterman[1]

1/ The interview was conducted in French.

RICHARD SHUSTERMAN: We met each other only very recently, in December 2007, and in no time at all, you suggested I be your interlocutor in an interview for an important book about your work. Your proposal enticed me, but it also surprised me by its spontaneity, which expressed a boldly impulsive mind, open to chance and risk. Your art, however, displays an extremely methodical spirit, full of deliberation. Your oeuvre seems to be governed by strict organization. For example, for 10 years (since 1997), your work has been structured around one central project, the *Bureau of Implicit Activities,* which includes several *Modules.* The terms "bureau" and "modules" evoke that spirit of extremely deliberate organization. What role do risk, chance, and impulse play in your creative work and in your artistic process?

TATIANA TROUVÉ: I feel the construction of a work demands that we remain exposed to any chance occurrence the work itself opens up for us, but also to the risk that the work might fail, succeed, or be wrong. Over and beyond that obvious aspect, which is the very essence of art, my *B.I.A.* was born as a project, both melancholy and bold, to give form to a feeling of disappearance or inexistence. The bold move was to build a space at whose heart that disappearance would not only be tangible, but also produce forms almost in spite of itself, against its own grain. I organize disappearance; I archive this void. What I invent is a kind of time that escapes our chronological measurements. By naming this work *Bureau* and grouping activities into different *Modules,* I was perhaps simply allowing myself to spend 10 years on it, and to help those years pass by.

RICHARD SHUSTERMAN: Does your apparent desire in *B.I.A.* for method—for organizing and classifying all kinds of implicit and forgettable elements in life—represent a critique of the bureaucratic compartmentalization of contemporary life, of its mechanical, exaggerated, arbitrary, and essentially false order? Is it perhaps even a *reductio ad absurdum* of the bureaucratic will that dominates our world? Or is your desire for order rather a way to compensate for the unclassifiable flow of experience? After all, experience can never be grasped entirely, and often it is not even conscious enough to be described and classified. I'm not necessarily talking about the Freudian unconscious. Even the flow of ordinary consciousness contains small, hardly perceptible, nameless moments of transition between those ideas that we can clearly recognize and can name and classify.

TATIANA TROUVÉ: There was both a desire to respond to a bureaucratic system using a logic proper to that system, and a desire to transform that response into an aesthetic experience. In 1995, when I decided to live in Paris as an artist, I started by looking for a job that would allow me to rent a studio or an apartment. The search for a job became its own full-time job. Rejection letters started to fill my mailbox. All of them started with "Madame, Mademoiselle, Monsieur, we regret to inform you," etc. I found it amazing that a rejection could all of sudden transform me into a man, a woman, and a young woman. This gave me the idea of writing cover letters and signing them with a specially designed stamp: "Madame, Mademoiselle, Monsieur, Tatiana Trouvé." In *B.I.A.,* I kept many of these rejection letters, carefully ridding them of all content. That boiled down to keeping that typical turn of phrase: "Madame, Mademoiselle, Monsieur, we regret to inform you . . ." Entire lists of regrets—regrets that, by accumulating, ended up negating whatever they were expressing. This was also the starting point for my decision to invent résumés, not by listing everything that I had already done in my life, but by listing everything I would never do. This "never" is absolutely irremediable, unlike many titles

Polder, 2000
Carpet, shards of glass, cement, wood, imitation leather, plastic foam, plastic, 35 x 125 x 85 cm [13¾ x 49¼ x 33½ in.]

Polder, 2000
Wood, plastic foam, fabric, paper, plastic, paint, 32 x 130 x 84 cm [12 x 51¼ x 33 in.]

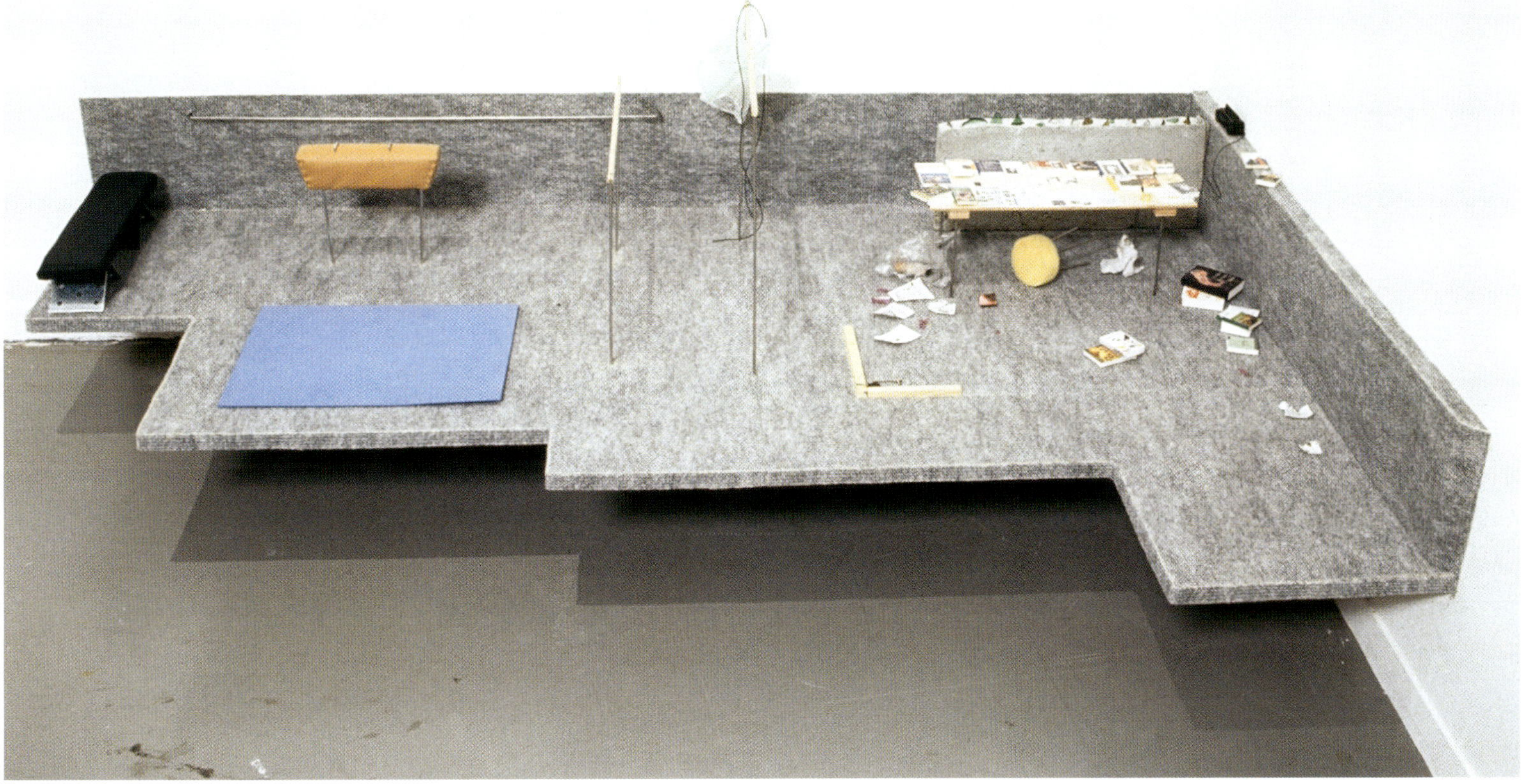

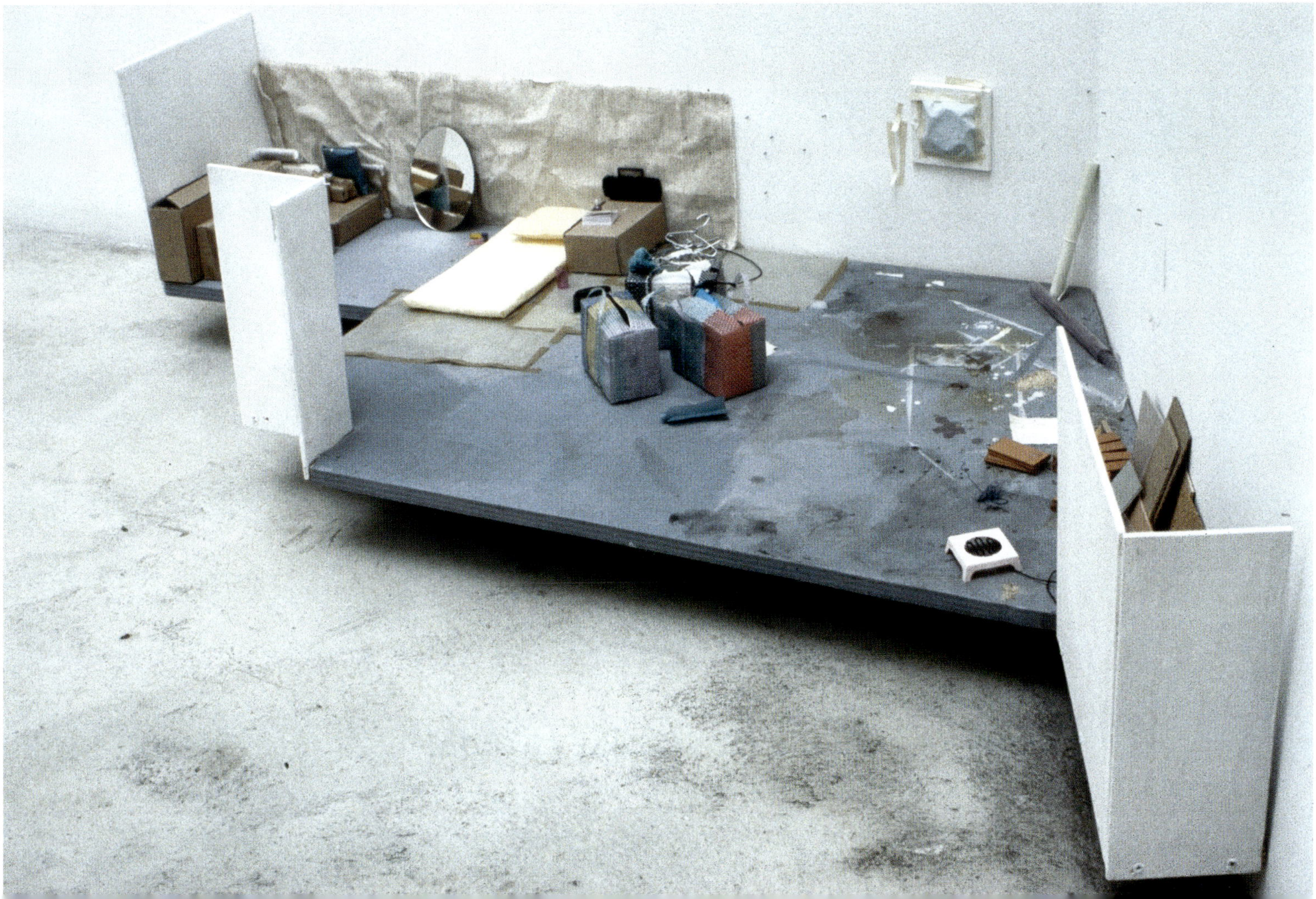

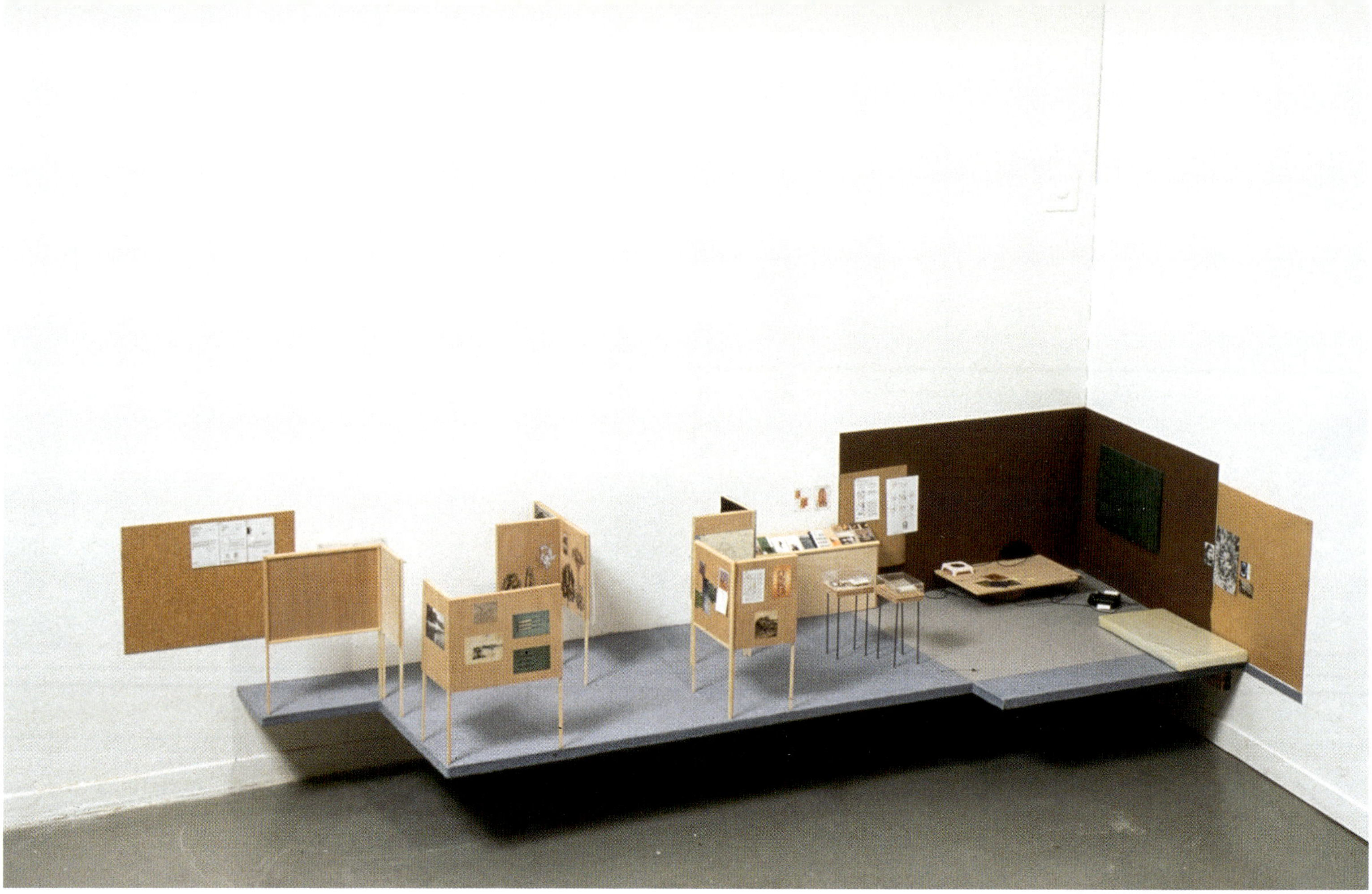

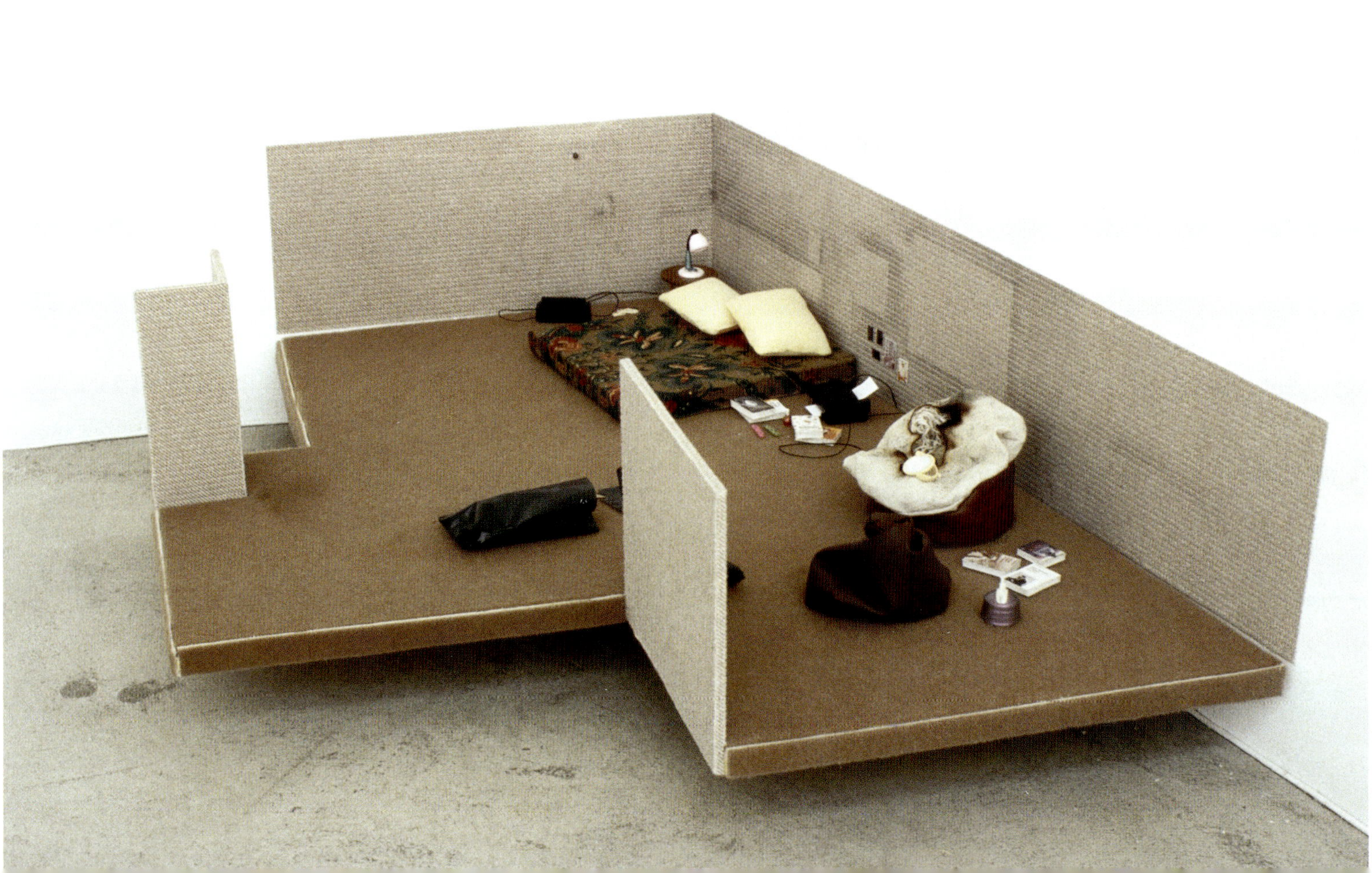

Polder, 2000
Carpet, wood, corkboard, plastic, metal, paper,
42 x 185 x 85 cm [16½ x 72¾ x 33½ in.]

Polder, 2000
Wood, plastic foam, felt, fabric, plastic,
35 x 105 x 73 cm [13¾ x 41¼ x 28¾ in.]

one takes on and subsequently has to prove. It's to my great regret, but I know I will never be a veterinarian. So I think the two aspects you've highlighted here have always crisscrossed through *B.I.A.,* because those responses to my situation in life had both social and aesthetic effects on me, because the response was fully and personally binding in my daily life, and because it involved a reflexive dimension. The *Modules* in the *B.I.A.* actually won out over other kinds of activity in which the daily dimensions of experience, like waiting, were directly implicated, with all that waiting also demands on the psychological level. How does the time we spend waiting construct us, what does it construct, and what elements of that time and that construction are we able to grasp? That's when I started working with sound recordings linked to my own experience of waiting, before constructing two *Modules* to be broadcast and an annex in which my archives could be consulted, and before finally beginning to collaborate with musicians who I asked to rework the available material and produce music for waiting.

RICHARD SHUSTERMAN: The notion of the archive seems to be a central element of your art, as does memory, which provides a guiding thread. One of your goals is to save ordinary experiences from oblivion, along with events, documents, and objects that might otherwise be regarded as worthless remnants from the flow of experience. Perhaps this artistic logic can be justified not only with respect to aesthetic interest, but also in terms of what it allows us to gain psychologically and cognitively: enriching our experience, making our consciousness fuller, our memories more extensive. But doesn't forgetting also have a psychological and cognitive value? And if it's possible to speak of an archive that isn't fully conscious, I also wonder what your relationship is to dreams and what role they play in your artistic process?

TATIANA TROUVÉ: My archives are somewhat peculiar and have developed on two different levels. On the one hand, they show that I'm not content with simply saving ordinary, everyday experiences—the flotsam and jetsam of our lives. The key is to conserve what is *produced* by some of these experiences: feelings, for example, whether related to glorious experiences involving success, or else painful ones associated with failure. On the other hand, my archives have developed as a way to conserve what produces the invisible movement where intuition can intervene, where an idea is formulated, before it assumes concrete form in a work, if at all. To my mind, that movement is powerful and essential. That's why I used to say things out loud—things I called "Secrets" and "Lies"—speaking the words into balloons, which I then cemented or froze and conserved in my archives.

In *B.I.A.,* I place great importance on forgetting, and I place just as much importance, in my life, on dreams, even if they don't necessarily intersect with my work. The unconscious element in dreams obviously helps me understand certain things about myself, without my feeling the desire to draw any magical formula from them, at least not in the surrealist and mechanical sense of the term. In contrast, I play much more readily with forgetting, primarily because I value its power to almost secretly organize and direct our existence. If I forget something, my mind does so because I'm then better able to remember something else; if I remember something, it's in order to be better able to forget the other thing: forgetting makes choices and affects selections in such a way that we could describe remembering and forgetting as two sides of the same coin. For me, forgetting has a creative charge. If I recall a party with guests and I describe it as I remember it, and then I repeat the same exercise a day later,

Polder, 2000
Plastic foam, paper, plastic, wood, 26 x 185 x 50 cm [10¼ x 72¾ x 19¾ in.]

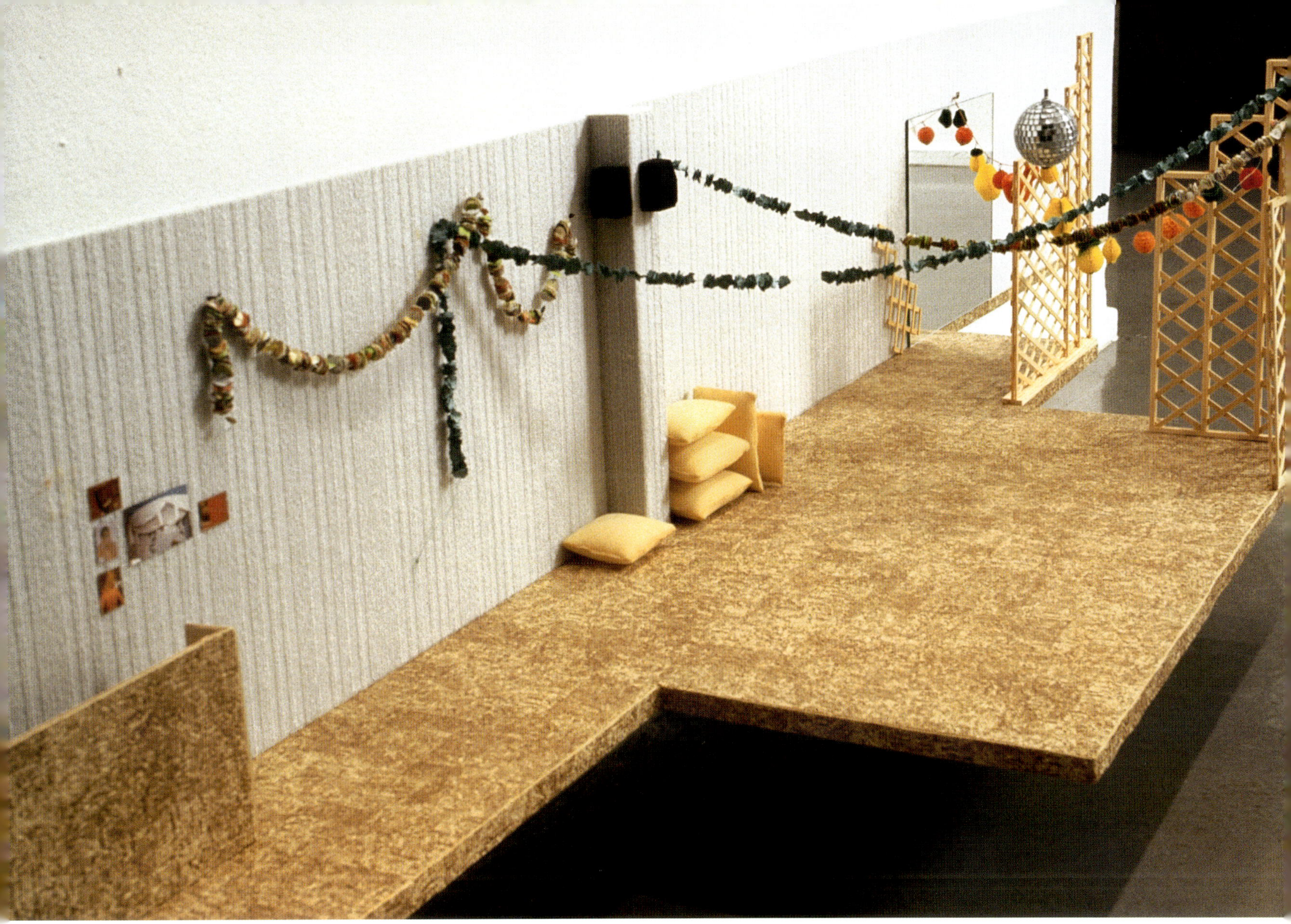

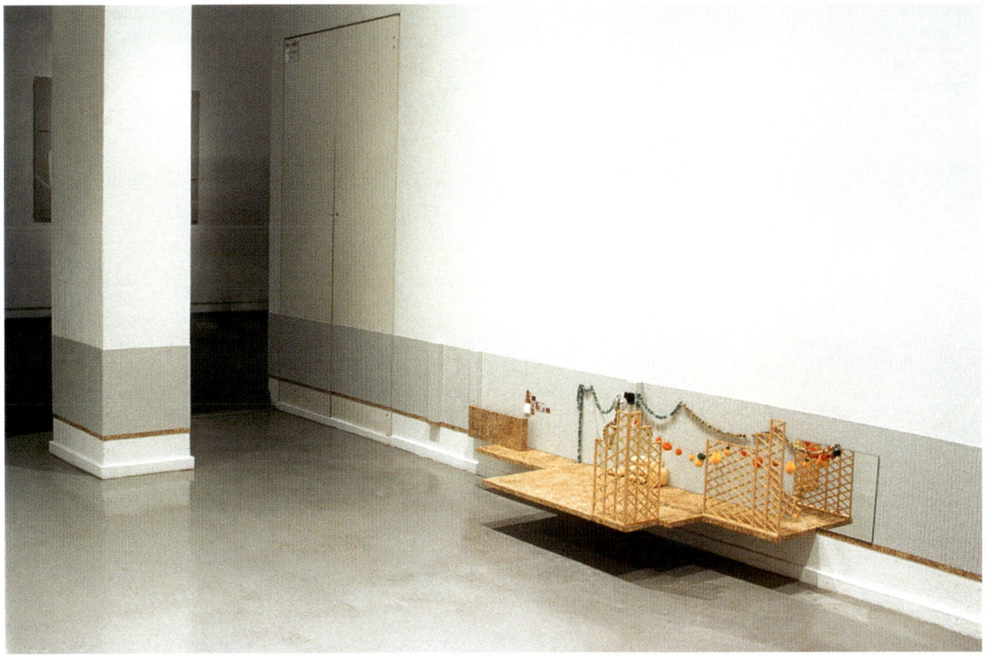

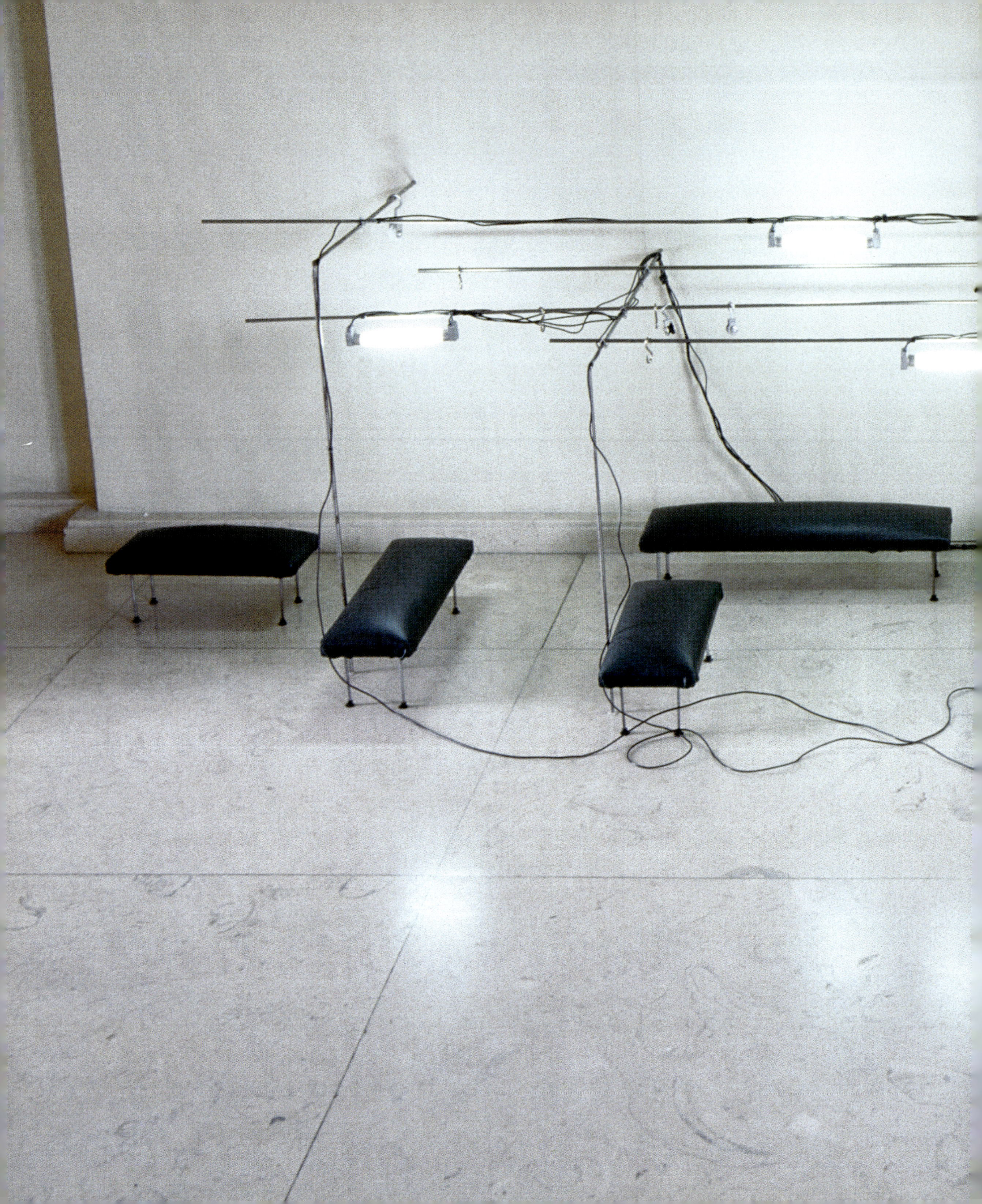

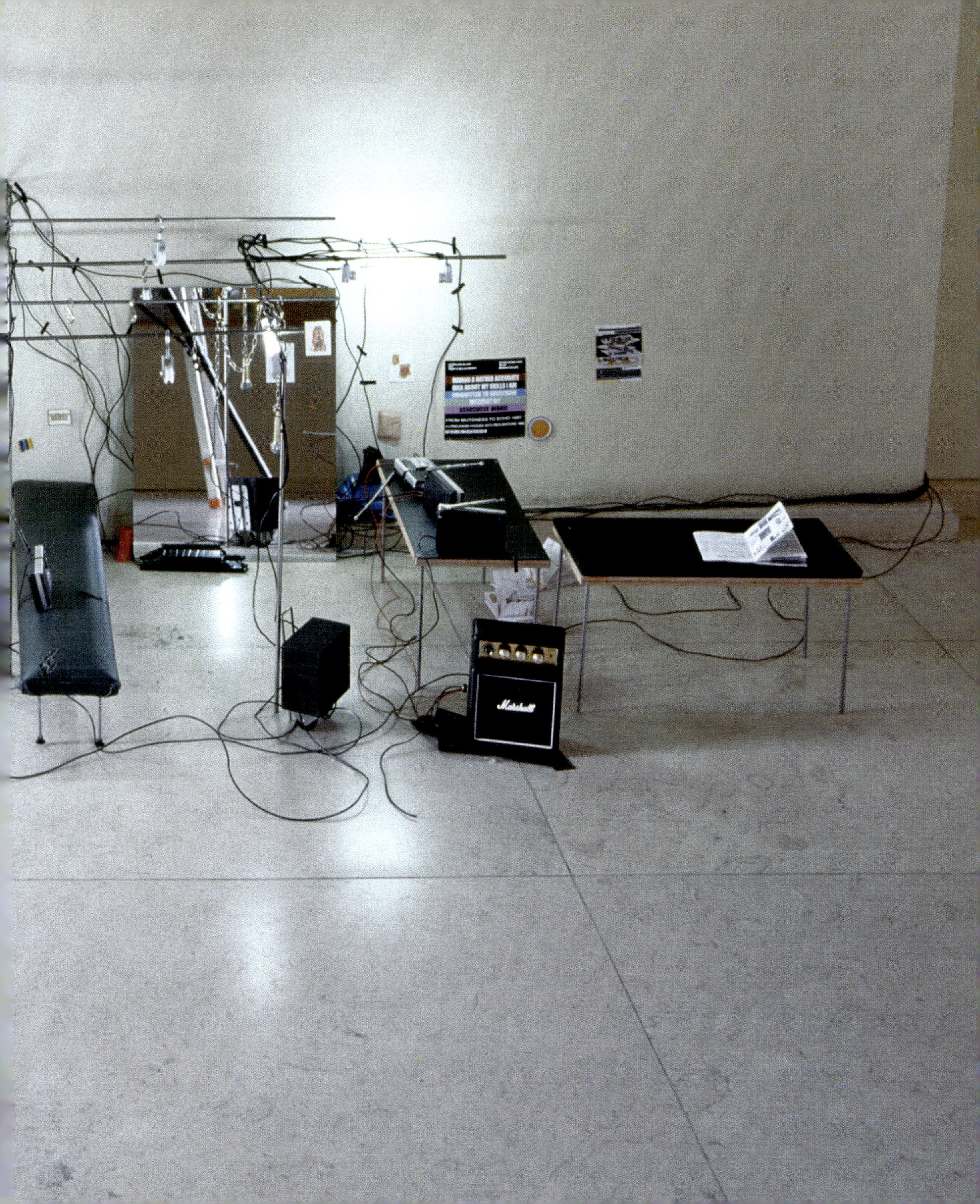
Marshall

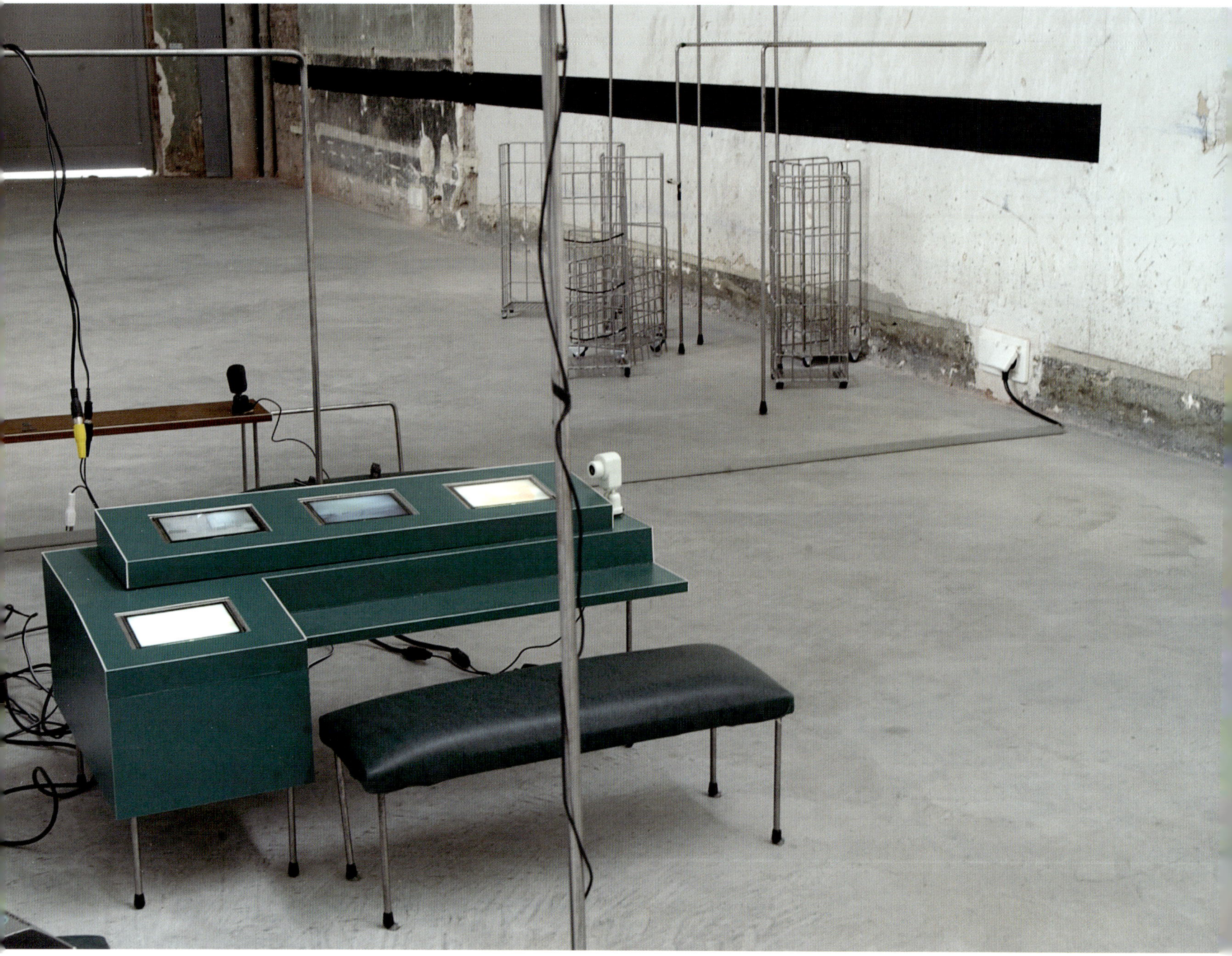

Previous pages:
Polder, 2001
Wood, imitation leather, metal, neon lights, mirror, mini-amplifier, radios, plastic foam, silicone, paper, 58 x 270 x 80 cm [22¾ x 106¼ x 31½ in.]

Above:
Polder, 2001
Paint, metal, mirrors, imitation leather, plastic foam, wood, chalk, plastic, video-surveillance cameras, amplifiers, rope, neon lights, 70 x 150 x 230 cm [27½ x 59 x 90½ in.]

I'll remember the party and the description I gave of it. However, if I continue the experiment, my first memory will gradually begin to merge with the various subsequent representations I've made of it, making facts that really happened appear as a kind of genre painting. This protocol implies that newness is one of the possible horizons of forgetting.

In *B.I.A.,* this operation is introduced in the *Sand Cell.* It's a little sand construction with a desk and chair. When you enter it, you find sand lying on the table, and there's a leather apron you have to put on to prevent the sand from falling to the ground. Everything you do inside this cell literally becomes a language, or discourse, of sand—inscribed without ever becoming permanent.

RICHARD SHUSTERMAN: Both in your interviews and in texts dealing with your work, you've often mentioned your interest in literature. *B.I.A.,* which you describe as the general matrix for your artistic creation, is itself described in terms of a project that has an underlying literary character. You also mention certain literary influences: Calvino, Borges, Perec, and others. However, I've never encountered any reference to philosophers. As a "professional philosopher," I'd be curious to know more about your relationship to philosophy.

TATIANA TROUVÉ: That's true. I described the *B.I.A.* as a matrix that has allowed me to produce multiple systems of creation and reflection. However, I didn't wish to assert that this matrix could reproduce, in its entirety, a project of a literary nature, but rather that, at several points, it might cross paths with elements and procedures identifiable in certain literary works. With these literary references, I was alluding to certain intersections with other artistic universes I think are particularly important. I've often taken the example of Dino Buzzati's *Il Grande ritratto* (1960), or else of Perec's *Les Choses* (1965). I also was delighted to discover Bela Tarr's films and Lynne Cohen's photography since they provided consolation for my universe. If both writers and philosophers have sometimes written about my work, it's yet again, I think, because of affinities most often discovered by surprise or through chance encounters. Talking and discussing things can lead to the desire to pursue a more elaborate conversation, and when the chance arises, I like to seize the opportunity. My relationship to philosophy is tied to these encounters and their ramifications.

RICHARD SHUSTERMAN: You sometimes speak of your artistic work of archives, representation, and doubling in terms of "fiction." In the philosophical tradition of the West, there's a strong tendency to define art as being contrasted to real life—contrasting the represented image to the thing itself, and verisimilitude to the truth. This opposition between art and life, like that between aesthetics and praxis, does not feature prominently in other cultures, for example in Asia or Africa. Couldn't one see your efforts to document real experiences—archiving real documents and sound recordings of real events—as a kind of epistemological labor? Does it express, in other words, a search for truth, an "art of living," in the sense of an artistic expression of the classical philosophical imperative to "know thyself"? I'm asking you this because your oeuvre and your artistic focus are often defined in close relationship to life, to your life. How would you situate your artistic project with respect to projects of caring both for the self and for the world? To put the question more bluntly, and in more commonplace terms, what are the ethical, social, and political implications of your artistic project?

Polder, 2001
Paint, metal, mirrors, imitation leather, plastic foam, wood, chalk, plastic, video-surveillance cameras, amplifiers, rope, neon lights, 70 x 150 x 230 cm [27½ x 59 x 90½ in.]

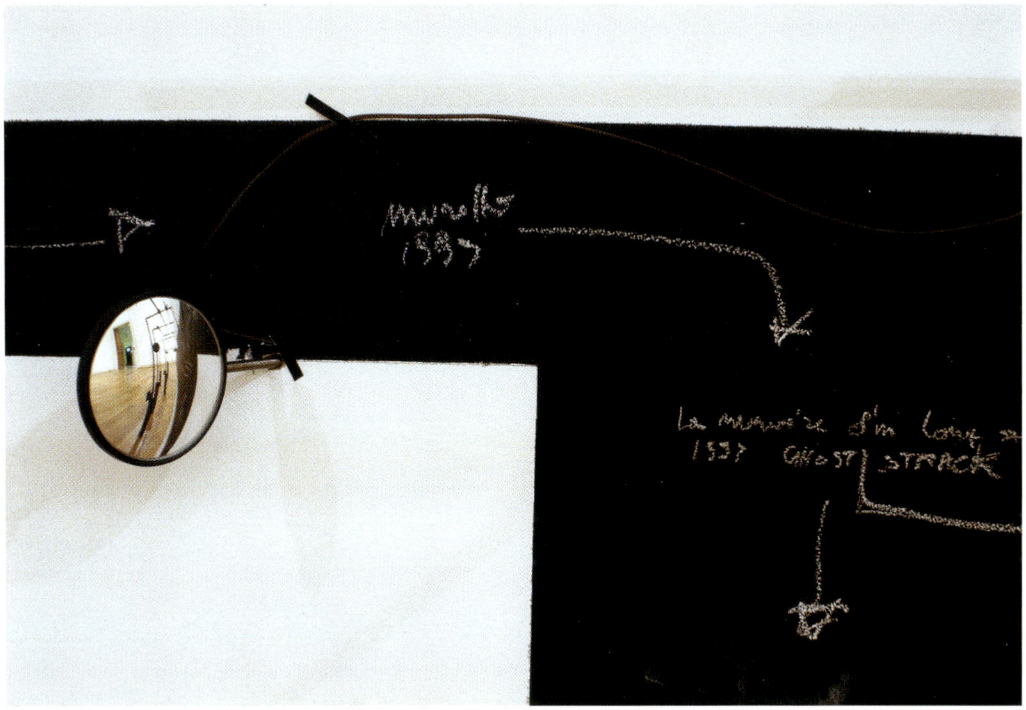
GHOST STRACK

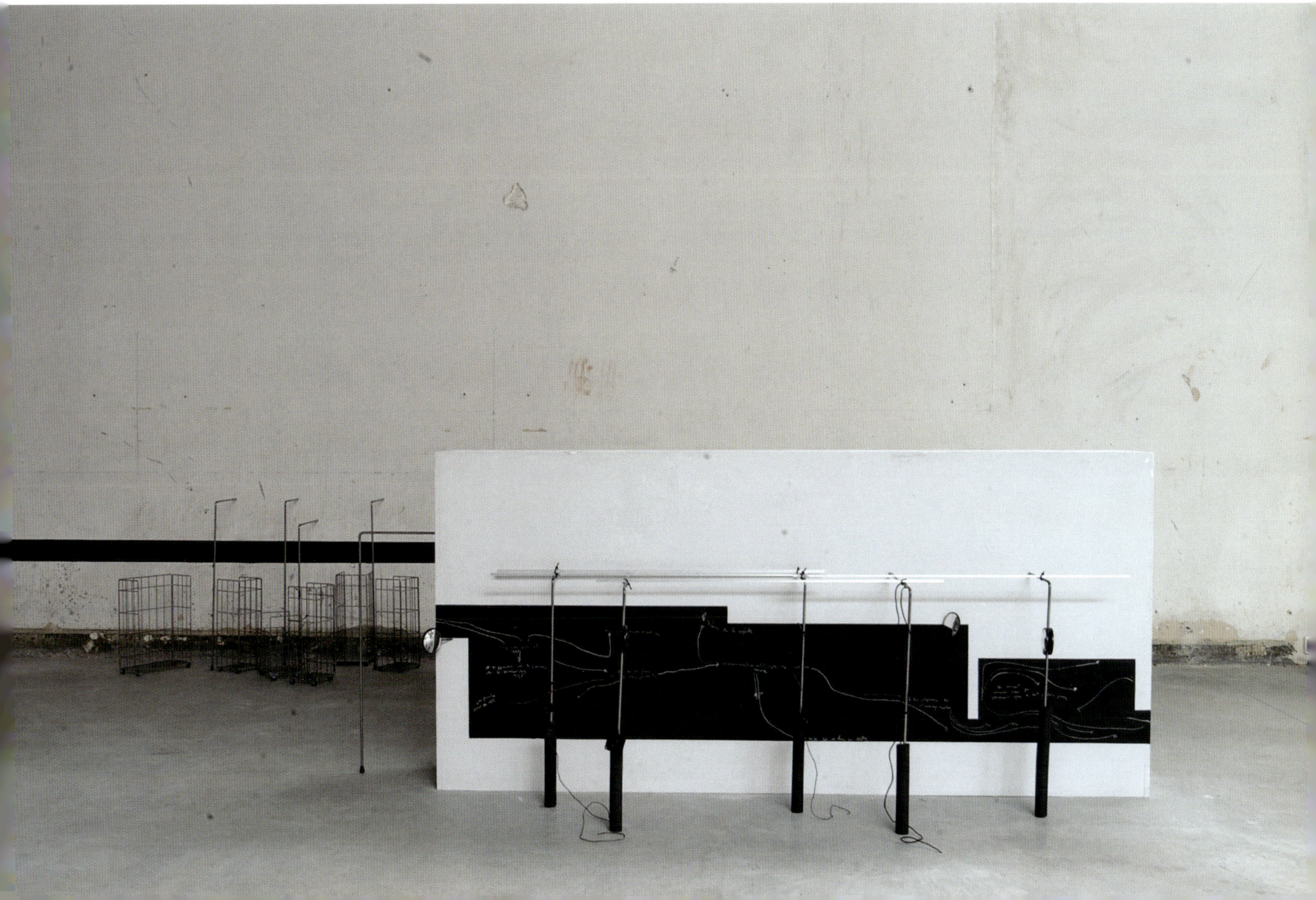

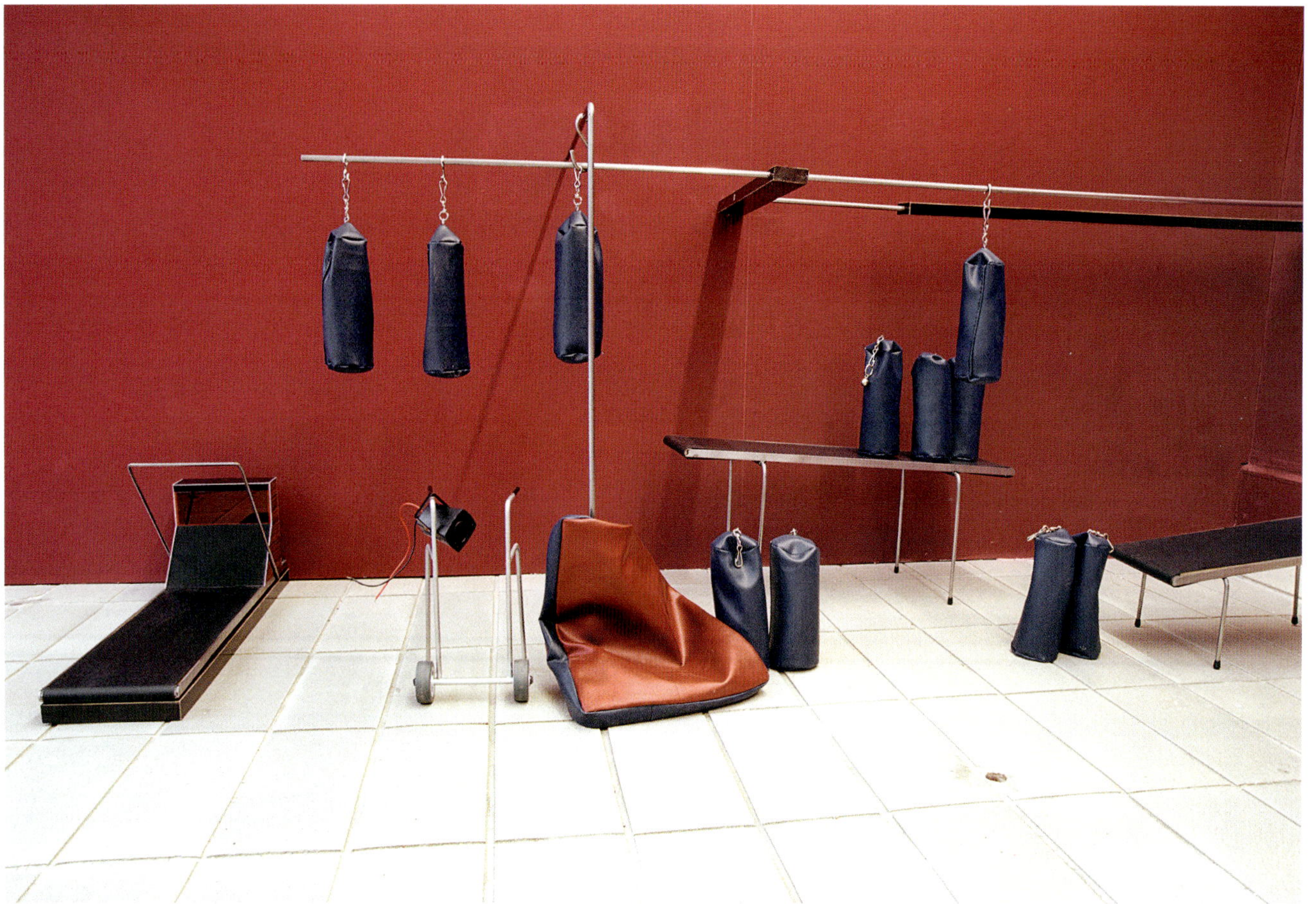

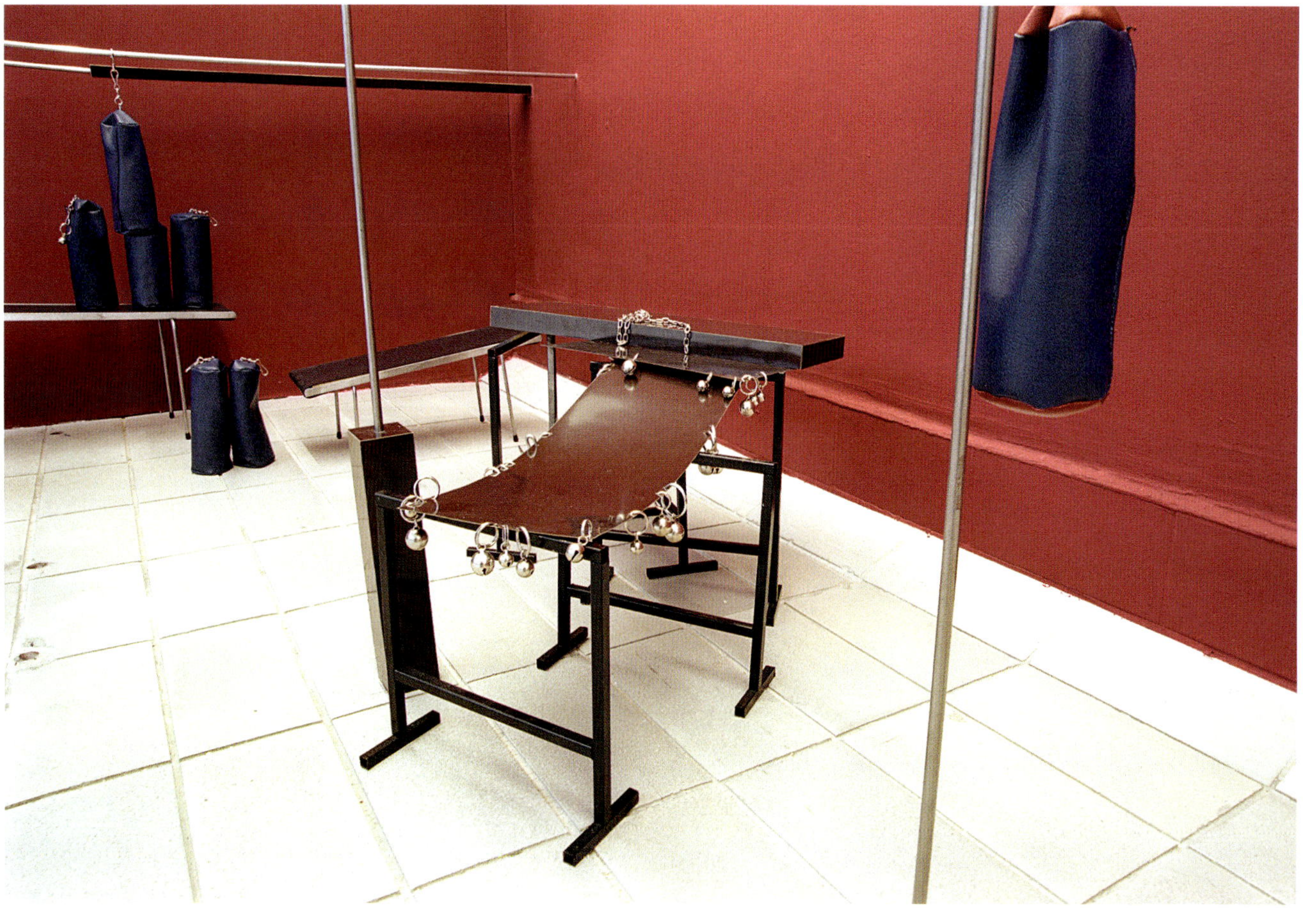

Polder, 2002
Paint, silicone, wood, metal, imitation leather, Bakelite, alarm siren, 120 x 215 x 117 cm [47¼ x 84¾ x 46 in.]

TATIANA TROUVÉ: I don't think my work belongs to the realm of fiction, even if, especially in the past, it does sometimes appeal to it. And although I gladly concur with your second suggestion, about knowledge of the self, I would speak of it without opposing it to forms of fiction. As far as I'm concerned, this relationship is expressed by a self-doubling that I have deliberately provoked. When I speak of doubling, I refer to the existence of two twin sisters—two Tatiana Trouvé's who take one another by the hand, encourage each other, and keep each other balanced enough to get things done together: one allows herself to follow her train of thought, while the other gets down to physical tasks; one gives in to the necessity of being quiet, while the other is convinced of the necessity of getting things done. At first, I brought about the separation in order to unify and organize my work: in a way, I had to be both the engineer and construction worker for the project I was undertaking. It went beyond the *B.I.A.* because this form of organization afforded me a lot of liberty in my activities. But this doubling never placed a living Tatiana on one side and an artist Tatiana on the other. No, the two are very much alive, and they are both artists who share the same world. I'd like to mention here that this doubling is an absolutely conscious strategy that has nothing to do with schizophrenia, as some people have sometimes hastily suggested. I therefore do not consider art to be on the one side and life on the other. For me, the two are essentially linked. But I don't think this relationship between art and life can be reduced to an "art of living," understood as the fusion of art and life. In the past, my work has sometimes been interpreted as an "art of survival," even if I have never proposed any methods nor given instruction to anyone in it. This art did not have the role of a manifesto. However, because elements stemming directly from social life were brought up, perhaps those who viewed my work were able to share my experience, perhaps they were affected or moved by them, and perhaps that was important for me. Although this doesn't give a social function to my art, it doesn't take any social dimension away from it either. Now that my works no longer offer direct links to the social, the implication is perhaps not quite the same. Actually, I don't think there is any more fiction to my current sculptures than there are love stories in abstract painting. But does that mean they're entirely separate from the social? I work with different forms of expression, and I use different experiences from my life. I've always concentrated on the spatial and temporal coordinates of those experiences as a way to create intermediate dimensions where these can be played out otherwise. My work's aesthetic and political commitment can probably be found within that field of research, which defines ways of world-making and ways of being in the world.

RICHARD SHUSTERMAN: You told me you redesigned your studio so that you could really live there to stay close to your works day and night. Do you have trouble separating yourself from your works, sending them to exhibitions, galleries, and collectors? The concept of project, which seems to be very important for your work, is essentially orientated towards the future. As indicated by its etymology, "project" means throwing forward. What relation do you have to your past works once they are completed and sold? Do you think of them as finished products or rather as elements or stages of a continuous project—temporary means for an ever-deferred and infinite end?

TATIANA TROUVÉ: I remodeled my studio so I could live and work there because, in a very concrete way, it allows me to stay concentrated without interruption over periods that are related to different projects. On the other hand, I have no trouble separating myself from my work. Quite the contrary, I think

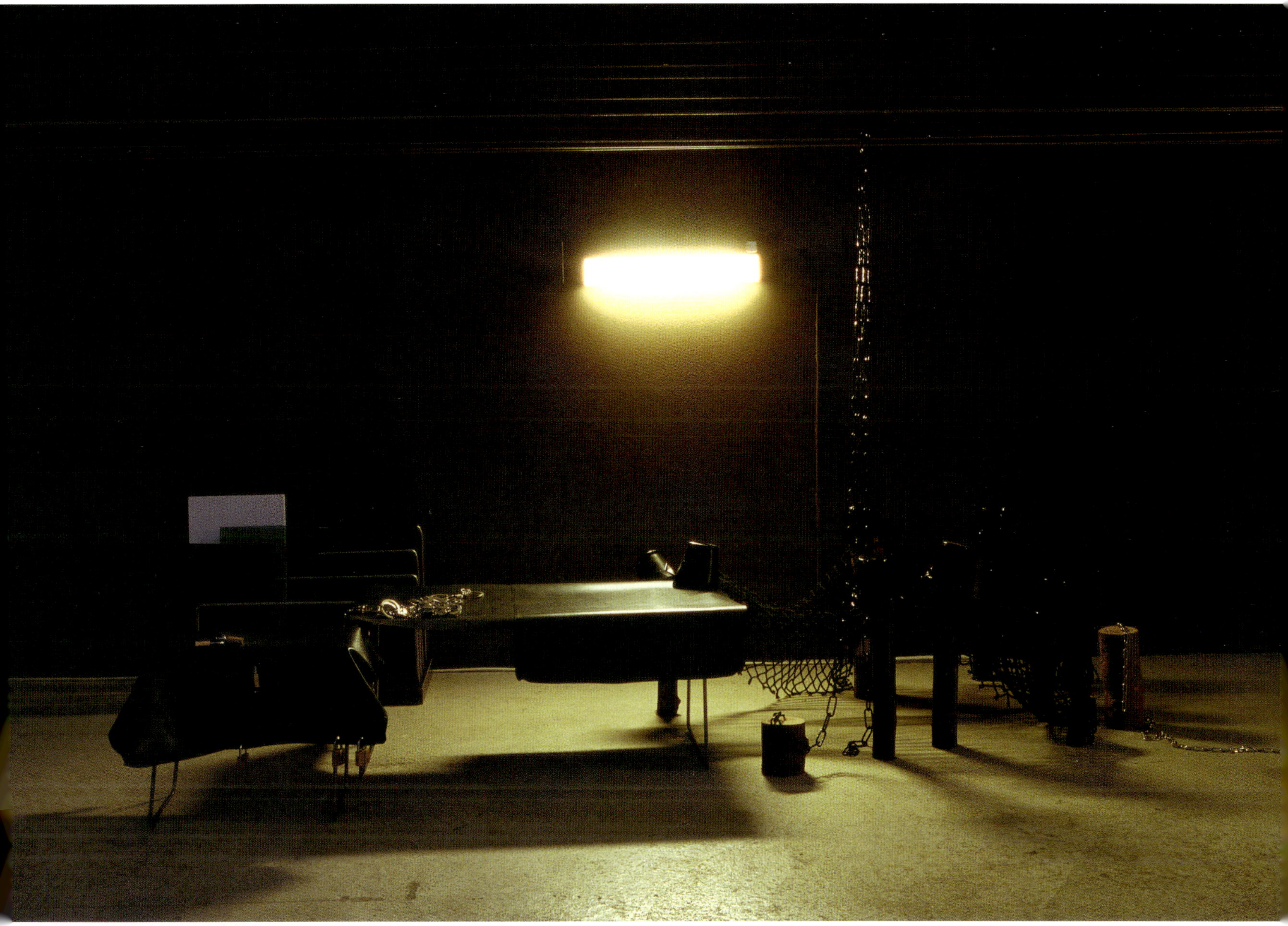

Polder, 2002
Wood, leather, PVC, metal, Bakelite, dried sausage, neon light, Plexiglas, silicone, paint, 120 x 600 x 80 cm [47¼ x 236 x 31½ in.]

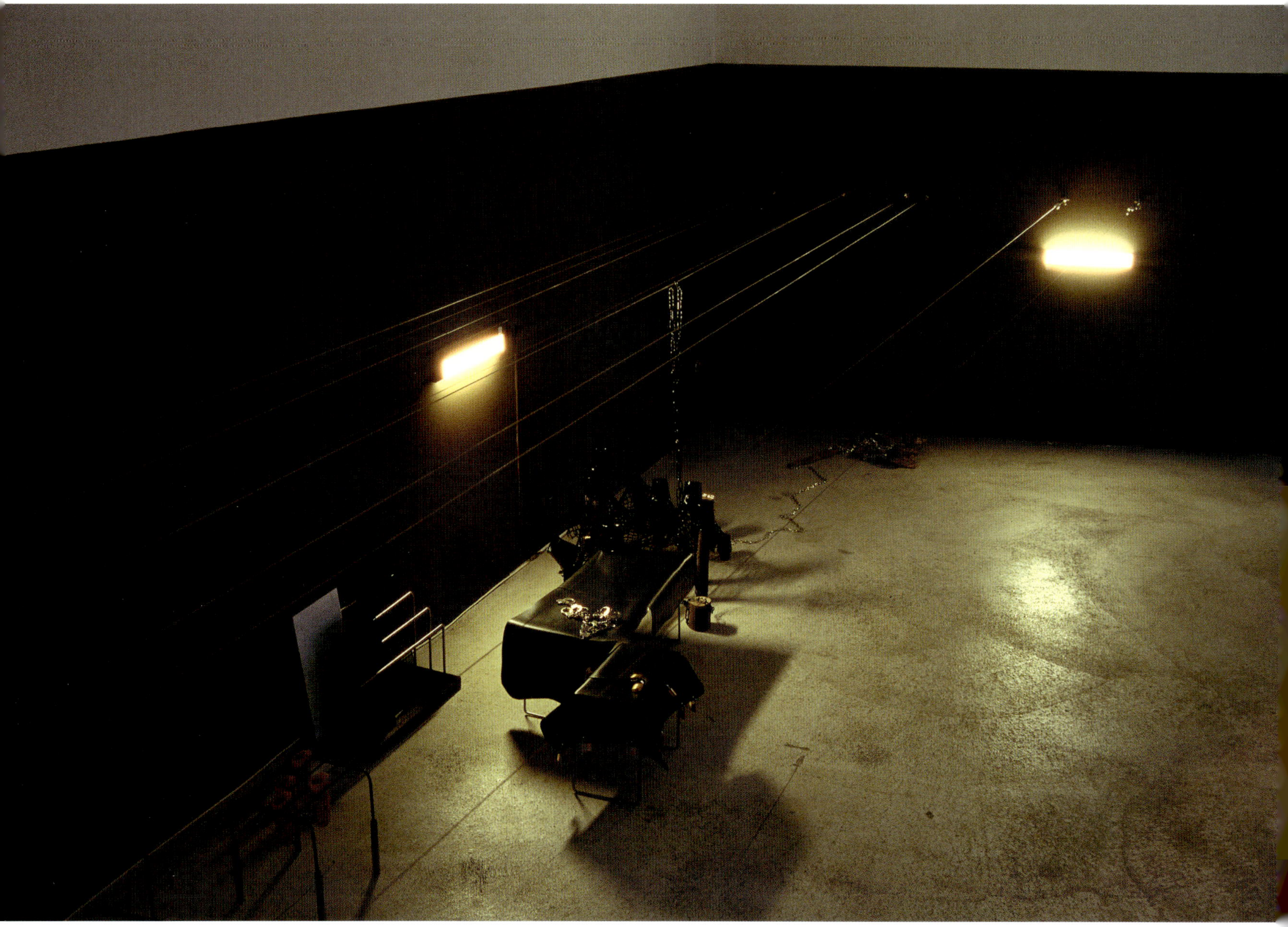

Polder, 2002
Wood, leather, PVC, metal, Bakelite, dried sausage, neon light, Plexiglas, silicone, paint, 120 x 600 x 80 cm [47¼ x 236 x 31½ in.]

that once things have been completed, they detach themselves from us of their own accord. The ideas and the media in which they are embodied are made to circulate, and I certainly hope that the people who own my work don't stop sharing it. If form is the sediment of content, then it only reaches its fullest sense in the experience it affords. The material separation therefore in no way brings about a rupture or disappearance. Works are enriched by our memory of them, whether of a form, a material, or an intuition. Sometimes we follow up on these memories and sometimes we don't. I don't keep works at home or in my studio, because it's important for me after an exhibition to return to an empty space that allows me to open up a new field of possibilities.

RICHARD SHUSTERMAN: You've mentioned that the body is very important in your art. Yet representations of the body seem entirely absent from it, even if a body is sometimes suggested in an indirect way (for example, in the exhibition *Time Snares,* at Galerie Emmanuel Perrotin, Miami, by a pair of shoes that can be seen behind a panel that doesn't quite reach the floor) or in a more analogical way (for example, again in *Time Snares,* through metal bars on which pieces of leather are corseted or merely hung, suggesting bodies, as in bones and flesh). Yet again, in *B.I.A.* and the *Polders,* the human body is essentially implied through the presence of mechanisms, projects, and archives that suggest an embodied subject who has to use his or her body to act, even for the most implicit activities. Elsewhere, you say that the *B.I.A.* is "comparable to a body" because of the fact that it is "modified by its growth and alterations." But I imagine that the role of the body in your work goes far beyond this model of growth and transformation. The body is the point that defines the subject's space; the body is also the basic medium for appreciating time and duration—the beating of the heart, the rhythm of breath. The body is also, of course, the archive of past time, and not only in the form of "muscle memory." Does body consciousness or, more precisely, *your* body consciousness play a role in the way you explore space, time, and memory—elements that are clearly important in your artistic work?

TATIANA TROUVÉ: All the hypotheses you've suggested strike me as important, and even very interesting, because they touch on my central concerns. They would, I think, provide enough material for an entirely separate interview. I'll limit myself to responding briefly to several of the points you've brought up. The *B.I.A.* is an architectural ensemble consisting of *Modules* on the scale of the human body. When it was exhibited, the viewer found him- or herself in the position of an intruder visiting a work site that had been abandoned by its user or users. Except for the *Modules* devoted to waiting, none of them were open to the viewer. The viewer is therefore the passive witness to an operative, but absent, body. The visitor is not a third wheel since he or she occupies the privileged place of the voyeur. But his or her body is not directly engaged.

The *Polders* are reduced spaces. They're too big to be architectural models, but too small to be usable. They put visitors out of step in relation to the environment they're entering. It's as if the scale of the objects were absorbed by the architecture that houses them, as if the forms of the objects had been absorbed by the material that composes them. The doors are sunk into the walls, and objects are frozen while apparently in the midst of falling, as if the emptiness of these spaces, their alterations and densities, created a recessed body. I could reverse your proposal that "the body is the point that defines the subject's space." In my work, where there is effectively no representation of the subject, space constructs the body of a potential subject.

I remember reading a story told by a dwarf about how he lived. He explained why he had decided to take on the manners and dress of a tourist. He talked about a relationship to space and architecture, affirming that tourists are visitors to a world to which they do not belong, through which they pass only to disappear, and from which they bring souvenirs back home. This dwarf had therefore constructed his life by taking note of a relationship to a space and a world in which the proportions of objects kept him from having an active life: in this world, it was no longer worth living except as a tourist. This could be a metaphor for the experience I'm offering the viewer.

RICHARD SHUSTERMAN: You sometimes seek to express and create aesthetic experiences that are troublesome in some way, experiences of disquiet (or "intranquillité," to refer to one of your titles). Your central image of the bureau is far from signifying a space of pleasure or an architecture designed for beauty: it's neither a beach nor a palace. But even if one finds an ascetic aspect in your work, this does not exclude the fact that there is also room for the beautiful and the pleasurable—because there is no real conceptual contradiction between asceticism and aestheticism, between discipline and pleasure. What is your relation to pleasure and the beautiful in art?

TATIANA TROUVÉ: If the *B.I.A.* provided the "central image" for all of my work, I think it has evolved. It has been in existence for 10 years now and engendered different *Modules* in which certain activities were developed. The *Polders* were part of one of my three "archives," and at that point it was a matter of reconstructing places in which I'd lived or something had happened: they were reconstructions of space and memory in the form of models. There was something very strange about them, no doubt because of the approximate way that memory interprets situations and places. That exercise subsequently engendered and developed increasingly large productions that my archives were soon no longer able to contain. The *Polders* ended up leaving the *Modules* and started to colonize the ensemble of the *B.I.A.* to such an extent that they ended up burying it and proliferating in exhibitions. Currently, even I no longer know if, when I do an installation, it's still a *Polder.* It is certainly true, though, that I have not realized a *B.I.A. Module* since 2003. In a way, it ended up disappearing into what it had produced. That disappearance is an expression of beauty: for me, the beautiful comes from the association of a form with a concept. We could say that the *B.I.A.*'s beauty is expressed in its very disappearance, which is also its completion. I also think of that poem by Baudelaire, who falls in love with a passerby that he sees only for a moment or two, since his desire for her is associated with the melancholic feeling of her irrevocable loss. Pleasure, here, cannot be dissociated from the ephemeral. I don't think beauty is strictly a matter of form, whether it be the form of beaches, coconut trees, or hospitals.

RICHARD SHUSTERMAN: To understand works of art, but also to sell them, there's a recurring tendency to identify artists with movements or specific artistic groups, or with national fields and traditions. What do you, whose experience is so international and transcultural, think of the artist's passport? You were born in Italy of an Italian mother and a French father, you lived in Dakar, in Africa, between the ages of eight and 15, and you studied art in France and Holland before returning to France to work. You don't seem especially eager to be labeled as a "French artist," and you say quite explicitly that "these identifications or geographic or cultural identities do not apply to what I put into place, just as I don't think that

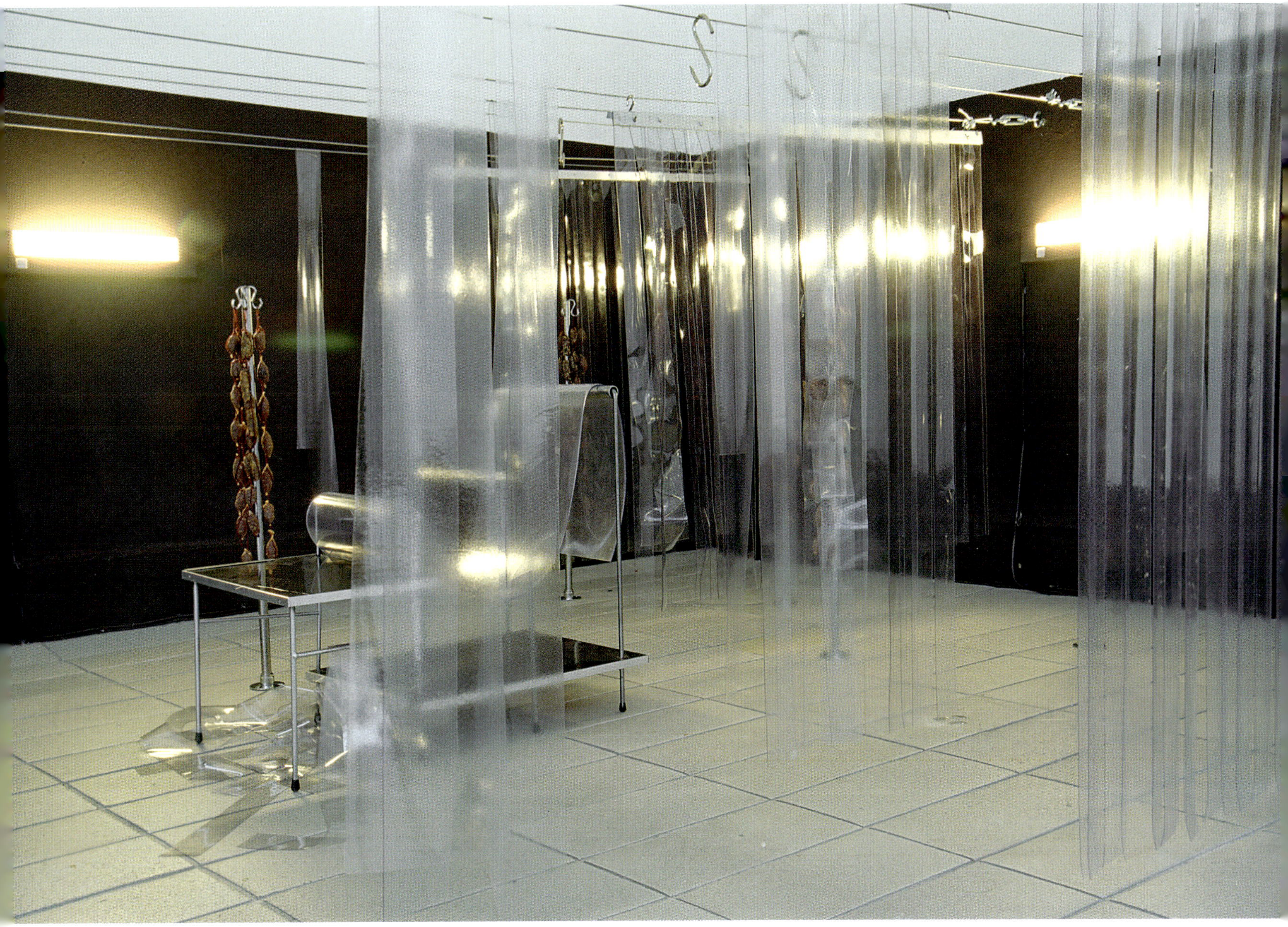

Polder, 2002
Wood, leather, PVC, metal, Bakelite, dried sausage, neon light, Plexiglas, silicone, paint, 120 x 600 x 80 cm [47¼ x 236 x 31½ in.]

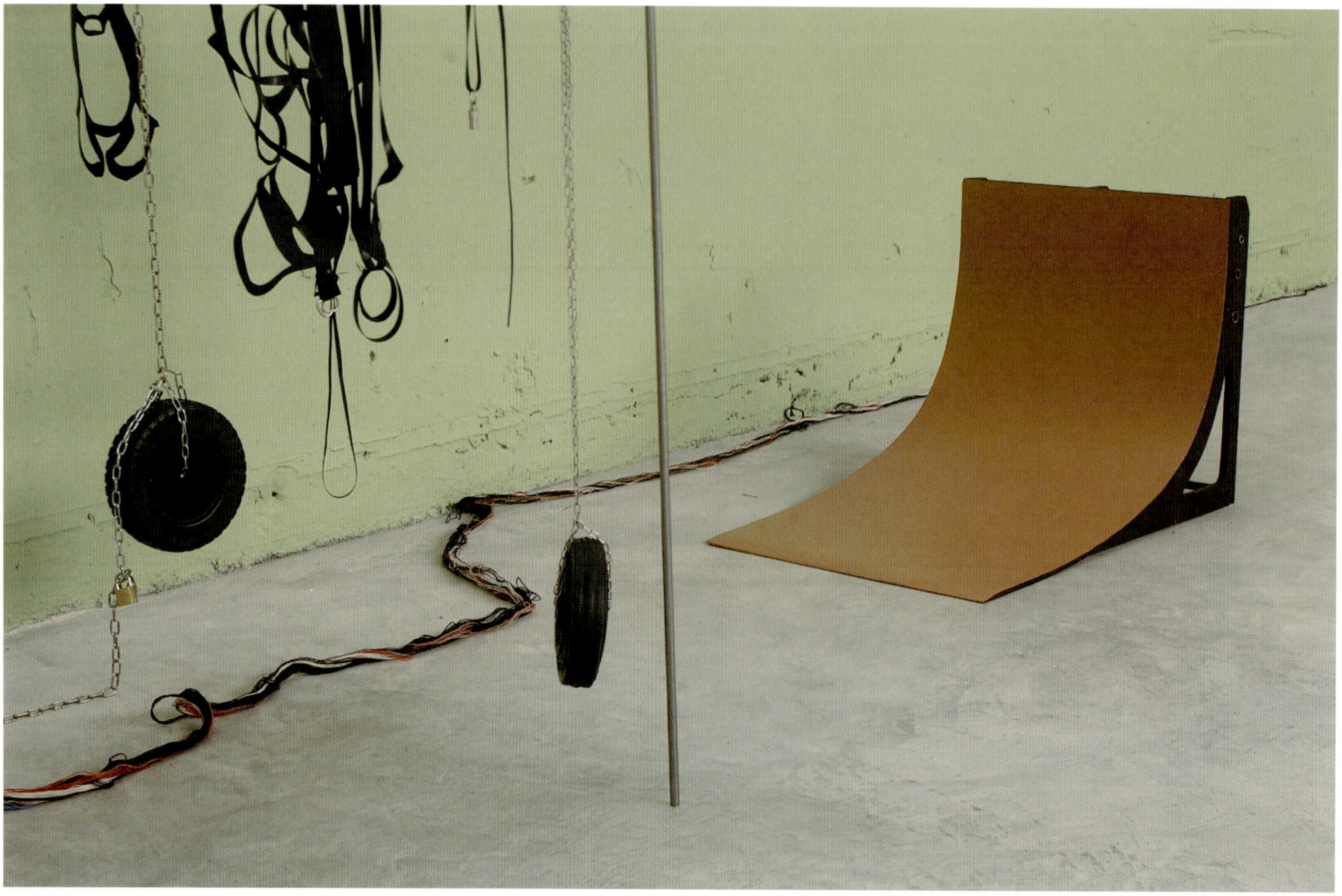

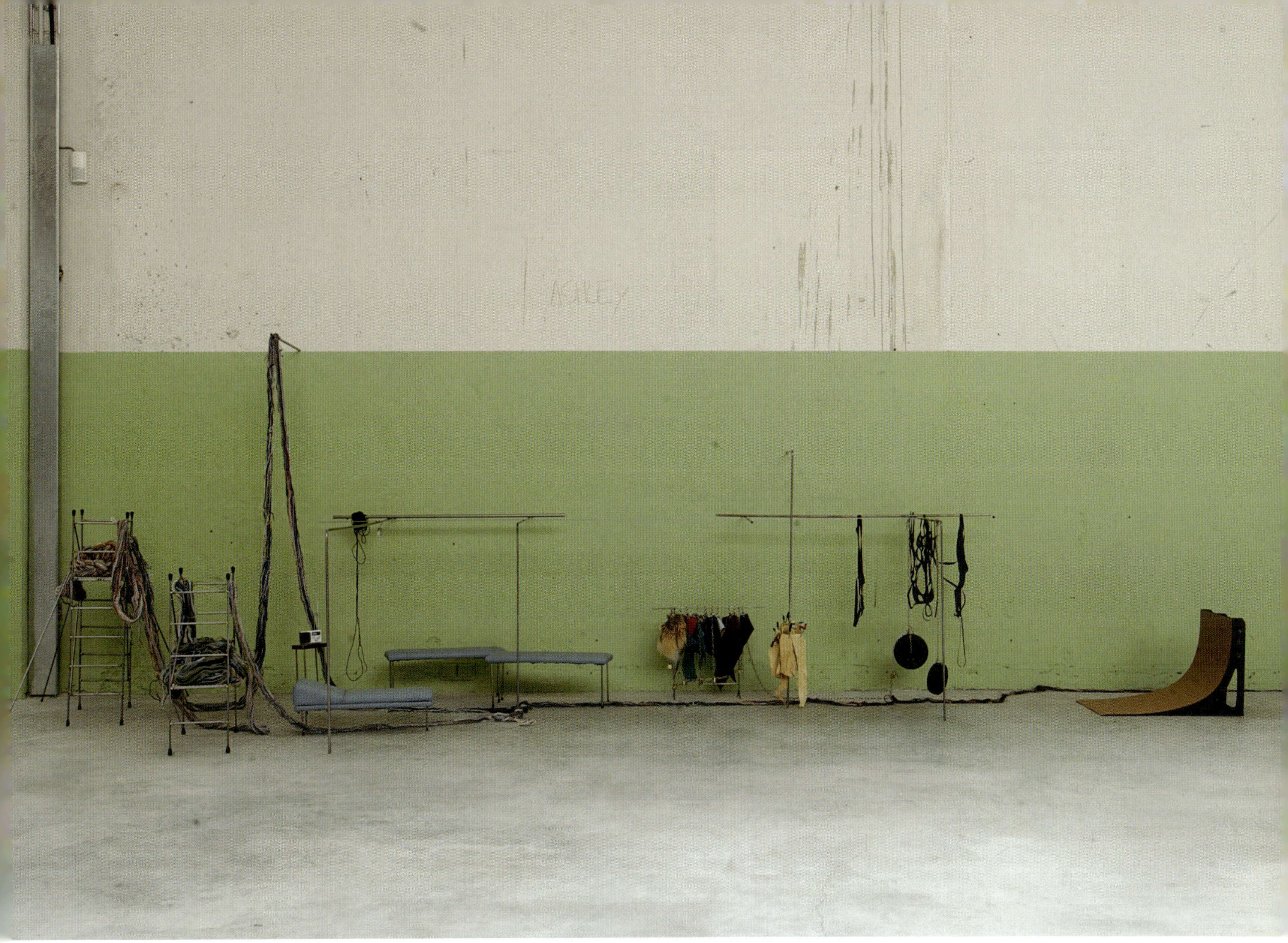

Polder, 2002
Paint, imitation leather, rubber, metal, plastic, wood, radio, fur, plastic foam, wool,
150 x 500 x 160 cm [59 x 197 x 63 in.]

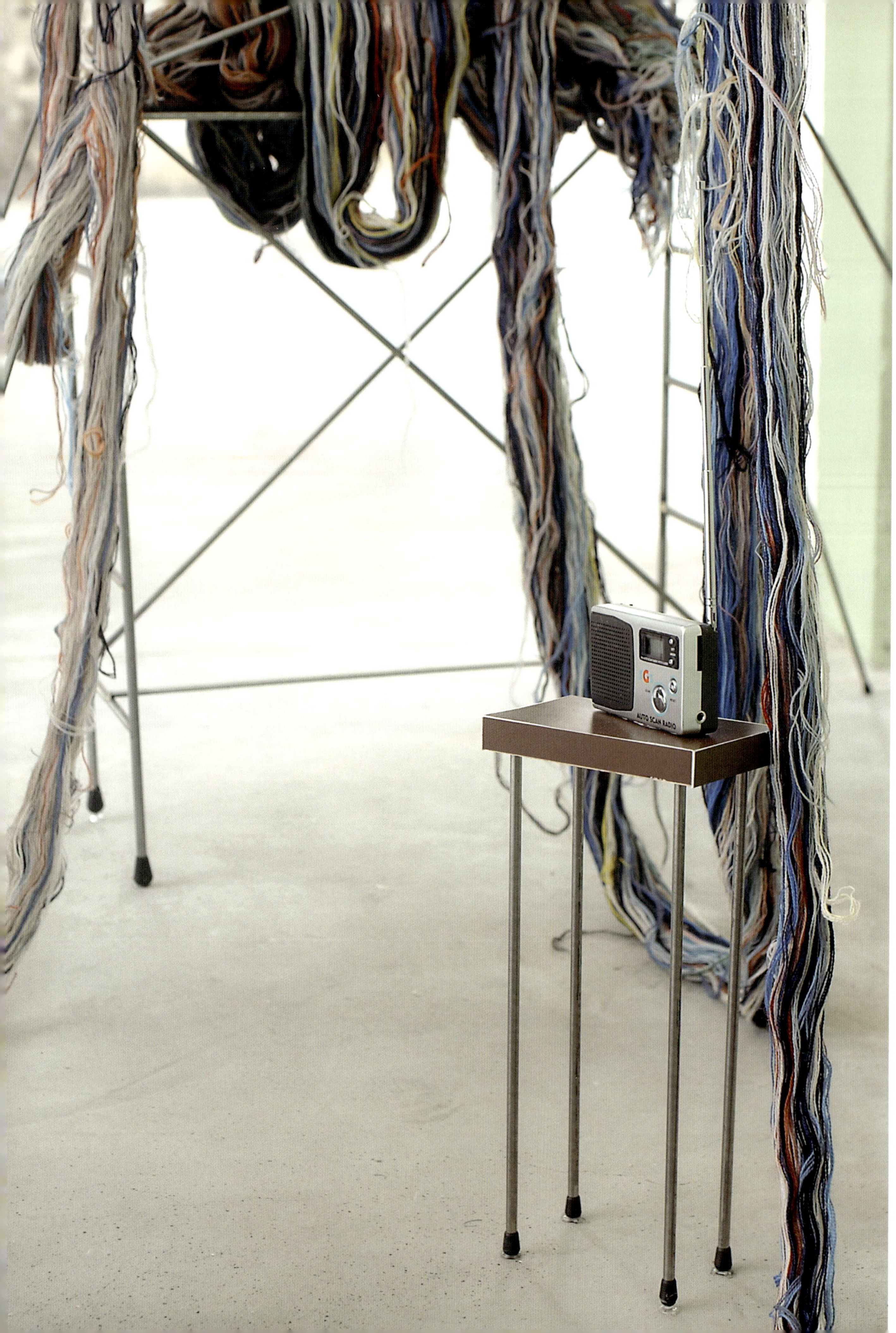
AUTO SCAN RADIO

Polder, 2002
Paint, imitation leather, rubber, metal, plastic, wood, radio, fur, plastic foam, wool, 150 x 500 x 160 cm [59 x 197 x 63 in.]

they are the motivation for my personal experiences." Your words remind me of Wittgenstein's remark: "A philosopher is not a citizen of any community of ideas. That is what makes him a philosopher." In your opinion, does the artist have to renounce all communities of thought, all cultural identifications to preserve his or her creative freedom?

TATIANA TROUVÉ: I don't think an artist has to renounce all communities of thought and cultural identifications, but I also don't think he has to see himself as a part of any particular one of them, or to submit to their laws and become a "citizen" of them, as Wittgenstein suggests in that beautiful quotation. Many of my contemporaries work with the idea of strict communitarian, cultural, ethnic, or sexual belonging. The identification of art with communities of thought or culture is one way that art works, and it has been at the center of artistic production for some time. Indeed, it has long since become a legitimate element of the art world, and it responds to the demand for new objects of desire. I fully agree with Wittgenstein's remark, but doesn't that already inscribe me in a new community?

RICHARD SHUSTERMAN: Like philosophers, artists are supposed to improve in their work through the maturity of age. How do you see your future artistic development? Do you already have plans for the work to come after your current projects? Are there subjects, media, or cultures that you would particularly like to explore and incorporate into your artistic oeuvre?

TATIANA TROUVÉ: Your comment is correct, but it's unfortunately not always the case in fact. Some artists lose their creativity with age; their sources of inspiration or reflection die out and their work loses all its interest. No plan, however strong, will be able to alter that mystery. I hope it won't happen to me: wrinkles don't scare me, but that certainly does. For years now, I have allowed myself to be guided by my work and my intuitions. I become interested in certain media and subjects once they find themselves justified by the content, thought, or idea of a piece. But here again, it's by looking back that I can more or less imagine where my work is likely to lead me. I believe more and more that the fields in which my sculpture and installations come together are opened by links between abstraction and architecture, between experiences of space and of the body. I'd like to do sculptures of echoes, falling, emptiness, depressurization, magnetism…

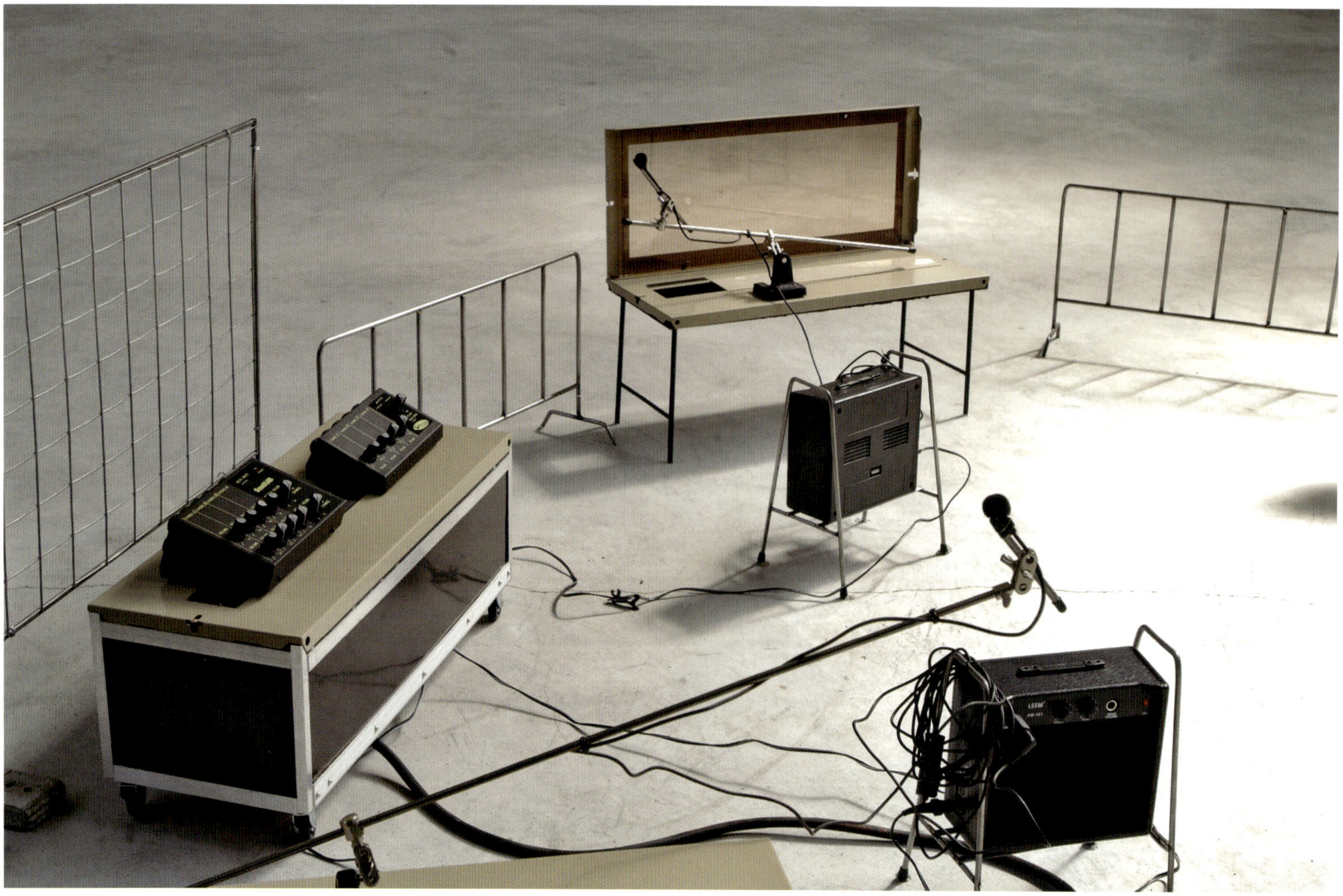

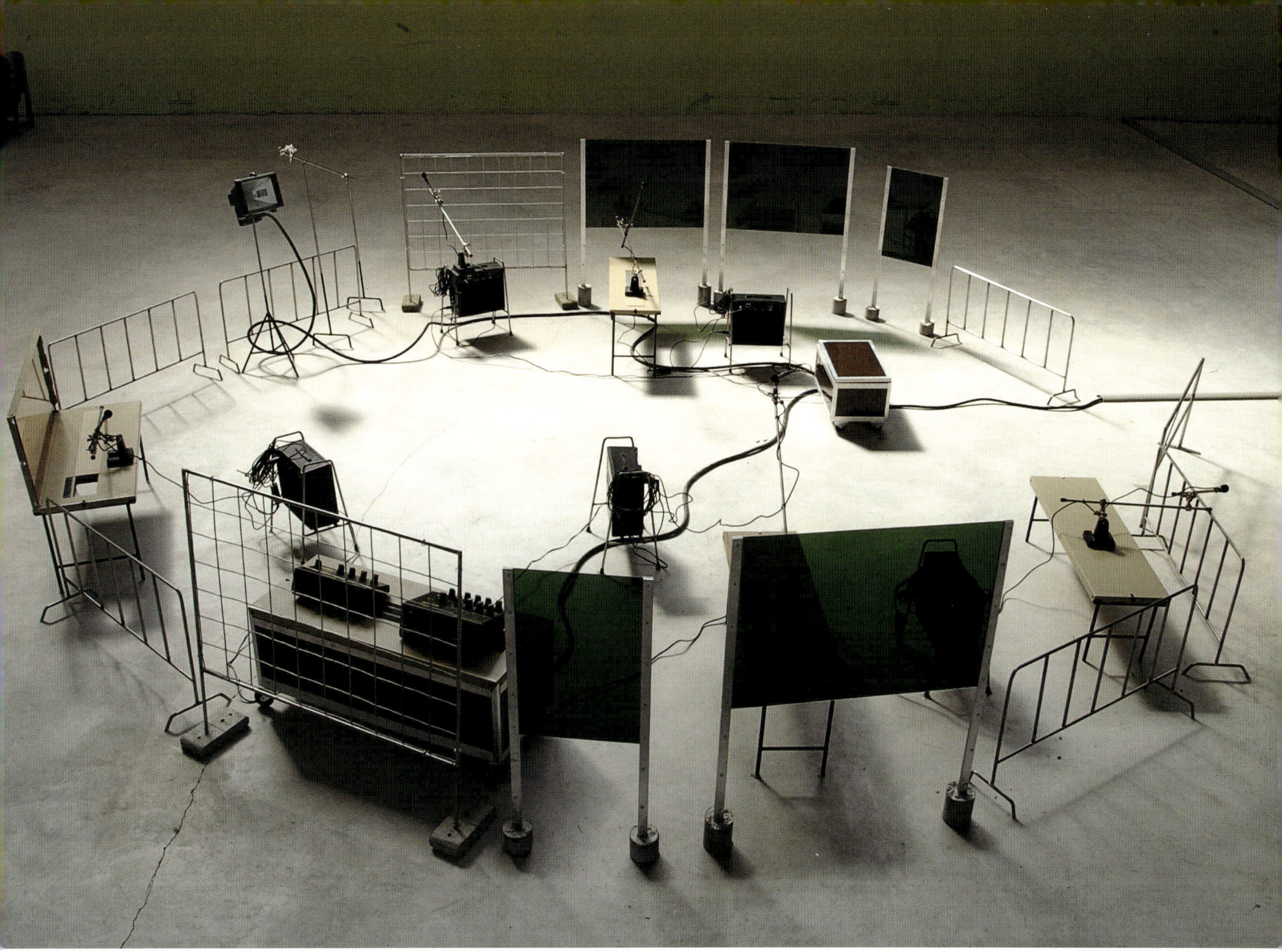

Polder, 2002
Metal, Plexiglas, halogen lamp, amplifier, cement, microphones, wood, mixing consoles, 60 x 230 x 230 cm [23½ x 90½ x 90½ in.]

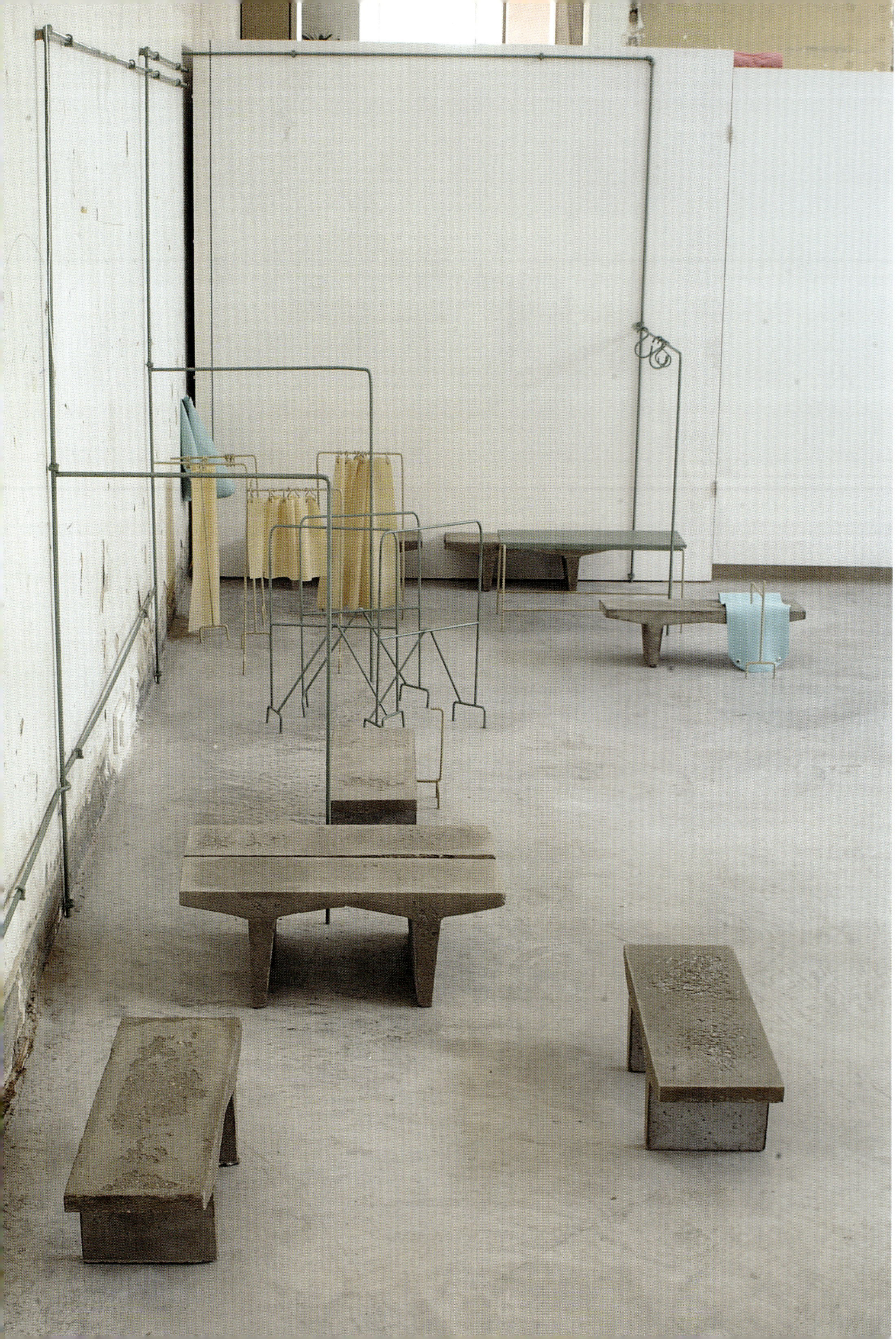

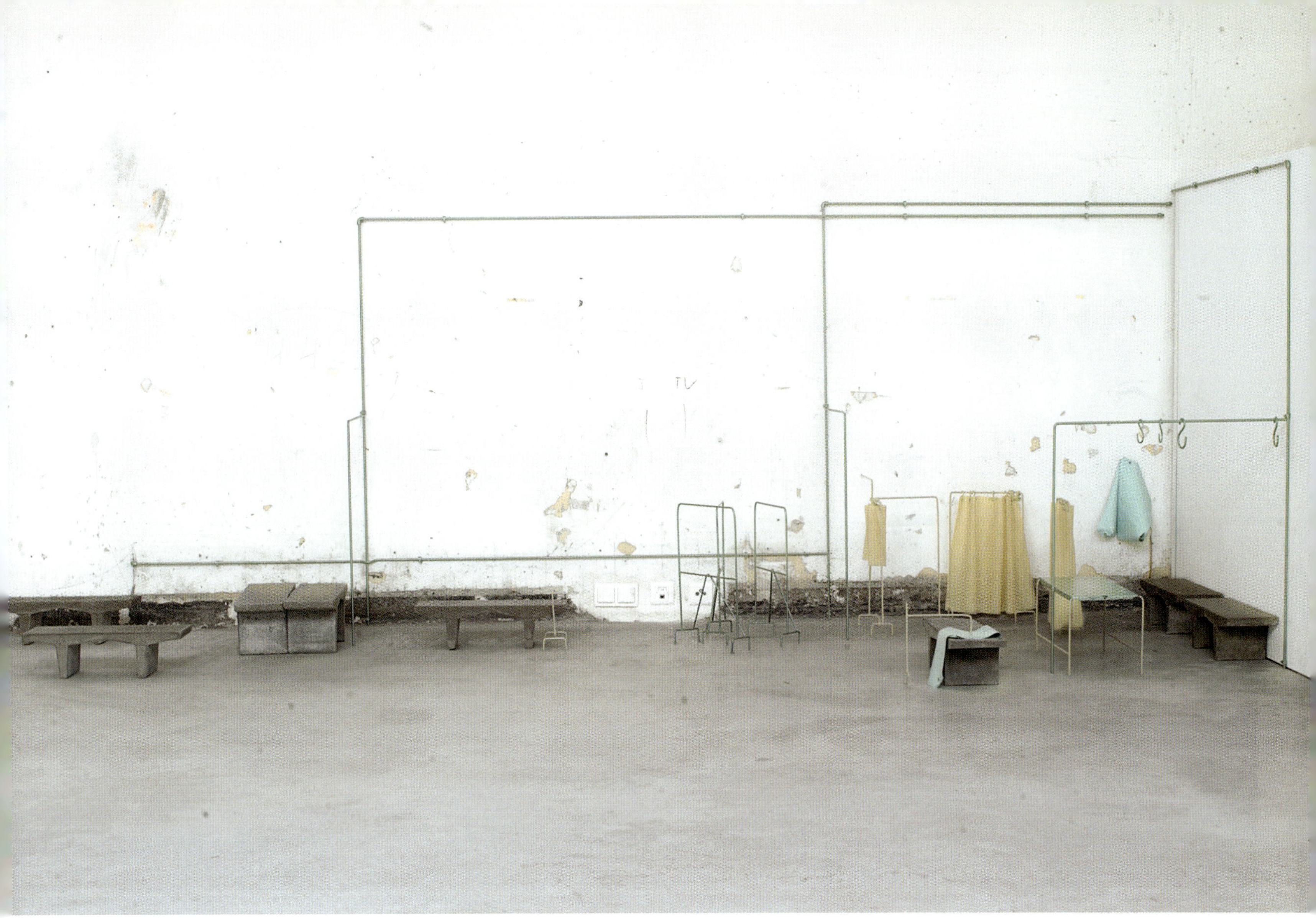

Polder, 2002
Metal, silicone, cement, 150 x 340 x 150 cm [59 x 134 x 59 in.]

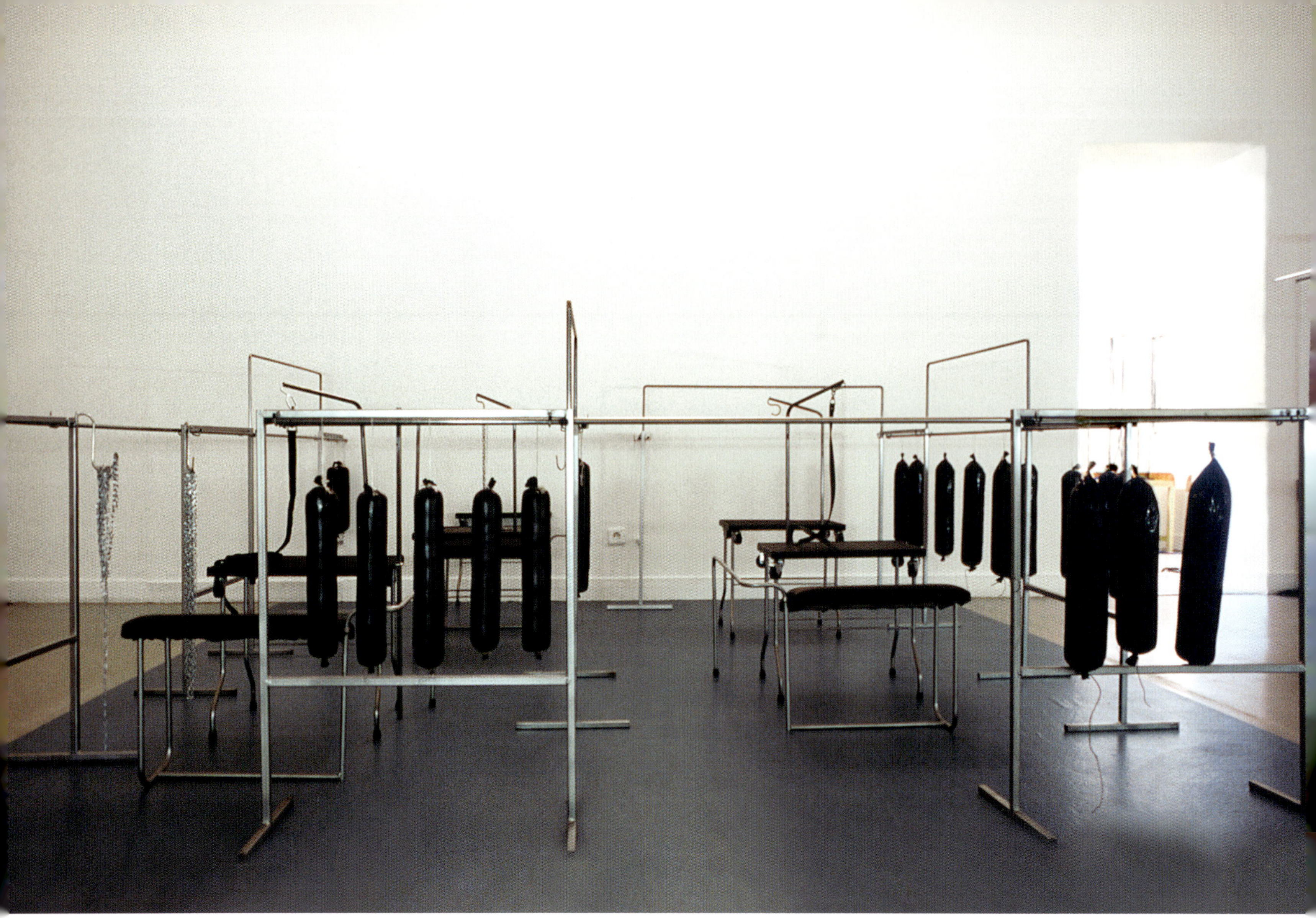

Polder, 2003
Iron, silicone, plastic, Formica, artificial bowels,
103 x 390 x 290 cm [40½ x 153½ x 114¼ in.]

Polder, 2003
Plexiglas, metal, wood, chocolate, imitation leather, rubber bands,
85 x 400 x 400 cm [33½ x 157½ x 157½ in.]

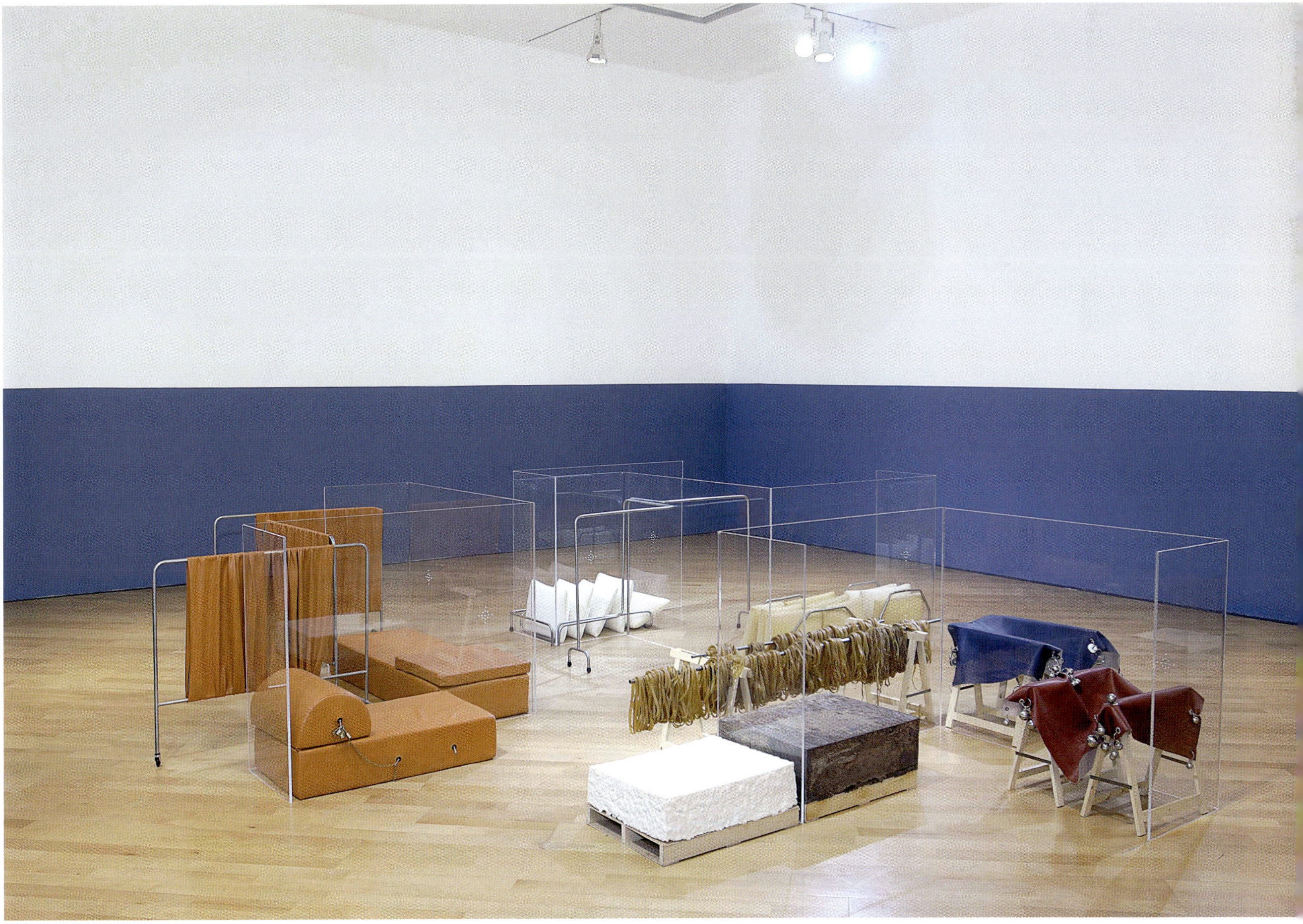

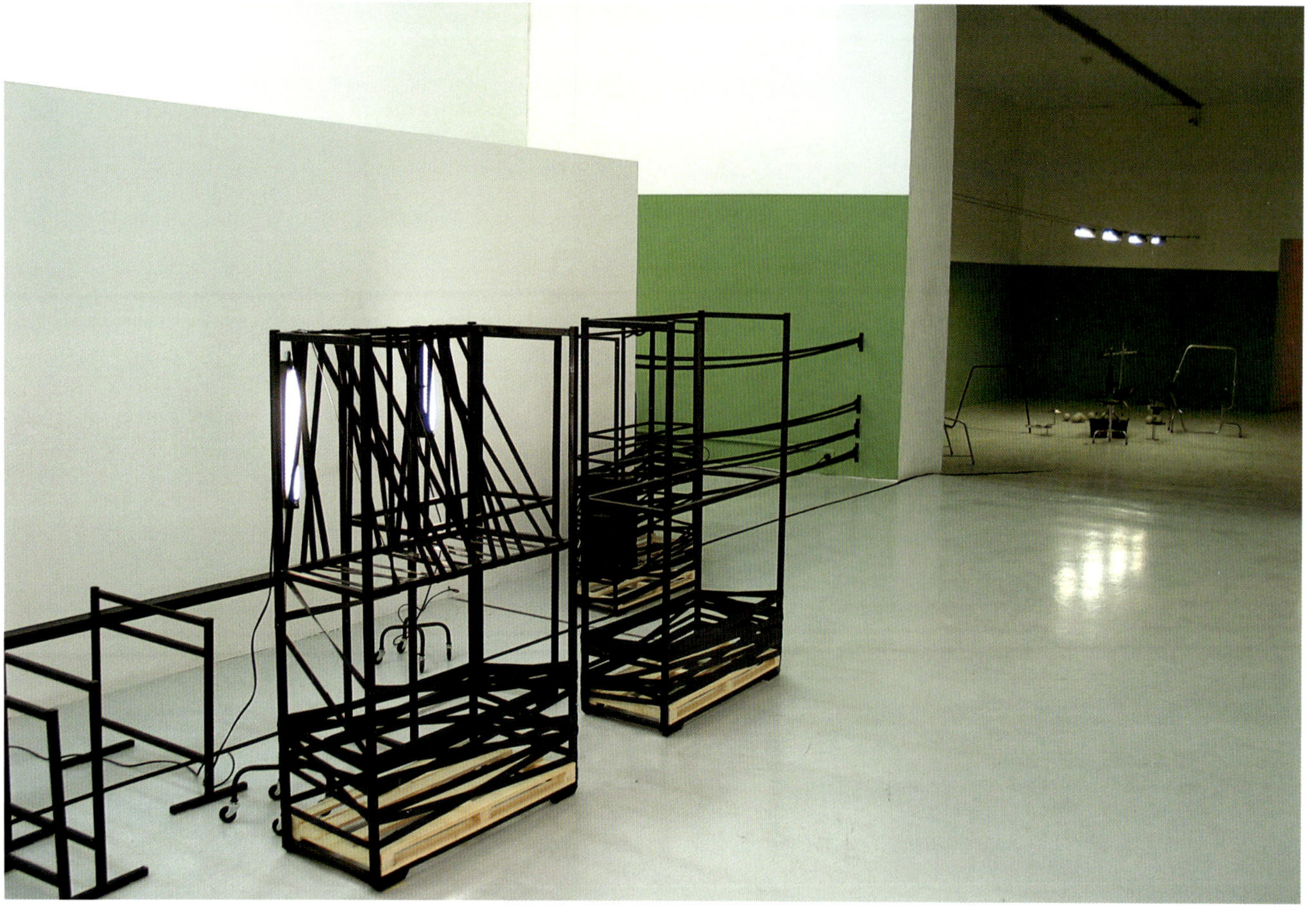

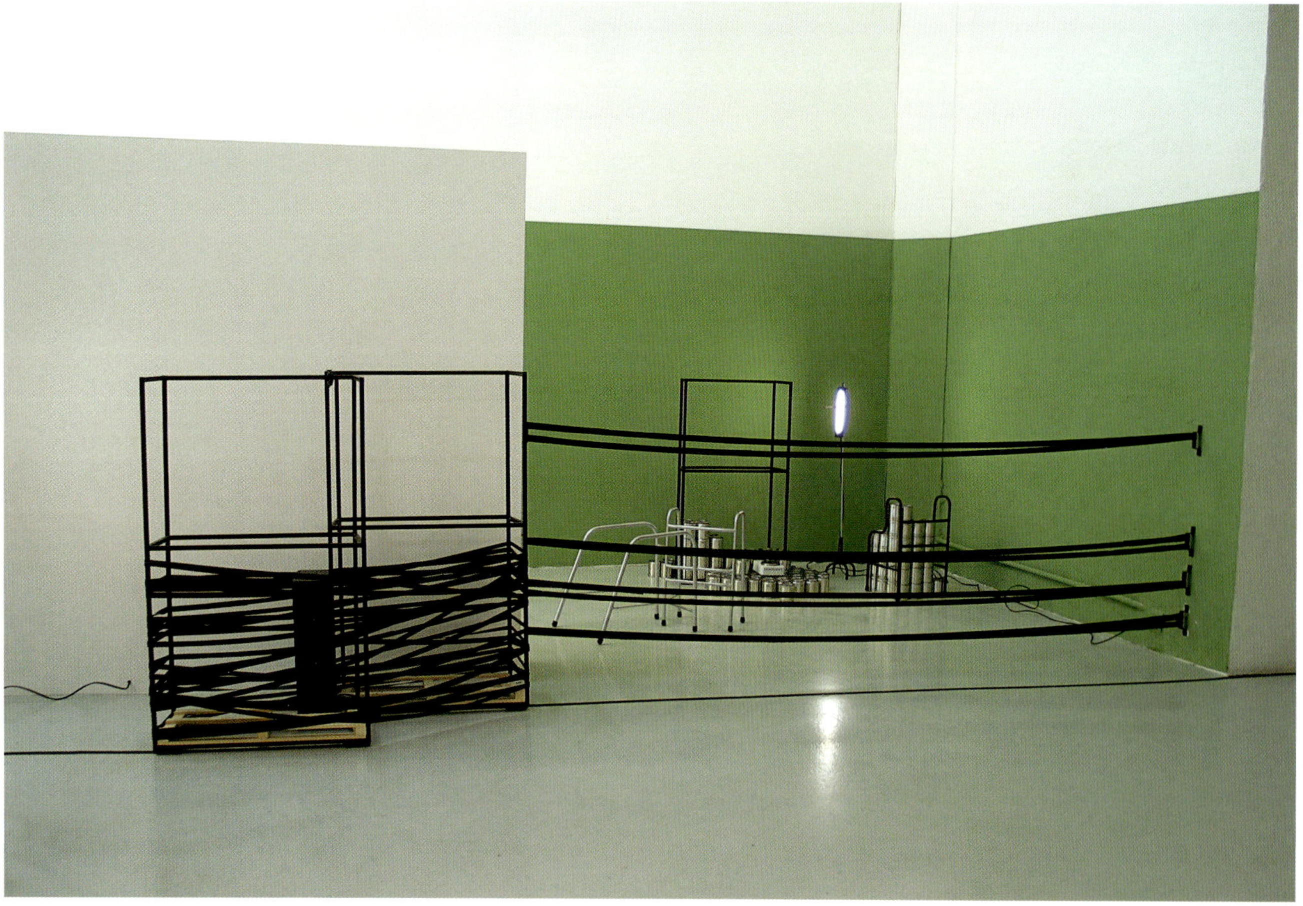

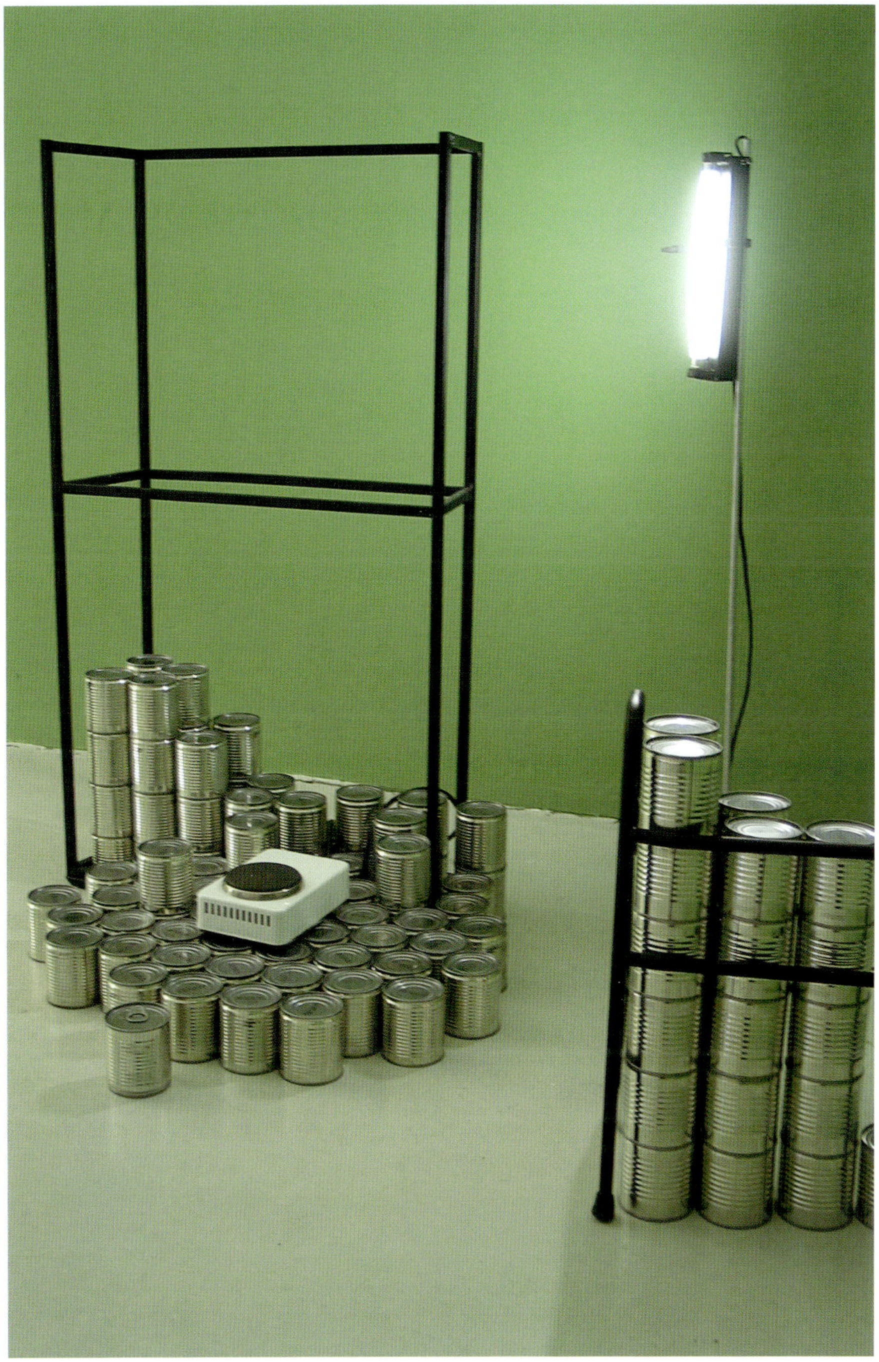

Polder, 2005
Metal, silicone, plastic, neon light, paint, soundtrack, variable dimensions

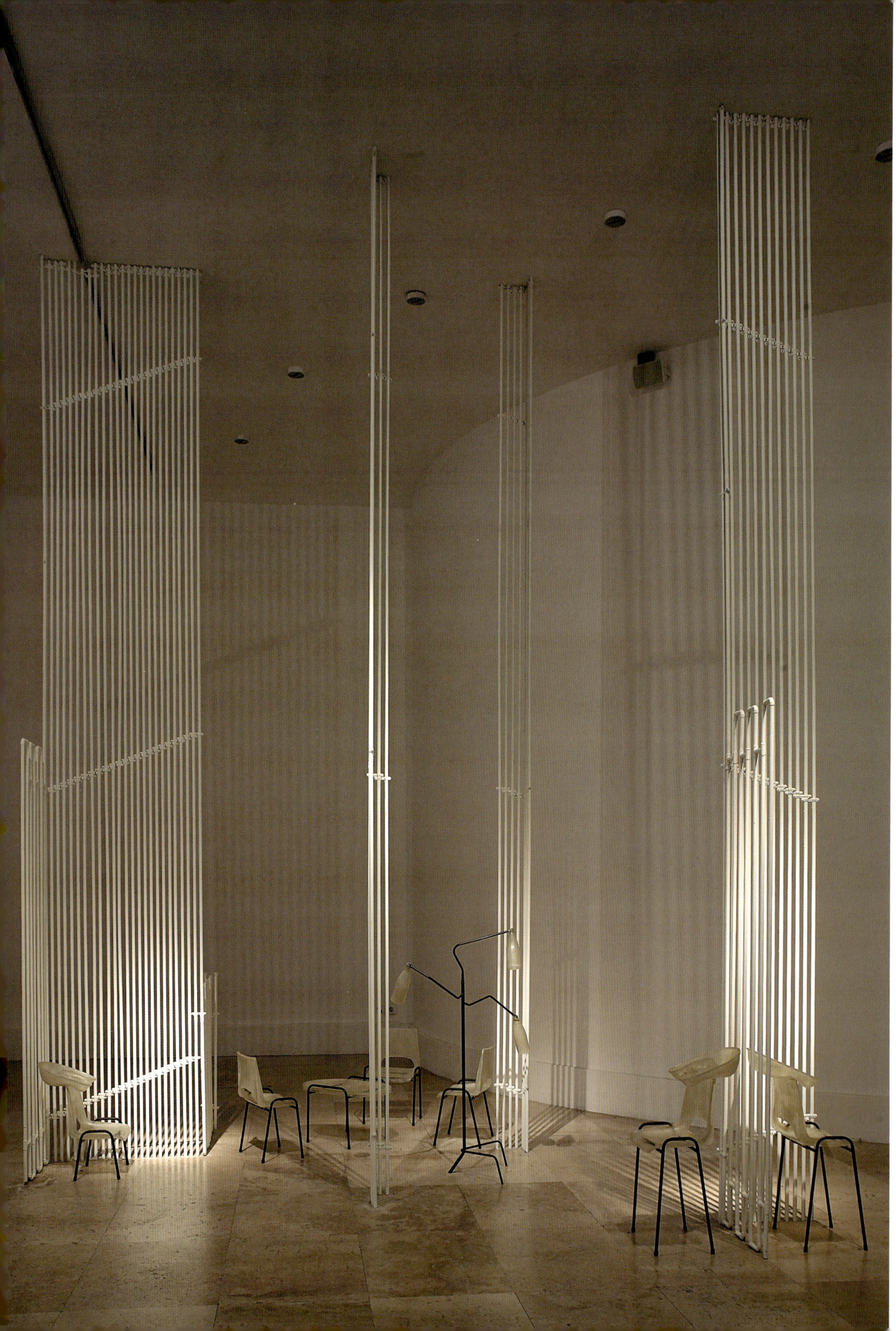

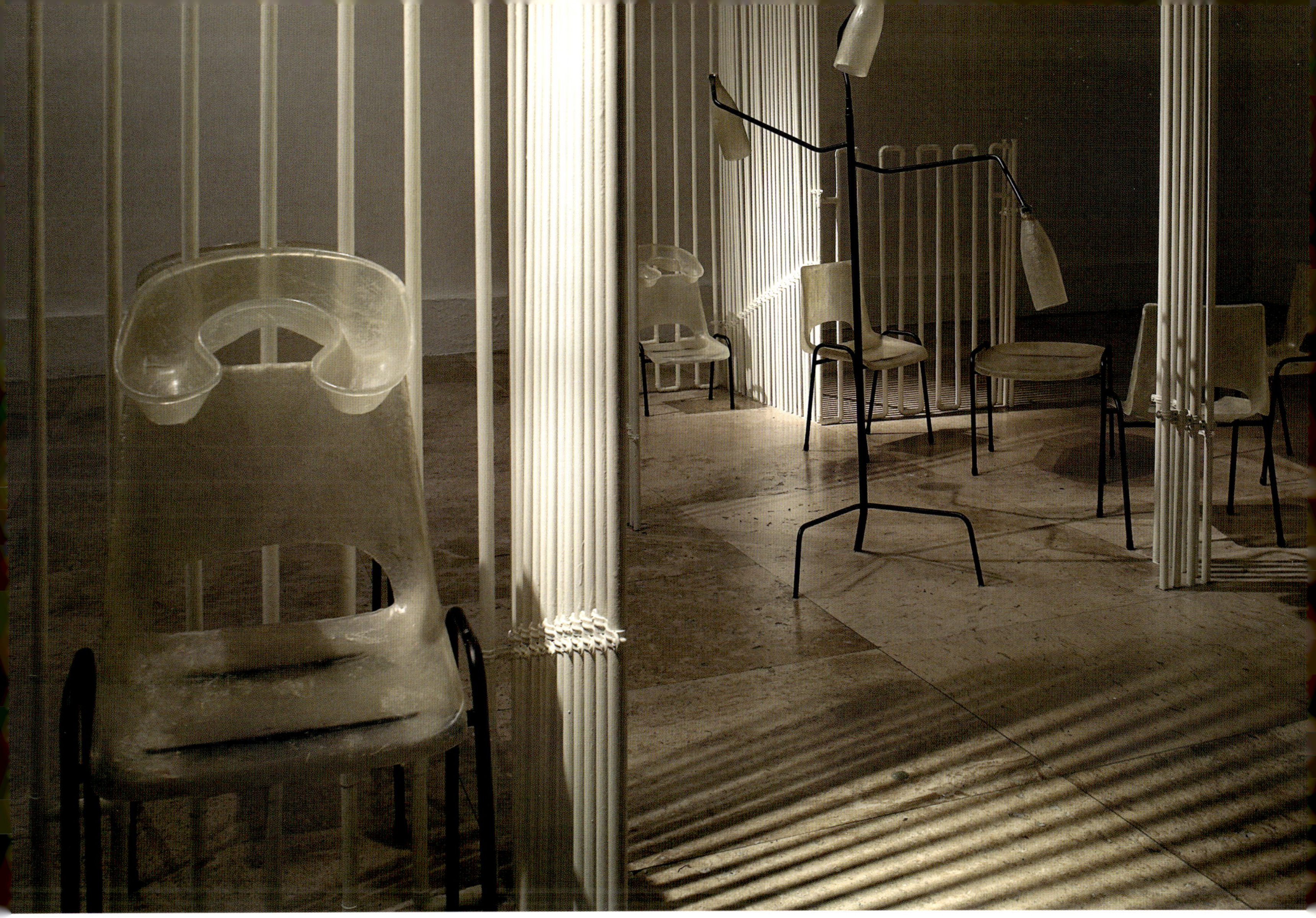

Polder, 2005
Copper, paint, resin, metal, 450 x 350 x 450 cm [177 x 138 x 177 in.]

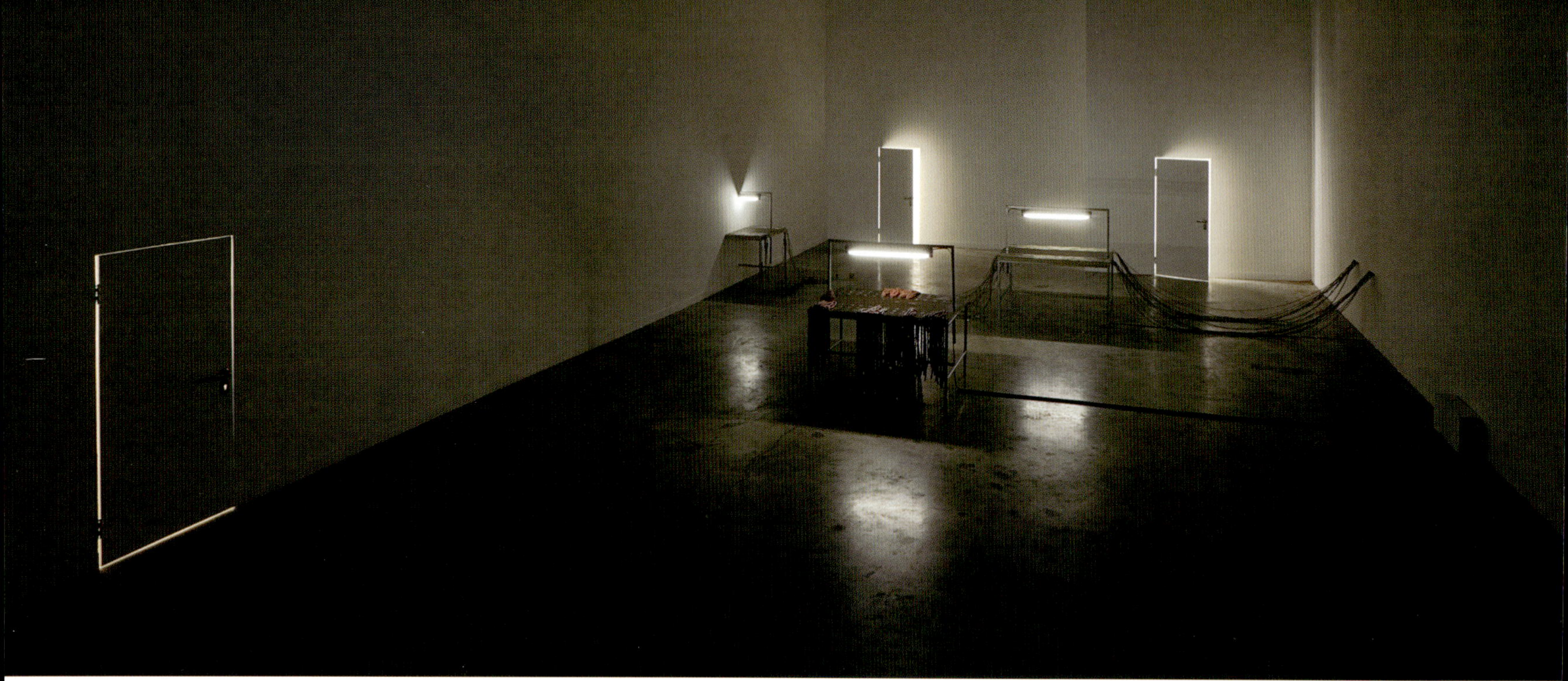

Polder, 2005
Wood, Bakelite, glass, metal, neon light, rope, variable dimensions

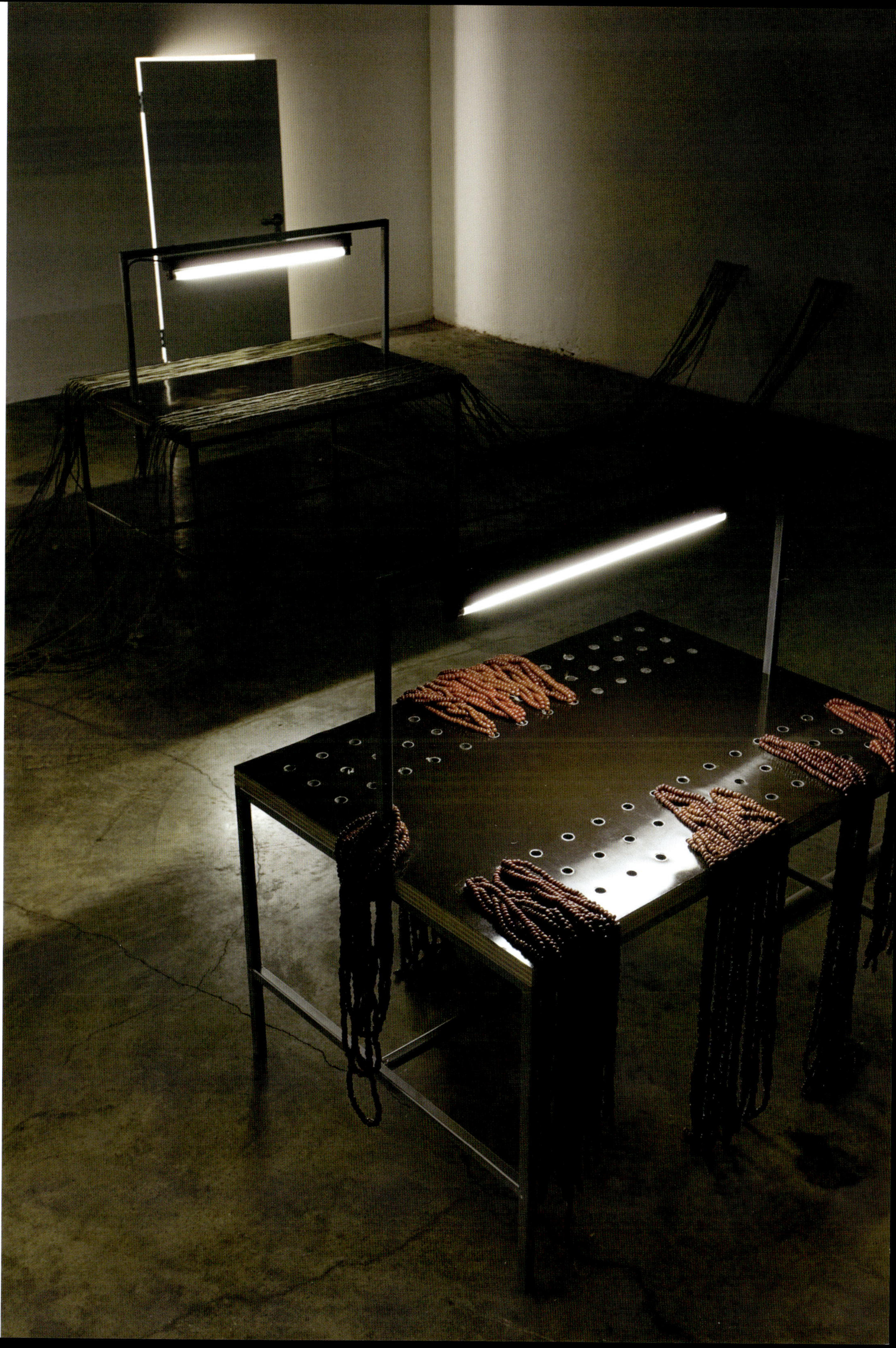

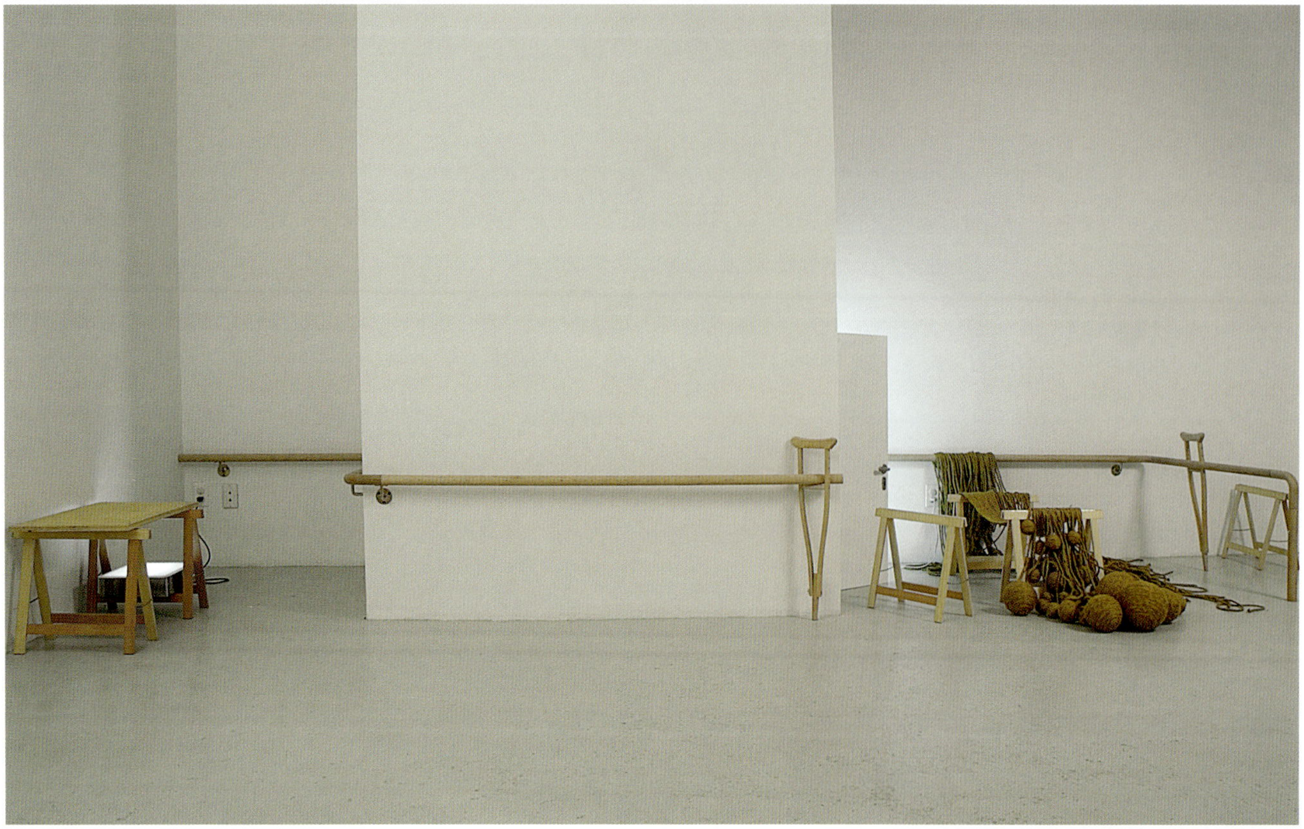

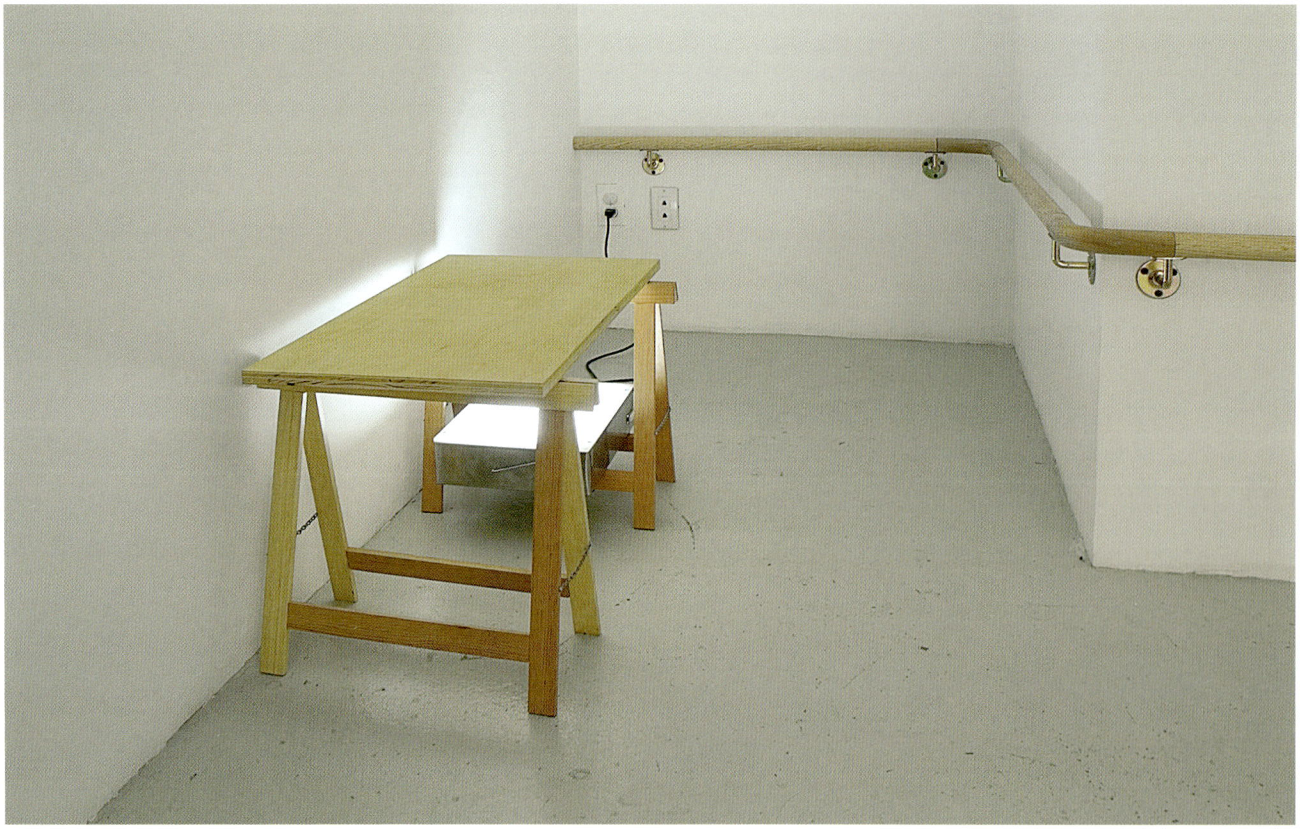

Polder, 2005
Wood, Plexiglas, metal, wool, light, 110 x 610 x 250 cm [43¼ x 240 x 98½ in.]

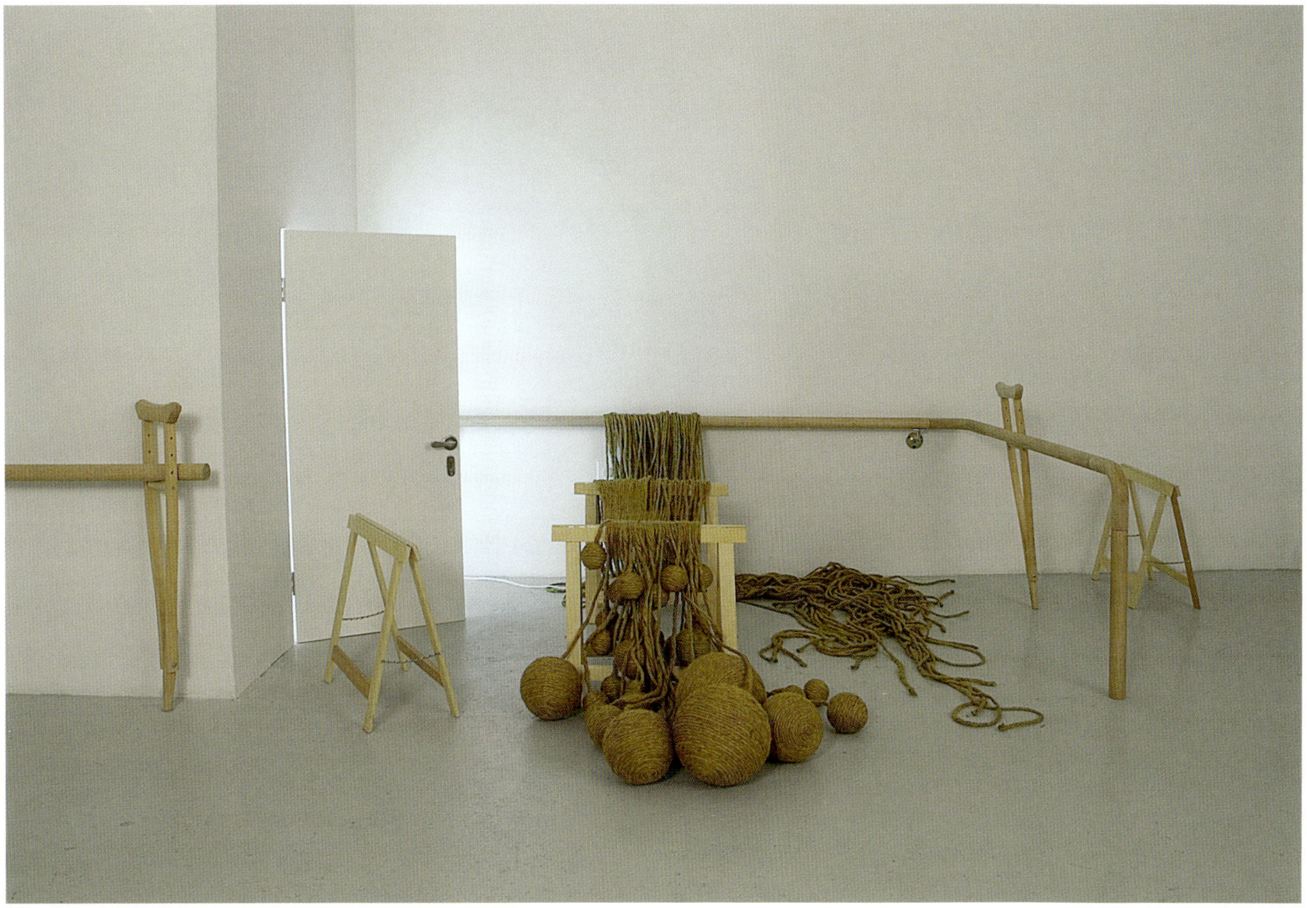

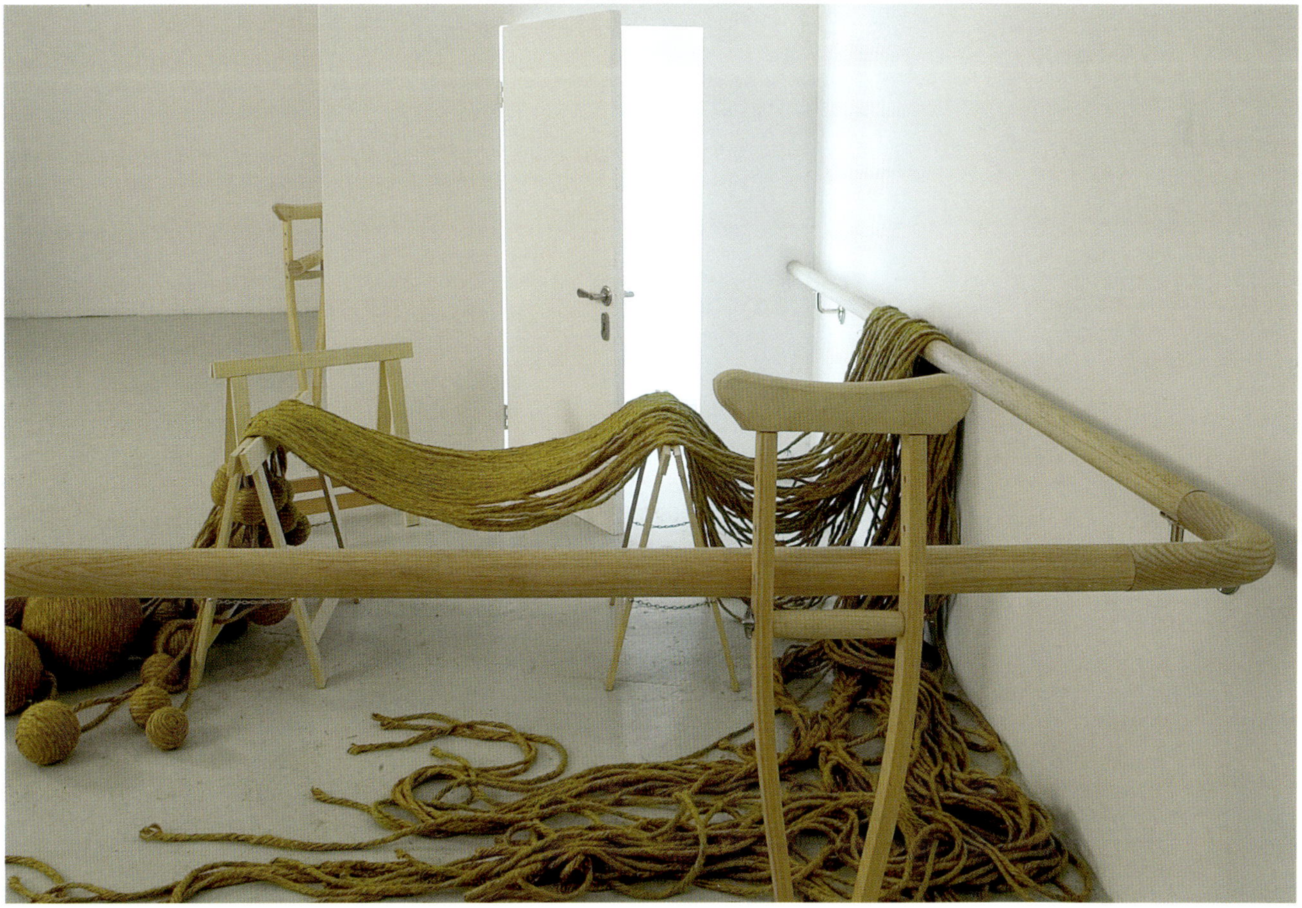

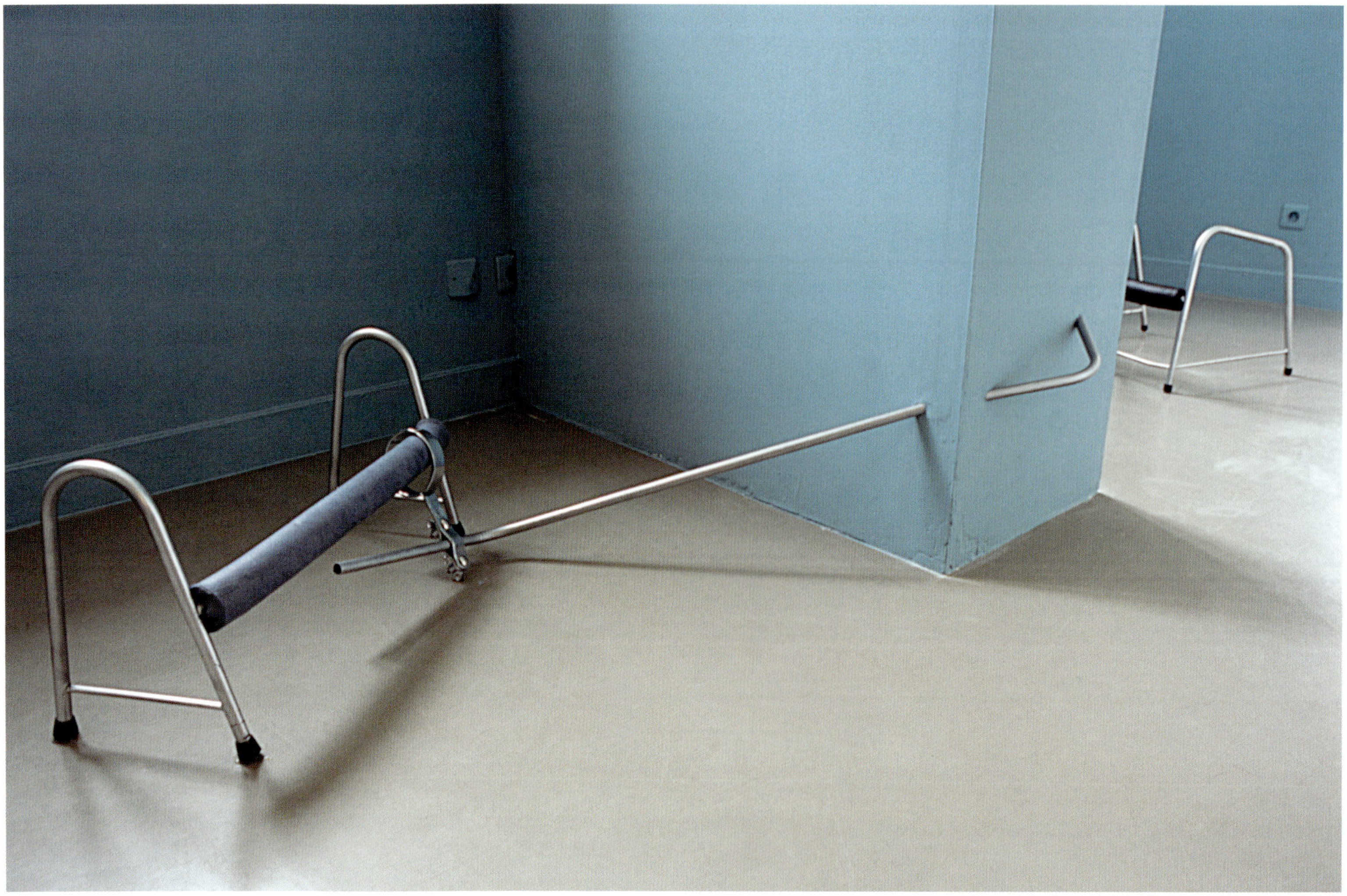

Polder, 2005
Metal, imitation leather, plastic, variable dimensions

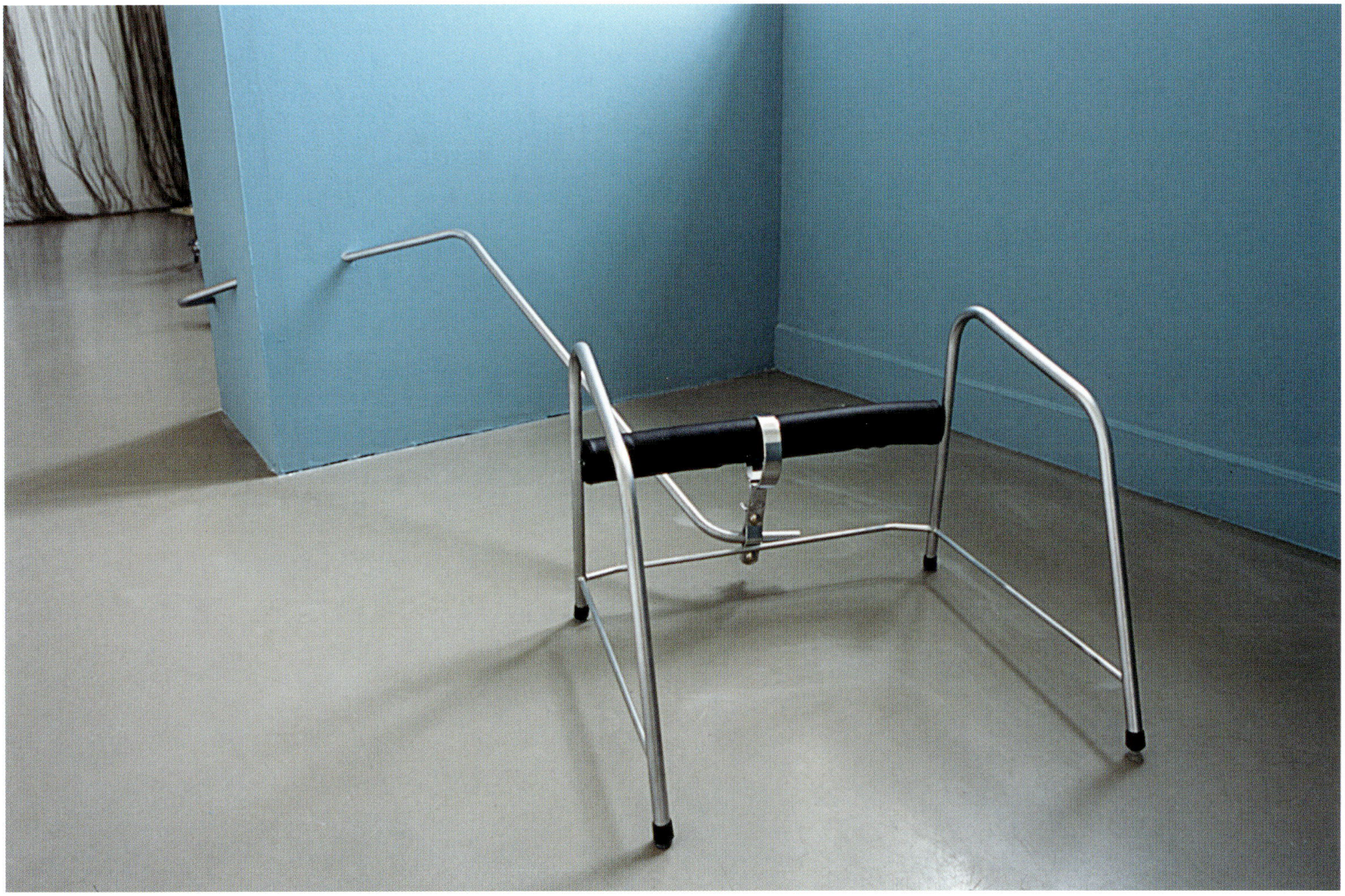

Following pages:
Polder, 2006
Metal, leather, plastic, wrought iron
Two components: 150 x 120 x 90 cm [59 x 47¼ x 35½ in.];
150 x 130 x 125 cm [59 x 51¼ x 49¼ in.]

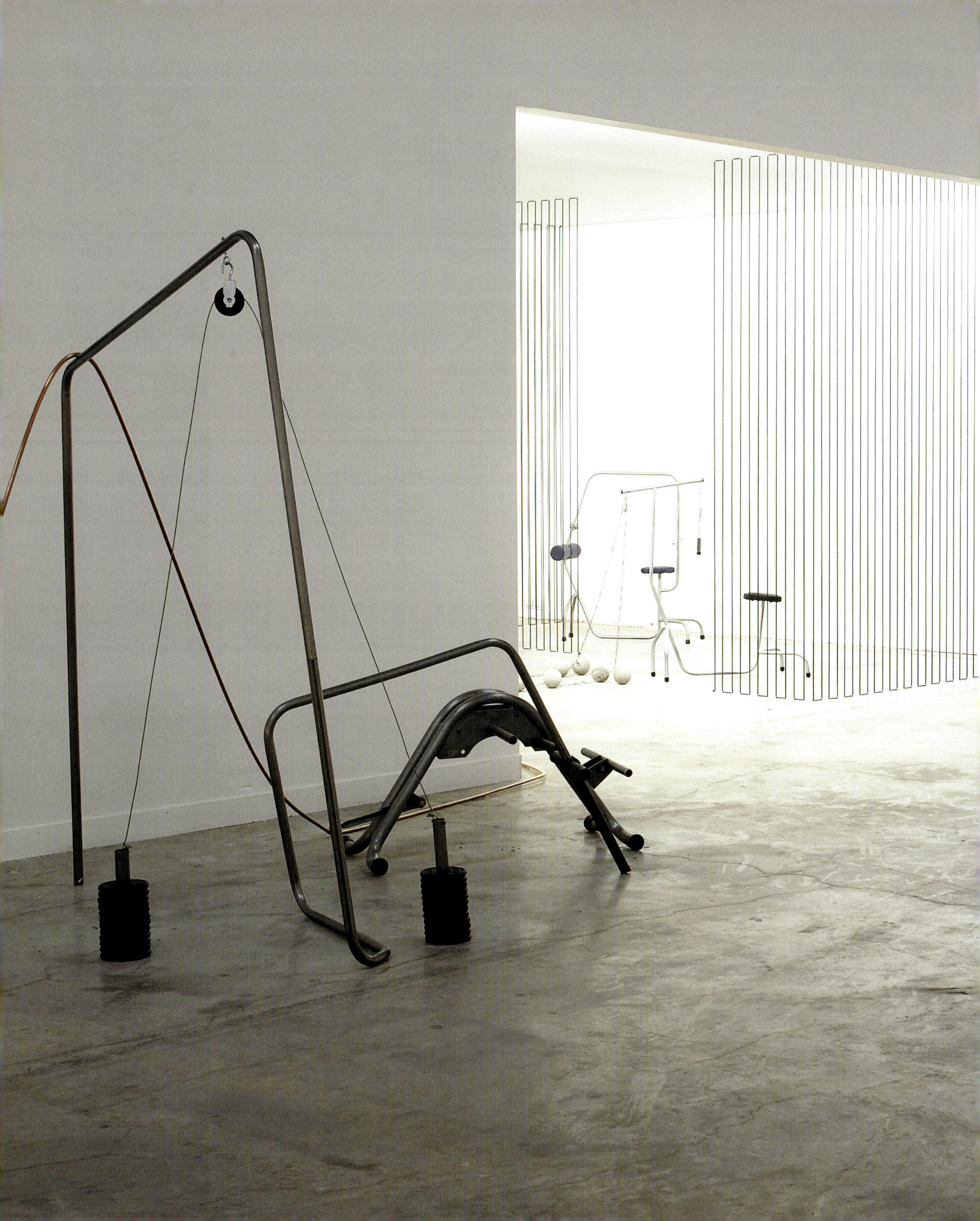

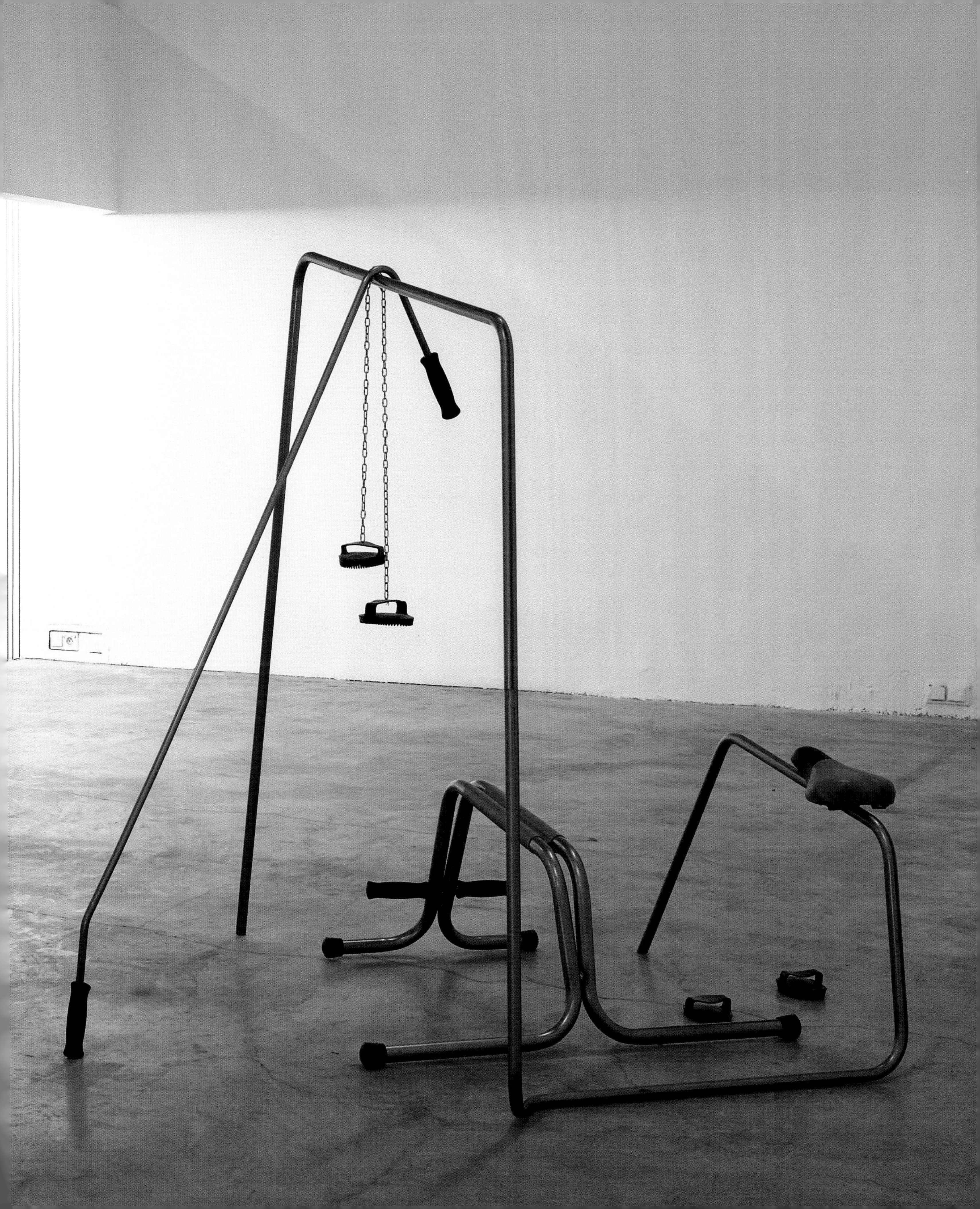

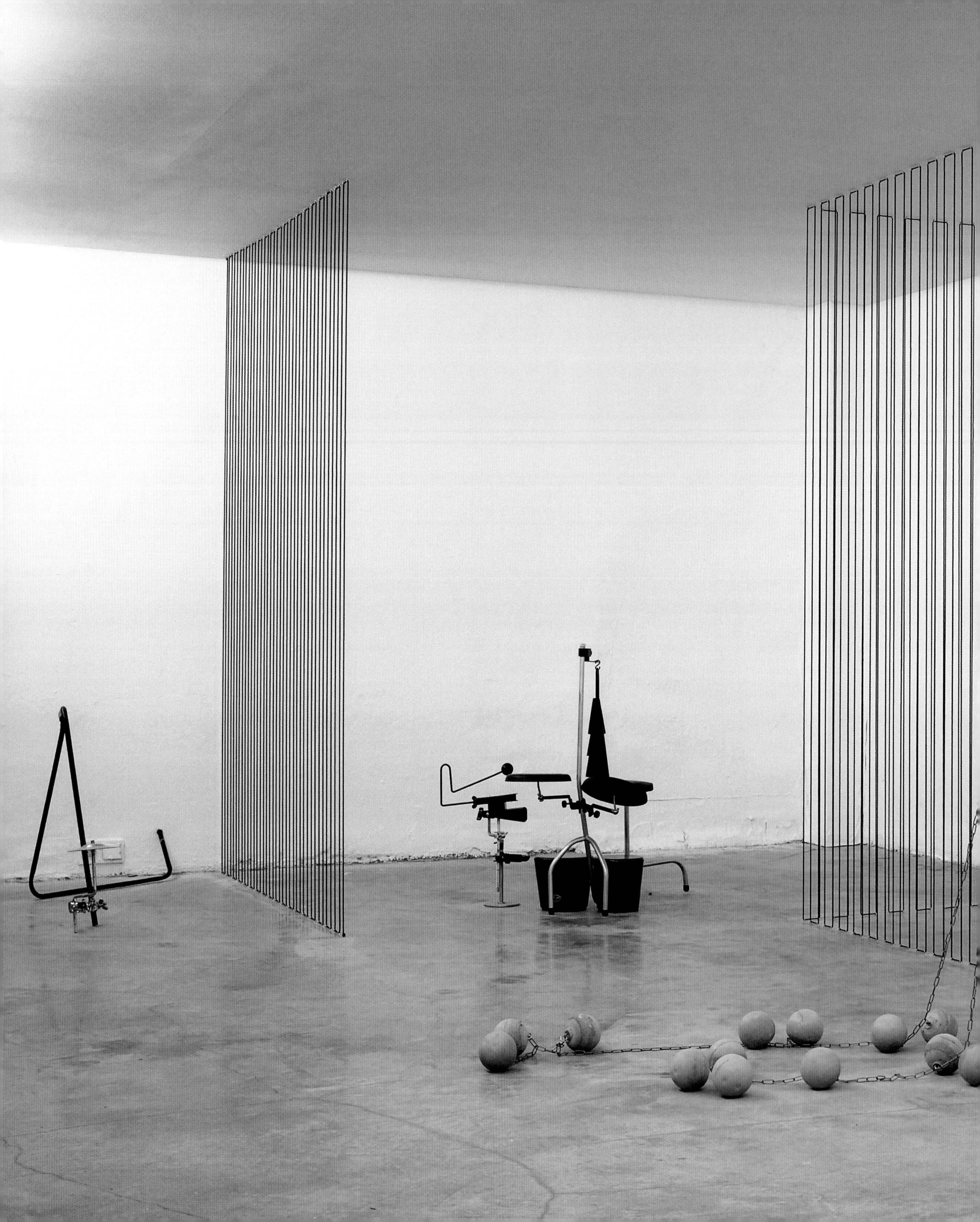

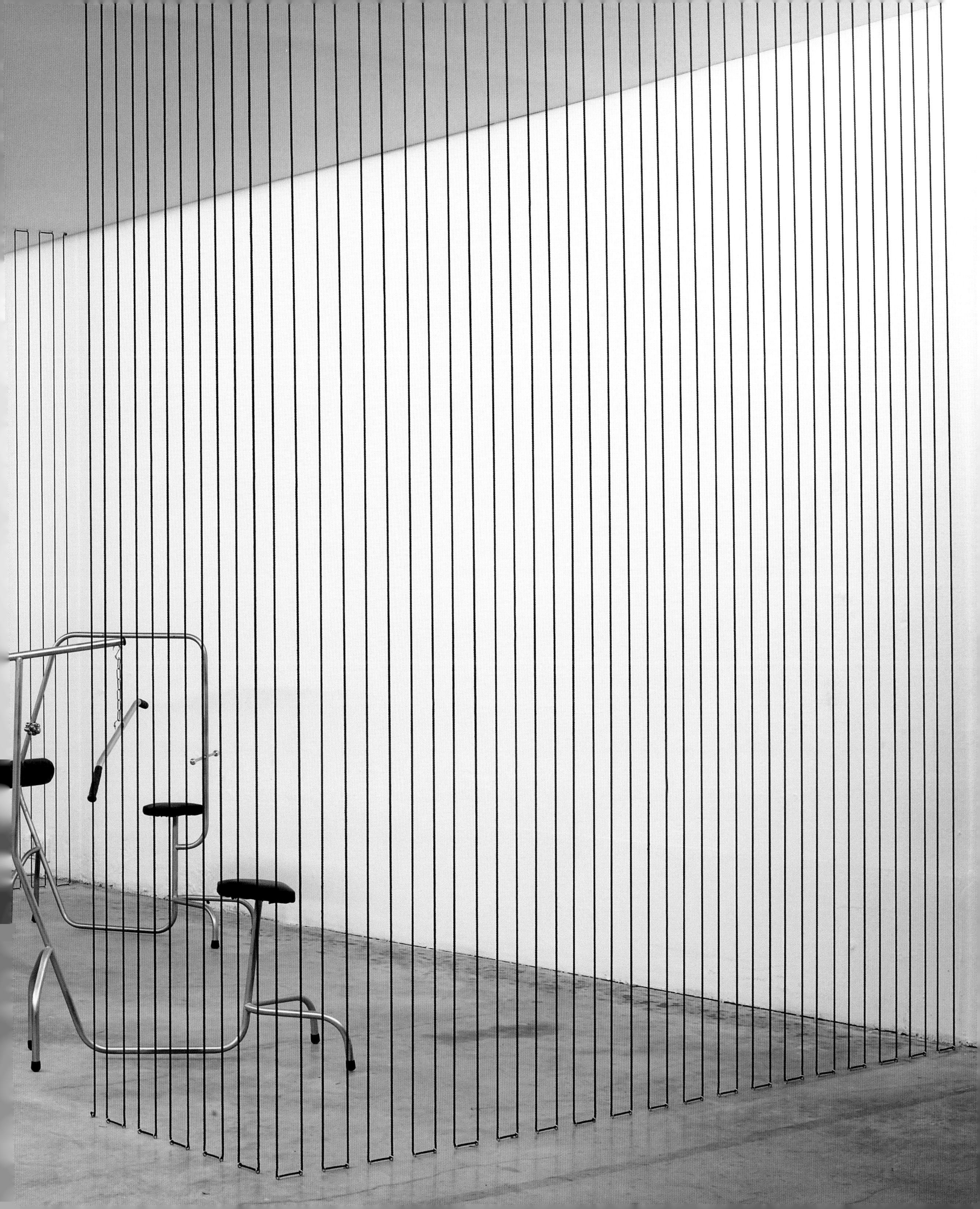

Previous pages:
Polder, 2005
Metal, cement, imitation leather, wood, rope, plastic,
210 x 350 x 500 cm [82¾ x 138 x 197 in.]

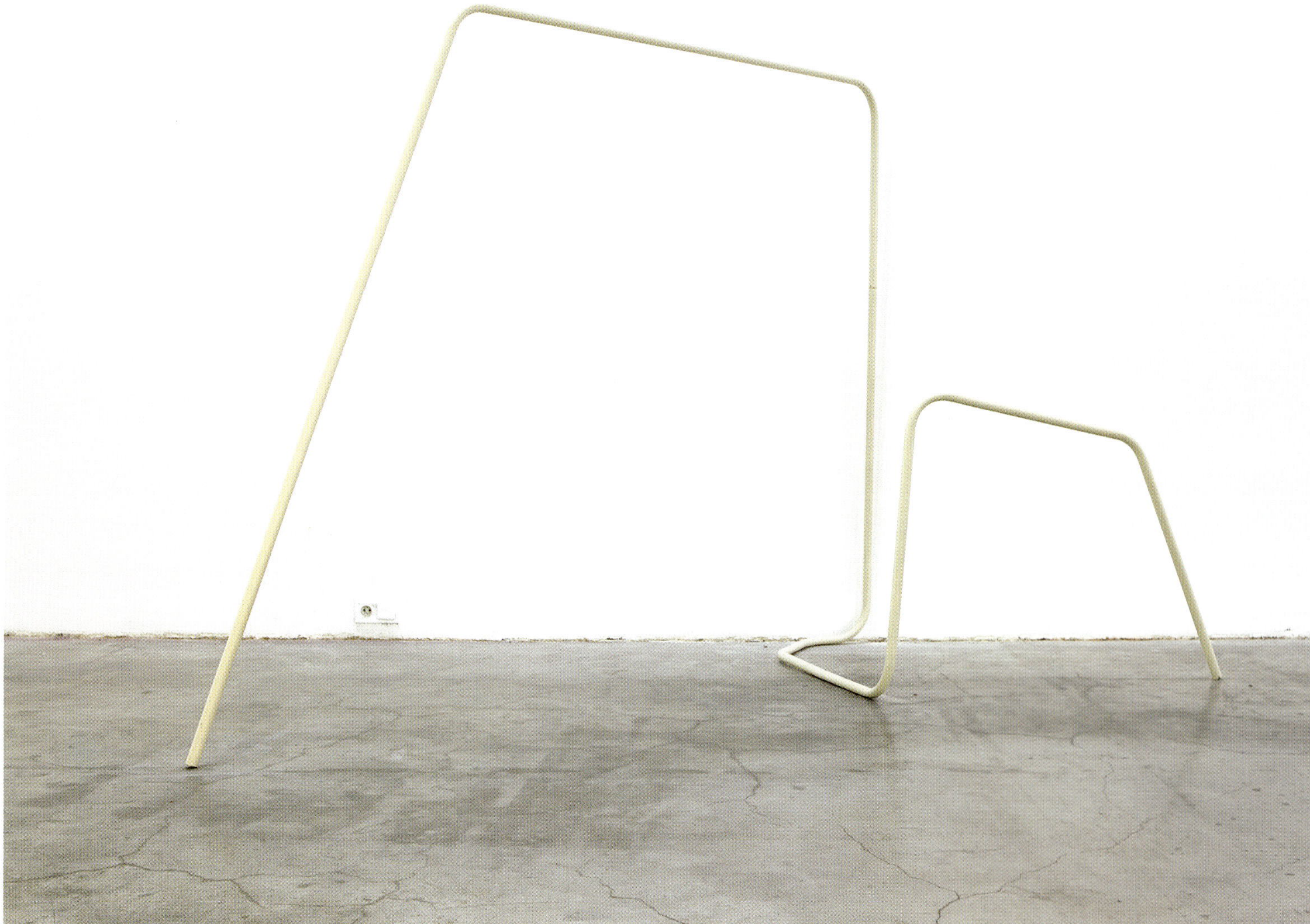

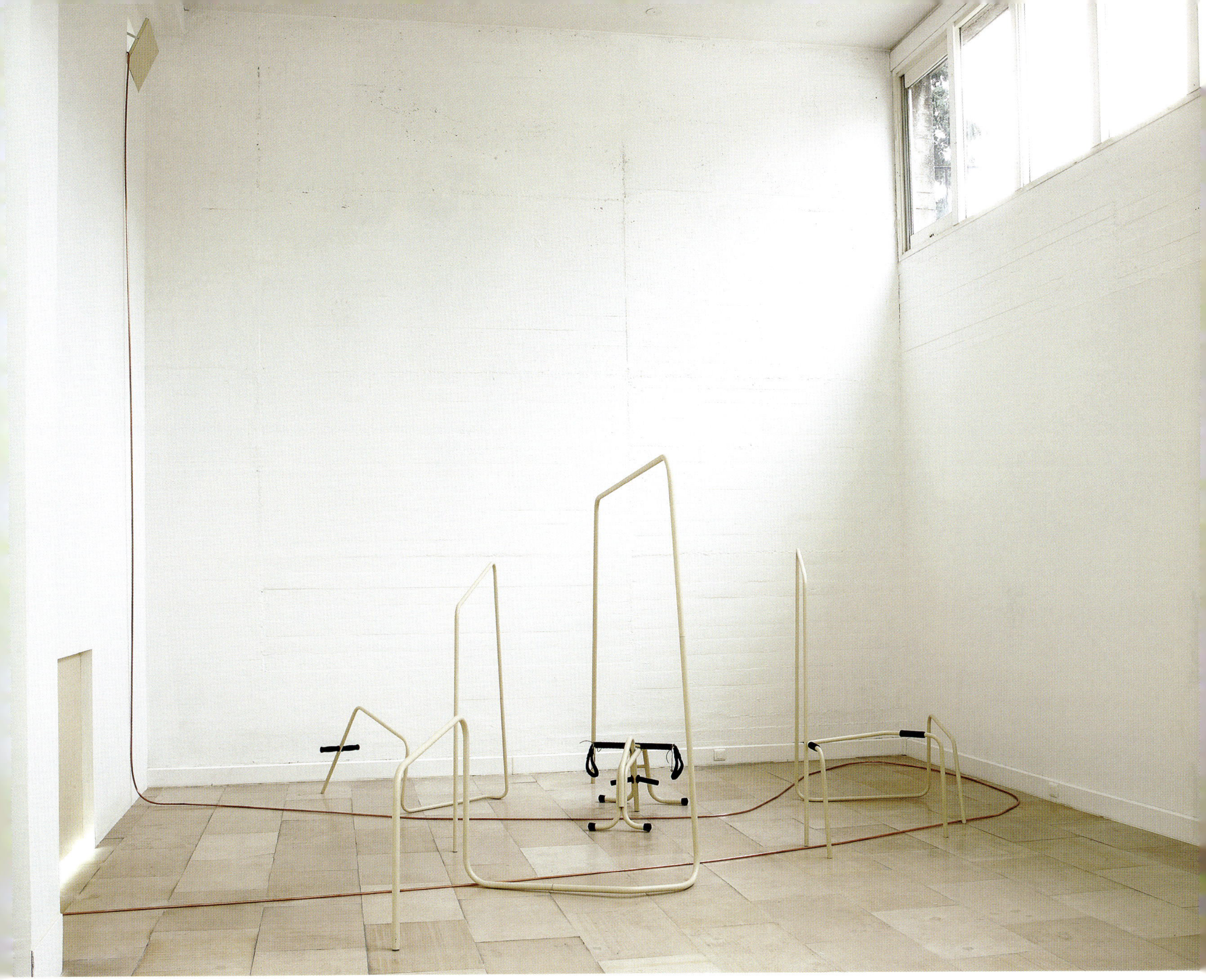

Left-hand page:
La Linea, 2007
Metal, epoxy paint, 186 x 109 x 339 cm [73¼ x 43 x 133½ in.]

Above:
Polder, 2007
Metal, leather, epoxy paint, wood, Formica, neon light, copper, variable dimensions

Priapus, 2007
Wood, leather, burn, 122 x 35 x 3.2 cm [48 x 13¾ x 1¼ in.]

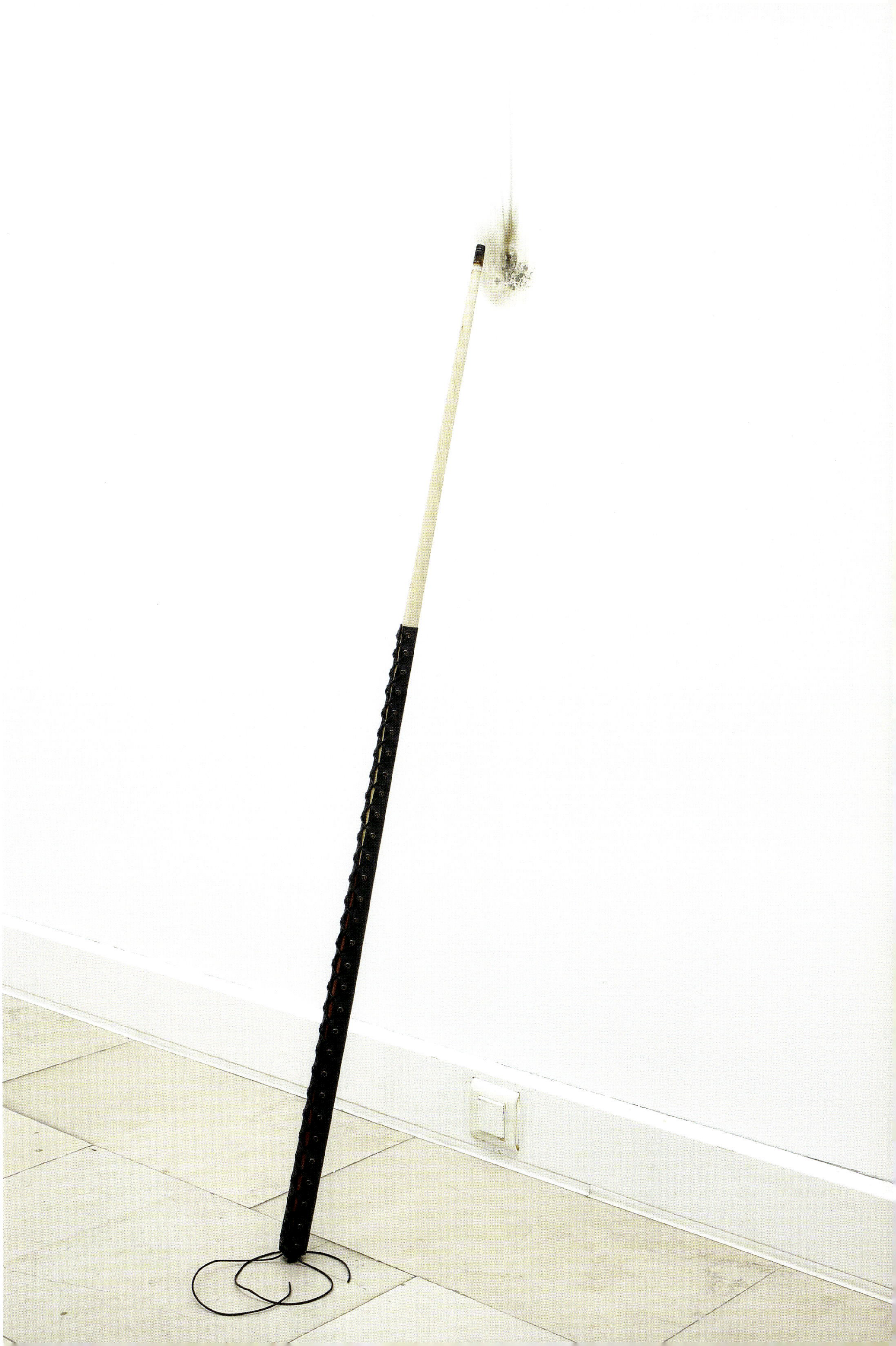

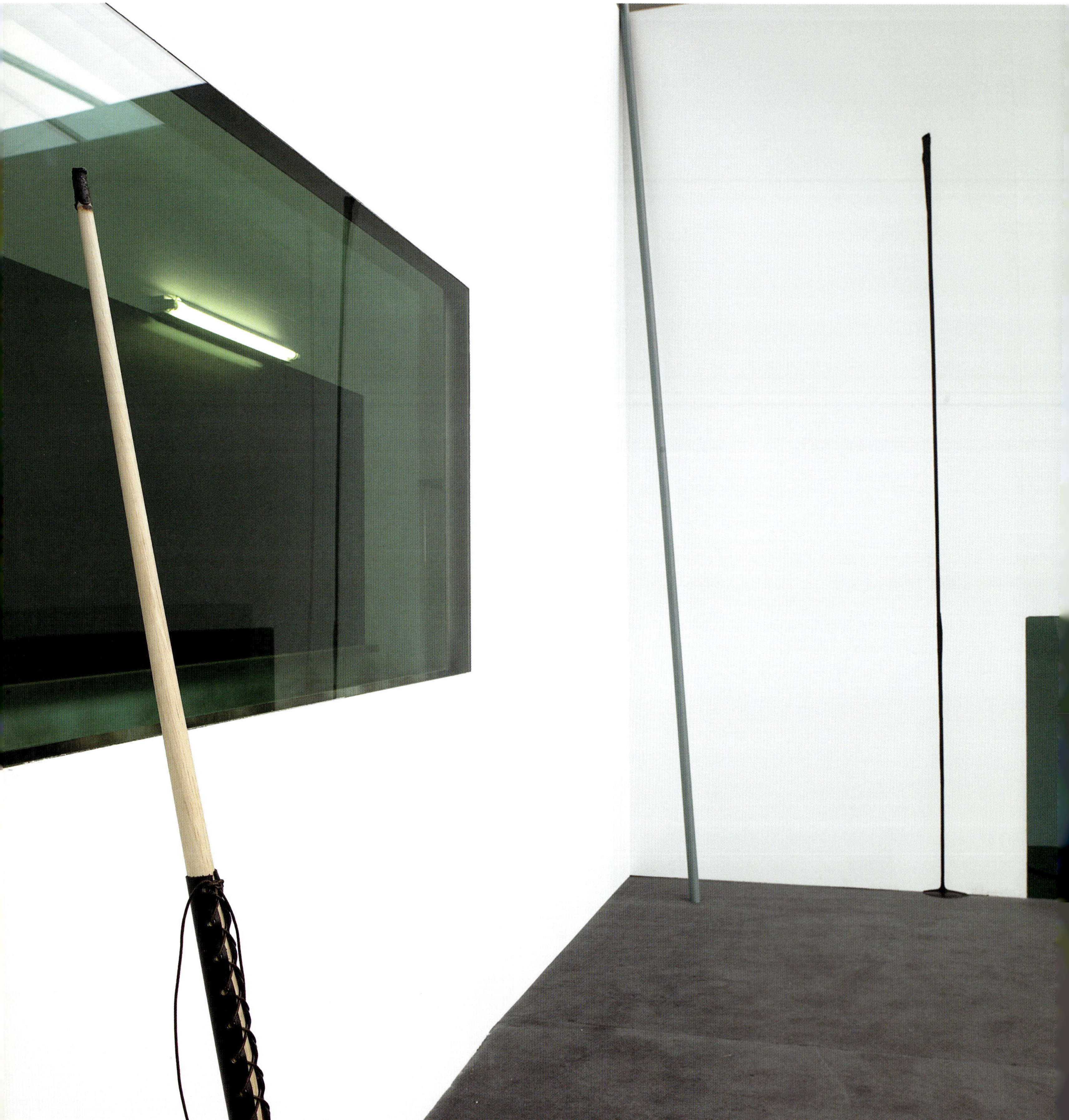

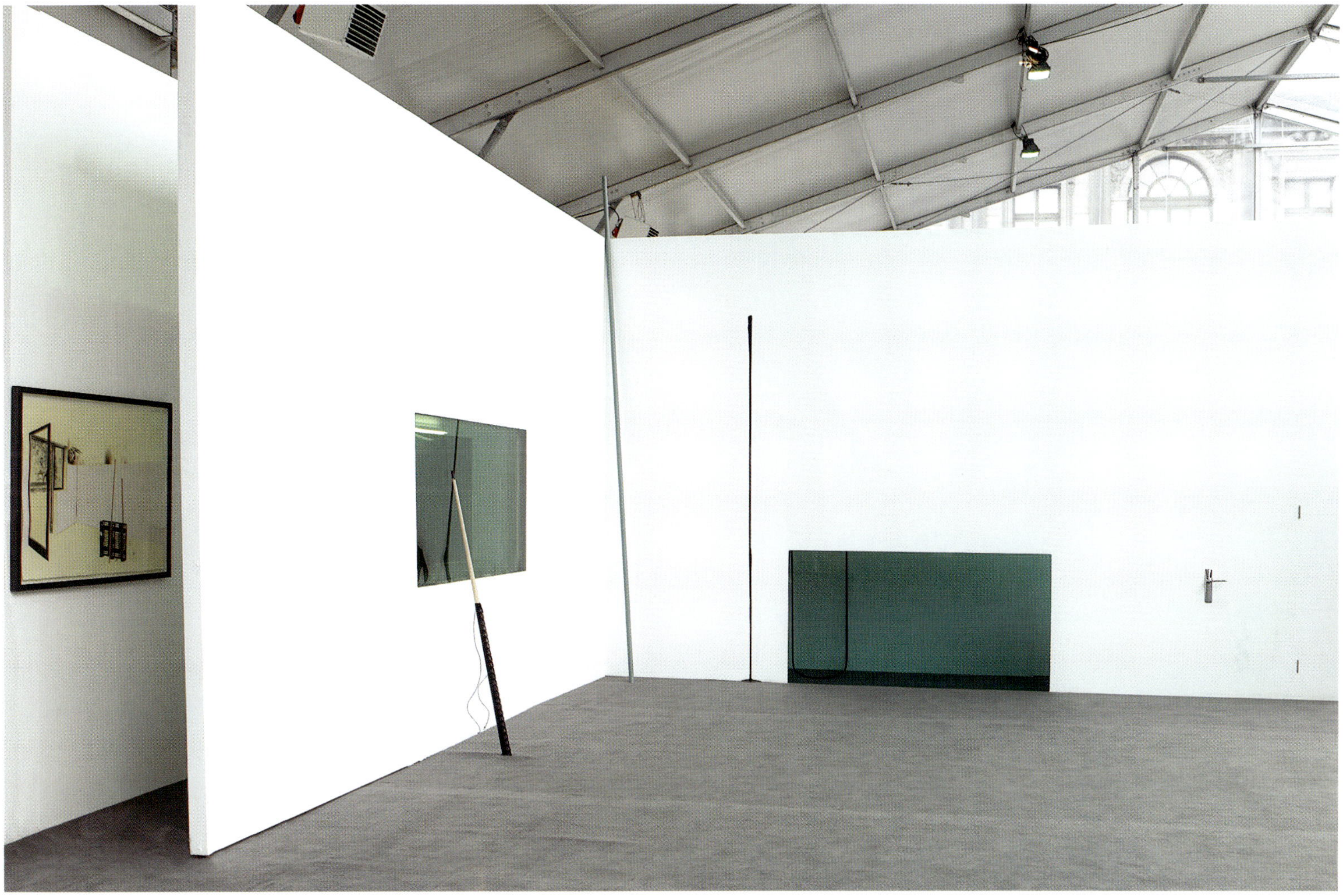

Untitled, 2007
Plexiglas, Formica, metal, leather, copper, mirror, wood, neon light, paint,
290 x 500 x 500 cm [114 x 197 x 197 in.]

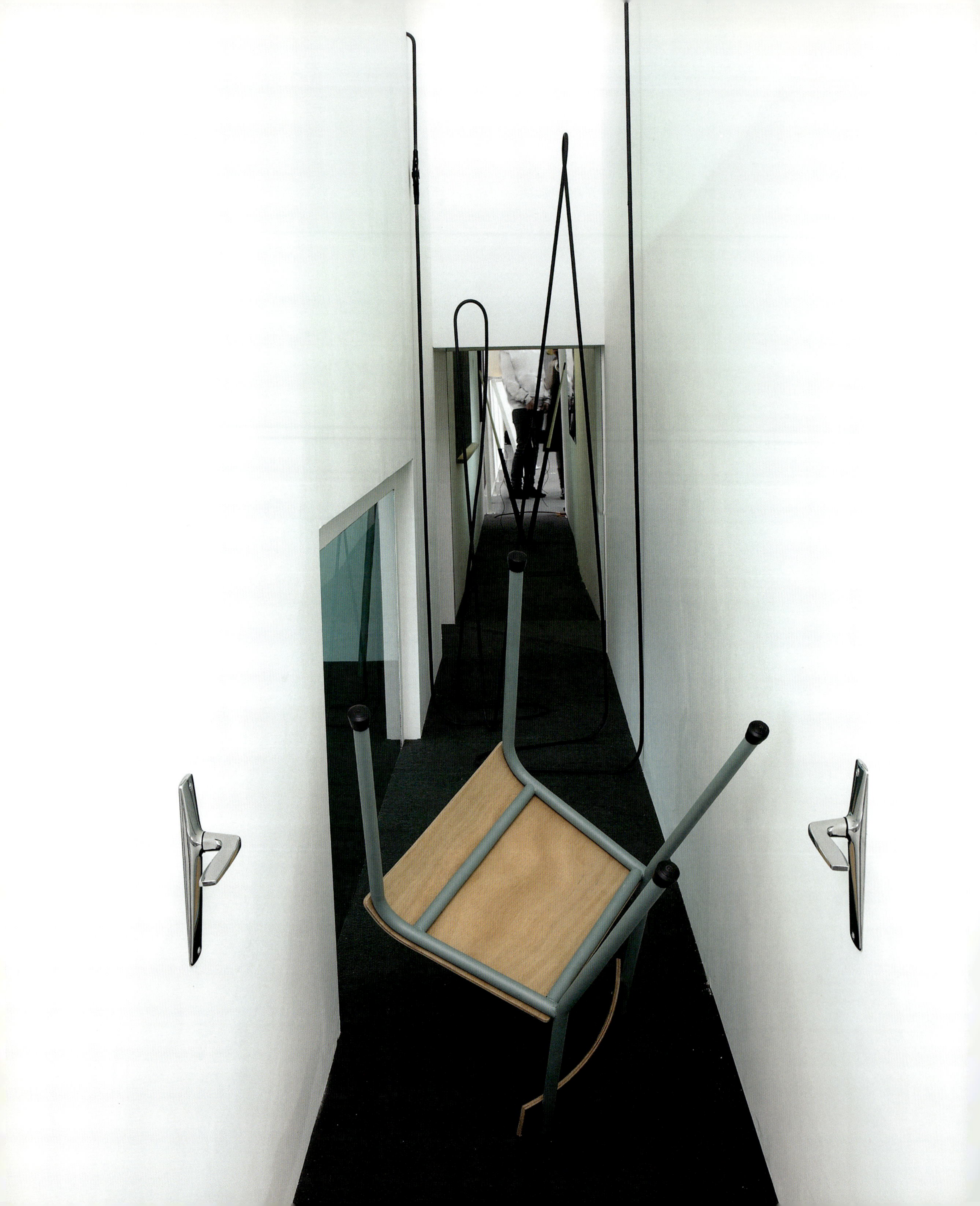

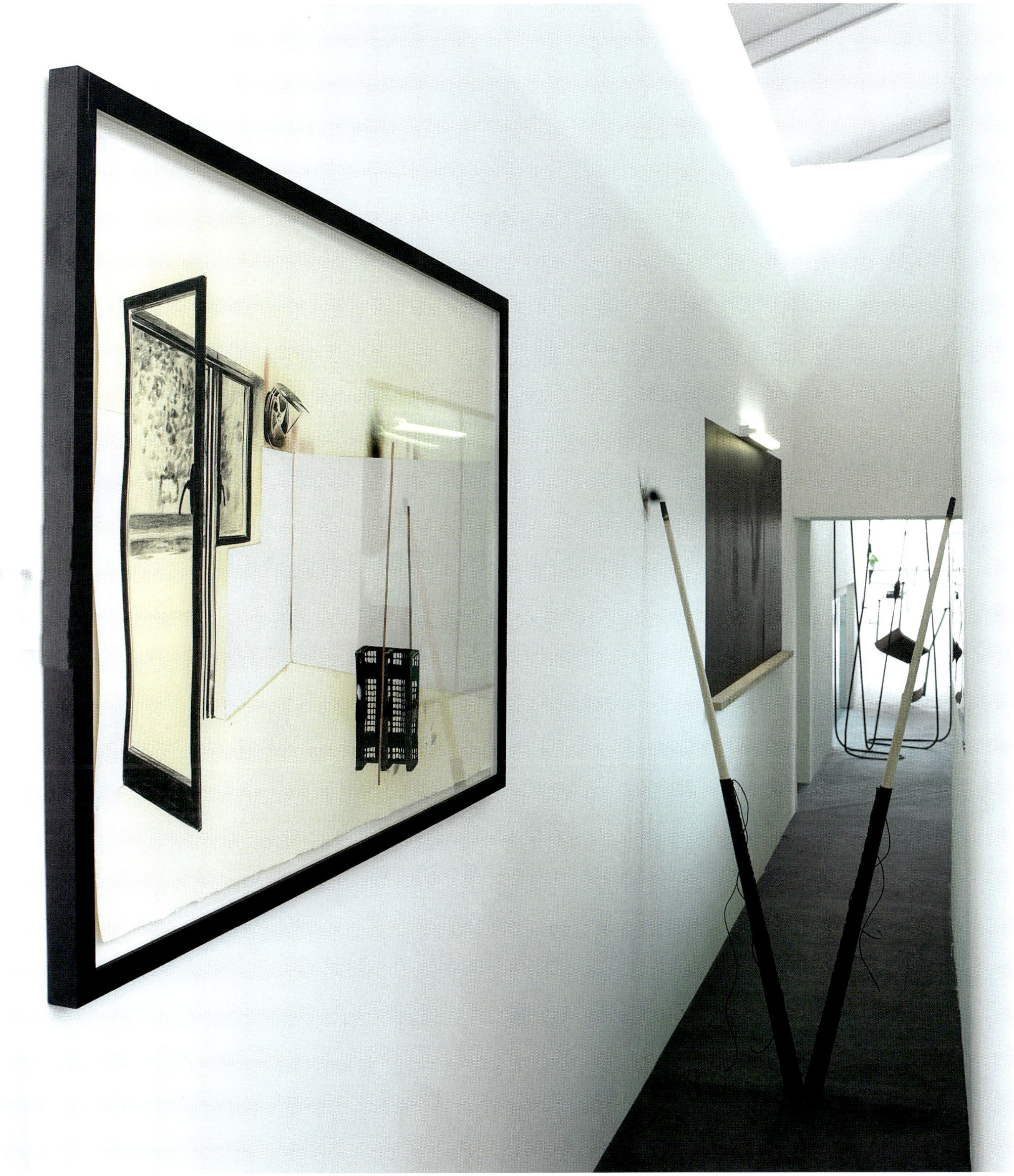

Detail from the installation *Untitled,* 2007

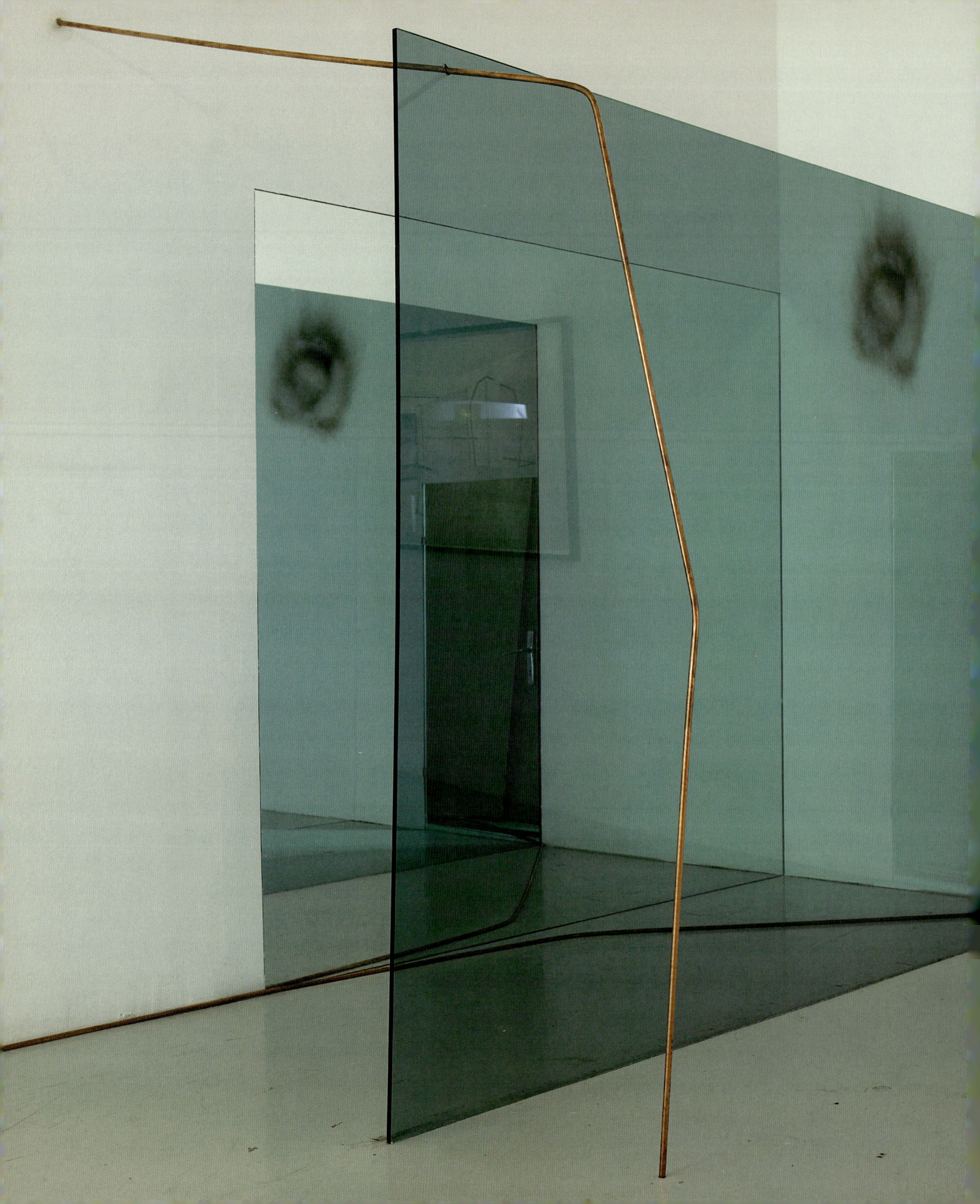

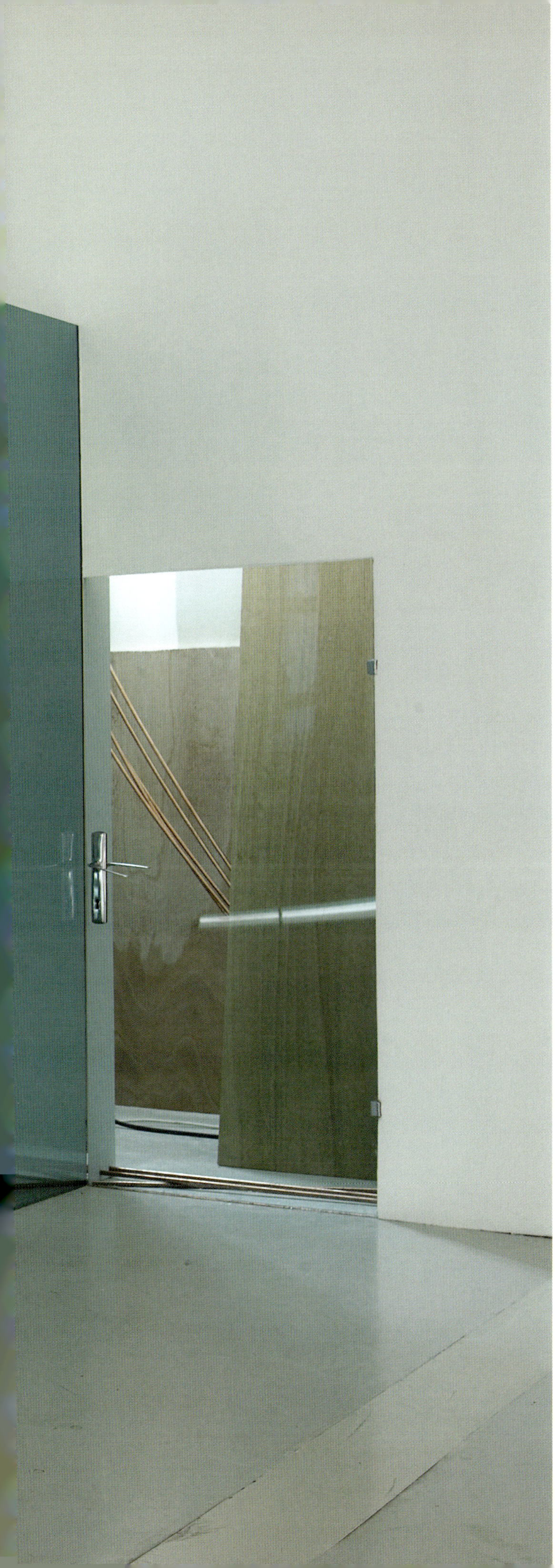

View of the exhibition *Airs de Paris,*
Centre Georges Pompidou, Paris, 2007

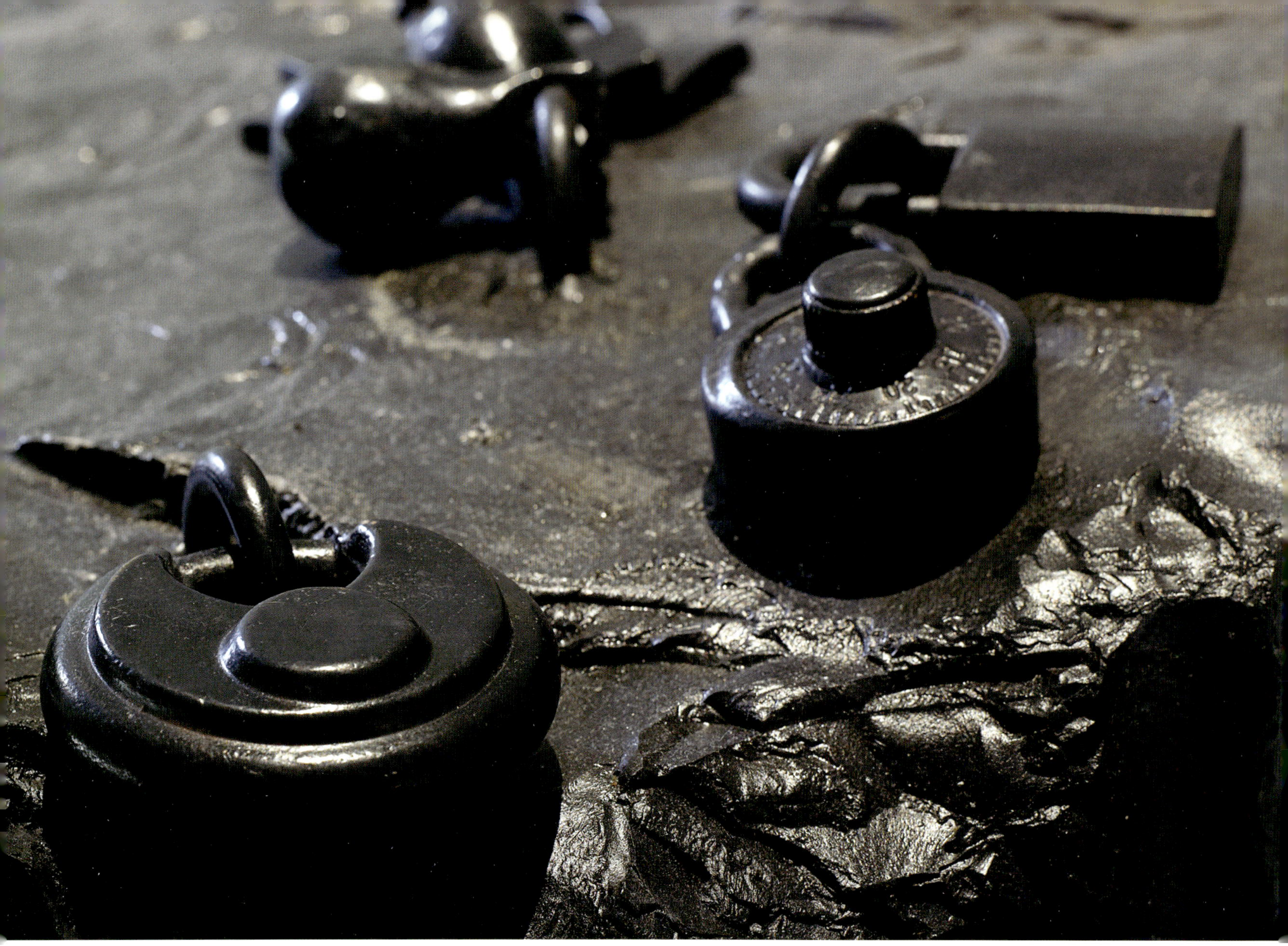

Rock (detail), 2007

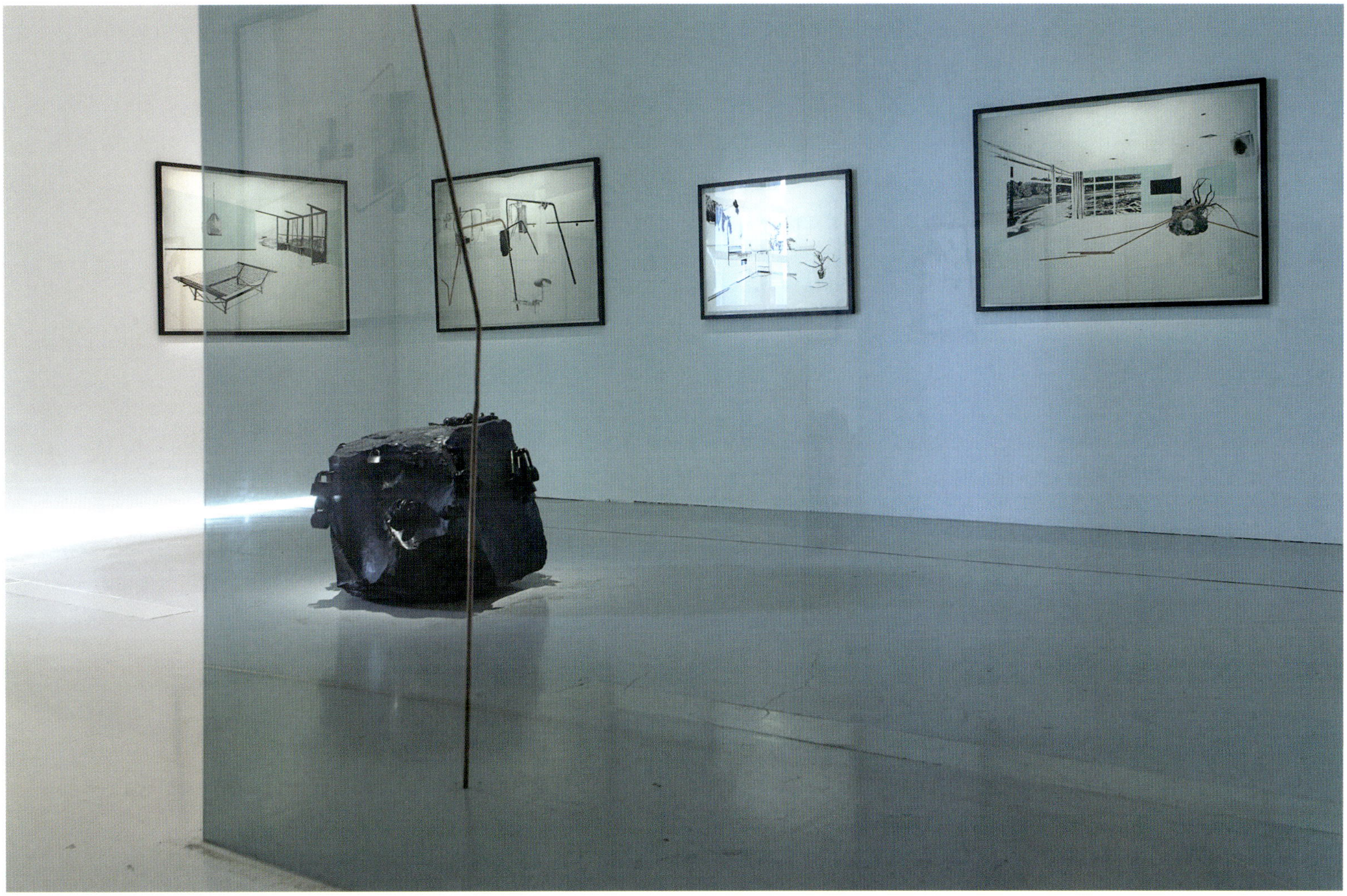

View of the exhibition *Airs de Paris,*
Centre Georges Pompidou, Paris, 2007

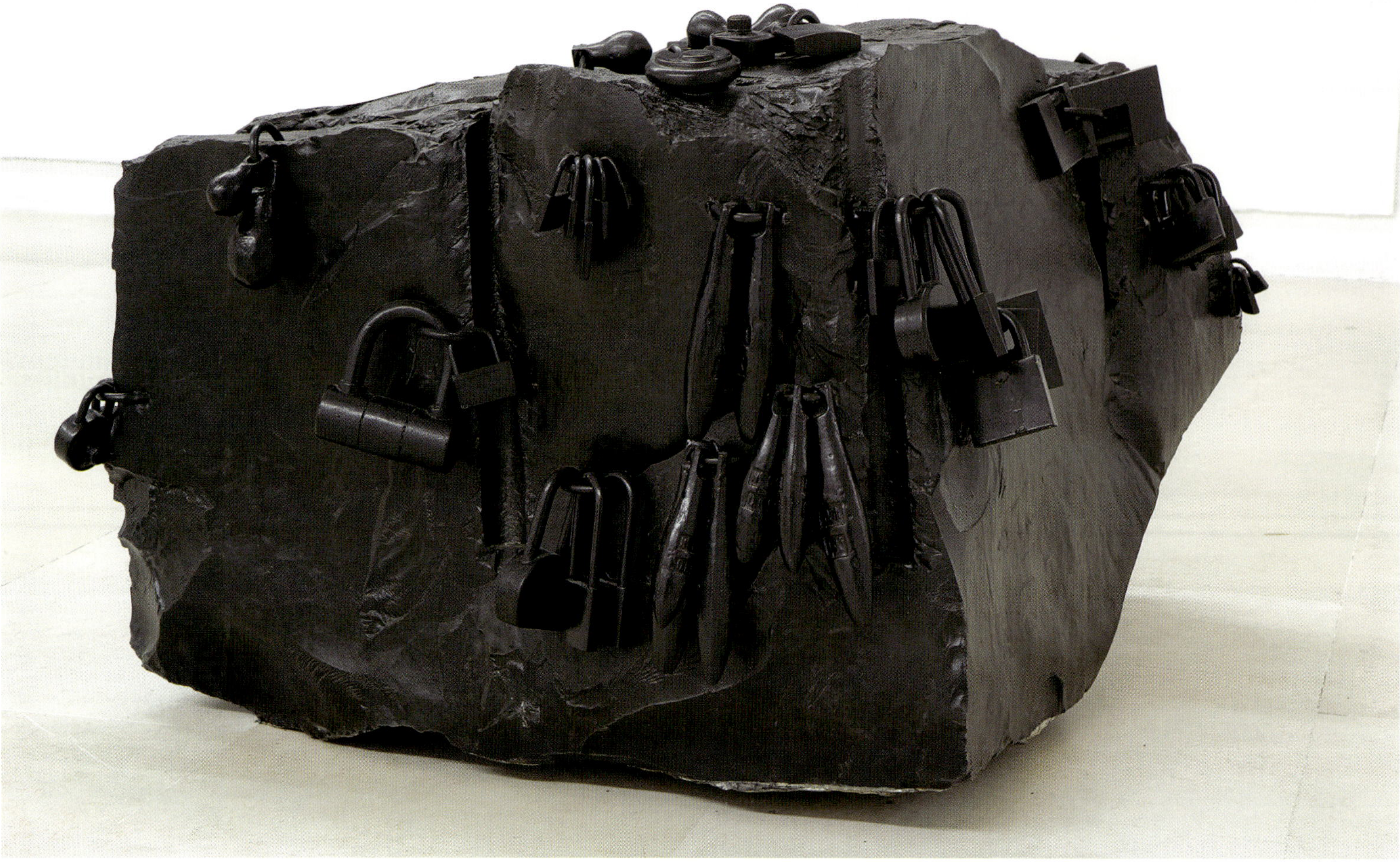

Rock, 2007
Fine black marble from Belgium, polished black bronze,
58 x 77 x 85 cm [22¾ x 30¼ x 33½ in.]

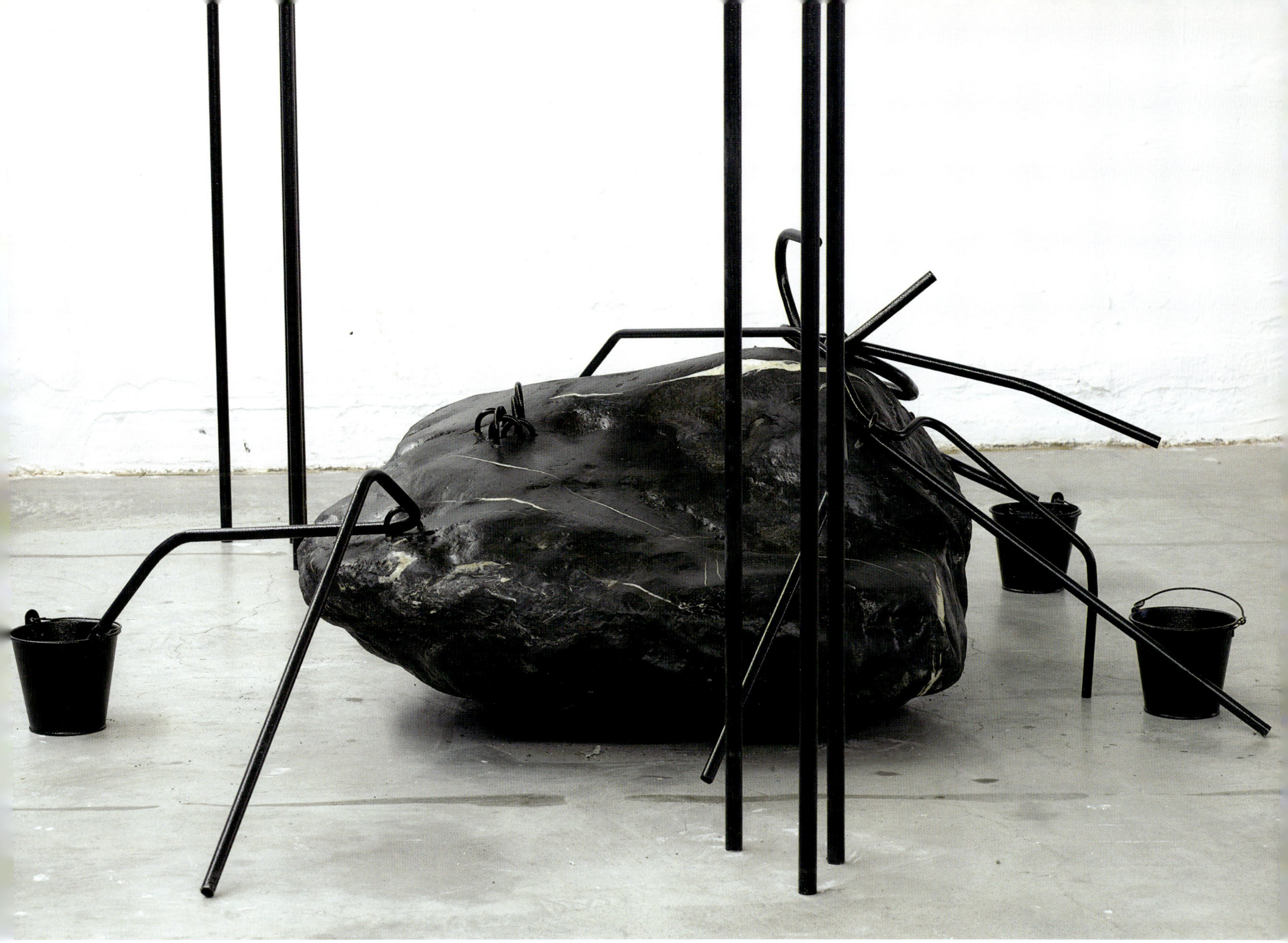

Above:
Polder (detail), 2007
Stone, painted metal, black epoxy paint, 260 x 450 x 300 cm
[102¼ x 177 x 118 in.]

Following pages:
View of the exhibition *Double Bind,* Palais de Tokyo, Paris, 2007

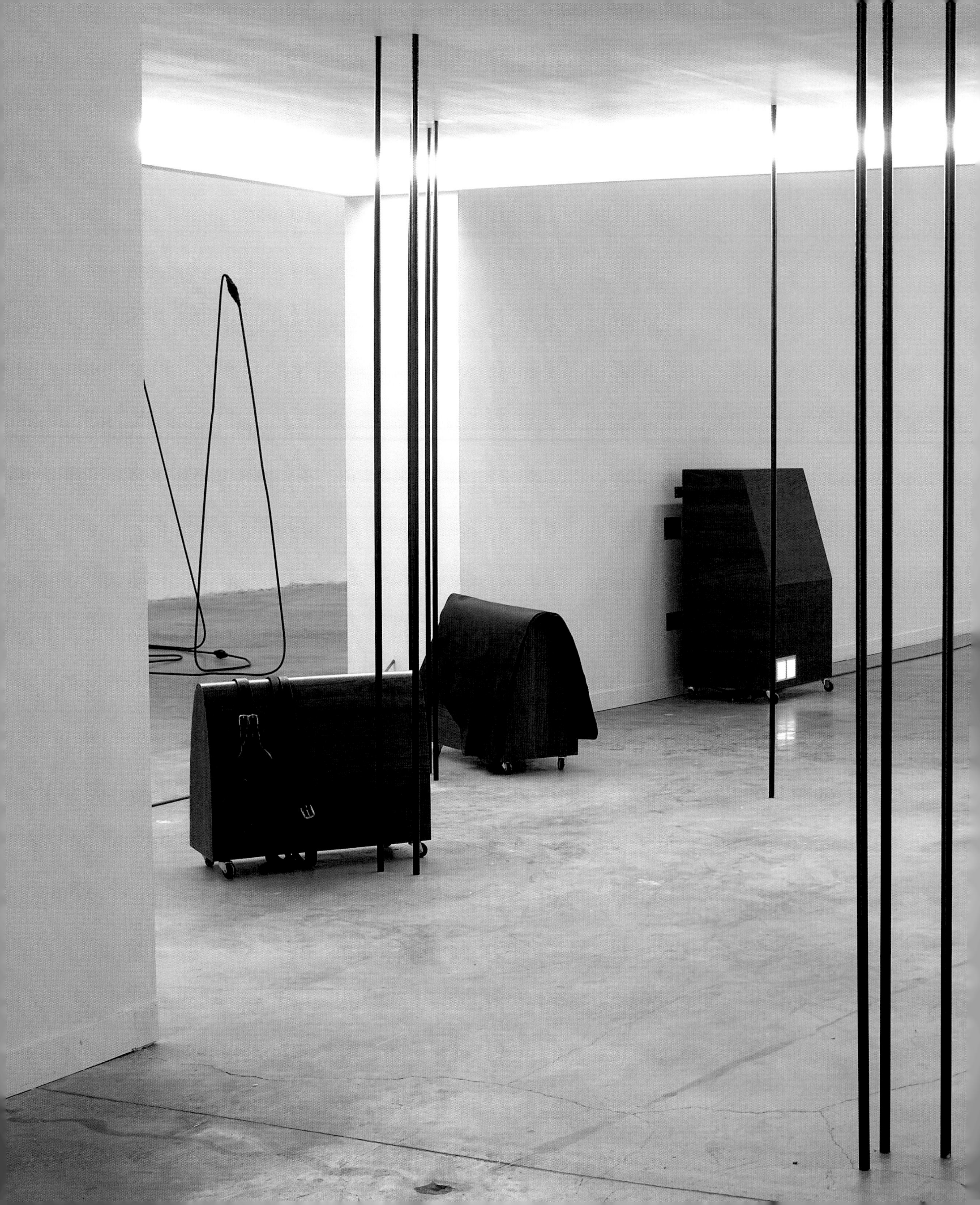

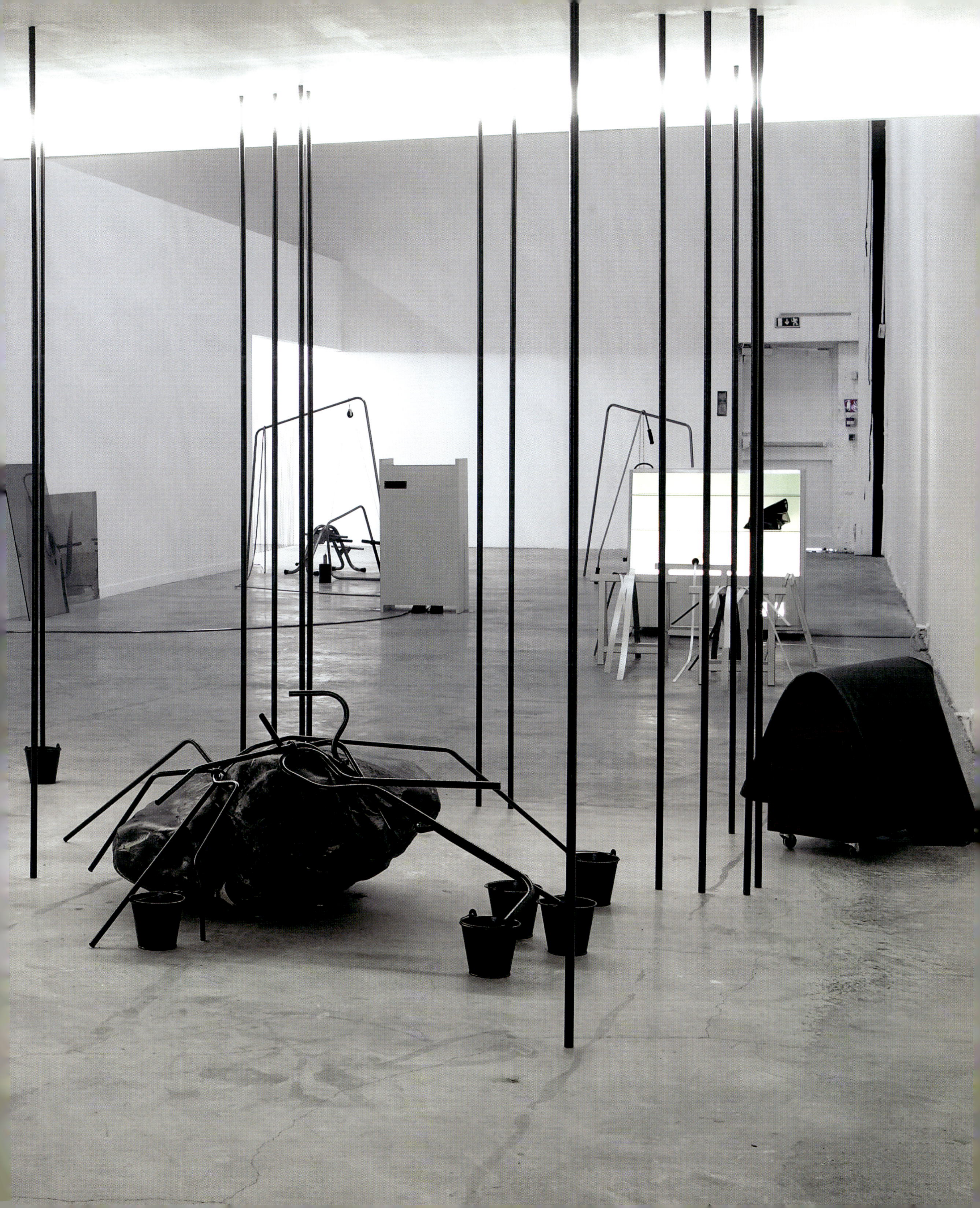

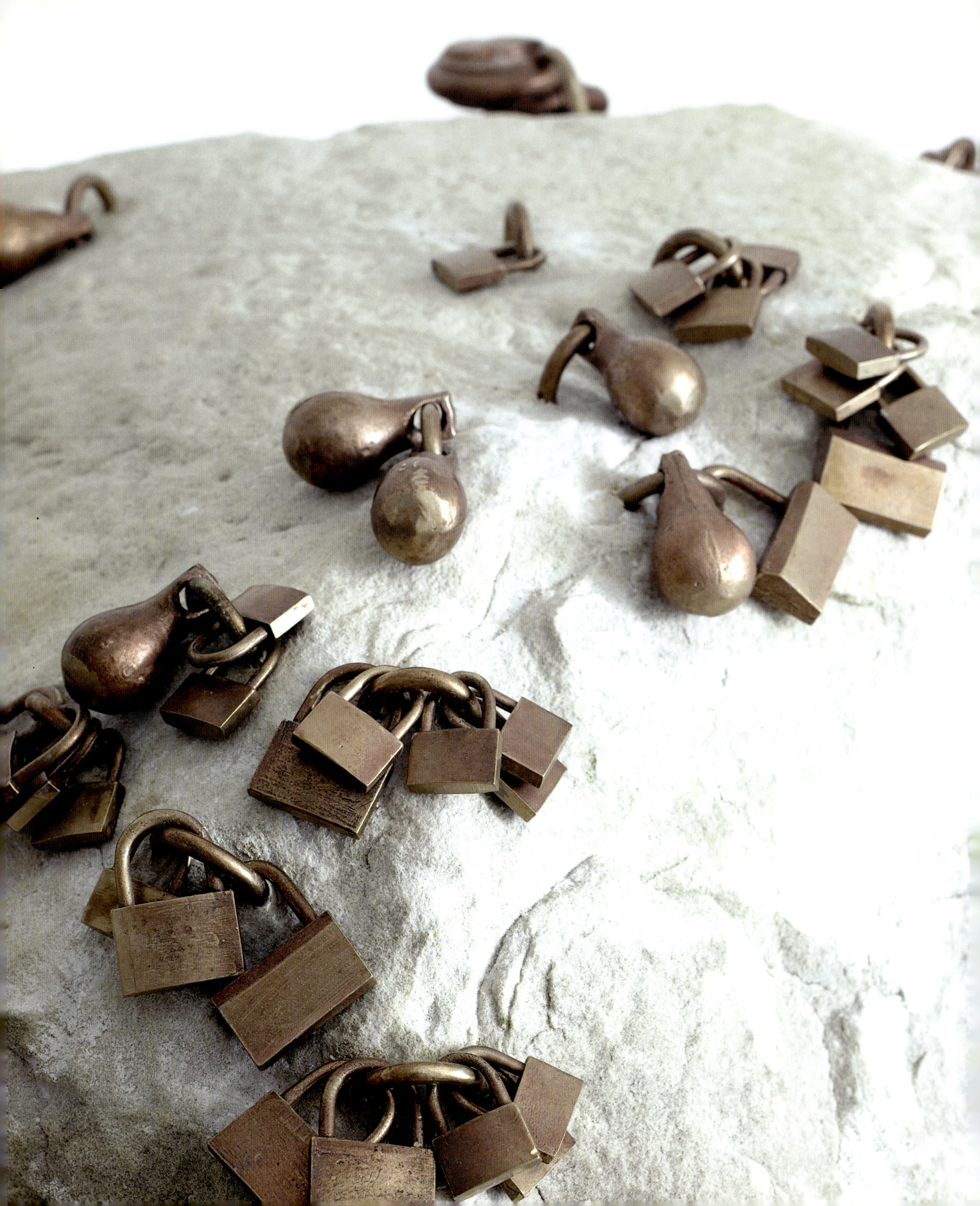

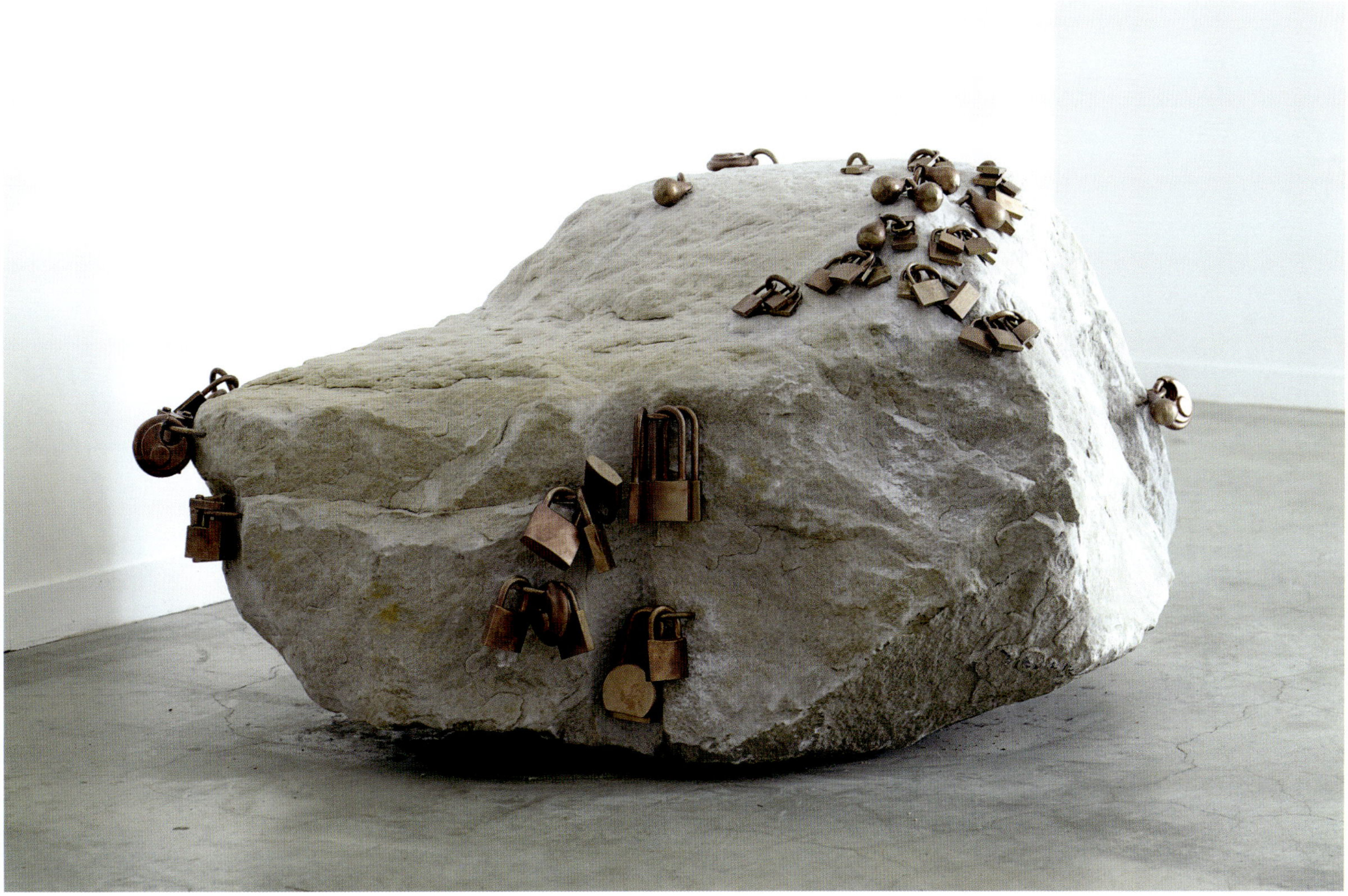

Rock, 2007
Fontainebleau stone, bronze, 63 x 106 x 122 cm
[24¾ x 41¾ x 48 in.]

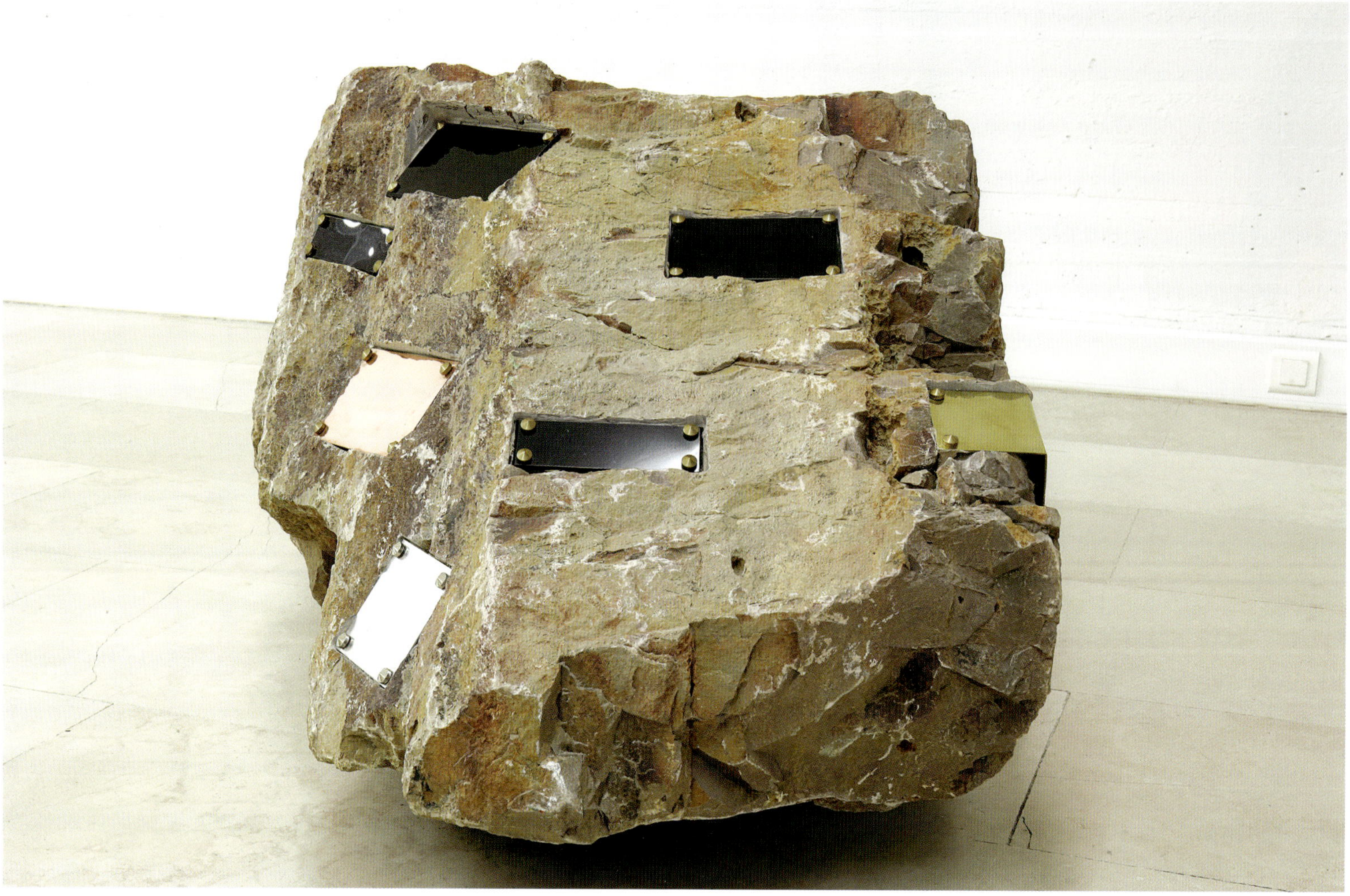

Rock, 2006
Stone, Plexiglas, aluminum, copper, brass,
63 x 147 x 72 cm [24¾ x 57¾ x 28¼ in.]

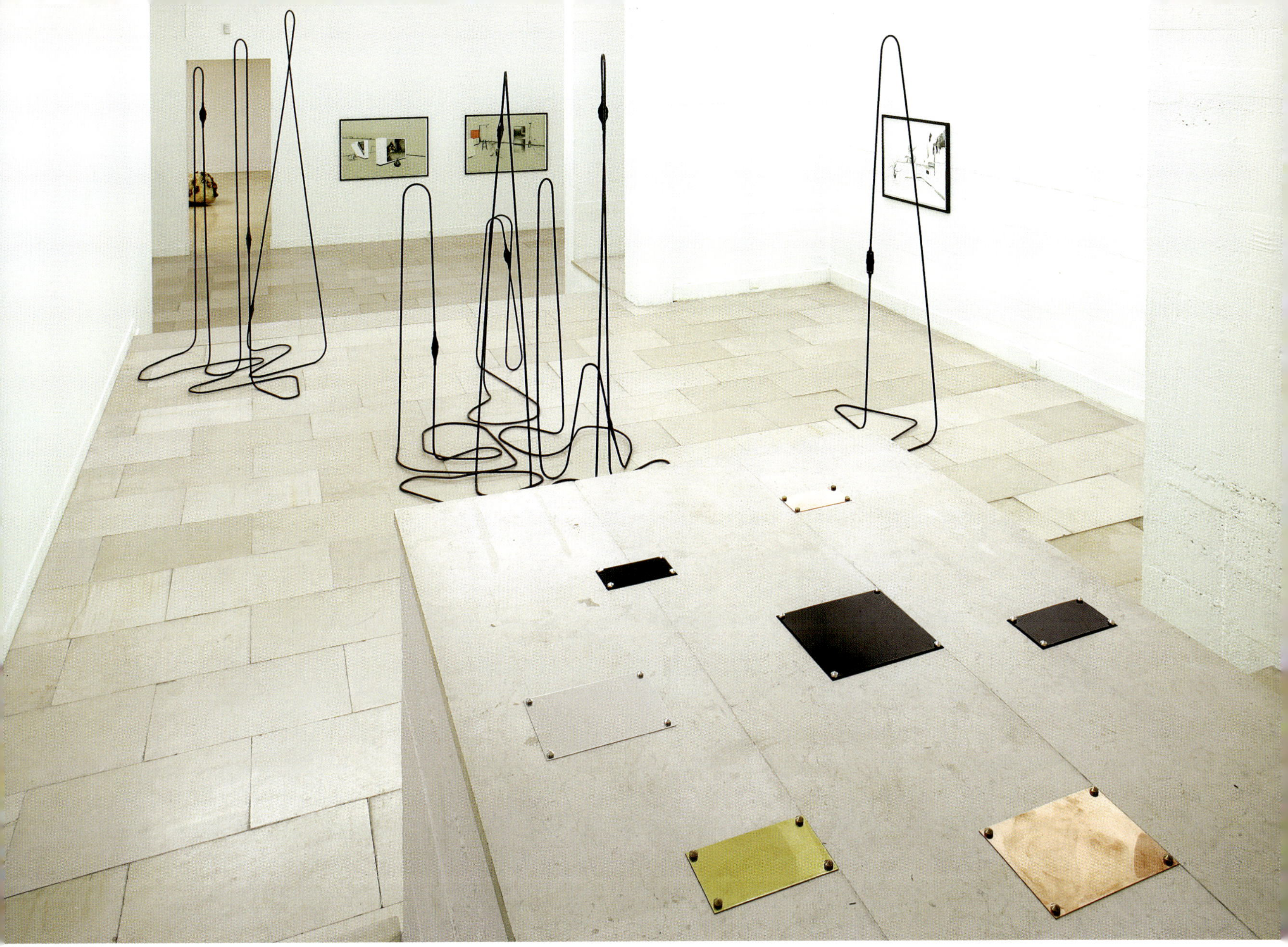

Above:
View of the exhibition *Tatiana Trouvé,* Centre National d'Art Contemporain de la Villa Arson, Nice, 2007

Following pages:
Untitled, 2007
Metal, rubber, 214 x 70 x 54 cm [84¼ x 27½ x 21¼ in.]
Untitled, 2007
Metal, rubber, 229 x 122 x 92 cm [90¼ x 48 x 36¼ in.]

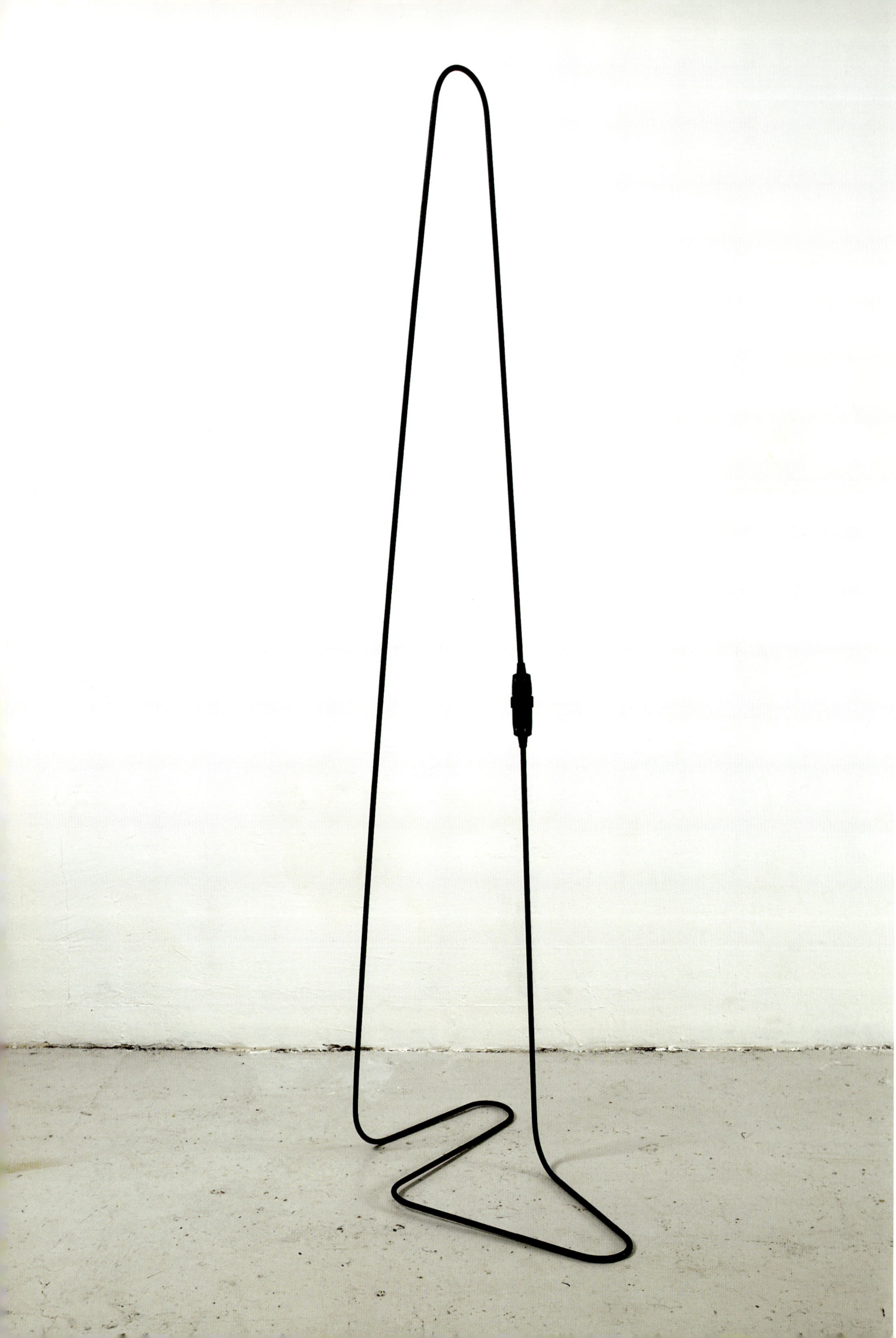

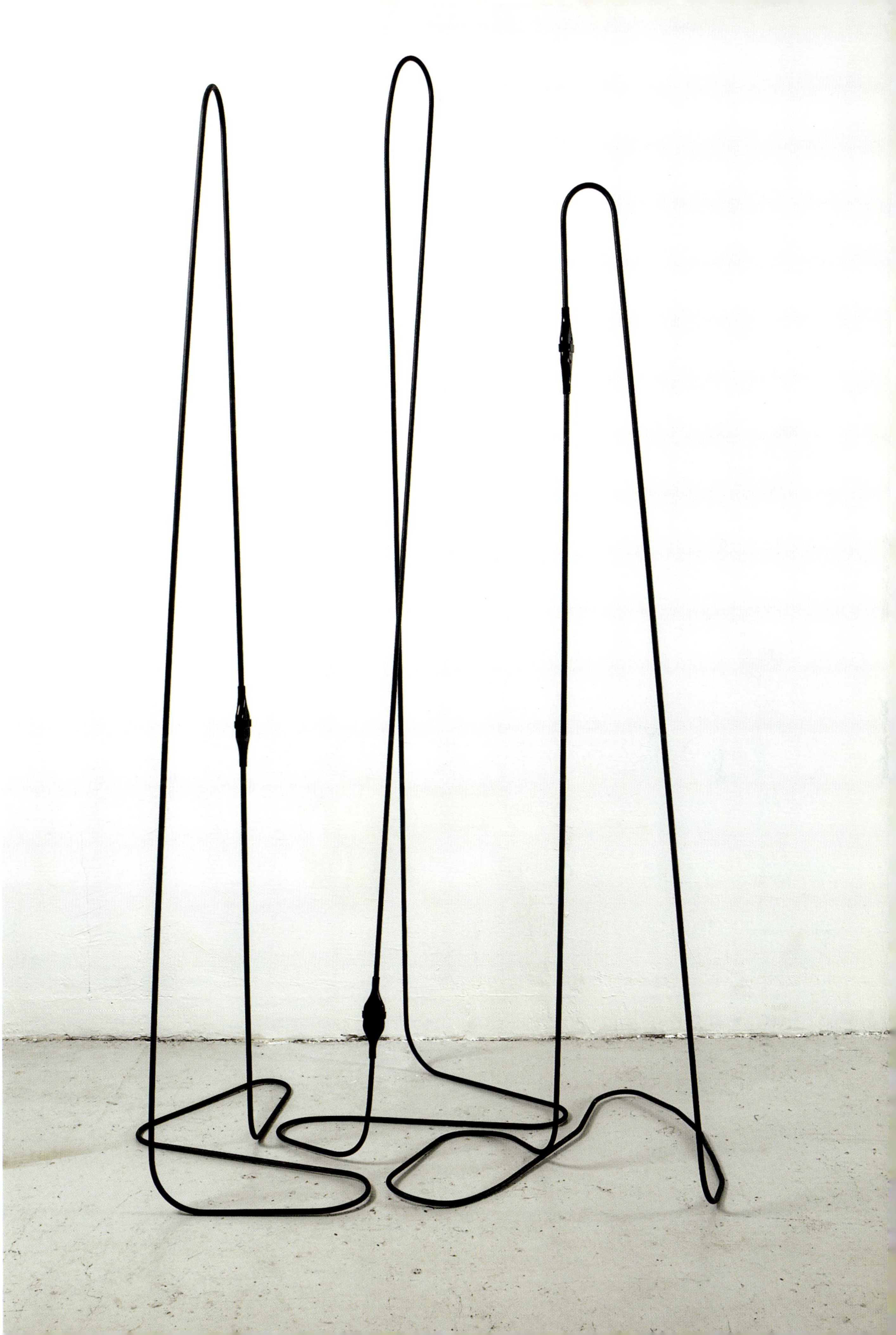

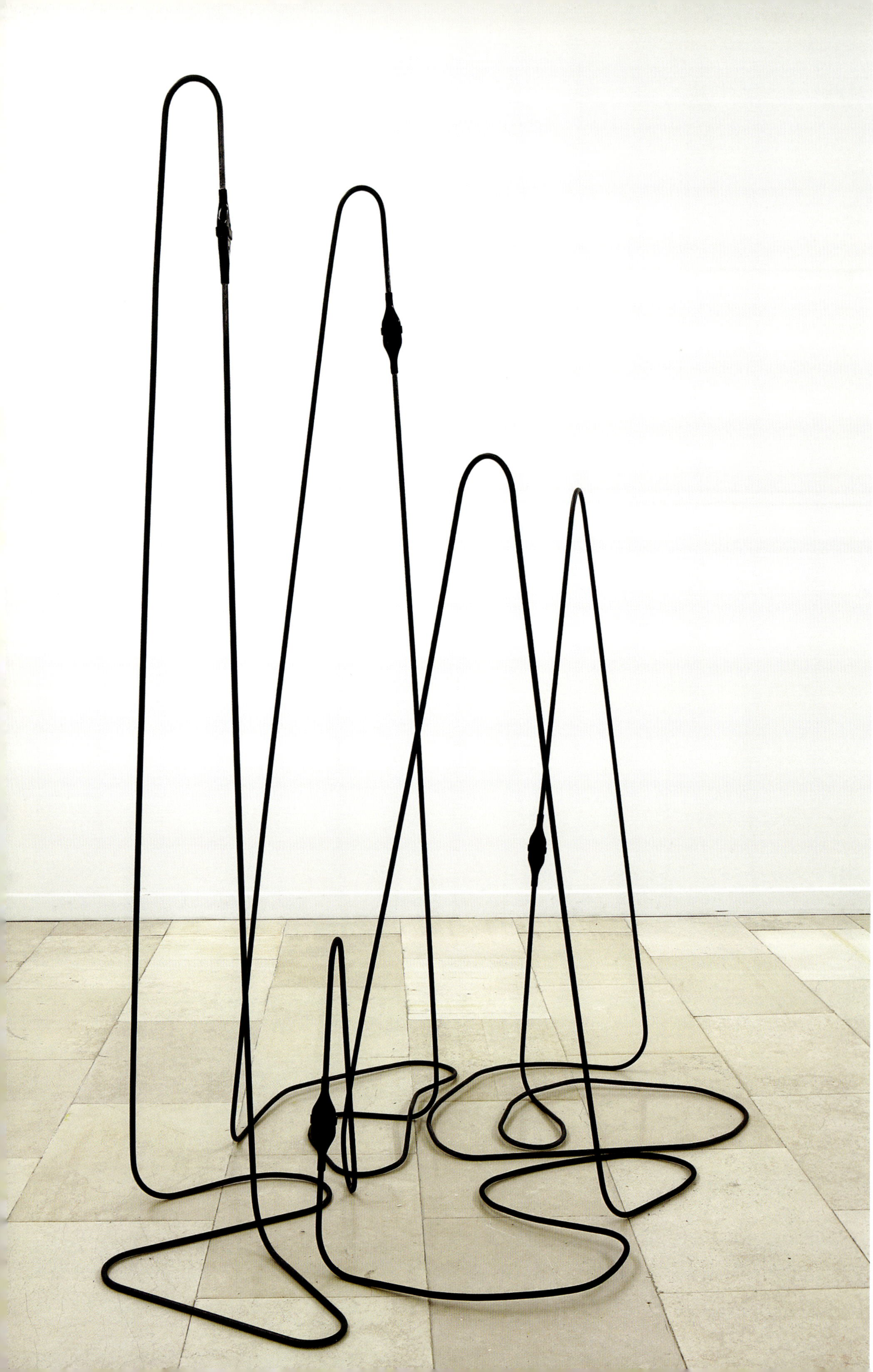

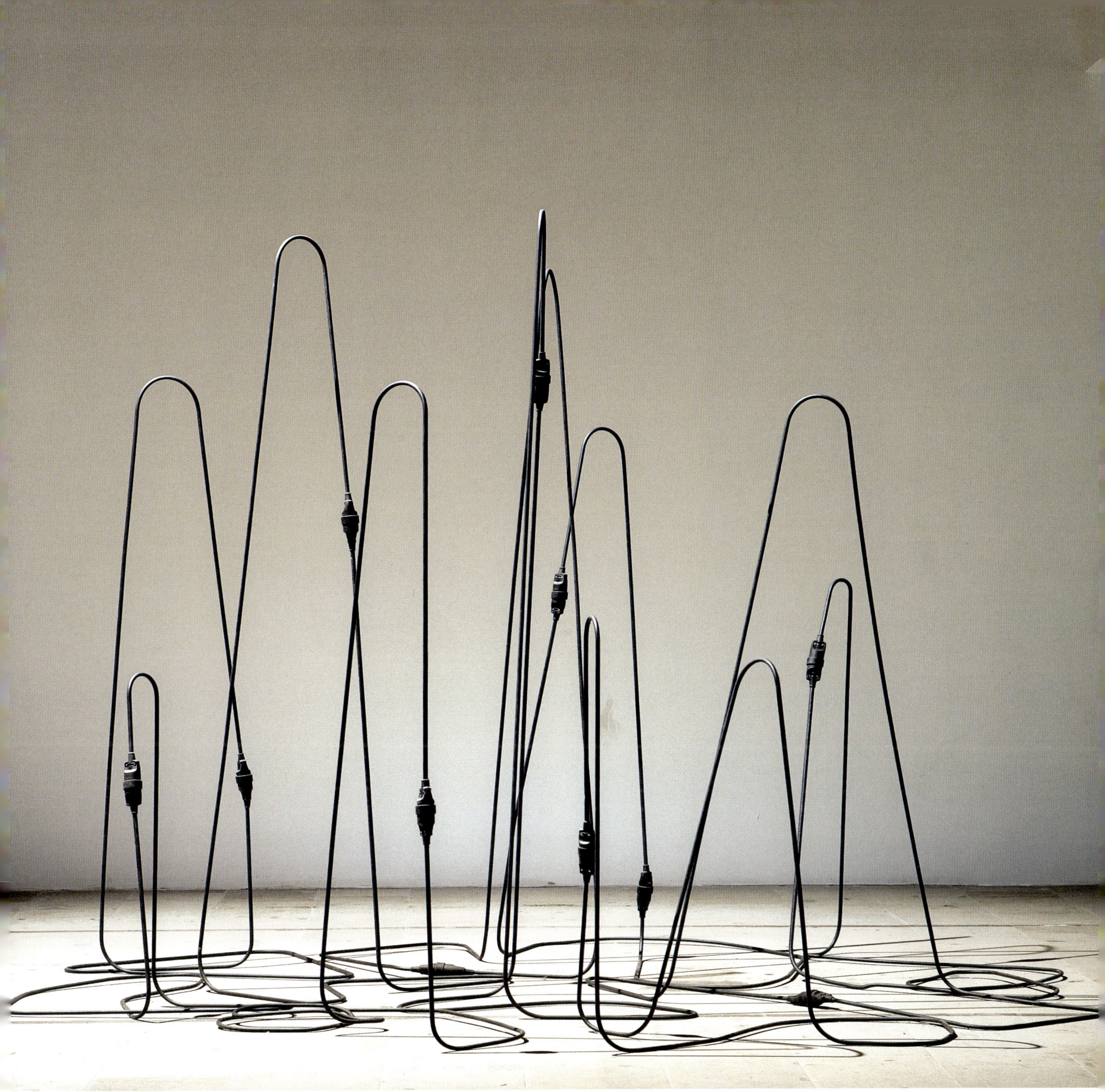

Untitled, 2007
Metal, rubber, 205 x 164 x 140 cm [80¾ x 64½ x 55 in.]

Above:
Untitled, 2007
Metal, rubber, 218 x 268 x 240 cm [85¾ x 105½ x 94½ in.]

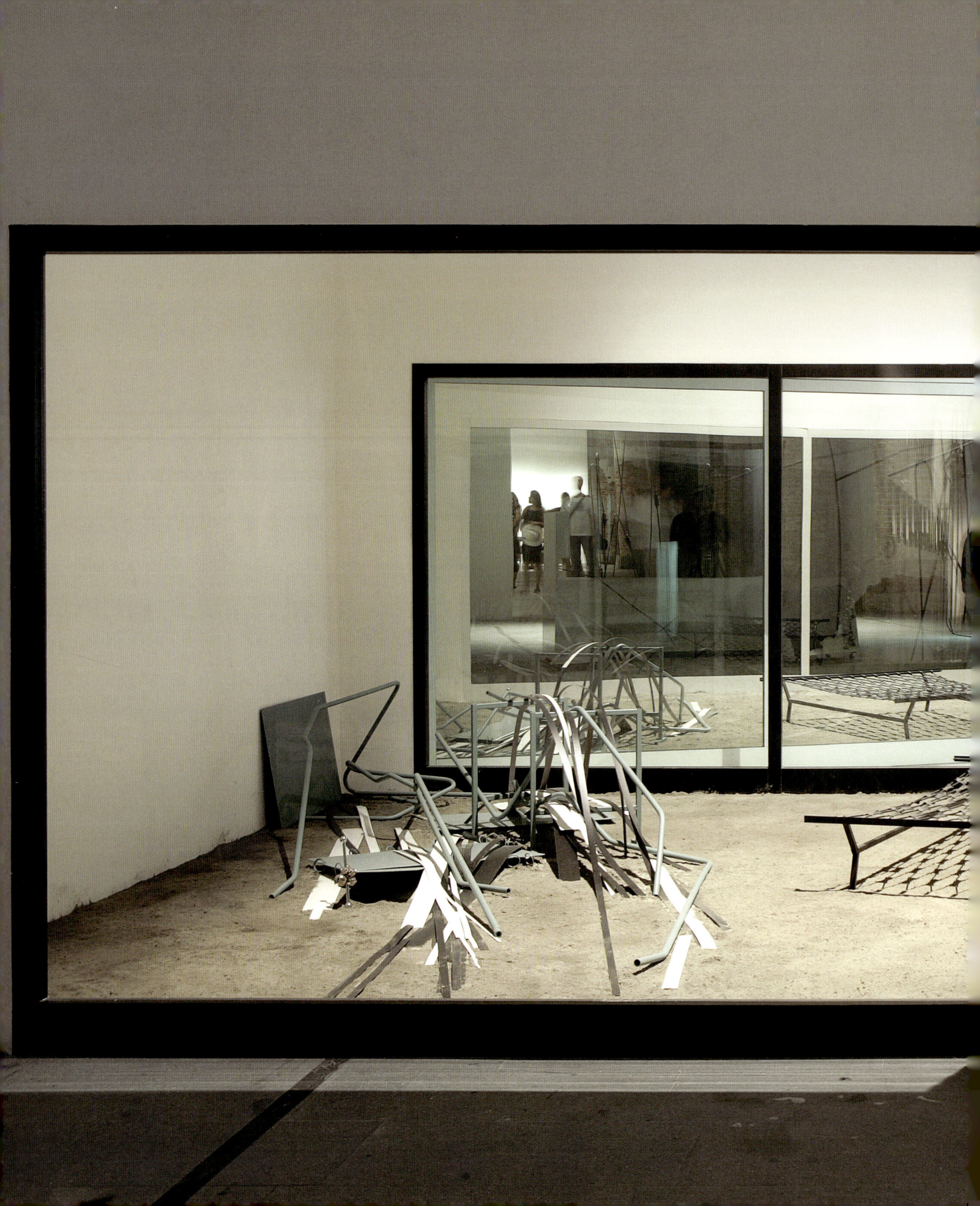

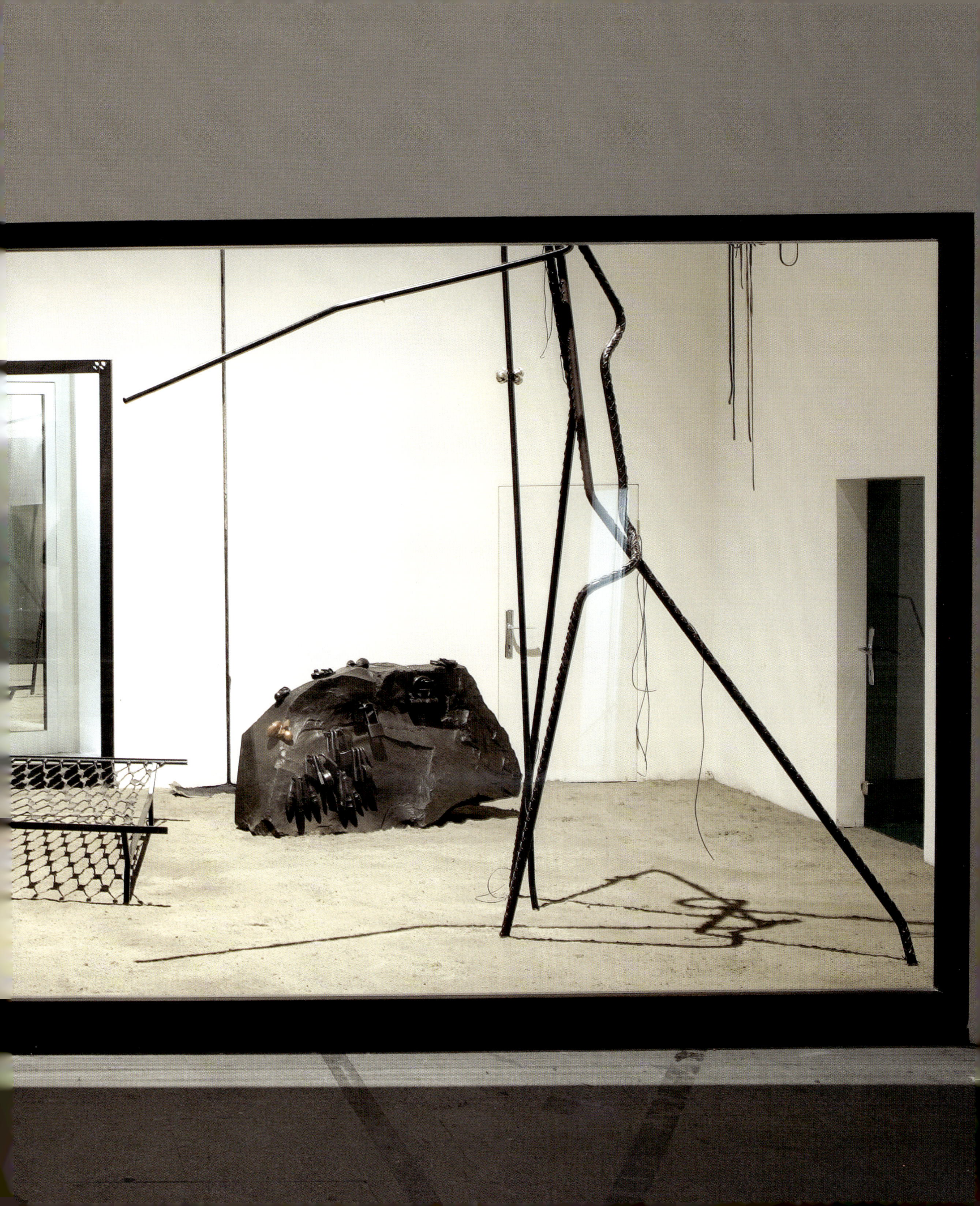

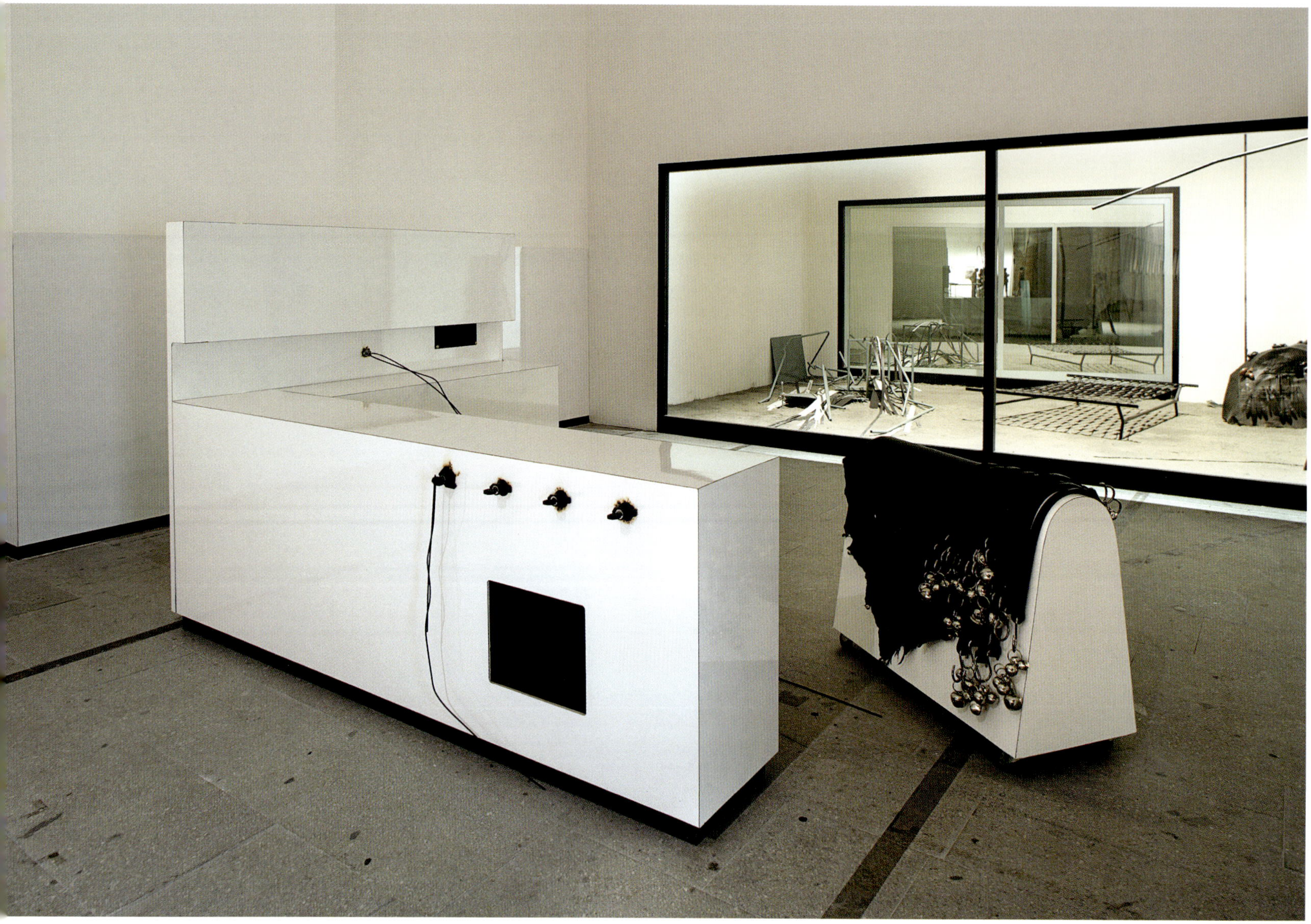

Previous pages:
Untitled, 2007
Cement, Plexiglas, Formica, metal, leather, marble, bronze, wood, 300 x 610 x 421 cm [118 x 240 x 165¾ in.]

Above:
View of the exhibition *Think with the Senses – Feel with the Mind,* 52nd Venice Biennale, 2007

Right-hand page:
Expansion of a Closure, step 0, 2007
Metal, Plexiglas, rubber, neon light, wood, Formica, 128 x 84 x 73 cm [50½ x 33 x 28¾ in.]

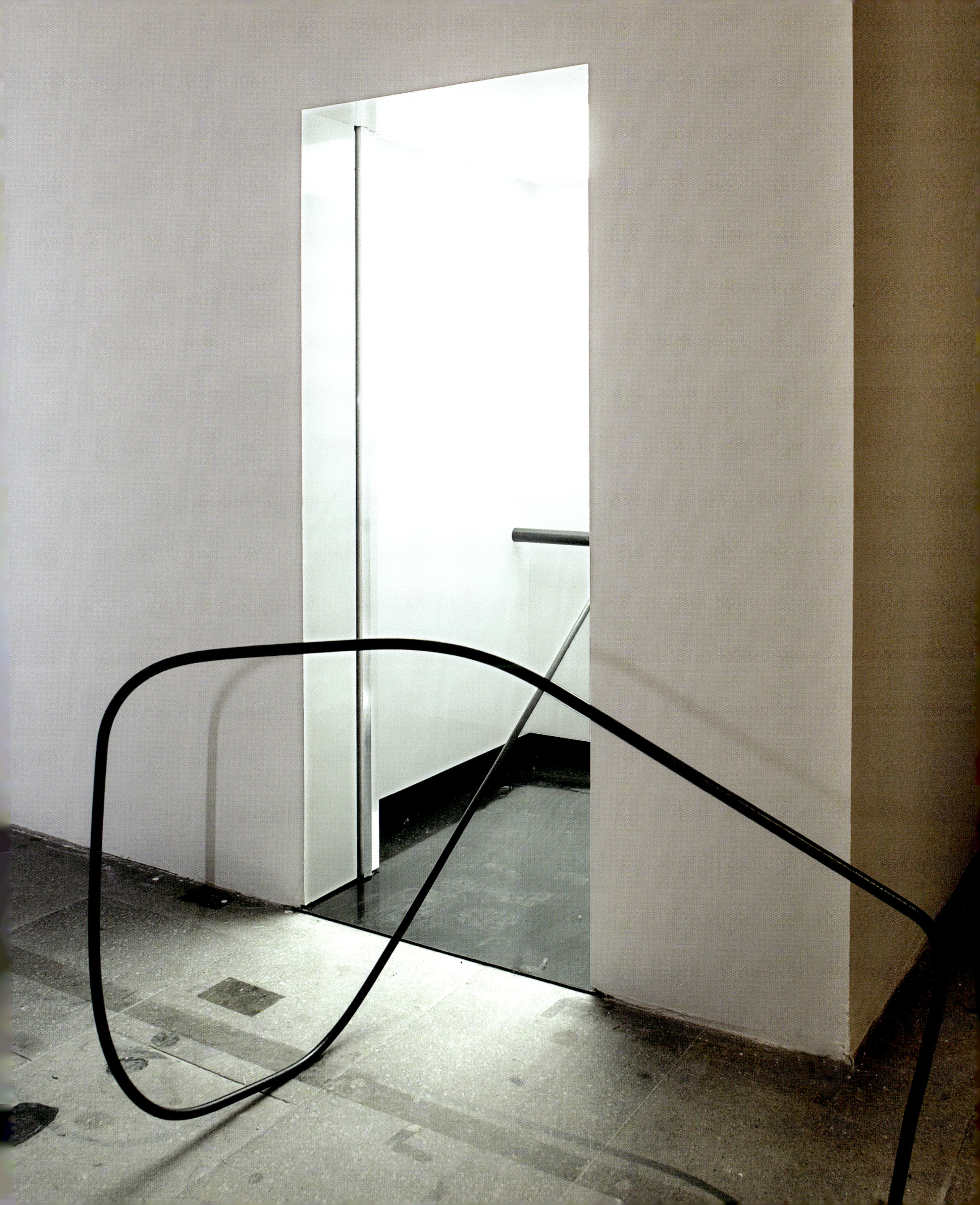

Expansion of a closure, step 1, 2007
Metal, Plexiglas, rubber, neon light, wood, Formica, 145 x 78 x 87 cm
[57 x 30¾ x 34¼ in.]

Following pages:
Polder, 2007
Formica, wood, Plexiglas, neon light, metal, paint, plastic, 96 x 100 x 360 cm
[37¾ x 39¼ x 141¾ in.]

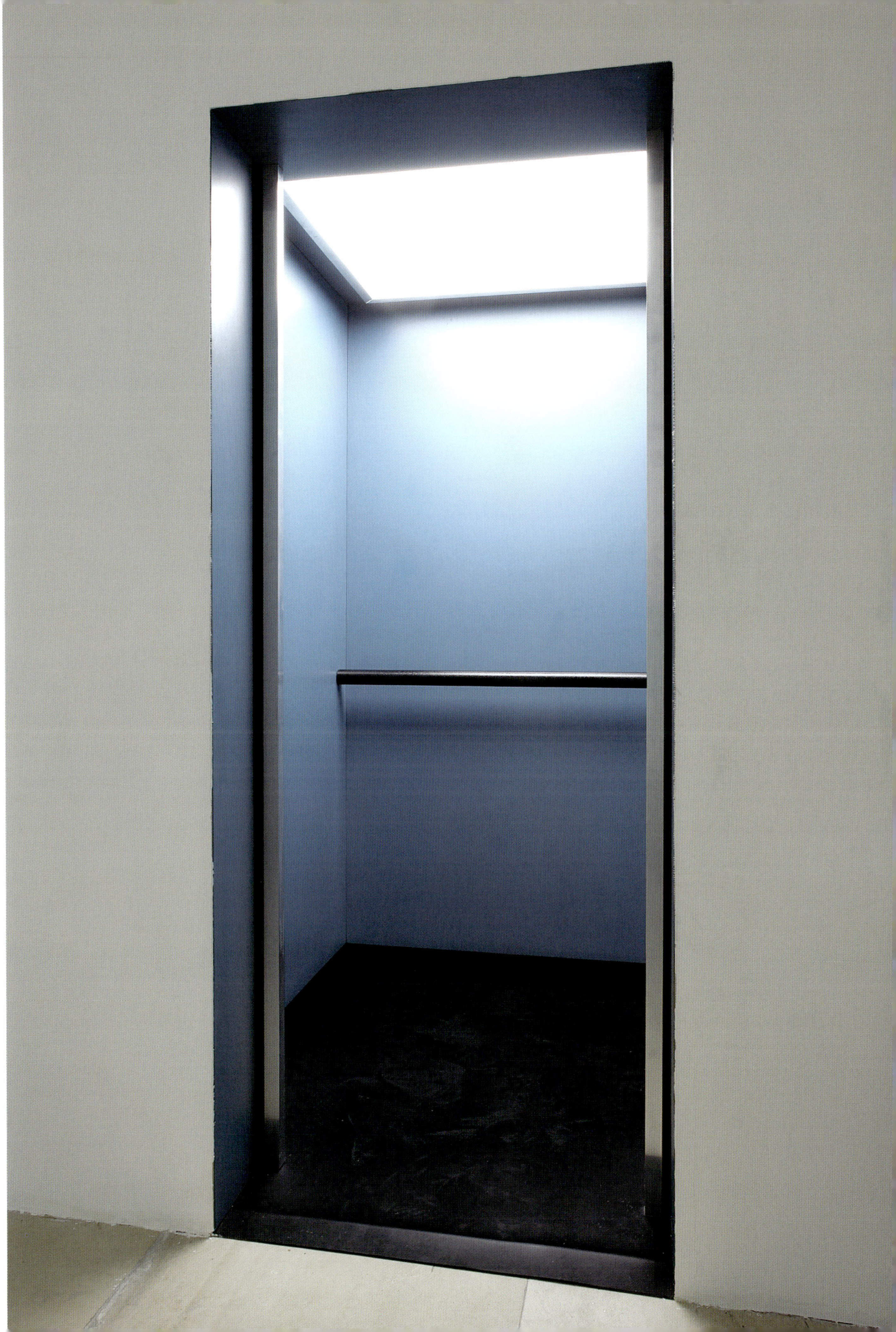

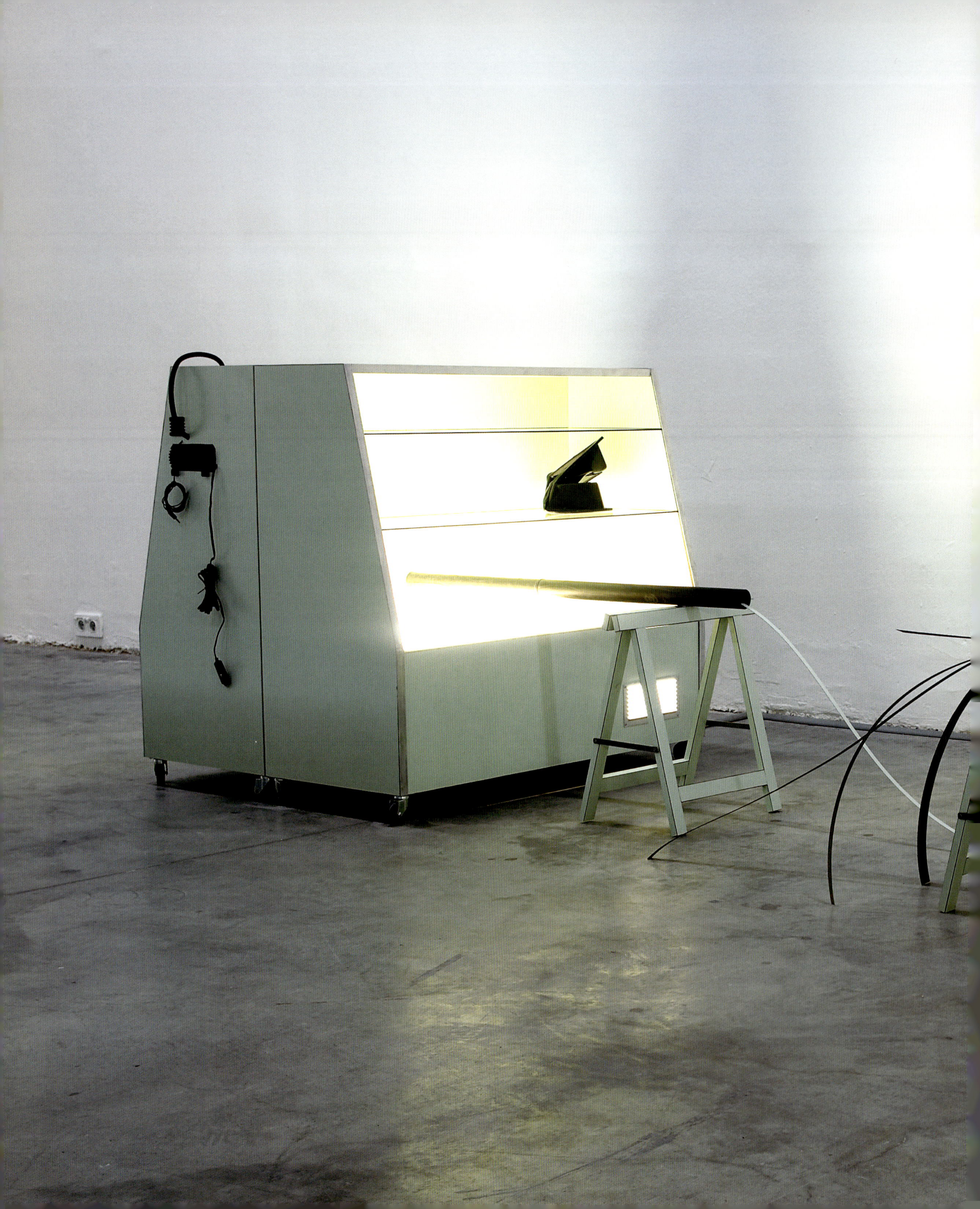

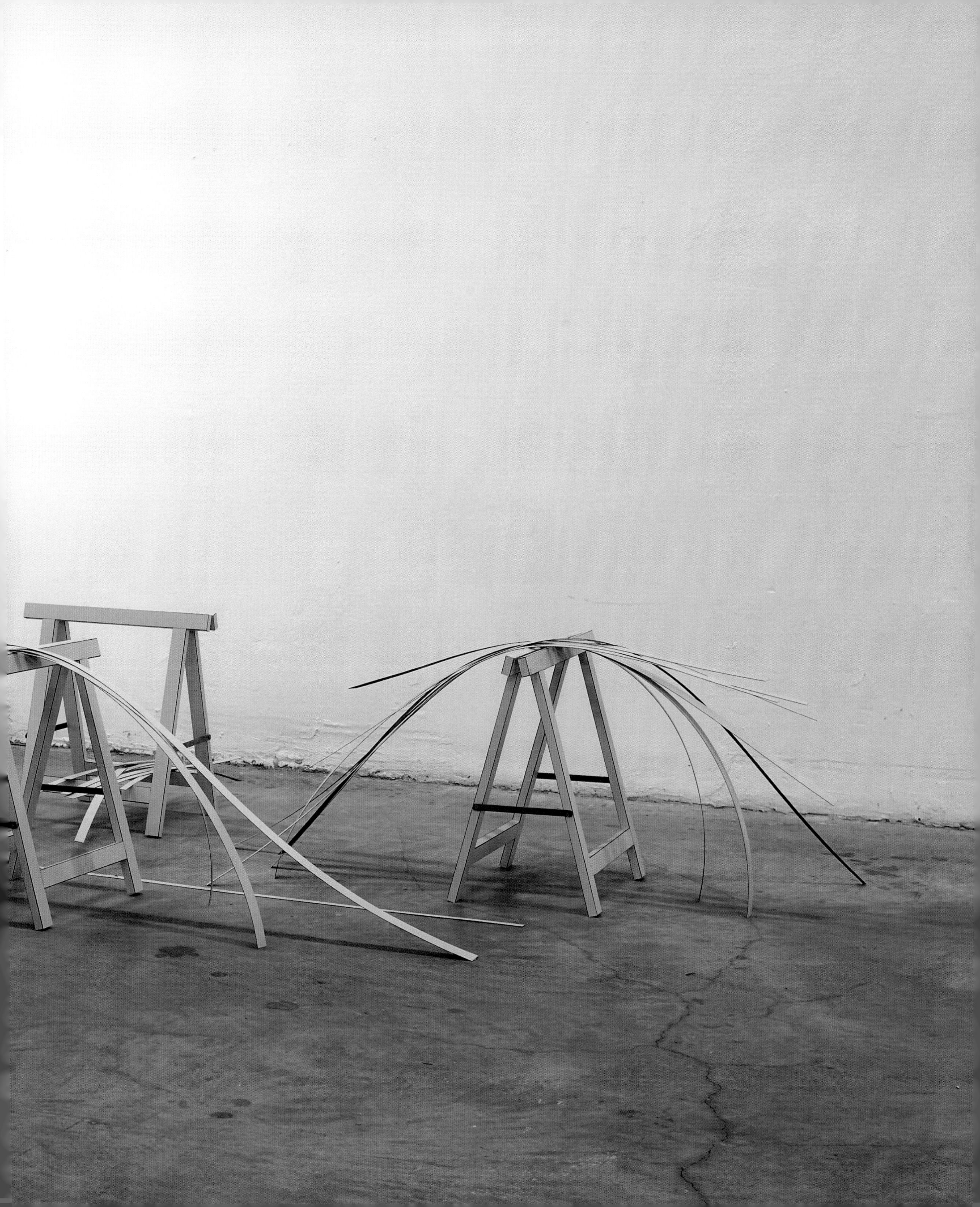

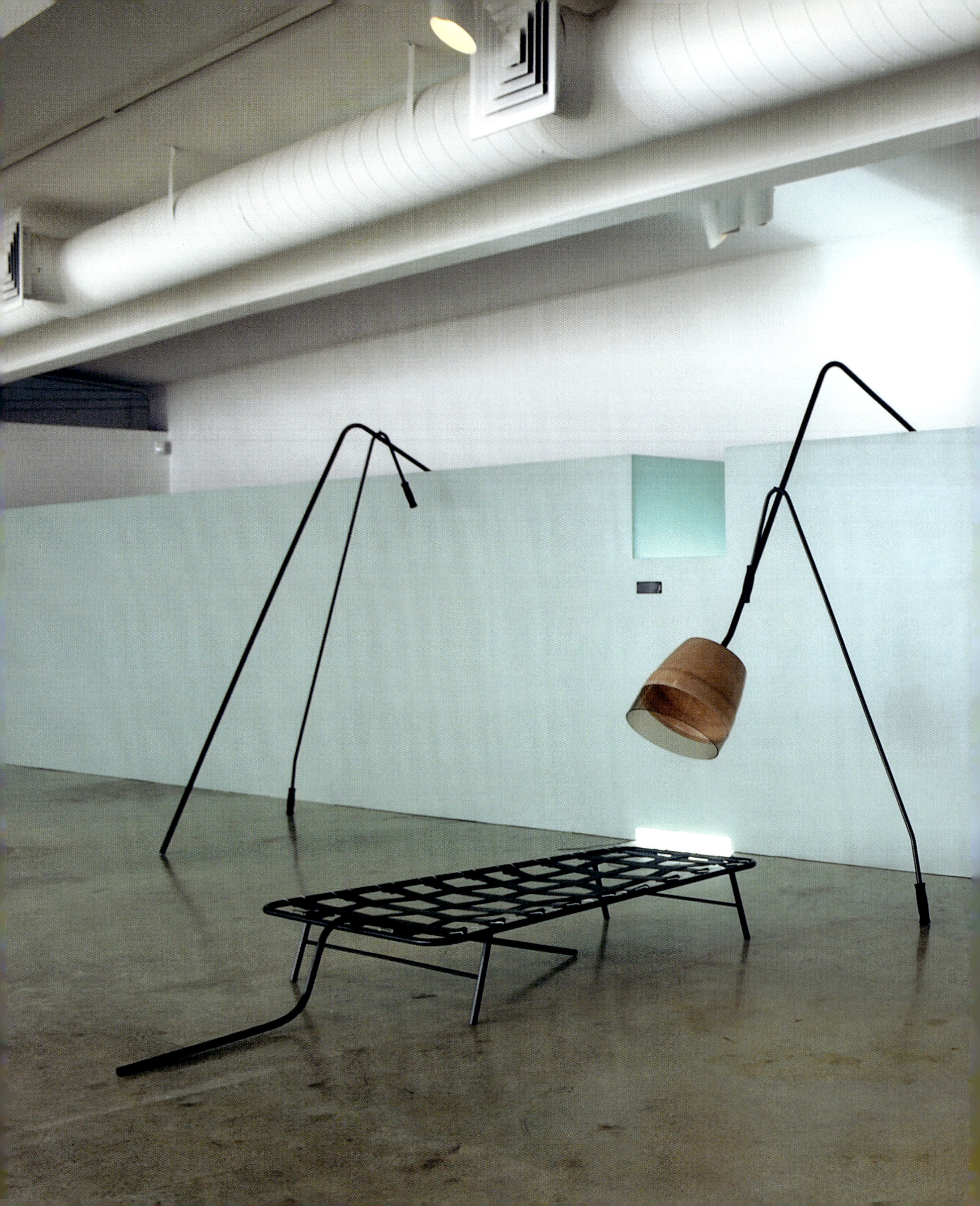

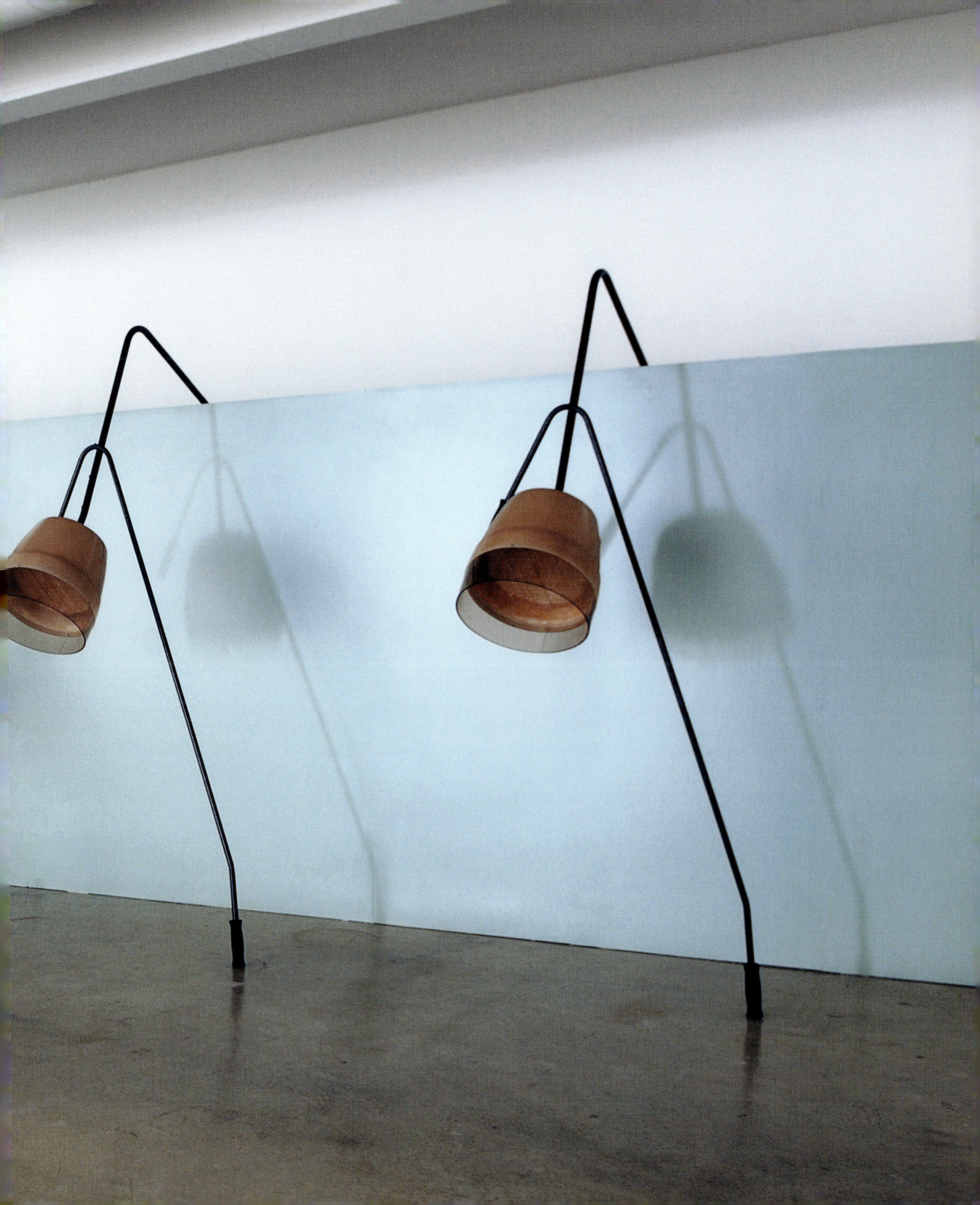

Previous pages:
Untitled, 2007 (view of the exhibition *Time Snares,*
Galerie Emmanuel Perrotin, Miami)
Metal, epoxy paint, Formica, wood, leather, resin,
190 x 800 x 500 cm [74¾ x 315 x 197 in.]

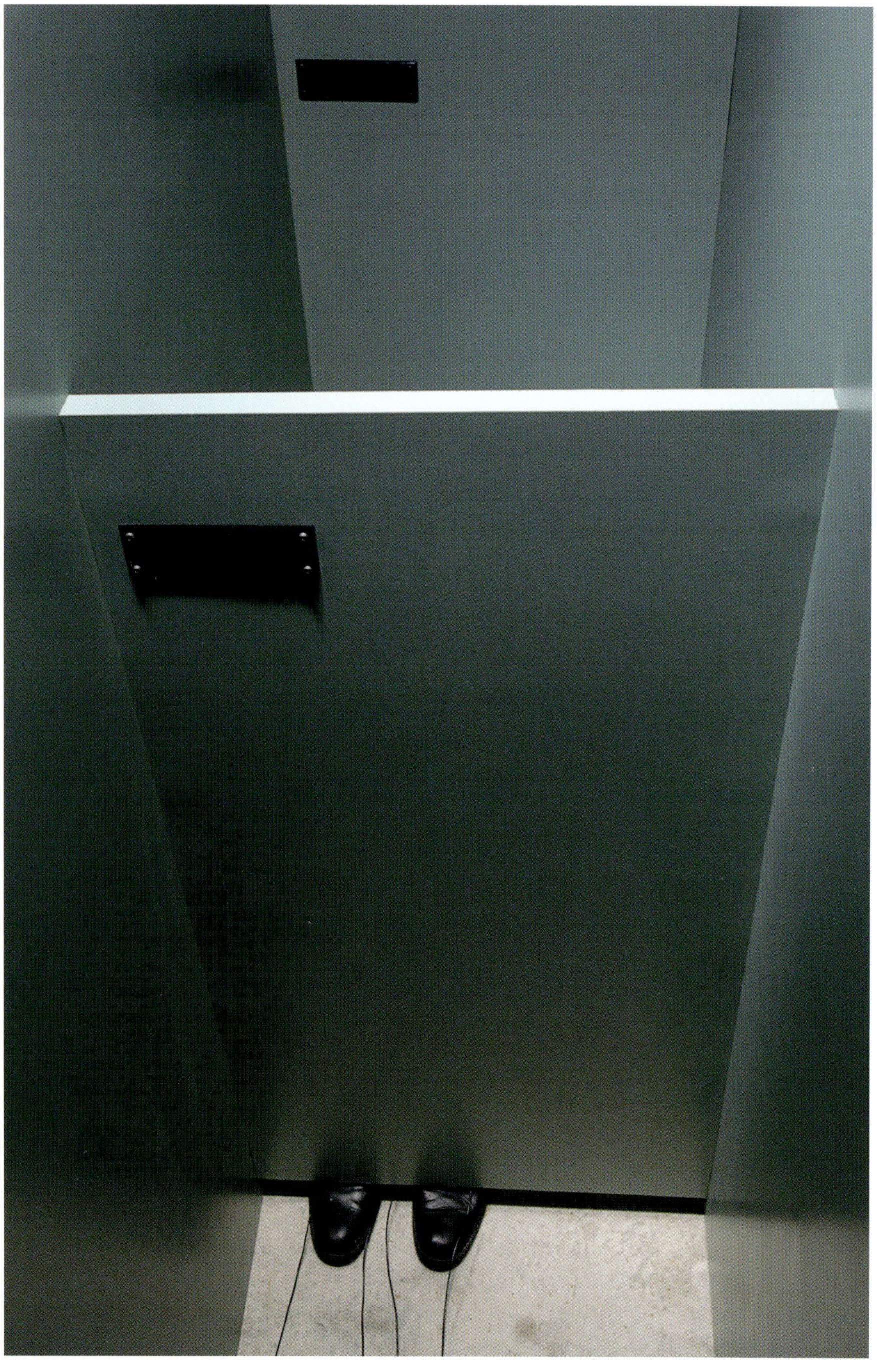

Untitled (details of the installation), 2007

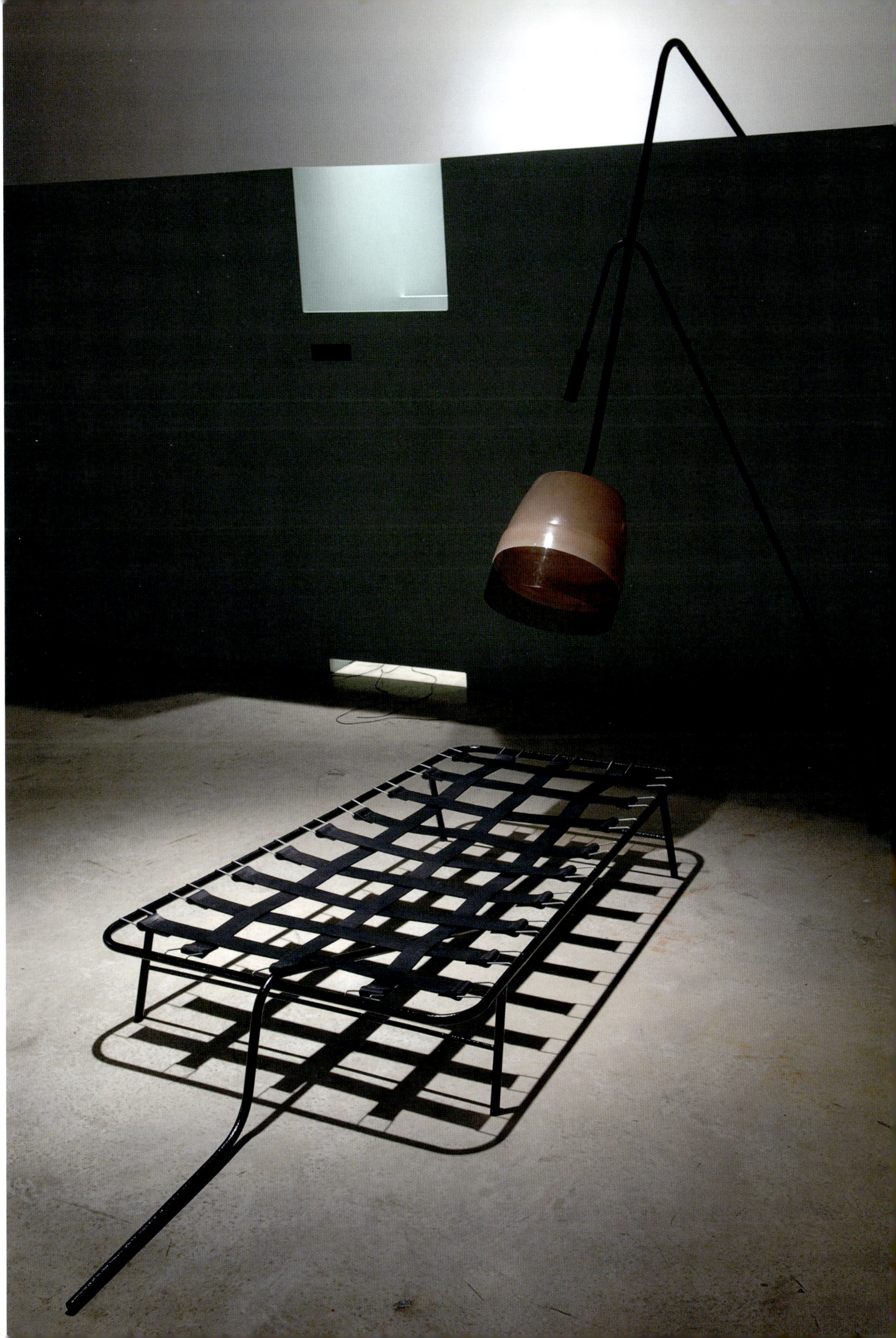

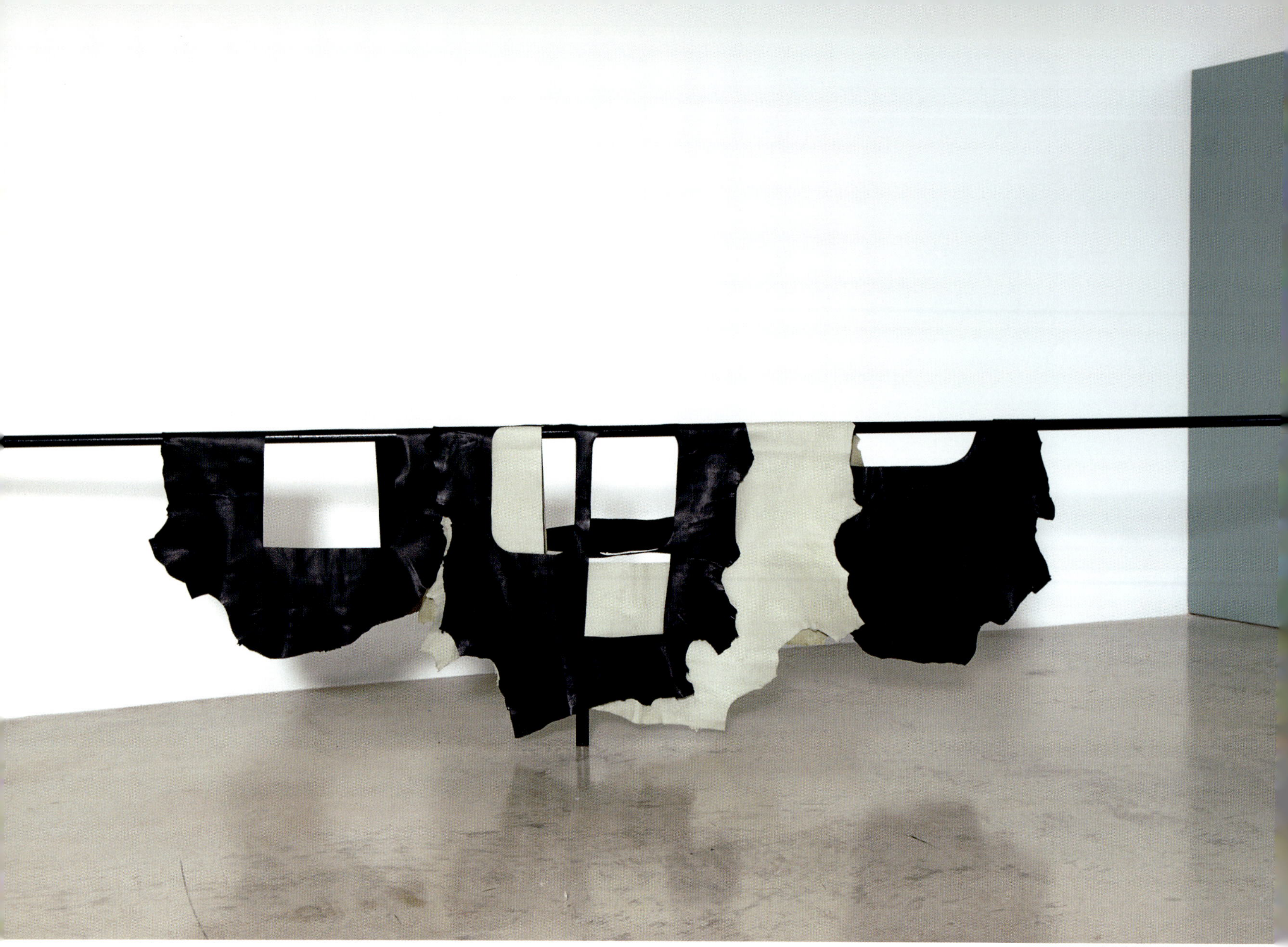

Detail of the exhibition *Time Snares,*
Galerie Emmanuel Perrotin, Miami, 2007
Metal, leather, epoxy paint, Formica, wood, variable dimensions

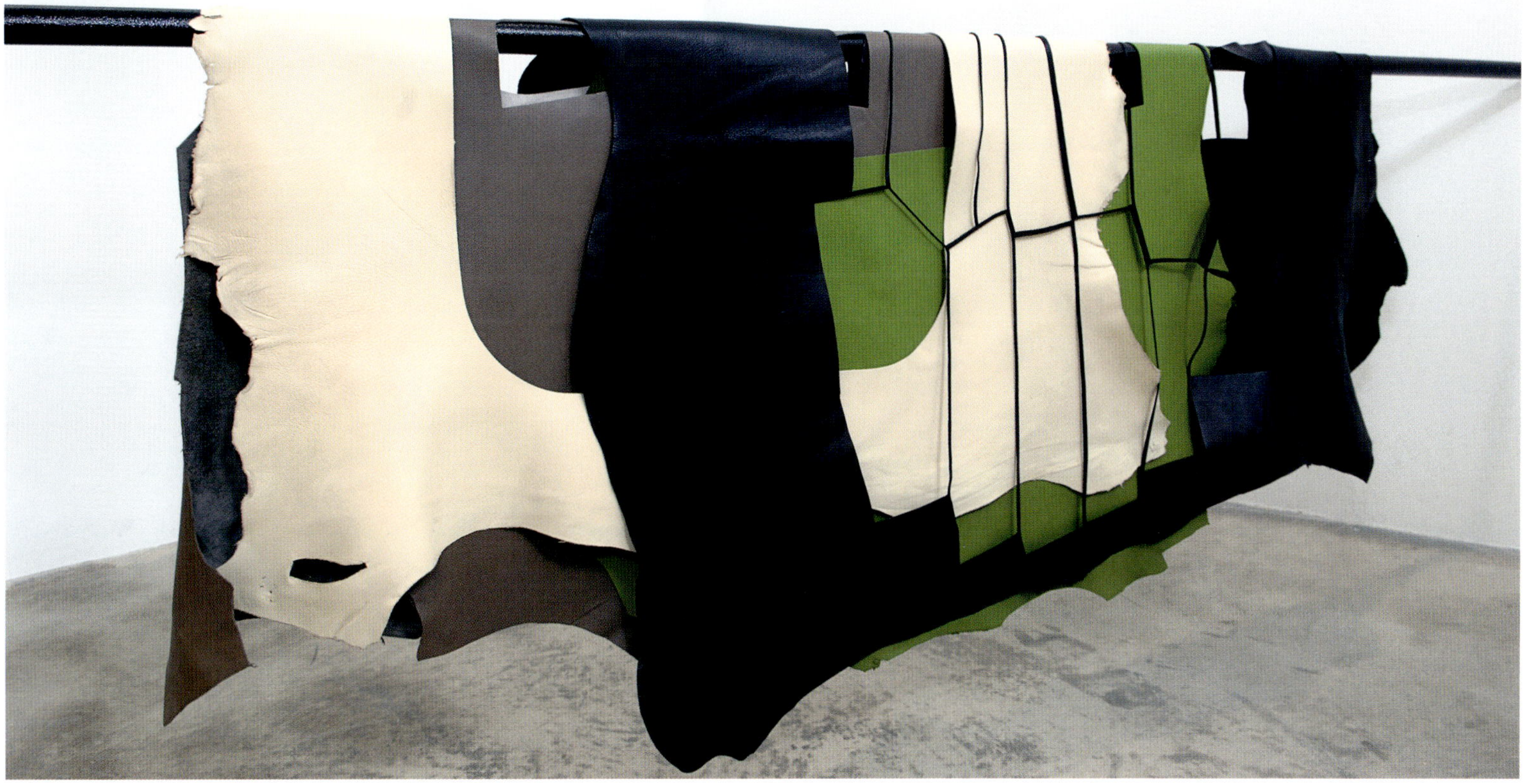

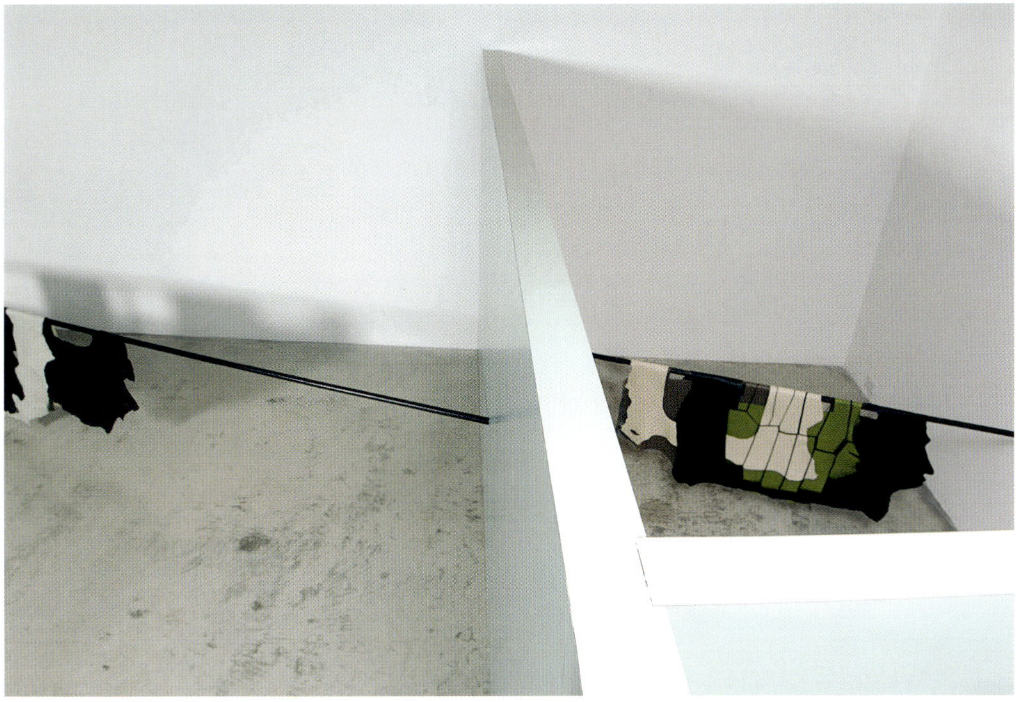

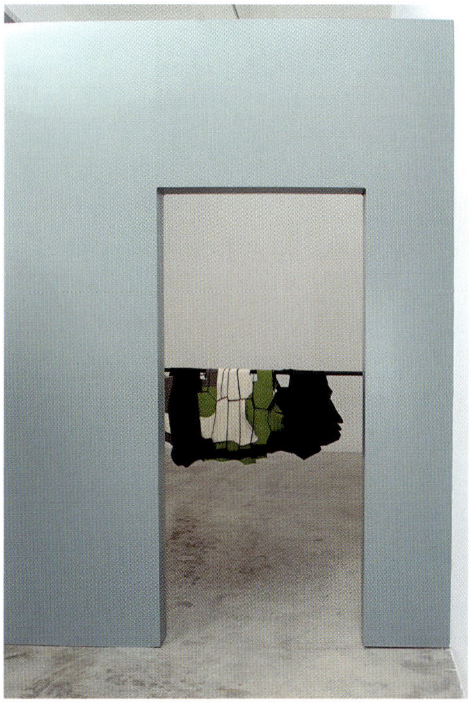

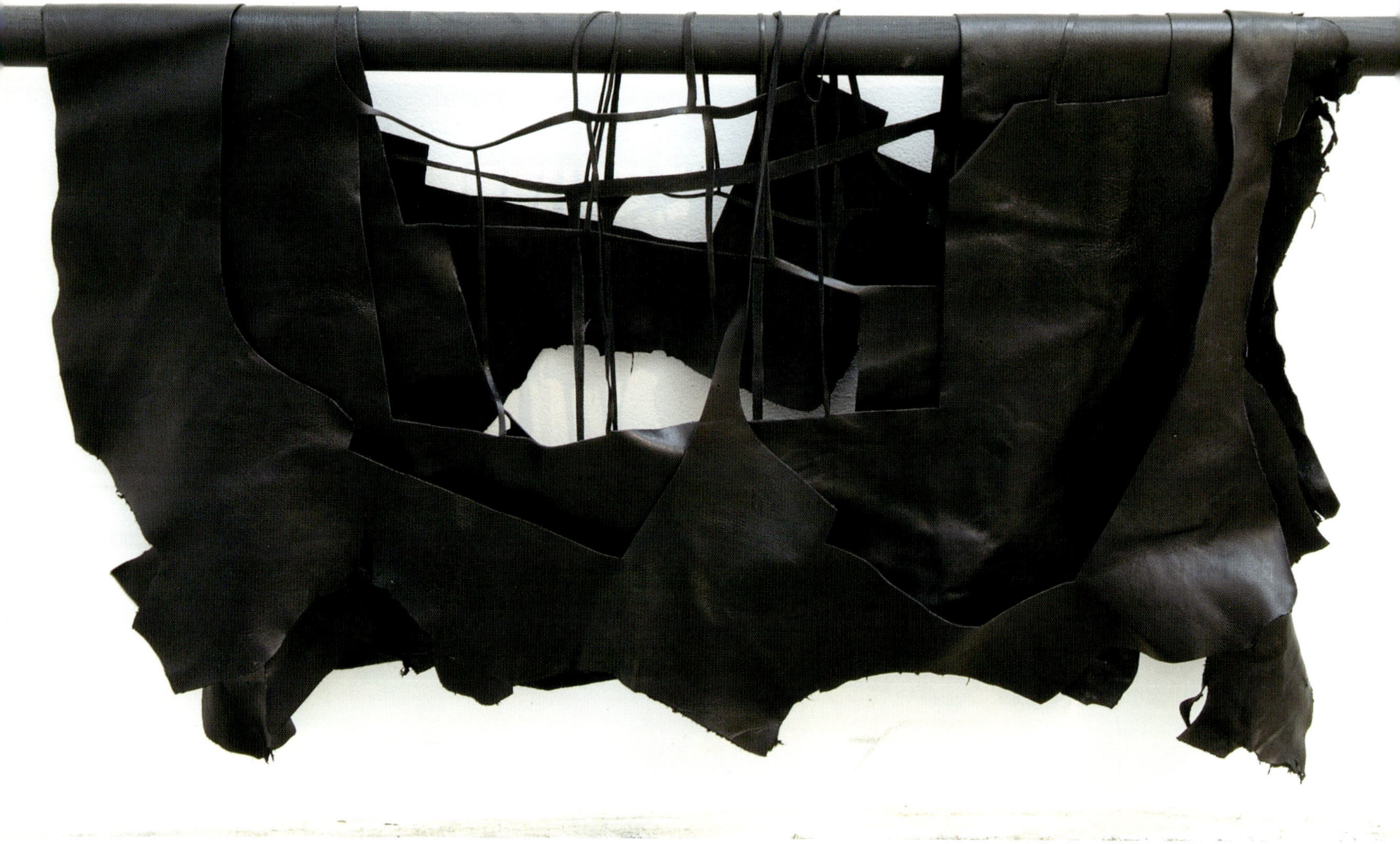

Untitled, 2005
Leather, wood, 70 x 120 x 8 cm [27½ x 47¼ x 3¼ in.]

Untitled, 2005
Leather, wood, 71 x 270 x 48 cm [28 x 106¼ x 19 in.]

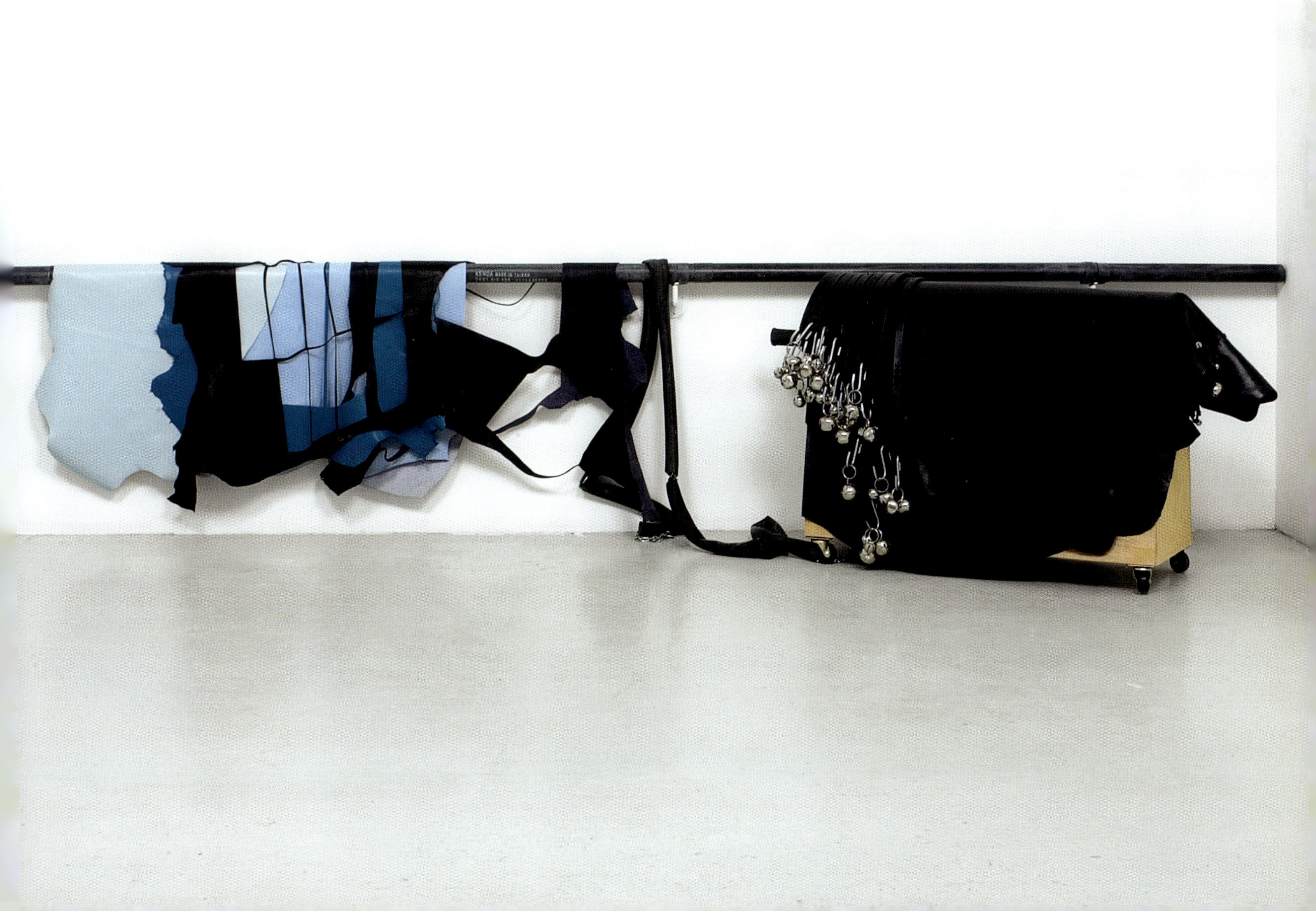

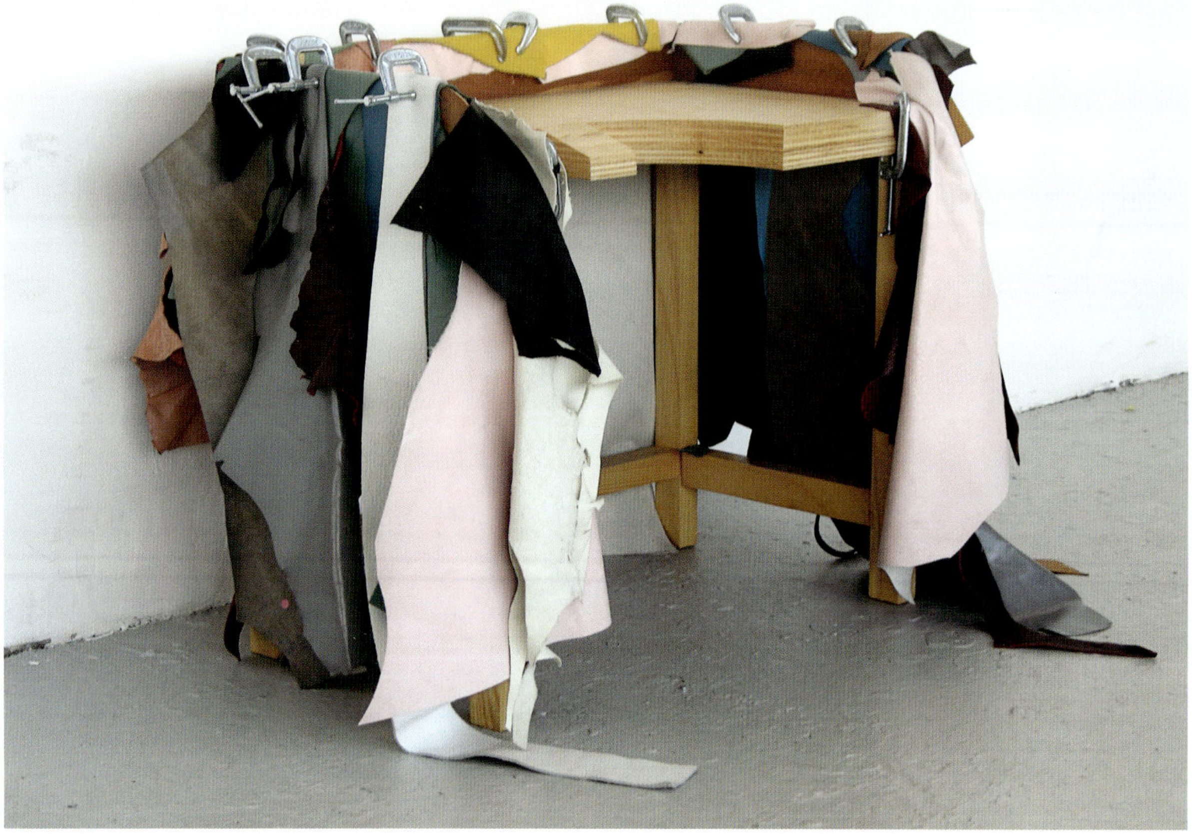

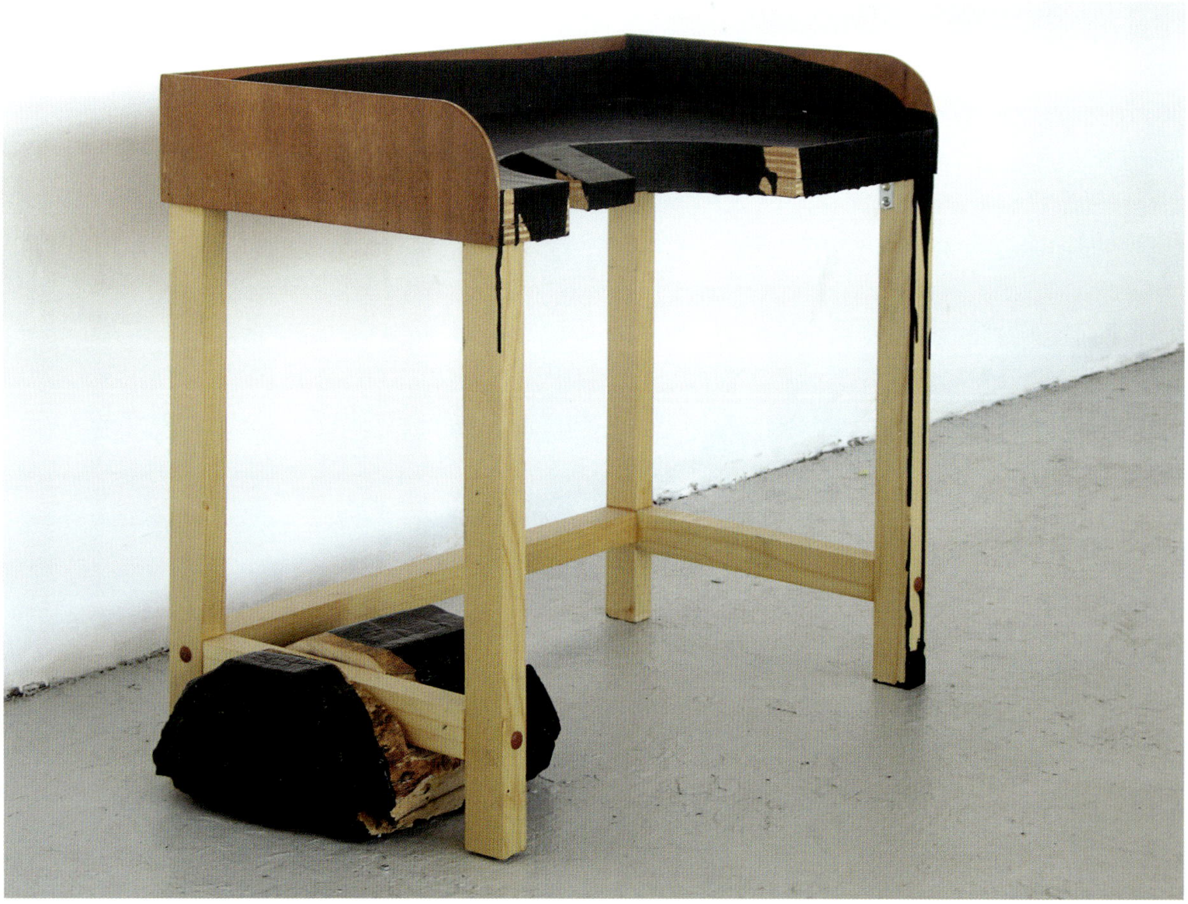

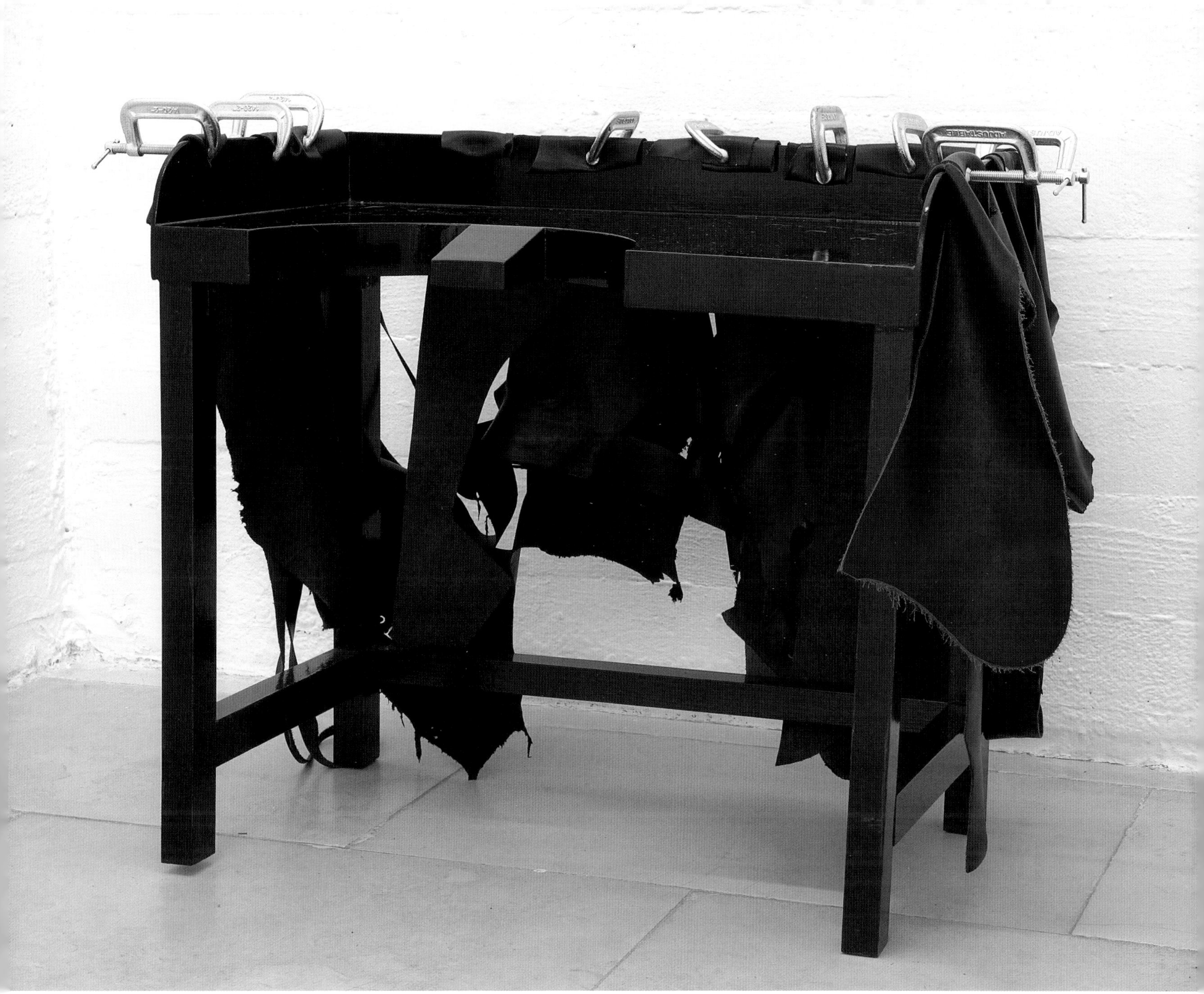

Above:
Untitled, 2007
Wood, leather, metal, 65 x 60 x 45 cm [25½ x 23½ x 17¾ in.]

Left-hand page:
Untitled, 2007
Wood, leather, metal, 65 x 60 x 45 cm [25½ x 23½ x 17¾ in.]
Untitled, 2007
Wood, acrylic, 65 x 60 x 45 cm [25½ x 23½ x 17¾ in.]

Following pages:
View of the exhibition *Time Snares,*
Galerie Emmanuel Perrotin, Miami, 2007

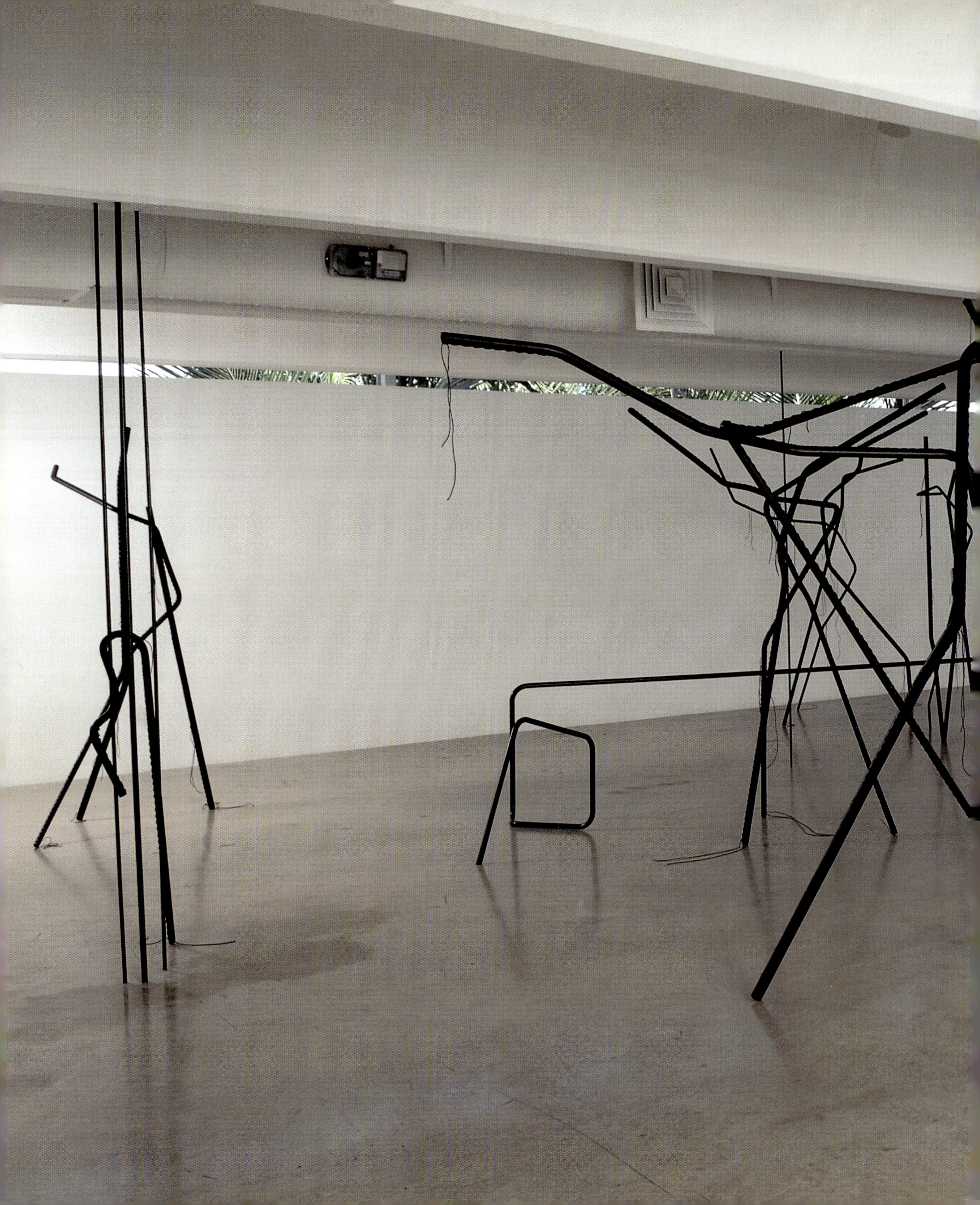

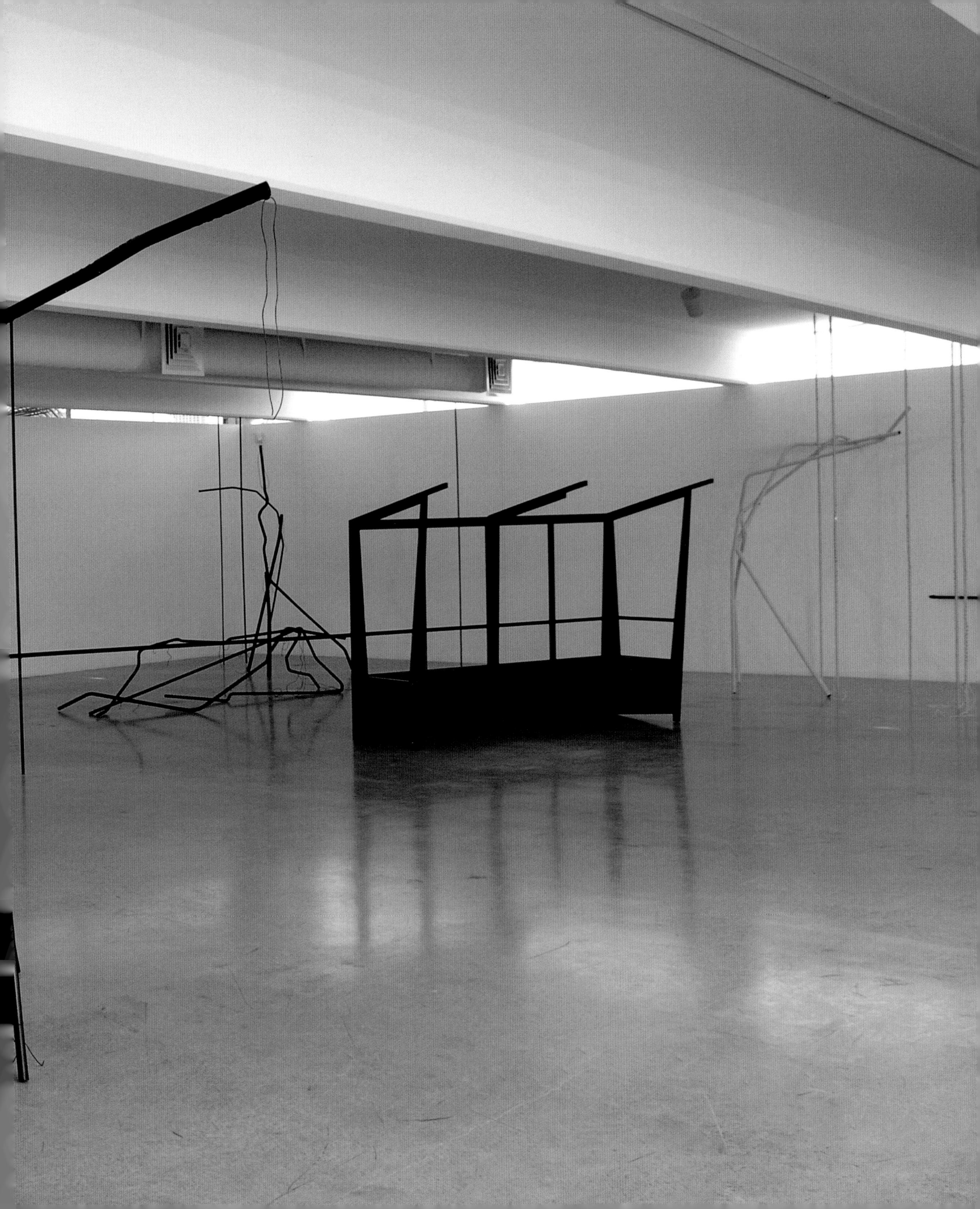

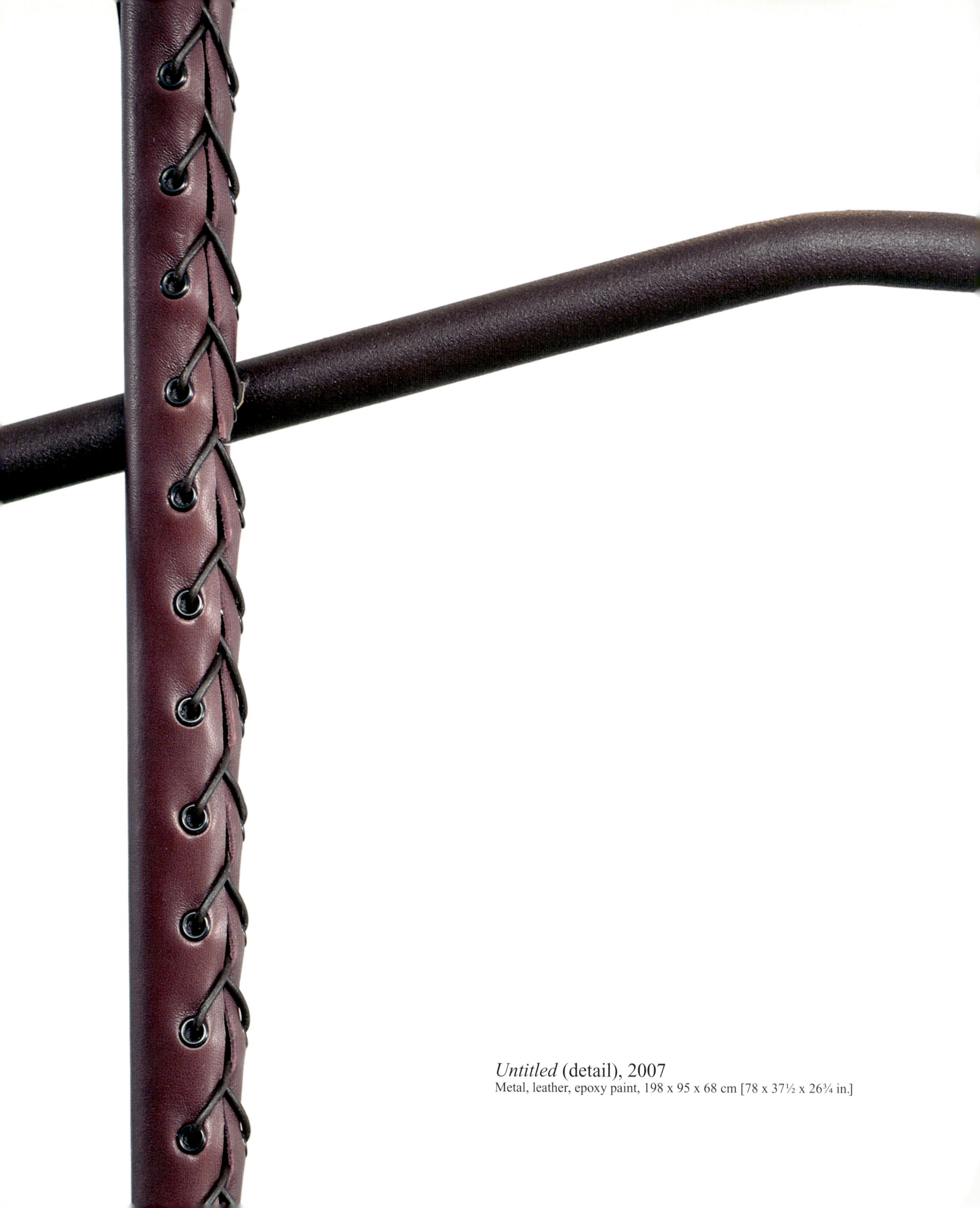

Untitled (detail), 2007
Metal, leather, epoxy paint, 198 x 95 x 68 cm [78 x 37½ x 26¾ in.]

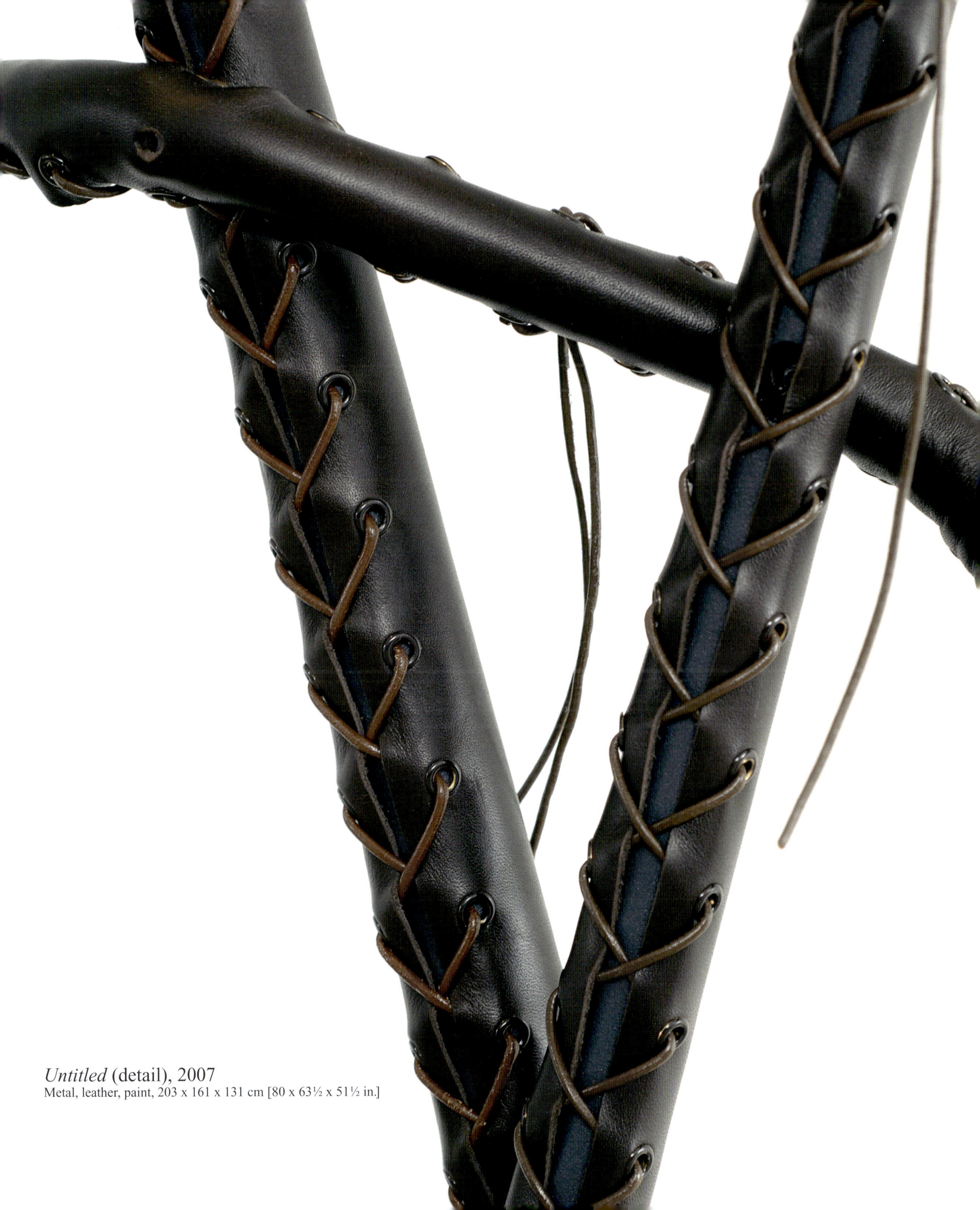

Untitled (detail), 2007
Metal, leather, paint, 203 x 161 x 131 cm [80 x 63½ x 51½ in.]

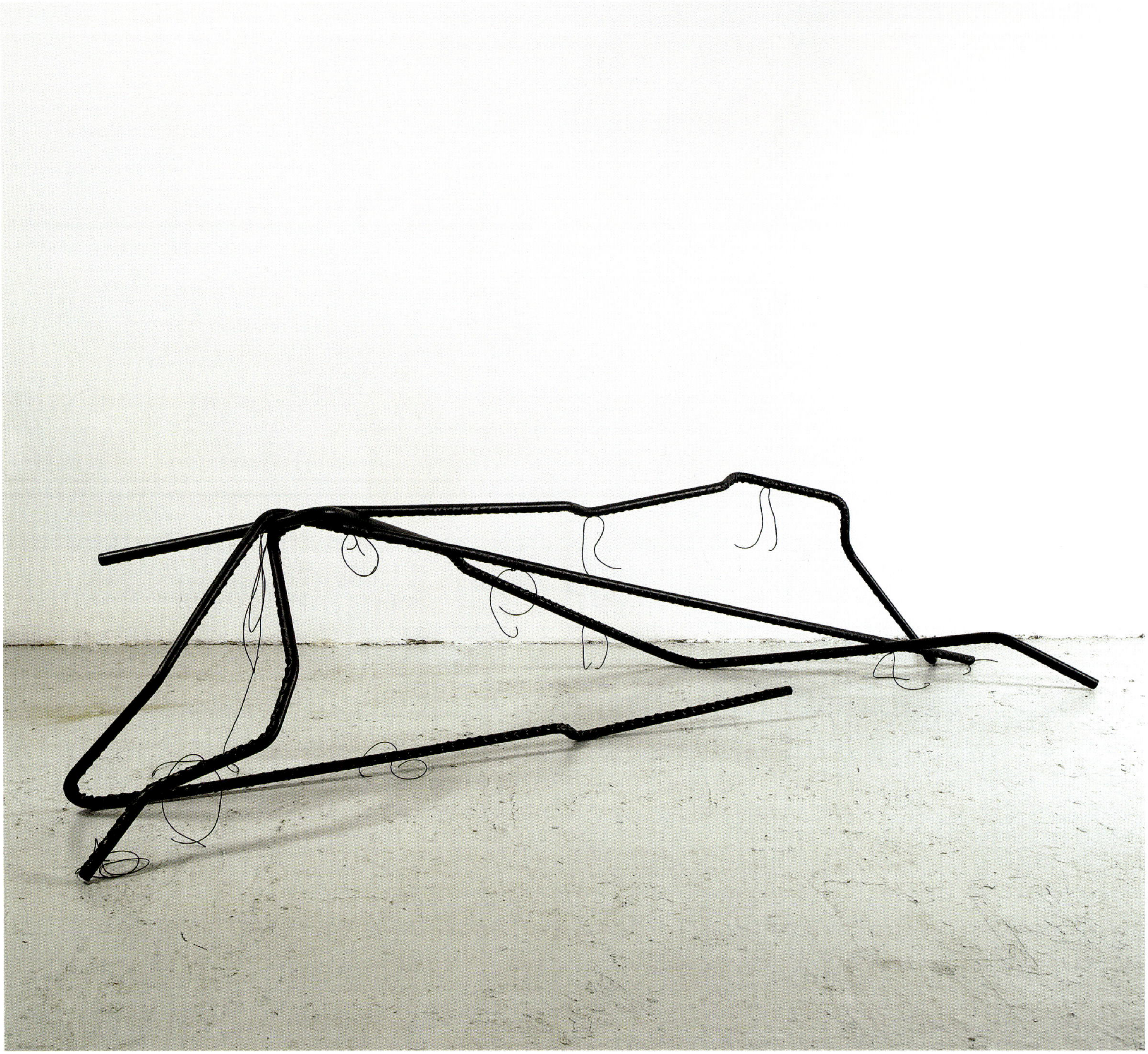

Untitled, 2007
Metal, leather, epoxy paint, 55 x 255 x 75 cm [21¾ x 100 x 29½ in.]

Right-hand page:
Detail of the exhibition *Time Snares,*
Galerie Emmanuel Perrotin, Miami, 2007

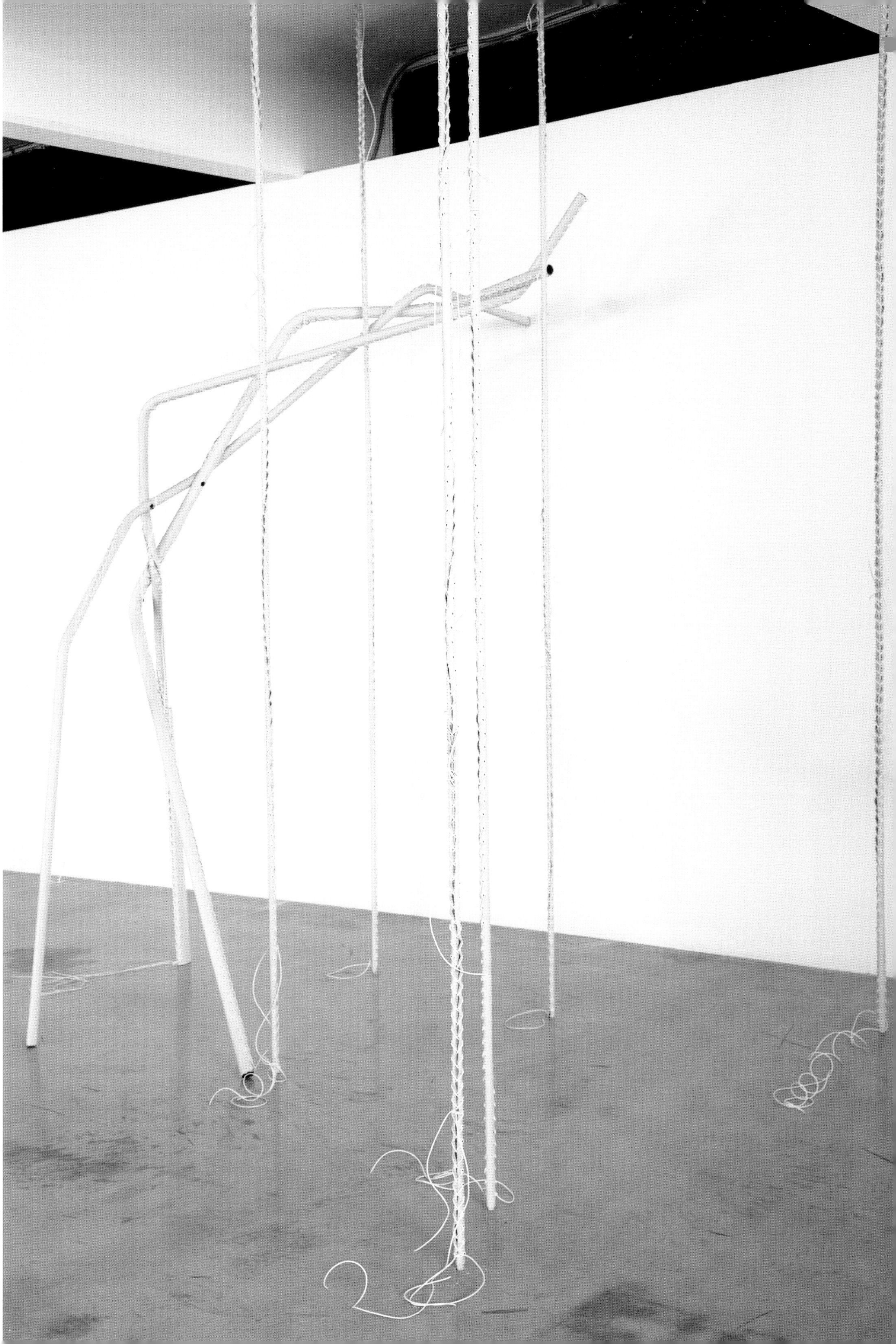

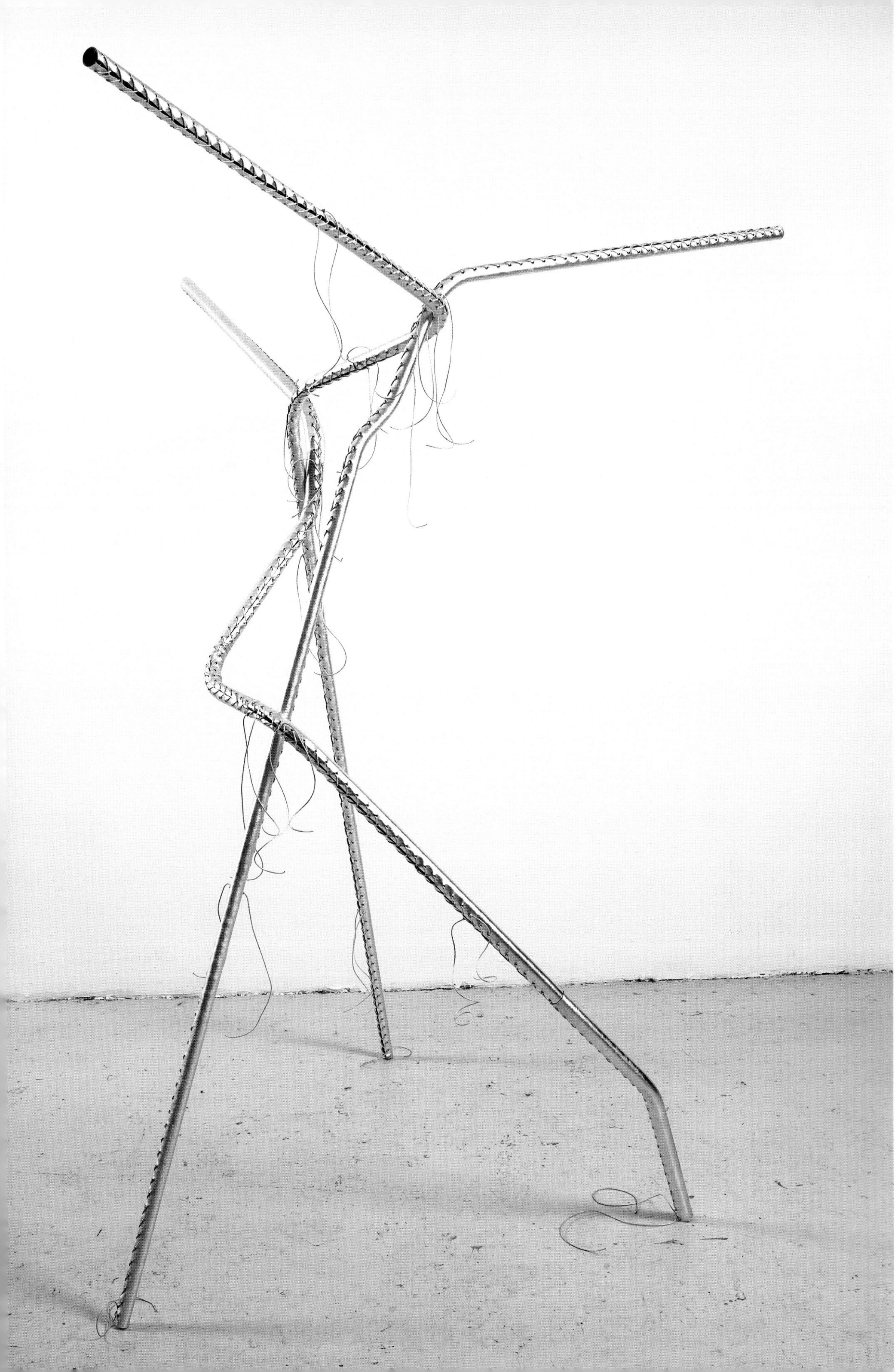

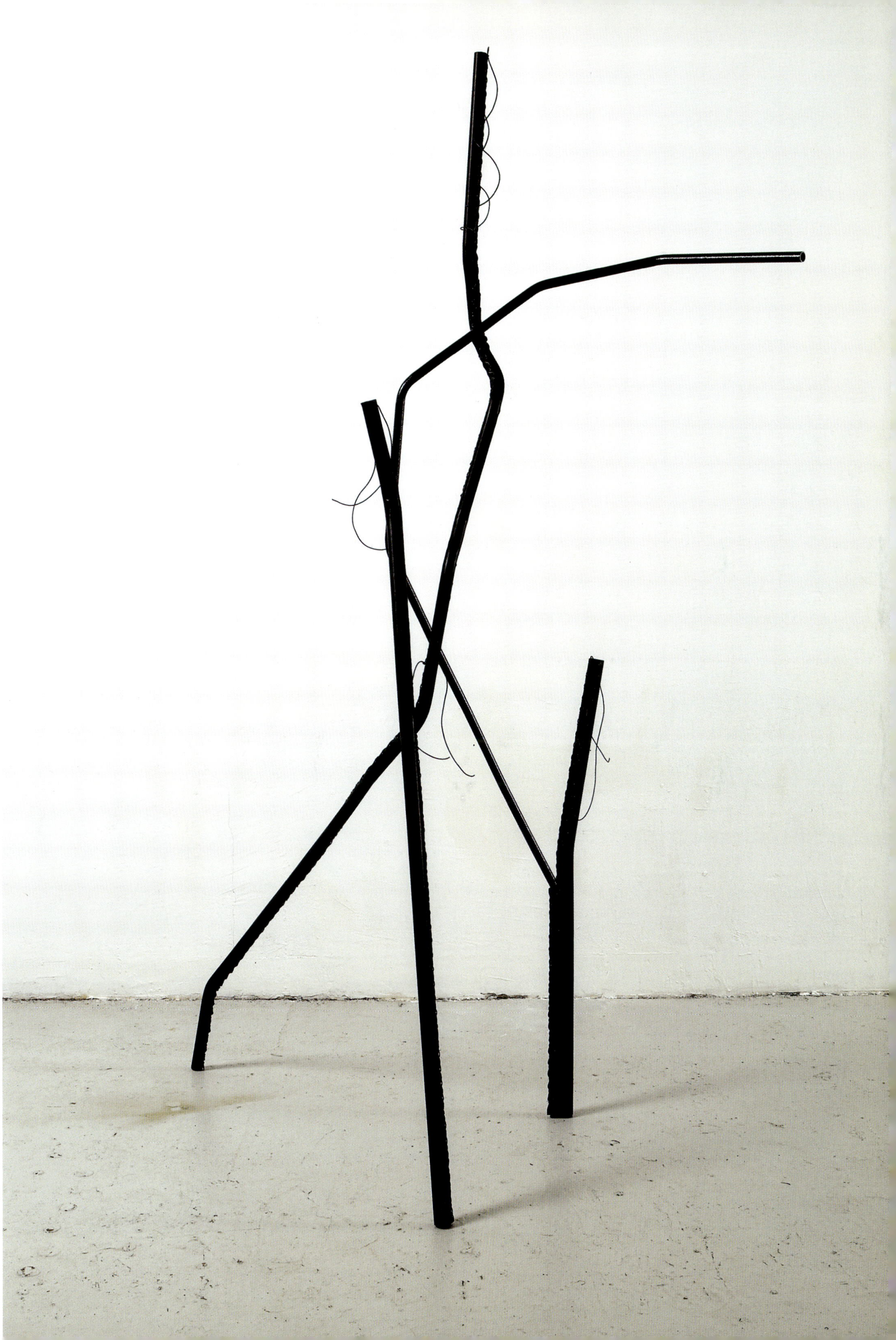

Previous pages:

Untitled, 2008
Metal, leather, epoxy paint, 207 x 147 x 130 cm
[81½ x 57¾ x 51¼ in.]

Untitled, 2007
Metal, leather, epoxy paint, 208 x 140 x 75 cm
[82 x 55 x 29½ in.]

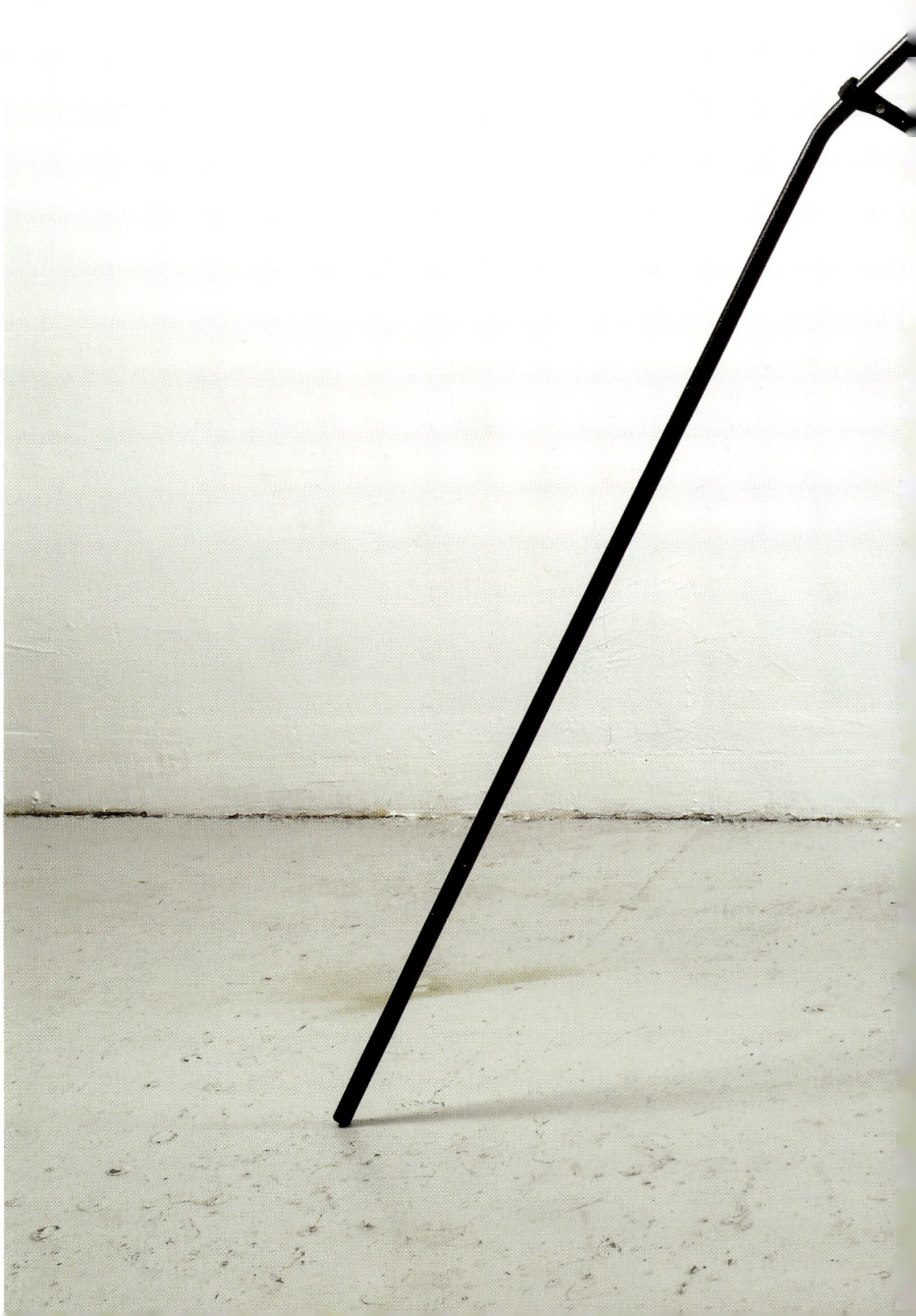

Untitled, 2007
Metal, leather, epoxy paint, 187 x 235 x 84 cm
[73½ x 92½ x 33 in

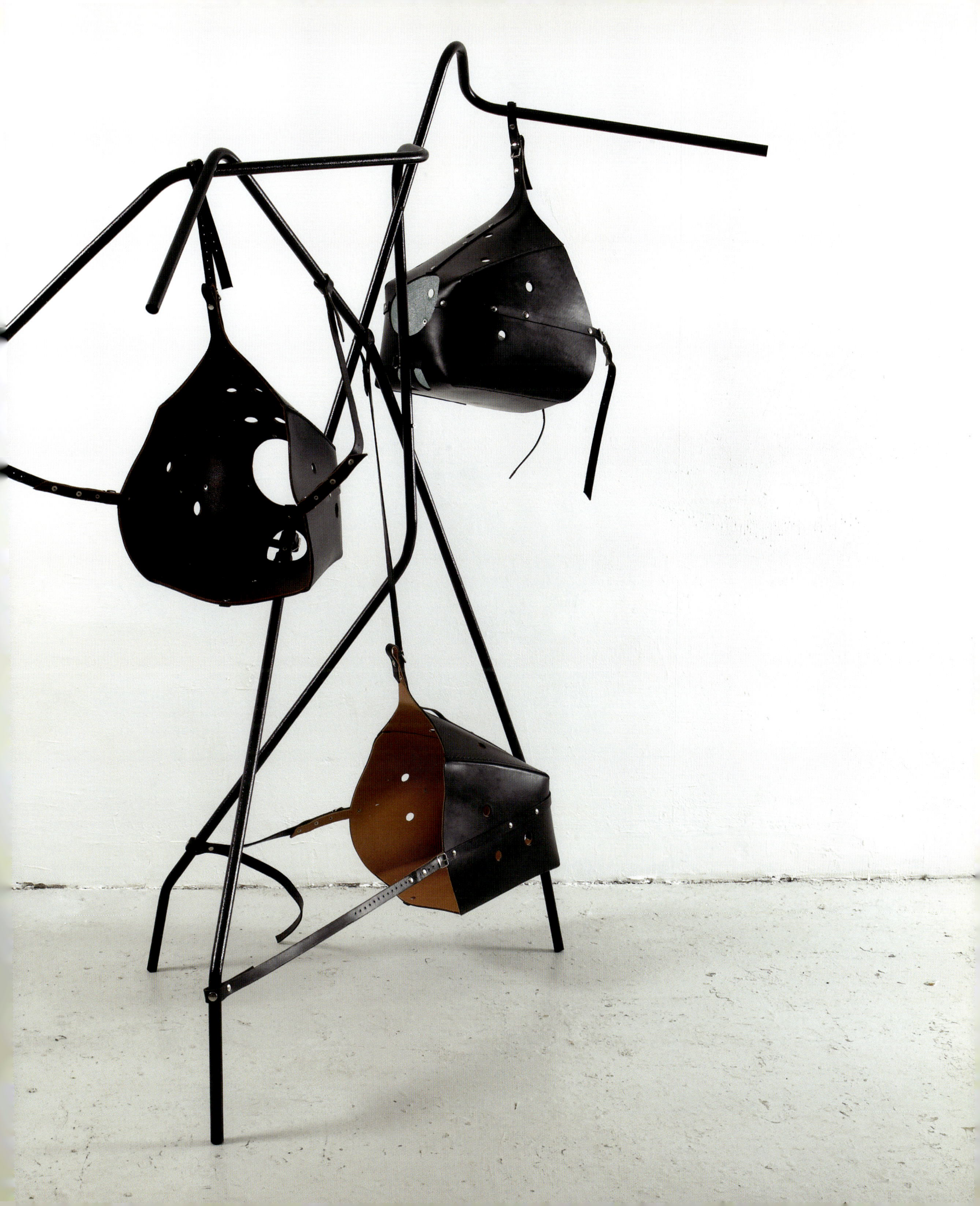

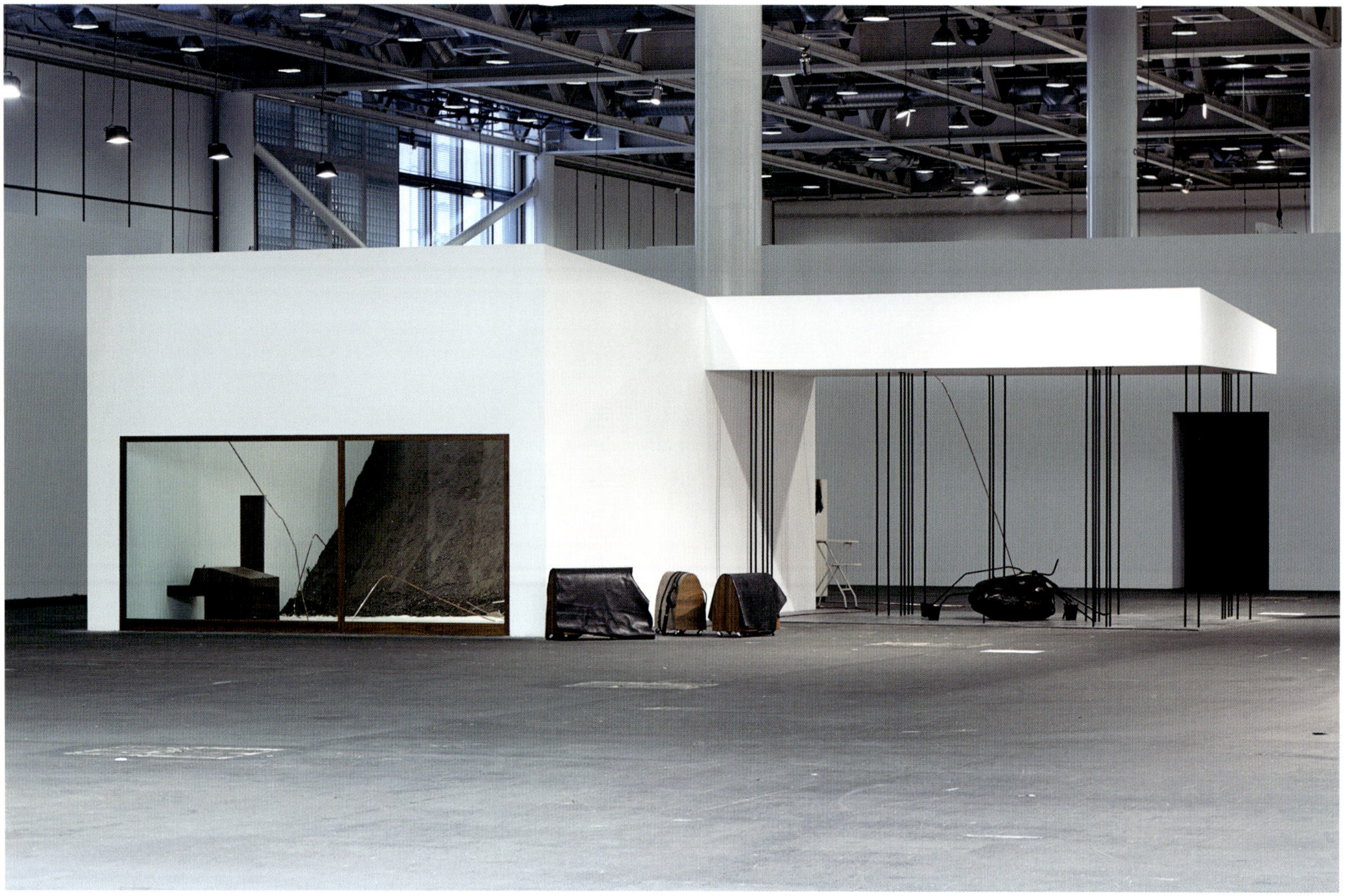

Untitled, 2007
Sand, copper, soil, Formica, wood, metal, Plexiglas, 310 x 425 x 650 cm
[122 x 167½ x 256 in.]

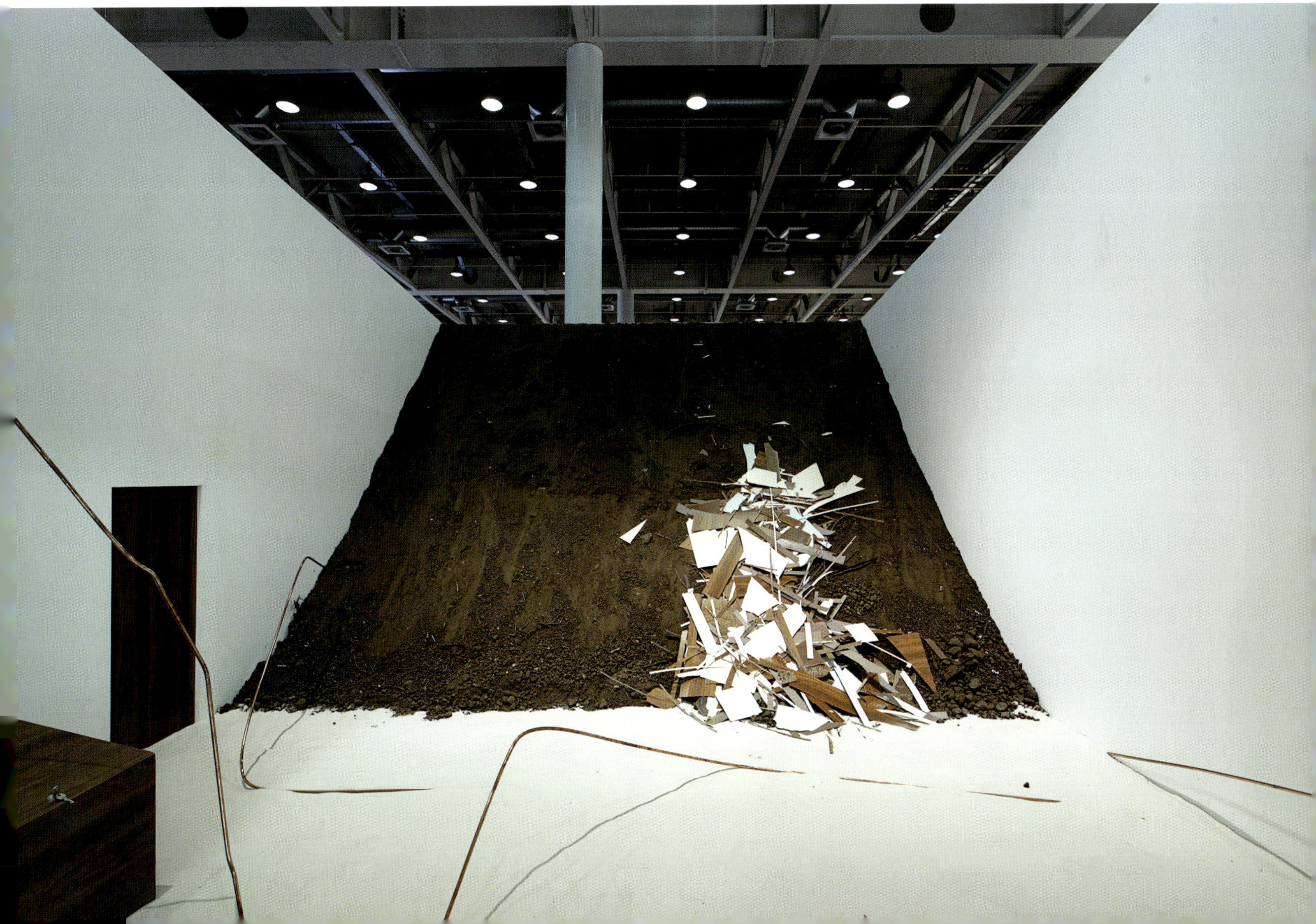

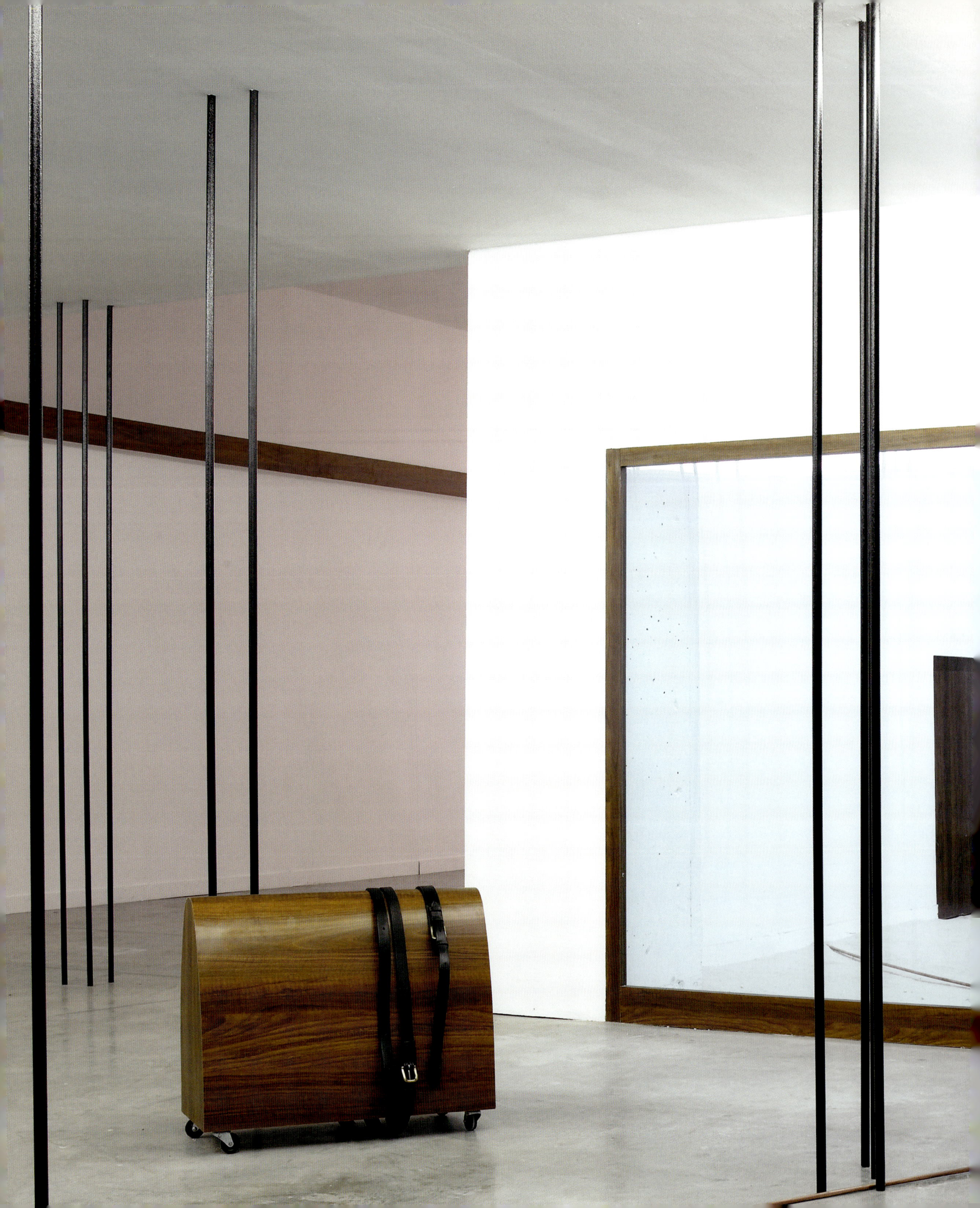

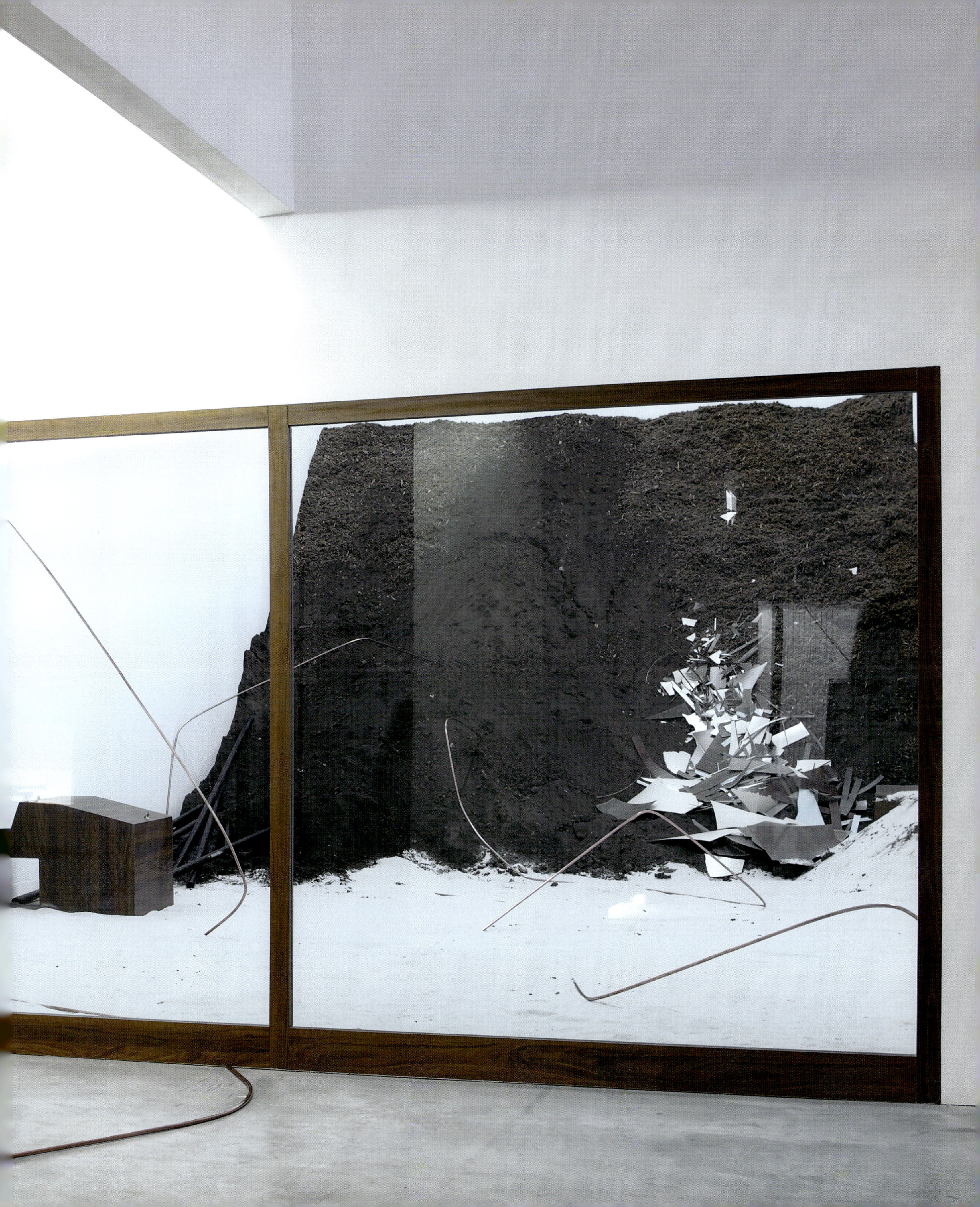

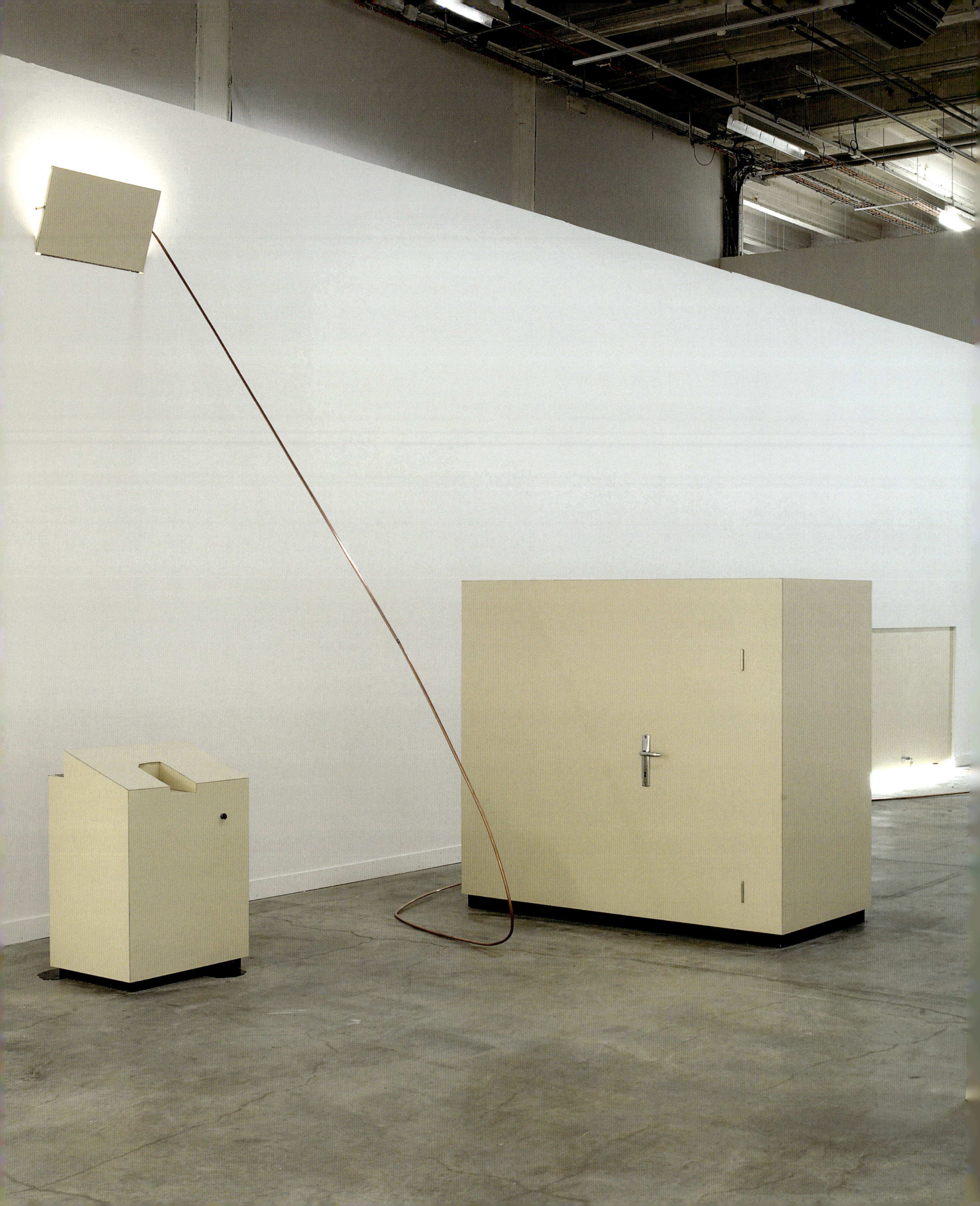

Previous pages:
View of the exhibition *Double Bind,* Palais de Tokyo, Paris, 2007

Polder, 2007
Formica, wood, metal, burn, paint, Plexiglas, neon light, copper, variable dimensions

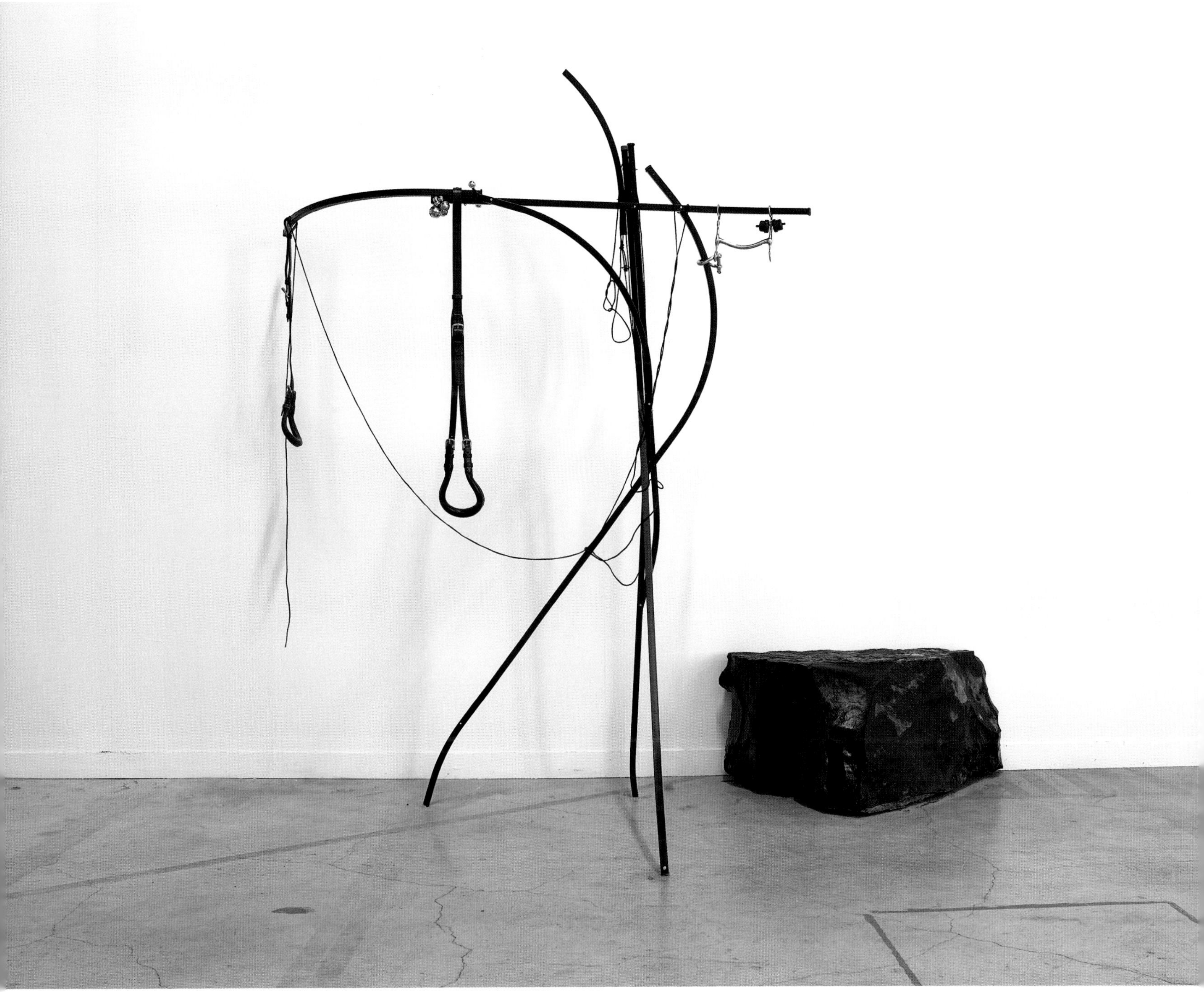

Totem, 2006
Metal, leather, piercing, rope, 195 x 165 x 90 cm [76¾ x 65 x 35½ in.]

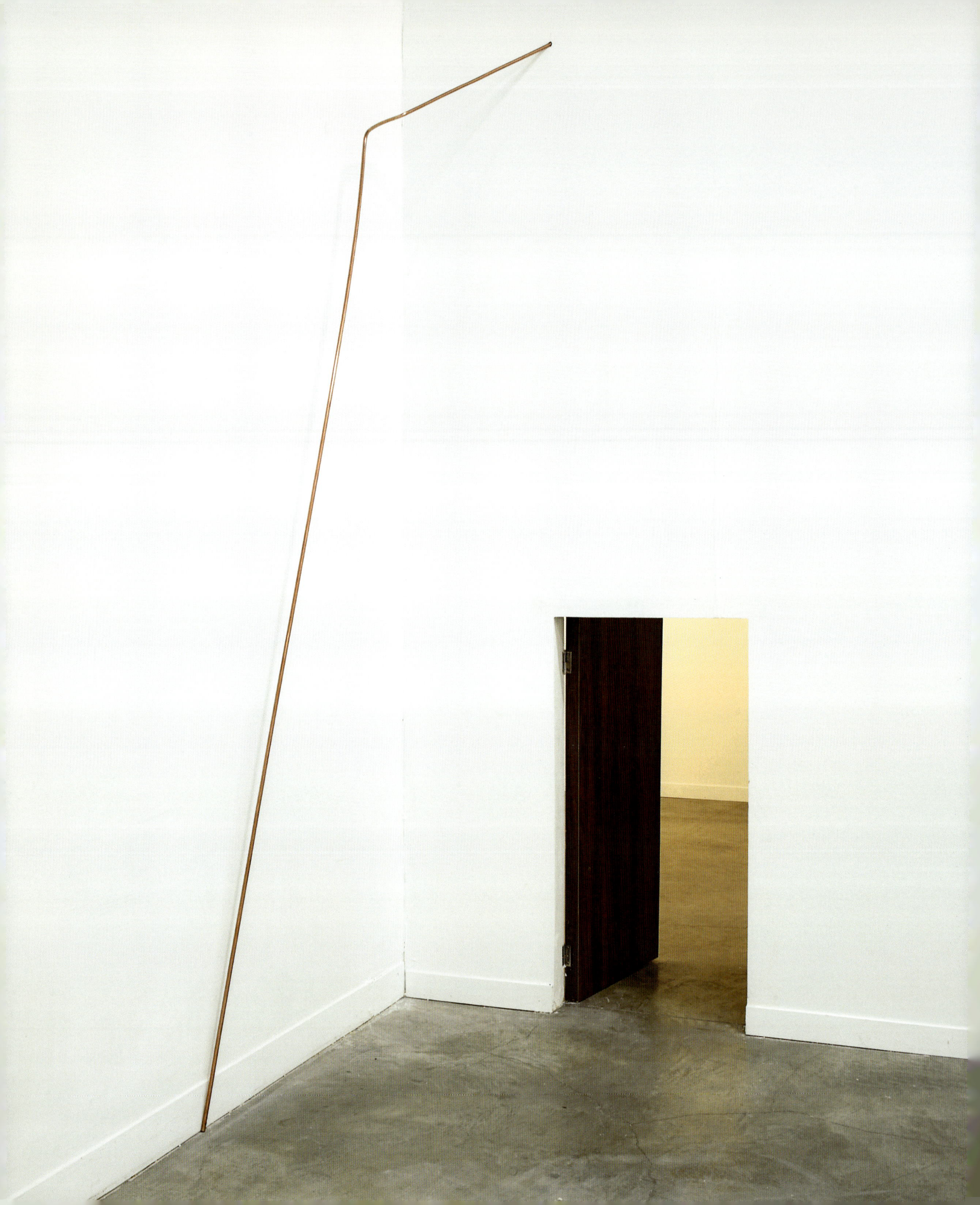

View of the exhibition *Double Bind,* Palais de Tokyo, Paris, 2007

APPENDIX

SLIPS OF THE TONGUE

Seeking paid training with a company in order to survive the logical training of my development.

Dear Mister or Madam Director, in the meantime please, I pray in the meantime, I pray in the meantime of this meantime.

Seeking a first level paid training, in order to benefit from the education in a qualified cursus, with hopes for a contract including opportunities to be offered a work contract.

I accept all types of employment concerning me if possible.

I possess varied knowledge in a sucker's imaginary. Available now or later, mobile and motivated, on the hot line.

Mrs, Miss, Mister,
Tatiana Trouvé
16, rue Lalande
75014 Paris

I do not remember very well the motives for my research, however I remember perfectly those of my expectations.

From the exile of my memory, I am on the spot for any occasional contact.

I would love it, occasionally, in case you would agree with me, though this is probably quite unnecessary.

I have a few first names, as well as a strong passion for some of them. Contact me for all projects concerning me.

I am seeking everything that could seduce me, suit me, or at least feed me, directly or indirectly.

It is only because no demand scopes as far as a proposition that I've always been up to the standards.

Tobacco, back, migraine, weight, anguish, stress and loneliness.
16, rue Lalande
75014 Paris.

Calabrian reflexology, well-being and relaxation, fitness for the body and the mind.
html/www.shortrelaxation@demon.co.uk

Qualified young woman, serious and passionate, seeking a realm of predilection.

Rich in relational and technical flexibility willing to exchange decision making tools with others.

Fights against anonymity and brings motivation back.
First visit free.

Soon, my future will be free.

Dear Madam, Dear Sir, please receive the expression of my sincere solutions

Cooperative firm of consultants: personalised and confidential studies from files, projects, photos, or simple request. Proven effective.

Quality control offer from individual to individual.

On-site woman worker, for 3 years on benefits, living in Paris with telephone, available now, by résumé only.

In the context of careers and employment, I am trying to solve all my problems in one week.

I have serious knowledge in the realm of motivation, for all positions with advancement possibilities and rest on Sundays, I am available at request.

In order to second the mission of my re-integration I am seeking good opportunities from inside help, preferably for sure. For all serious inquiries, leave a message, thank you.

Customised travelling salesperson, natural language, professional look, to fill immediately.

Young woman, excellent dexterity, offers courses to users of a wide range of products from the most difficult to the most simple (43 p./mn).

Seeking special employee position, beginner or experienced, part-time or full-time, possibly for an undetermined period of time.

Seeking position to be filled with a list of careful know-hows.

Young woman offers her work skills, between more or less long periods of inactivity.

Following a long period of absence during which I was somehow there, I am trying to re-position myself if possible.

I own many résumé manuals in order to obtain an authentic professional experience. People with similar experiences need not apply.

It is in the perspective of a positive motto summing up a career to accomplish that my full motivation comes out.

I know I am intelligent, effective, responsible, full of initiative sometimes audacious, but at the end of the day, it is impossible to get you on the phone.

For years now, I've been marking time, would you be kind enough as to keep me informed of your decisions.

100% ready to use, eager applicant perfectly bilingual, specialist of sleepless nights with a handkerchief.

Would I dare ask you, you who barely knows me, to push my request by a word, a response, in the shortest possible delays?

I will be back.

Having a rather accurate idea about my skills, I am committed to succeeding without my Associates' degree.

Please leave a message after the beep.

How to succeed in everything through hope in a world of opportunities.
With all my gratuity.

Not quite up to the level but light-hearted, such are my profile and my mission.

Thanks to your attention, your interest, as well as your desire for action, I have always survived the scope of my own demands.

I will do everything I can to keep trusting you. Please believe in the expression of my greatest motivation.

Seeking young woman or young man with social skills congenial with welcoming me.

I have read many want ads, I thought about sending my application in, which seems worthy of interest, I feel obliged to arrange an RDV for myself.

About to retire from benefits at the age of thirty, I want to get into social life, would you please tell me how. Thanks for believing me.

Young lady fonded with great hopes for life in Paris seeks any information related to debts/reimbursements systems while waiting for the situation to stabilise.

Dear Jacques, dear Paul, dear Marc,
dear François and Bruno.
Yours faithfully with all my gratuity.

I'm not really autistic, but I will probably die from cancer.
Seeking serious gallery.

During my stay between the enclosure and the space, I never received a visit from any relative, and no one is waiting for me outside or in.

I am against the system.
But the system will turn me into a heroin.

TITLES

AND IF NEVERTHELESS,
AND IF EVER,
AND IF SUDDENLY
1990

REECREEAATIOOON
1990
cakes, bread and other burns

THE GREAT INTERNAL FROSTS
1990–1997
miscellaneous frozen goods

SUBJUGATED AND SWALLOWED
BY HIM
1990
prostheses

PRE-SELECTION, SELECTION,
PRESENTATION
1990

AMOR CH'OL COR GENTIL
RATTO S'APPRENDE
AMOR CH'A NULLO AMATO
AMAR PERDONA
1990

TROPHY WITHOUT
MEMORIES
1990

WHICH MEANS EITHER
1990

()…?
1990

DORMIVEGLIA DI PROGETTI
1992

DYSLEXIC PHOTO ESSAY
1992
videos

AESTHETIC CORRECTIONS
1992

TITLES, BRIEF THOUGHTS,
AND SHORT IDEAS
1992

ALL MATERIALS TO WRITE
TO NOBODY
AND TO SEND NOWHERE
1992
mixed media

YOUNG GIRL ASLEEP AT
THE HOSPITAL
1992

I VENTI PIU FORTI DEL NORD
1992
fans

FLAGS ANTI FLAGS
1992
fabrics

I WANT TO BE WHAT I AM NOT
FOR NOBODY LIKES YOU
1992

CURRICULUM VITAE
1992

GIOCATTOLO PER MAGALI
1992

STUDIES FOR THE INFINITE
TUNNEL
1992

RECOVERY FOR THE GREAT VOID
1992
oxygen and plastic

0° CONNECTION WITH INFINITY
1992

BANCARELLE
1993

MURETTO
1993

ALTALENE
1993

TWENTY FOUR ARRIVALS FROM
A CHOLERA STRUCK REGION
1993

CONCEPT FOR A UNIQUE REALM
STRICTLY INAPPLICABLE
1994

TUTTI I GIOIELLI DI MARESA
1994

EMPTY AND BENT SPACE
1994

THE LONGEST ECHO
1994

STUDIES FOR STUDYING
1994
pencil on paper

MOBILE HOME WITHOUT WHEELS
1994

THERE IS ONLY ONE STEP
THAT SHE WOULD HAVE
PLEASANTLY MADE
FOR ALL THE REASONS
YOU CAN GUESS
1995
batteries, Scotch tape

A TISSUE OF UNTRUTHS
1995

EVERYTHING I DO NOT SAY
1995
microphones, foam, walls

A NAME WHICH ERASES
ANOTHER ONE
1995
erasers

I LIVE IN PARIS
1995

ACTIVITY WITHOUT A PROJECT
1995
Tape recording, magnifying glass,
mirror, light

PROJECT FOR A POSSIBLE BLISS
1995
confetti, beads, sequins

PARIS ON THE 28-11-95
AN UNKNOWN

SOMEWHERE ON THE 18-12-95
AN UNKNOWN

MILANO IL 22-12-95
UNA SCONOSCIUTA

AMSTERDAM, ON THE 29-12-95
AN UNKNOWN

A YOUNG DWARF DEAF AND DUMB
1996

A LONELINESS PADDED
WITH REALISATIONS
1996
shingles and gelatin

HE ALWAYS TAKES HER OVER
1996

TO A SELF WHO IS NOT WORTH
A THING, TO ANOTHER ONE
WAITING TO SHOW ITSELF
1996
invisible performance

DRUNK PRISONER AT THE WINDOW
1996
urine and urine

I EAT LIFE IT DRINKS ME
1996
chocolate, beer

LIQUID SMILE AND BURNING EYES
1996

BETWEEN HER AND HER,
I HER AND SHE HERSELF
1996

TOLERANCE FOR THE UNDESIRABLE
1996

I CANNOT TALK TO YOU I WOULD
LIKE VERY MUCH TO ASK YOU
1996

99 AFFIRMATIONS ON
THE LADDER
1996

A LOST POINT
1996

PERFORMANCE
BY MY SHADOW AND ME
1996
virtual shadow video

A PUBLIC SERVANT OF
THE UNIVERSAL
1996
photograph

YOUR BRAIN IS NOT WELL,
IT LOOKS LIKE NOTHING ELSE,
THERE IS NOTHING LIKE IT
ON THE FACE OF THE EARTH
1996 (…?)

EXECUTION OF CURIOUS
MOVEMENTS AND
STRANGE GRIMACES IN THE VOID
(W.G)
1996

A DEATH FAR FROM OVER
1996
styrofoam, ash, light

MY BELOVED YOU BROKE
MY HEART,
BANG BREAK MY HEART BROKEN,
MY SWEET LITTLE BANG BANG
1996 (I.B.)

A FEMALE CHAMPION
OF UNSOLVABLE ANSWERS
1996

A LONELINESS PADDED
WITH REALISATIONS
1996
shingles and gelatin

PARIS ON THE 31-12-96
AN UNKNOWN

PARIS ON THE 28-01-96
AN UNKNOWN

GREAT EXTENTS OF WEAKNESS
1997

A NEW BELOVED WHO
DOES NOT SHATTER A THING
ANYMORE
1997

THE HYPER SHORT-SIGHTED
CONQUEST OF
A DISENCHANTED NIGHT
1997

TITLES NAMING THE ABSENCE
1997

LIGHTS UP, EXPLODES, SCREENS
1997
lawn, urine, wind

PARIS LAUGHS AND SURVIVES ME
1997

A FAILED PROSECUTOR CHASING
A FAKE VICTIM
1997

FULFILLED TEARS
1997

AN ARTISTIC AND EMOTIONAL
PERSONALITY
1997

A SMALL GROUP IN WHICH
EVERYONE IS
THE PLAYTHING OF THE OTHER'S
IMAGINATION
1997

OBSTINATELY CHOOSING NOT
TO CHOOSE,
CHOOSING TO DRIFT AND
DRIFTING ON
1997
miscellaneous edges and borders for scale
models

GOING TO HELL IN ORDER
TO KEEP CURSING
1997

DAYS OUTSIDE OF MEMORY
ONE AFTER THE OTHER
1997
virtual agenda

TEARS CRYING FOR
NOT BEING
1997 (J.M.)

SYNCOPATION OF LINEAR TIME
1997

A SUBMISSION TO DEATH
1997

A PERSPECTIVE ON THE WORLD
WITH FOUR VANISHING POINTS
1997

WITH ALL MY TENDERNESS
1997
cotton, alcohol, tears

-Yes
- (Let's go)
THE END
1997
overexposed VHS tape, mixed media

GROUP PHOTO OF THE POWER OF
THE ONES OVER THE OTHERS
1997

HE ALL LIT UP
SHE ALL WOOD AND STRAW
1997
wood and straw

ARTIFICIAL INSEMINATION
OF DUST
1997
alcohol, glass, dust

ACCOMPLISHING DESIRE
OF INDEFINITE DURATION
1997
mixed and indefinite techniques

MAYBE YOU COULD
IN CASE YOU AGREED TO
IT SEEMS TO ME THAT PERHAPS
1997
pencil on paper

INTENTIONS FOR
AN APPOINTMENT
1997

PROMISES THAT SELF-DESTRUCT
WHILE REALISING (J.M.)
1997

IT WAS LITTLE LONG
WAY DOWN
1997
toboggan samples

DESIRES CONTAINING
THE POSSIBILITIES
OF ALL SITUATIONS
1997

THE RETURN OF DEFEAT
1997

TEARS AND SOBS FESTIVAL
1997
water samples, lights

THE BLOSSOMINGS
OF ANONYMITY
1997

NEITHER WOMAN, NOR MAN IN ME
1997
miscellaneous pills

ALWAYS THE IMPOSSIBLE
AS STUPID AS REALITY
1997 (F.P.)

A WOOLEN RAFT
1997
wool, polystyrene

A RAGING SEA OF LAUGHS ON
BURNING DESIRES
1997
super mixed technique

THE SPARKLE OF ABSENCE
1997
virtual shadow

A LITTLE BIT MORE…
D.F.

THE GREAT INTERNAL FROSTS
1990–1997
miscellaneous frozen goods

SUSPENDED IDEA OF FALLING
1997 (J.M)

FLAT BUT FORTHCOMING DESIRE
1997
mirror and thread

THE AFTERNOON OF "THE FIANCEE
RETIRES"
1997

HER ARM SWELLS, MY HEAD
EXPLODES
SHE'S THE ONE WHO IS
SPEECHLESS
I'M THE ONE SNAPPING IN
THE WIND
1997

ANTICIPATION OF SILENCE OVER
ACHIEVEMENT
1997

A WINDOW WITH GREAT
HORIZONS
1997

THE BRAIN, THE HEART
AND THE SEX OF A WOUND
1997

HOLLYWOOD DOES NOT WANT ME
1997
carrots, mirror

I WOULD LIKE IT TO BE
RARELY TRUE,
I WOULD LIKE IT TO BE
SOMETIMES TRUE
1997

IT WILL BE ME, IT WILL BE HER,
IT WILL BE US,
IT WAS NEVER US
1997

HE HAS THE PRESENT SITUATION
SHE HAS WISHES
1997

I AM IN FRONT OF HIM AND
HE CANNOT FIND ME
1997
lenses, glasses and wigs

ON THE 10-06-97
AN UNKNOWN

PARIS ON THE 17-06-97
AN UNKNOWN

THE RECOMMENDATIONS
1997
tape recording of applause

AN ACHIEVEMENT EXHAUSTED
BY ITS OWN NECESSITY
1997
without form or technique

UNA VISITA
1997
confetti

FORGOTTEN BETWEEN USE
AND EXCHANGE
1997
handkerchiefs

A POSSIBILITY INDICATED
AND EXILED TO THE CONFINES
1997

FROM MUTENESS TO ECHO
1997

RESERVE ARMY
1997

A GREAT LOVE THAT DOES NOT
EXCEED
A GREAT SILENCE
1997

A PERFORMANCE THAT YIELDS
MY PLACE TO MY SHADOW
1997

EVERY MORNING, DISTANCE,
REMOTENESS, ABSENCE
1997

A BREATHLESS QUICK BREEZE
1998
1968 fans

ONE, TOO LATE NEVER PERHAPS
1968–1998

IMPORTANT FAREWELL TRANSFER
1998
Électricité de France

THE COMING THEYS, ALWAYS
ALREADY GONE, STILL HERE
1998

A WATERMAN BLOODY
WITH SALIVA
1998

A FACING THREE STEPS FROM A
BEHIND
1998
shadow and light

AMOROUS MOORED MASS
1998
mixed media

WHAT HAPPENED?
WHY DID IT HAPPEN?
HOW WAS IT POSSIBLE?
1998
appearance of various memory stratums

THE LOGICS OF DESOLATION
1998
sun, mirror and arson

A SUITCASE THAT PACKS AND
UNPACKS ITSELF
1998
logics of wandering

HE ALL TURNED OFF BY COURAGE
SHE ALL EXCITED BY FEAR
1998
fear and courage

HE LOOKS ME IN THE EYES
IT'S OVERWHELMING
I FALL, SPLASH
1998
crutches

THE INTENSE TIREDNESS OF THE ONE
WHO WEARS HERSELF OUT SEDUCING
1998
young girl

HE WILL BE, HE IS
1998
the future of an illusion

LOCATED IN THE VOID, SHE DREAMS
OF BEING THE ORIGINAL VERSION
1998
images from oblivion

THE EVENT ILLUMINATING
ITS OWN PAST
1998
68 cm of smoke

AN UNLIKELY DESTINY
1999
concrete, secrets

GENEALOGY OF A SECRET
1999
plaster and lies

MY NONSENSE YEARS
1999
1968–1999

4500 FRS
1999
plaster, wood

9700 FRS
1999
mixed media

160 000 FRS
1999
cotton and wool

e
MY SILENCE YEARS
1999
digital video

DEPARTURE INTO
THE SURROUNDINGS
RETURN TO
THE NEIGHBOURHOOD
1999
group photograph

450 FRS
1999
oil on canvas

250 FRS
1999
embroidered paper

GREY FACE
1999
lead led

A NUMBER OF SWITCHES
AND SHORTS
1999
galleries, museums and art centres

PLEASE DO NOT TOUCH
ANYTHING
1999
without media

THE REMEMBERANCE OF
A LONG SILENCE
1999
ghost track

THE EXILE OF MEMORY
1999
1968–1973 ; 1996–1998

DURING MY STAY BETWEEN THE
ENCLOSURE AND THE SPACE, I
NEVER RECEIVED A VISIT FROM
ANYONE, AND NO ONE IS WAITING
FOR ME OUTSIDE OR IN
2003

TUNNEL AIRLINES
Thursday, October 3

ME NEAR MY DESTINATION
2004

DJINNS
2005

SOMETHING HAPPENED
2005

TIME SNARES
2007

DOUBLE BIND
2007

INTRANQUILLITY
2005–2008

MISTER, MRS., MISS
TATIANA TROUVÉ
1990–2008

MISTER, MRS, MISS
TATIANA TROUVÉ
14, RUE LALANDE
75014 PARIS
1990–2008

SERENDIPITY
2008

EXPANSION OF A CLOSURE
2007–2008

TATIANA TROUVÉ

Born 1968 in Cosenza (Italy)
Lives and works in Paris (France)

SELECTED SOLO EXHIBITIONS

2008

4 between 3 and 2, curator Jean-Pierre Bordaz, Centre Georges Pompidou, Paris, France

Tatiana Trouvé, Galerie Johann König, Berlin, Germany

2007

Time Snares, Galerie Emmanuel Perrotin, Miami.

Double Bind, curator Marc-Olivier Wahler, Palais de Tokyo, Paris, France

Tatiana Trouvé, curator Éric Mangion, Centre National d'Art Contemporain de la Villa Arson, Nice, France

2005

Djinns, curator Sylvie Boulanger, Cneai, Chatou, France

2004

Tatiana Trouvé, Juste assez coupable pour être heureuse, curator Christian Bernard, Mamco, Geneva, Switzerland

2003

Tatiana Trouvé, Aujourd'hui, hier, ou il y a longtemps, capcMusée d'art contemporain de Bordeaux, France

2002

Tunnel Airlines, Galerie GP & N Vallois, Paris, France

Polders, curators Nicolas Bourriaud and Jérome Sans, Palais de Tokyo, Paris, France

SELECTED GROUP EXHIBITIONS

2007

Chalet de Tokyo, curator Marc-Olivier Wahler, Centro cultural Recoleta, Buenos Aires, Argentina

Art unlimited, Alphaville, curator Simon Lamunière, Galerie Almine Rech, 38th Art Basel, Switzerland

Think with the Senses – Feel with the Mind, curator Robert Storr, 52nd Venice Biennale, Venice, Italy

Airs de Paris, curator Christine Macel, Centre Georges Pompidou, Paris, France

2006

Printemps de septembre, curators Jean-Marc Bustamante and Pascal Pic, Les Abattoirs, Toulouse, France

La Force de l'Art, Grand Palais, Paris, France (Paul Ricard prize selection)

Notre Histoire..., curators Nicolas Bourriaud and Jérôme Sans, Palais de Tokyo, Paris, France

Re-opening, Musée d'Art Moderne de la Ville de Paris, France

2005

Singuliers – Art contemporain en France, curator Thierry Raspail, Guandong Museum of fine arts, Canton, China

2004

Tour-détours de Babel, curator Christian Bernard, Mamco, Geneva, Switzerland

2003

Clandestini / Clandestines, curator Francesco Bonami, 50th Venice Biennale, Venice, Italy

2002

New hanging up of the collections, Musée National d'Art Moderne, Centre Georges Pompidou, Paris, France

2001

Squatters, curators Miguel Perez and Vicente Todoli, Museu Serralves, Porto, Portugal

Troubler l'écho du temps, curator Thierry Raspail, Musée d'art contemporain de Lyon, France

2000

Voilà, le monde dans la tête, curator Suzanne Pagé, Musée d'Art Moderne de la Ville de Paris, France

BIBLIOGRAPHY (SELECTION)

Monographs

2008

4 between 2 and 3, text by Élie During, ed. Centre Georges Pompidou, Paris

2007

Lapsus, interview with Frank Lamy, ed. MAC/VAL, Vitry-sur-Seine

2005

Djinns, interview with Hans-Ulrich Obrist, ed. Cneai, Chatou (artist book)

2003

Tatiana Trouvé, Aujourd'hui, hier, ou il y a longtemps..., texts by Élie During, François Poisay and Maurice Fréchuret, ed. capcMusée d'art contemporain de Bordeaux, Bordeaux

2002

Polders, texts by Gianfranco Maraniello, Palais de Tokyo, edited by Caisse des dépôts et consignations, Paris

1997

Tatiana Trouvé, texts by Charles-Arthur Boyer and Joseph Mouton, ed. Centre National d'Art Contemporain de la Villa Arson, Nice

CREDITS

MODELS OF THE BUREAU OF IMPLICIT ACTIVITIES

pp. 14–15: Private collection, Paris; Photo: J-C. Lett.
p. 16: Private collection, Paris; Photo: Laurent Édeline.
p. 17: Collection MAC/VAL, Vitry-sur-Seine, France; Photo: Laurent Édeline.
pp. 18–19: Produced by MAC/VAL, Vitry-sur-Seine; Photo: Marc Domage.

BUREAU OF IMPLICIT ACTIVITIES

p. 23: Dépôt Mamco, Geneva, Switzerland; Photos: Marc Domage.
p. 27: Dépôt Mamco, Geneva, Switzerland; Photo: Ilmari Kalkkinen.
pp. 28–29, 30: Jumex Collection, Mexico; Photos: Ilmari Kalkkinen.
p. 33: Jumex Collection, Mexico; Photo: Marc Domage.
pp. 34, 37: Jumex Collection, Mexico; Photos: Laurent Édeline.
p. 38: Dépôt Mamco, Geneva, Switzerland; Photo: Marc Domage.
p. 41: Photos: Laurent Édeline.
pp. 42–43: Dépôt Mamco, Geneva, Switzerland; Photo: Ilmari Kalkkinen.
p. 44: Photo: Jean Brasille.
pp. 46, 47: Photos: Frédéric Delpech.
p. 51: Photos: Laurent Édeline.
pp. 52–53: Collection CNAP, Paris; Photo: Marc Domage.
p. 54: Private collections; Photo: DR.
p. 57: Collection Fnac, Paris; Photo: Bernhard Strauss.
p. 58: Photo: Bernhard Strauss.
p. 63: Collection Fnac, Paris; Photo: Bernhard Strauss.
p. 64: Photo: Marc Domage.
p. 67: Photo: Laurent Édeline
pp. 68–69: Photo: Marc Domage.
pp. 70–71: Photo: Marc Domage.
pp. 72, 73: Collection Frac Paca, Marseilles; Photos: Jean Brasille.
pp. 74, 75: Collection capcMusée d'art contemporain, Bordeaux; Photos: Marc Domage.
p. 76: Collection Frac Paca, Marseilles; **left:** Photo: Laurent Édeline; **right:** Photo: Marc Domage.
p. 77: Collection Frac Paca, Marseilles; Photo: Laurent Édeline.
pp. 78, 79: Collection Frac Poitou-Charentes, Angoulême; Photos: Marc Domage.
pp. 82–83, 84: Photos: Marc Domage.

DRAWINGS

p. 86, top: Collection Claude Berri, Paris; **bottom:** Collection of the artist; Photos: Serge Veignant.
p. 87, top: Private collection, Paris; Photo: Serge Veignant; **bottom:** Collection Claude Berri, Paris; Photo: Serge Veignant.
p. 88: Private collection, Paris; Photo: Serge Veignant.
p. 89: Collection of the artist; Photo: Serge Veignant.
p. 90: Private collection, Paris; Photo: Serge Veignant.
p. 91: Private collection, Paris; Photo: Serge Veignant.
pp. 92–93: Collection Guillaume Houzé, Paris; Photo: Serge Veignant.
p. 94: Private collection, Paris; Photo: Serge Veignant.
p. 95: Collection Claude Berri, Paris; Photo: Serge Veignant.
p. 96, top: Collection Mnam, Centre Georges Pompidou, Paris; Photo: Christopher Burke; **bottom:** Private collection, United States; Photo: Christopher Burke.
p. 97, top: Private collection, Paris; Photo: Christopher Burke; **bottom:** Collection of the artist; Photo: Christopher Burke.
p. 98: Collection Mnam, Centre Georges Pompidou, Paris; Photo: Marc Domage.
p. 99: Private collection, Paris; Photo: Marc Domage.
p. 100, top: Private collection, United States; Photo: Marc Domage; **bottom:** Private collection, Paris; Photo: Marc Domage.
p. 101, top: Collection of the artist; Photo: Marc Domage; **bottom:** Collection Mnam, Centre Georges Pompidou, Paris; Photo: Marc Domage.
pp. 102–103: Collection Claude Berri, Paris; Photo: Marc Domage.
p. 104, top: Collection Almine and Bernard Ruiz-Picasso, Brussels; Photo: Marc Domage; **bottom:** Collection Guerlain, Paris; Photo: Marc Domage.
p. 105, top: Collection JMS, Paris; Photo: Marc Domage; **bottom:** Collection Andrea Succo, Milan; Photo: Marc Domage.
p. 106, top: Collection JMS, Paris; Photo: Marc Domage; **bottom:** Collection JMS, Paris; Photo: Marc Domage.
p. 107, top: Collection Samuel Georges Levy, New York; Photo: Marc Domage; **bottom:** Private collection, Paris; Photo: Marc Domage.
pp. 108–109: Collection Beth Rubin DeWoody, United States; Photo: Marc Domage.
p. 110: Collection Michel & Isabelle Fedoroff, Monaco; Photo: Marc Domage.
p. 111: Photo: Marc Domage.
pp. 112, 113, 114–115: Photos: Marc Domage.

POLDERS, SCULPTURES, INSTALLATIONS

p. 119, top: Photo: Marc Domage; **bottom:** Photo: Laurent Édeline.
p. 120, top: Photo: Marc Domage; **bottom:** Collection Bob Calle, Paris; Photo: Laurent Édeline.
p. 123: Photos: Marc Domage.
pp. 124–125: Private collection, Paris; Photo: Rita Burmester; © Fondation Serralves.
pp. 126, 129: Collection Mnam, Centre Georges Pompidou, Paris; Photos: Marc Domage.
p. 130: Private collection, Paris; Photos: Bernhard Strauss.
pp. 133, 134: Photos: Laurent Édeline.
p. 139: Photo: Bernhard Strauss.
pp. 140, 141, 142: Collection Frac Limousin, Limoges; Photos: Marc Domage.
pp. 146, 147: Collection JMS, Paris; Photos: Marc Domage.
pp. 148, 149: Collection Frac Île-de-France, Paris; Photos: Marc Domage.
p. 150: Jumex Collection, Mexico; Photo: Ania Freinoorf.

p. 151: Private collection, Paris; Photo: Blaise Adilon.
pp. 152, 153: Collection Guillaume Houzé, Paris; Photos: J-C. Lett.
pp. 154, 155: Collection Musée d'Art Moderne de la Ville de Paris; Photos: André Morin.
pp. 156, 157: Photos: Florian Kleinefenn; © Palais de Tokyo, Paris.
pp. 158, 159: Private collection, United States; Photos: Christopher Burke.
pp. 160, 161: Photos: Ania Freinoorf.
pp. 162–163: Photo: Marc Domage.
p. 164–165: Collection Guillaume Houzé, Paris; Photo: Marc Domage.
p. 166: Collection Almine and Bernard Ruiz-Picasso, Brussels; Photo: Marc Domage.
p. 167: Photo: Jean Brasille.
p. 169: Private collection, Paris; Photo: Jean Brasille.
pp. 170, 171, 172, 173: Collection Heinz Peter Hager, Italy; Photos: Fabrice Gousset.
pp. 174–175, 176, 177: Collection Mnam, Centre Georges Pompidou, Paris; Photos: André Morin.
p. 178: Collection Mnam, Centre Georges Pompidou, Paris; Photo: Jean Brasille.
p. 179: Collection Hauser & Wirth, Switzerland; Photo: Marc Domage.
pp. 180–181: Photo: Marc Domage.
pp. 182, 183: Collection Almine and Bernard Ruiz-Picasso, Brussels; Photos: Marc Domage.
p. 184: Collection Guillaume Houzé, Paris; Photo: Jean Brasille.
p. 185: Photo: Jean Brasille.
p. 186: Collection Caroline Thompson, Paris; Photo: Marc Domage.
p. 187: Collection Beth Rubin DeWody, United States; Photo: Marc Domage.
p. 188: Photo: Jean Brasille.
p. 189: Collection Günter Lorenz, Germany; Photo: Daniele Resini.
pp. 190–191: Photo: Daniele Resini.
p. 192: Photo: Daniele Resini.
p. 193: Collection Jean-Michel Attal, Paris; Photo: Daniele Resini.
p. 195: Photo: Jean Brasille.
pp. 196–197: Photo: Marc Domage.
pp. 198–199, 200, 201: Private collection, Paris; Photo: Mariano Peuser.
pp. 202, 203: Photos: Mariano Peuser.
p. 204: Photo: Marc Domage.
p. 205: Private collection, Paris; Photo: DR.
p. 206, top: Collection Grigoris Papadimitriou, Greece; Photo: DR; **bottom:** Collection Gunter Lorenz, Germany; Photo: DR.
p. 207: Photo: Jean Brasille.
pp. 208–209: Photo: Mariano Peuser.
p. 210: Private collection, Bologna; Photo: Mariano Peuser.
p. 211: Collection Hauser & Wirth, Switzerland; Photo: Mariano Peuser.
p. 212: Photo: Marc Domage.
p. 213: Photo: Mariano Peuser.
p. 214: Collection Clémence and Didier Krentowski, Paris; Photo: Marc Domage.
p. 215: Collection Claude Berri, Paris; Photo: Marc Domage.
pp. 216–217: Photo: Marc Domage.
pp. 218–219: Photos: Simon Vogel.
pp. 220–221: Photo: Marc Domage.
p. 222: Photo: Marc Domage.
p. 225: Collection Guillaume Houzé, Paris; Photo: Marc Domage.
p. 226: Photo: Marc Domage.
p. 244: Photo: Marc Domage.

ACKNOWLEDGMENTS

I would very much like to thank Maria Muhle and Jérôme Saint-Loubert Bié for assembling this catalogue, and Nora Orallo and Raphaël Gatel for their invaluable assistance.

Thank you to Catherine Millet, Robert Storr, and Richard Shusterman for their contributions.

The following people have helped me, in different ways, in realising, showing, and producing my works, for which I am particularly grateful: Bruno Rousseaud, Christine Macel, Alexia Fabre, Laurence Gateau, Marc-Olivier Wahler, Maurice Fréchuret, Almine Rech, Emmanuel Perrotin, Johann König, and Kirsa Geiser.

I would like to mention, as well, the encouragement and support I received from Annette Messager, Christian Boltanski, Élisabeth Lebovici, Christian Bernard, Élie During, Joseph Mouton, Martin Szekely, Myriam and Jacques Salomon, Didier and Clémence Krzentowski, Guillaume Houzé, and Bob Calle.

My thanks to Lorelay, Maresa, and Jacques Trouvé, Christophe Kihm, and Éric Mangion, who have believed in my work from the beginning.

Thank you to Sarah (see verso), whose loyalty and courage have accompanied me for many years, in my different studios.

(and thank you, as well, to all those I have forgotten to thank…)

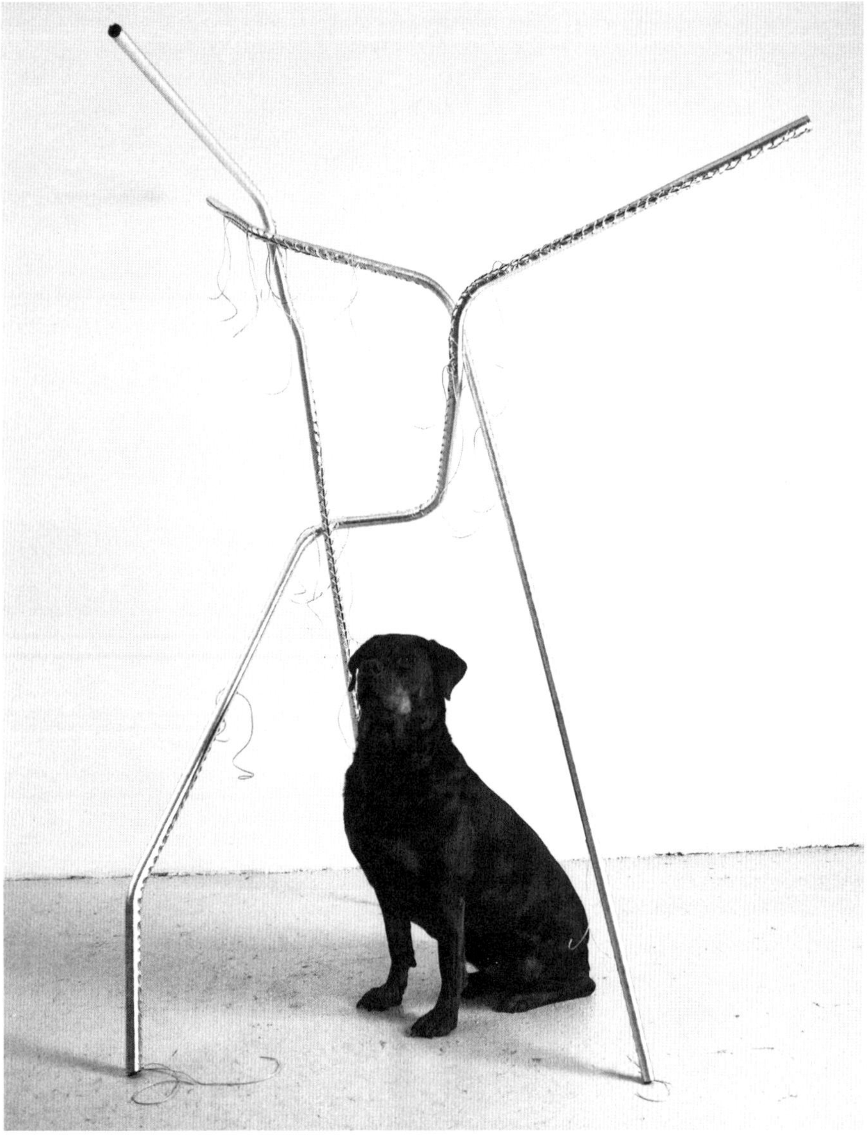